Gerhard Preyer
Donald Davidson's Philosophy

Gerhard Preyer

Donald Davidson's Philosophy
From Radical Interpretation to Radical Contextualism

HUMANITIES
ONLINE

Bibliographic information published by the Deutsche Nationalbibliothek
The Deutsche Nationalbibliothek lists this publication in the
Deutsche Nationalbibliografie; detailed bibliographic data are available
in the Internet at http://dnb.d-nb.de

© 2006 Humanities Online
Frankfurt am Main
Germany
www.humanities-online.de
info@humanities-online.de

Second Edition
© 2011 Humanities Online
ISBN 978-3-941743-11-3

Cover: Uwe Adam, Bruchköbel
Printed in Germany

E-Book edition available on our website: www.humanities-online.de

To *Bruce Aune*

Contents

Preface

This book is a part of the projects on the philosophy of language and epistemology from the project and journal ProtoSociology (www.protosociology.de). It stands on the shoulders of the researches dealt with in our book *Language, Mind and Epistemology. On Donald Davidson's Philosophy.* Edited by G. Preyer, F. Siebelt and A. Ulfig (1994). But the background of studies published in *The Contextualization of Rationality.* Problems, Concepts and Theories of Rationality. Edited by G. Preyer and G. Peter (2000), *Logical Form and Language.* Edited by G. Preyer and G. Peter (2002), E. Rogler, G. Preyer *Materialismus, Anomaler Monismus und mentale Kausalität.* Zur gegenwärtigen Philosophie des Geistes bei D. Davidson und D. Lewis (2001), *Concepts of Meaning.* Toward an Integrated Theory of Linguistic Behavior. Edited by G. Preyer, G. Peter and M. Ulkan (2003) has also taken effect on these considerations. Also to mention here are our projects on contextualism in philosophy (G. Preyer, G. Peter (2005 a, 2007).

I have to thank many people, in particular Georg Peter, Louise Röska-Hardy, Erwin Rogler, Michael Roth for their comments and corrections. In particular the studies together with Erwin (Rogler) and Michael (Roth) of parts of Davidson's writings were helpful over the years. In this English version of *Donald Davidsons Philosophie. Von der radikalen Interpretation zum radikalen Kontextualismus* (2002) I have not included the third part on a radical theory of agency because I intend to continue this part from an expanded frame of reference. Furthermore it is to mention that the English version was extended by re-systematizing Davidson's philosophy. In the chapter "Radical Contextualism" I go along with parts of D. Wunderlich's speech act theory of 1976. In the eighties I lectured regularly on semantics and speech act theory. From our contemporary point of view it seems that speech act theory was overrated as semantics in general. Yet, regarding the contemporary horizon in semantics also the conception of a modified speech act will be fruitful, framing an integrated theory of linguistic behavior. Within such a frame semantics plays a significant role. This is in harmony with the unified theory of thought, meaning and action and its development. Furthermore it is to mention that the English version is extended in the re-systematization of Davidson's philosophy. It should be mentioned as well that my looking for *basic theories* in semantics and epistemology was inspired by my teacher in philosophy in the first part of the 1970s, Herbert Schnädelbach. In particular I would like to thank Ilse Maria Bruckner for skillfully checking the language of this book to bring it in its final shape.

Introduction

Since the seventies of the last century Donald Davidson, besides Willard van Orman Quine, has been the most famous American philosopher of analytic philosophy. Until the year 2004, more than nine volumes were published on his building a unified theory of thought, meaning and action (= *unified theory*) and its ontological implications (2004 (1980)).[1] His *unified theory* has systematized parts of classical analytic philosophy. Davidson goes along with B. Russell's doctrine: "I propose to consider whether anything, and if so, what can be inferred from the structure of language as to the structure of world." (B. Russell 1950: 3) The *unified theory* gives classical analytical philosophy a new turn: "...it is plausible to hold that by studying the most general aspects of language we will be studying the most general aspects of reality" (Davison 1984 (1977): 201). Davidson does not go along with an analytical theory of meaning as put forward by R. Carnap according to Quine's critique of the two dogmas

---

1 A part of Davidson's articles was published in: D. Davidson Vol. 1 1980, Vol. 2 1984, Vol. 3 2001, Vol. 4 2004, Vol. 5 2005. On Davidson's philosophy grounded in his theory of meaning and philosophy of language E. Lepore, K. Ludwig (2005); on Davidson's theory of language, action, and epistemology K. Ludwig ed. 2003, U. M. Zeglen ed. 1999, G. Preyer, F. Siebelt, and A. Ulfig eds. 1994, J. Brandl and W. Gombocz eds. 1989, E. Lepore, B. P. McLaughlin eds. 1986, E. Lepore ed. 1986, Vermazen, and M. B. Hintika eds eds. 1985, G. Evans, and J. H. McDowell eds. 1976; C. Amoretti (2008); on Davidson's philosophy of mental J. Heil, and A. I. Mele eds. 1993; on Davidson's program M. Root, and J. Wallace (1982); on Tarski and Davidson D. Larson 1988; on an overview of Davidson's philosophy G. Preyer, F. Siebelt, A. Ulfig 1994, K. Ludwig 2003; on Davidson's theory of language E. Lepore 1982; on criticism B. Loar 1976; M. Dummett 1975, M. Platts 1979, J. J. Katz 1975; on logical form R. M. Martin 1978, W. K. Essler 1984; E. Lepore, K. Ludwig 2002 have given Davidson's semantics a further turn with an interpretive fulfillment theory, on further continuation and research G. Preyer, G. Peter eds. 2002a, on new research on the slingshot argument S. Neale 2001. On Neale Protosociology Vol. 23 2006: Facts, Slingshots and Anti-Representationalism. On Stephen Neal's Facing Facts. Preyer and Peter eds. On a "Bibliography of Davidson's Publications", Ludwig 2003, 207-213, on a "Selected Commentary on Davidson," 214-15, on "Bibliographic References", 216-31; an "Interview with Donald Davidson by E. Lepore", 231-65. In: Davidson 2004.

of empiricism. He considers this to be a consequence of breakdowns of classical analytic philosophy, the logical atomism (Russell, L. Wittgenstein *Tractatus*), and also of the semantics of logical empiricism of the Wiener Kreis, the so-called Sinnkriterium. The *unified theory* evolves from Quine's work; he has responded extensively to Davidson in his Pursuit of Truth (1992 rev. edn).

It is one of the main subjects of the theory of meaning and linguistic behavior to explain the ascription of propositional attitudes; evaluative attitudes like desires, intentions, hopes, moral convictions, views about duties, and obligations also count as propositional. Davidson calls all propositional attitudes *thoughts* because true beliefs play a significant role among them. They have semantic properties or specifiable content. Understanding speech is bound by the ascription of propositional attitudes, that is, it is the way of making behavior intelligible. The problem is arising in the continuation of Quine's philosophy of language. He has shown that in principle there is an interconnection between belief and meaning, and our understanding of meaning is bound by sentence meaning. In this context, Davidson has developed a *unified theory* as a *total* theory of behavior, that is, a connected theory of desires and beliefs, and consequently of all propositional attitudes to explain both linguistic and non-linguistic behavior.

RI and its holistic truth-centered theory is initiated by radical translation (Quine) and leads us to a theoretical revised version of this fundamental problem in the theory of language. Speaking in terms of terminology, I call the finitely axiomatizable, semanticly compositional theory of truth: *holistic truth-centered theory*. This theory is not definitional or epistemic. At first I will give an outline of Davidson's philosophy with its systematic intent. This means that all the main themes of his philosophy of language, mind, rationality, and communication emerge from radical interpretation (*RI*). In the following steps I will analyze the hard core of his philosophy of language and action with respect to the relationship between *interpretation (language)—rationality* (charity)—*triangulation* born from the holistic truth-centered theory. This shows how the mental (attitudes), language, the social and the rest of the world are connected. It is my goal to make comprehensive that there is just no contingent connection between the concept of language given by *RI* and the distal theory of meaning (reference) and cognition (thought), that is, the epistemological turn in his philosophy. The epistemological turn in his philosophy as an anti-foundationalism is: the system of beliefs and other propositional attitudes is to relate to external circumstances not epistemologically but semanticly. From the triangulation point of view, the certitude of beliefs of our own propositional attitudes is not a foundation of knowledge. Consequently the foundation of interpretation, but not the foundation of knowledge, is that the interpreter has to treat first person authority of speakers.

It is to mention here that the key to link the theories of language, mental, action and epistemology is the *coarse-grained* concept of events. I will mention here that events are also significant for our theory of time. In contemporary philosophy the concept of event plays a dominating role in the philosophy of mind, language and action. Yet it seems to me that the concept of event in contemporary philosophy is *too* coarse and, at the same time, *too* fine-grained.

The step from *RI* to the theory of action and the rationalization of behavior is taken with Davidson's concept of reason and his ontology of events: actions are events and, as such, body movements that we redescribe with an intentional vocabulary. This shows that ontology, interpretation and the conceptual/linguistic dualism work together in his philosophy. Yet, in order to understand Davidson's modified concept of causal explanation of action it is useful to look back to the three background theories he claims to reject: Hart's ascriptivism, the logical-connection argument (A. I. Melden), and Danto's theory of basic acts. In this context I will also discuss the critiques of Davidson's identity thesis of I. Talberg and A. I. Goldman. I have reached the conclusion that the relationship of act-pairs *A-A'* like, for example, moving the hand and turning on the light, is not one of the acts themselves but between *up-shots* (results). In this context I will introduce a radical theory of agency. An outline has been given in Preyer (2002 b). Analyzing the route from *RI* to triangulation I expand the frame of reference of *RI* by taking steps to an analytical contextualism, and I take into account the epistemic capacity as the limit of so-called *explanatory redescription,* of linguistic behavior and actions.

In the analytical philosophy of langugage and semantics, since the nineties a schism has emerged between semantic minimalism, for example S. Somas (2002), E. Borg (2004) and H. Cappelen, E. Lepore (2005) on the one hand and radical pragmatism (contextualism), for example R. Carston (2002), F. Recanati (2004), S. Neale (2004) on the other hand. The reason for this aggravate disagreement is born from the analysis of sentence meaning (see Preyer 2006 b). What I called radical contextualism a long time ago is not a so-called original utterance centrism which argues that there is no significant *basic set of content sensitive expressions* and there is no autonomy of meaning. Therefore the technical term *radical contextualism* is misleading in the contemporary scene of the philosophy of language. I have not changed the terminiology in this book because for me it is a matter of intellectual honesty not to modify something theoretically only from an opportunistic point of view. Therefore it must be pointed out that I use the expression "contextualism" with a particular meaning, that is, we theorize the meaning of the utterance of a single sentence *s* by the sentences *s** that just *s* implies. This is not to be constructed for a language in general, but for the uttered sentence. This way I will give *RI* a further turn. This turn is not truth-conditionally pragmatic or linguistically pragmatic in any of its versions. Furthermore I will also mention here the new researches on contextualism of K. Bach (2003). My old view was that linguistic communication and understanding only work if we assume any concept of linguistic meaning semanticly and not in essential pragmatically. This is not in any conflict with my use of the technical term in this book. We are in a continuous conversation about the problem of context sensitivity in semantics which gives the analysis of the relationship between semantic content a non-semantic content (G. Preyer and G. Peter eds. 2005 a, 2006 a). Every analysis of this relationship has to answer the question "On what level do we refer to the social frame of reference when understanding linguistic behavior (communication) basically?" That is not a trivial question because there may be some truth in "we are not born, speaking a language" (Davidson). The principle of autonomy of meaning is a hint to give us an answer.

We have to reckon that there is no total understanding and comprehensibility of linguistic behavior and consequently not of people either. Yet this is no defect of theories of interpretation and understanding in general. Both are a matter of *degree*, *contexts* and *background* theories. Just this is in harmony with the principle of autonomy of meaning. Therefore we are faced with the fact that the degree of understanding does not mean that we understand a natural speaker as a whole. We are black boxes in the case of successful interpretation also. I conclude this from Davidson's *unified theory*. Possibly this is a bit bulky to grasp. In Quine's philosophy it is valid: from the ontological point of view reference is scrutable, from the radical translation point of view (epistemological, behavioral) it is not. In a reversal of this: we are black boxes ontologically but not epistemologically, that is, if the ascription of attitudes works, the indeterminacy between the ascription of attitudes and the given interpretation of the speaker's words is limited (also in cases where discrepancies are). But from the point of view of radical interpretation we cannot discover the attitudes themselves, because from our theory of interpretation we conclude what attitudes are: attitudes cannot be located (principle of *non*-location). To be a black box ontologically takes also effect on rationalization behavior—the "climber-example"— because there is no way to explain how our attitudes cause an action that may also be caused in *another* way (Davidson 1980 (1973)): 79). That is my belief in contrast to many other colleagues. Yet it is to mention in this context that *RI* is not an inferential account.

It is in harmony with the autonomy of meaning that we link the mental, language and the social by *compositionality* (sub-sentential aspect). This is the *new* linguistic turn in philosophy partially followed from *RI*. Compositionality is built in on every stage of *RI*. This is the basic *theory* of the unification of both a theory of meaning and a theory of action. The language that we speak shows us sufficient structure to analyze the meaning of sentences and their parts; our thoughts and beliefs could not be completely false, so we have true world views at our disposal, and our actions and communications are not absolutely unsuccessful, therefore we have an understanding of people. The picture to link the mental, language and communication (the social) is built in compositionality because, if the theory of meaning is compositional, then (and only then) we ask how it is possible that the utterances of individual speakers are to redescribe by the specific compositional theory. Coping with the circle between belief and meaning by the evidence of holding a sentence true we find considerable insight into the nature of propositional attitudes, language and the mental. Therefore it follows from the truth-centered theory of *RI* as a semantic theory for a language that *satisfaction conditions, compositionality, translation (RI)* and *intentional explanation* work together. Firstly, a semantic theory assigns satisfaction conditions to semanticly valuable expressions and, in the same way, a theory of action assigns intentional contents to behavior. Such content is semanticly valuable as a quality of propositional attitudes. Secondly, the theory explains how the satisfaction conditions for complex linguistic expressions are determined by the satisfaction conditions of their parts. This explains us the nature of systematicity and productivity of natural languages. Thirdly, meaning is given by a successful translation, that is, in the procedure of *RI*. Here also pretheoretic intuitions come into play because speaking a language is also a skill. Fourthly, the *unified theory* applies the notion of content of attitudes to explain behavior intentionally. These issues of a semantic theory are accepted among the interpretive truth theorists. Philosophy of language has made progress in substance because we have realized that the traditional distinctions between "linguistic (conventional) meaning versus use", "truth-conditional versus non-truth-conditional meaning", and "context independence versus context dependence" do not work in principle. This is also something we can learn from the *unified theory*. I speak of understanding as knowing what something means. This implies skills also, and the knowledge of how to do something. An agent realizes his understanding in his first person authority immediately but an interpreter in a third person perspective has to theorize it. Yet this necessary, selective understanding of behavior is not contrary to the claim that making behavior intelligible is a matter of objective truth. And so our knowledge is grounded in truth. One central problem in philosophy of language must be mentioned, namely whether *RI* is possible and what consequence there is if there is no *RI*. The answer to the question "Is *RI* possible?" is dependent on how strong the epistemic restrictions of interpretation are assumed to be. And this leads to the question whether the concepts of meaning and propositional attitudes are theoretical in principle. Davidson's philosophy is significant in a *trans*disciplinary way. From the *unified theory* an orientation evolves to show us that the theories of language, communication, decision, epistemology and also ontology work hand in hand.

Part I
Radical Interpretation, Logical Form and Events

1. Donald Davidson's Philosophy: An Overview

Quine's post-empirical theory of meaning has shown the interconnection between beliefs and meaning. This can be considered to be a new paradigm in semantics. By developing a *unified theory* thought, meaning and action, Davidson clarifies the context of understanding linguistic behavior. (2004 (1980)) His theory of meaning is of interest in particular because *RI* as a semantic orientated radical translation (Quine) gives a particular solution to the interconnection between belief and meaning that cannot be eliminated, or in general, all propositional attitudes conspire to intelligible redescription: *RI* has to develop a theory of belief and meaning in one step, and it has to do so by a unified truth-centered theory of thought, meaning and action (Davidson 2004 (1980)). This is the theoretical frame of *RI*. From this point of view, a theory of language is in fact "pure semantics" (Rorty 1979), but the aim of *RI* is a "comprehensive theory of action and thought", that is, a *total* theory of behavior interpreting sentences and assigning propositional attitudes (Davidson 1984: 163).

From there, the guiding question is: what is meaning? Davidson was disappointed by the answers of C. K. Ogden and I. A. Richards, C. Morris, B. F. Skinner, G. H. Mead, also of the later Wittgenstein, and others. He replaces the question by another—more fruitful—one:

What would it suffice an interpreter to *know* in order to understand the speaker of an alien language, and *how* could he come to *know* it? (Where I look mainly at the interpreter, others have asked the analogous question about a speaker, but for various reasons the difference isn't very important at this degree of abstraction). (Davidson 1993a: 83, my italics)

A theory of meaning must explain to us *how* an interpreter can grasp an infinite set of sentences he has never heard before. Therefore he has to pick out a semantic structure of sentences. This must be elaborated without knowing any attitudes of the speaker under study. Such account is initiated paradigmatically by the interdependence between belief and meaning that every intelligible redescription must overcome. The independent availability of the evidence of interpretation that copes with the circle between belief and meaning is a generalization of *holding a sentence true*. A radical interpreter holds the belief constant and concludes from this assumption to the semantic content of what a speaker has said. Holding true immediately corresponds to the belief of a speaker and is itself to be generalized, because it is always the same attitude. Yet the task of a *unified theory* is not the natural description of behavior but a truth-centered *theory* of redescription of linguistic behavior, thought and actions (the theoretical framework is introduced in Davidson 2004 (1980)). Davidson also speaks of a "unified theory of belief, evaluation attitudes and language" (*Leuven Lectures* 17.10. – 15.12. 1994) because the *unified theory* is at the same time a theory of evaluative attitudes. Propositional attitudes are a part of the comprehensible reconstruction of speech acts and reasons for actions. The epistemological turn of the theory leads to a particular version of externalism:

There is no doubting, of course, the importance of showing how meanings and intentions are connected. Such connections give structure to the propositional attitudes and suit them to systematic treatments. But the interdependence of the basic intentional attitudes is so complete that it is bootless to hope to understand one independently of understanding others. What is wanted, then, is an approach that yields an interpretation of a speaker's words at the same time that it provides a basis for attribution beliefs and desires to the speaker. Such an approach aims to provide a basis for, rather than to assume, *the individuation of propositional attitudes*. (Davidson 1990: 316, my italics).

Davidson's philosophy is to be systematized in such a way that the theory of truth, the ontology of non-reducible (fundamental) events and the triangulation model of *RI*, that is, externalism of individuation of propositional attitudes, are joined. The key elements of the unification are the coarse-grained concept of non-reduce events, their causal power and a conceptual dualism in ontology born from *RI* and its holistic truth-centered theory. The different parts of the *unified theory*—the theory of thought, meaning and action (communication)—follow from *RI* and its holistic truth-centered theory of meaning in a Tarskian style and its conceptual dualism in ontology. The nature of first person authority, the myth of subjective, and the third dogma of empiricism are also conclu ded from coping with the difficulties of *RI*. The *unified theory* is a total theory of behavior, a connected theory of desires and beliefs in order to explain behavior in general. With its epistemological turn, an answer will be given to the individuation of propositional attitudes.

All the major topics of the *unified theory* are to group around *RI* in such a way that we arrive at a panorama of understanding linguistic behavior. In the following I will outline Davidson's philosophy along linking *interpretation (language)*, *rationality* (charity), the *explanatory redescription* of behavior counting as action, and the direct individuation of contents of attitudes by *triangulation* (as a non-foundational epistemology). That shows us how the mental, language, communication and the rest of the world are connected.

If this was shown, the traditional Cartesianism and empiricism epistemology (sense data, phenomenalism, the postulation of objects of thoughts, transcendental syntheses of an epistemological ego) would have to be given up; there is, for example, no difference to Putnam (1992) on that. It is the claim that this chapter in epistemology is to close. The end of a representation of the world outside us is, at the same time, the end of the modern Russellian correspondence theory of truth: there are no facts (or particular states of affairs, situations, or circumstances) to which true sentences refer. Just this is the epistemological turn of the *unified theory*. This is explained by the truth-centered basic theory of the triangulation model of *RI*.

1.1. The Initial Theoretical Situations

Two projects lead to Davidson's *unified theory*, the theory of agency and the semantics of natural language. At the beginning of his career as a philosopher, Davidson was confronted with a *problem*. In the cooperation with P. Suppes and S. Siegel, he intends to verify F. Ramsey's theory of decision. Ramsey made a suggestion to solve the problem of the disentangling role of subjective probability as the degrees of belief and the utility (the desire) in the case of decisions under uncertainty. Davidson reports that he was not successful in constructing a formal theory that explains the change of preferences of experimental subjects by the influences within the course of the experiment under study, and he decided to become a philosopher. In the end Davidson comes to the result that the power of the explanation of action in decision theory or of reason explanation does not arise from their axioms, but from the attribution of propositional attitudes (1980 (1976): 273). The unification with *RI* implies that the interpreter reads in the network of the agent under study that the single attitudes play a role within it. The ascription of attitudes is to compare with the measurement of different quantities. The other project is the semantics of natural language. Lepore, K. Ludwig (2005) have systematized Davidson's philosophy of language. They make the distinction between the *initial project* in *Theory of Meaning and learn-able Language* (1984 (1966)) and the *extended project* in *Truth and Meaning* (1984 (1967)). The first has introduced a compositional theory of meaning of natural languages, the second suggests that a Tarski-style truth theory solves the task of a compositional theory of meaning and discharges the first project. This is called *replacement-theory*. The step to *RI* as a reformulation of the *extended project* is the empirical turn of the theory of truth as an intelligible redescription of linguistic behavior introducing the principle of charity as a requirement of every inter-pretation of observable behavior. The short mention of Lepore's and Ludwig's approach shows the initial situation from which Davidson's theory of meaning emerges (see also 1.10., in this chapter).

The step to a *total*, connected theory of behavior, be it linguistic or not, as a *unified theory* is taken by the assumption that propositional attitudes have a structure within which true beliefs play a central role. Therefore Davidson has argued that Bayesian decision theory and the theory of interpretation are *made for each other*. It leads back to the beginning of Davidson's career as a philosopher when a theory of in-terpretation (meaning) was added to Ramsey's and Jeffrey's version of the Bayesian theory of decision—Davidson co-operated with him at the beginning of the sixties. But he does not argue for a utilitarian conse-quentialism in general (2004 (1995): 41). The unification is not brought about by a speaker who knows that he holds a sentence true, but it is his knowledge in the *degree* of the truth of belief. The theory of meaning works together with the theory of decision because the entities of the attribution of attitudes are *sentences*, not propositions as R. Jeffrey has argued. The compositional theory works on every level of *RI*. Davidson describes the interpersonal comparison of values within the decision theory grounded in the norms of consistency and of what is valuable in itself as well. This is a *normative* judgement that we do not choose. Therefore:

There is no reason we cannot judge the relative strengths of our own interests and those of others, or compare the interests of two others. My point has been that we do not have to establish, argue for, or opt for, a basis for such judge-ments. We already have it. (Davidson 2004 (1986): 74)

The overall aim of Davidson's philosophy is to elaborate a method of the semantic analysis of counterfactuals, subjunctives, probabilistic and causal statements, adverbs, attributive adjectives, quotations, mass terms, propositional attitudes, action sentences and descriptions, reported speech, perceptions and intentions (intending conceived as forming an intention).

Davidson's work is unified by the theory of truth serving as a theory of meaning. Many commentators agree that, when analyzing Davidson's philosophy, the following problems emerge: Why do truth conditions determine a significant interpretation? Is the application of the principle of charity as a requirement of the ascription of attitudes the guarantee of the selection of the correct correlation between the attitudes of the agent and his behavior caused by the physical environment? Is the application of the principle of charity the limes of the semantic compatibility of intelligible redescription? Therefore one must ask: is the normative claim of the epistemic assumption applying the principle of charity really fundamentally so that we all subscribe to it?

1.2. Truth and Meaning

For the understanding Davidson's philosophy it is to emphasize that the clarification of the concept of meaning explains the continuation and the modification of his philosophy as a whole. For him, propositions, properties, senses, relations and semantic universals are of no benefit in the theory of language and are not a requirement for a compositional semantics. Following Quine's radical translation and the rejection of the myth of the museum in semantics, a theory of language and action takes off from *RI*. This is the starting situation for all understanding of linguistic behavior (on Davidson's program and theory, M. Root, J. Wallace 1982, Lepore 1982, Lepore, K. Ludwig 2003). Entities of the theory of meaning and the truth-centered theory of *RI* are types of utterances and inscriptions but it is not the part of *RI* to analyze individual words. The theory of truth occupies oneself with the utterance of sentences. Sentences are the instances that 1. allow us to speak of all real utterances und inscriptions of the same type at the same time and 2. are the vehicles to which we would state types of the truth-condition of utterances and inscriptions if they were uttered. Therefore we technically speak in the case of acts of inscriptions and their companions of utterances. The basic assumption is that the translation of a speaker's words into an interpreter's words is the condition for the ascription of attitudes. The task of *RI* is the intelligible redescription of behavior, not its observation. Some behavioral items count as action. The problem is to give any propositional attitude a propositional content we do not observe. Therefore, if we apply truth to observable behavior this means, at the same time, assigning a *content* to all attitudes. The key to assigning intelligible items is the connection of truth and therefore of meaning of the way in which we *directly* individuate attitudes of someone else. *RI* is asymmetric in nature because an interpreter cannot immediately observe the propositional attitudes including the intentions also that partly determine the meaning of utterance (Davidson 2001: 210).

For *RI*, utterances of natural speakers are the subject of the redescription of a radical interpreter. A natural speaker realizes this understanding immediately, but a radical interpreter of his behavior has to theorize it from evidence. The model for analyzing sentential structure is Tarskian. Tarski's method is to define the satisfaction of complex open sentences in terms of simple sentences. With this concept we have an explanation at hand of *how* the meaning of composed sentences depends on the meaning of its parts. All expressions of a natural language are to interpret with the first-order quantification theory (plus identity). In this point Davidson agrees with Quine (1995 a: 278): "Quantification theory is home ground for bound variables. Since to be is to be the value of a bound variable, existential considerations are of the essence here." (Quine 1995 a, 278; on the limits of power of this account, see W. K. Essler 1994). This is also Davidson's option. It is the claim to give with this logical means an analysis of the propositional structure of *saying that…* in the framework of a truth-centered theory of interpretation.

Davidson's uncovering the logical form of a natural locution like *saying that …* results in applying Tarski's method of defining truth as revealing an effective structure. This means: from a recursive characterization of the truth-predicate like "is true in L" for every sentence s of L a sentence in a metalanguage it is to conclude that it is given from the form "s is true in L, if and only if p" insofar as we make the assumption that "s" is to substitute by a canonic description of a sentence of L, and "p" is to substitute by a sentence in the metalanguage by our stating the truth-condition of the respective sentence. We have a "deep explanation" if it is shown *why one sentence entails the other*, that is, *how* the meaning of sentences is systematically dependent on their *structure*. The logical form is represented by the logic of quantification, for example, adverbial constructions are to be analyzed as quantification over events as well (on the role of logical form and the ontological significance of events in the theory of language, see R. M. Martin 1979). Therefore it is essential that adverbs (non-extensional sentences) are to be constructed as predicates of events. This is derived from the quantificatory nature of logical form and from the introduction of the ontology of events. The paraphrasing of event sentences into quantification will give them their truth-conditions within the theory of truth.

Theorizing on understanding one's language does *not* require entities such as the meanings of expressions like Carnap's intensional entities. From an epistemological point of view, a proposition cannot determine both the content of propositional attitudes and their epistemic (subjective) assurance. In this point Davidson follows Quine's and Russell's critique of Frege, and there is an agreement on that among T. Burge, Putnam, Dennett, J. Fodor, Stich, Kaplan and many others. The claim of a truth-conditional-semantics is to explain the critical notions of a theory of meaning, as there are "is significant", "is synonymous with", "analytical", "means" (intensionally) in extensional terms like "satisfy", "is true", "designates". This implies: the interpretations of "...is true ..." and "...means..." are coextensive—for two sentences. This was Davidson's account in *Truth and Meaning* (1984 (1967)). In continuation Davidson has clarified and modified this project. The modifications are well discovered. One of the prominent critiques was Forster's objection (1976). Davidson has replied to him (1984 (1976), see also Lepore, Ludwig 2005: 114-18). One of the main problems was whether T-sentences are interpretive and not simply trivial without any benefit in semantics because they *express our intuitive concept of truth*. Davidson has clarified his proposal that the Convention T is not a surrogate of a general definition of truth but an application of the pre-theoretical concept of truth. The claim of the truth-centered theory of RI is empirical in nature, that is, we test the theory by the relevant conclusions of the implicit T-sentences, that is, an uttered sentence is true iff the utterance satisfied certain conditions. Therefore the theory of truth describes, explains (understands), predicts features of human behavior. T-sentences have the form and function of laws of nature. They are valid contrafactually and verified by examples. But T-sentences have no reference terms as its parts. Reference and satisfaction are theoretical constructs. The problem of the reformulation of the extended project by RI is whether the attitude of holding a sentence true relates belief and interpretation in principle. But Davidson's main correction of his project in *Truth of Meaning* (1984 (1967)) is that a *definition* of truth in a Tarskian style gives us both *at the same* time: what we can necessarily know about what truth is, and that the definition is to use as a definition of the description of the factual linguistic behavior. In this article, however, he discusses the problem how we make the assumption that such a definition is *valid*. And just this was a contradiction, he argued (Davidson 1984, *Introduction*: xiv-vi).

The *RI* itself relativizes Tarski's theory of truth to speakers (utterances) and time-points: *truth is taken as a property of utterances* (on Tarski and Davidson, see D. Larson 1988, R. L. Kirkham 1992, on further elaboration of Davidson's theory of meaning Lepore, Ludwig 2002). This is called *Davidson's Convention T* (Lepore, Ludwig 2002: 48, 49, 50, 54). But to do this,

The verification of instances of the *T*-sentences, or rather their surrogates in a theory relativized to speakers and times, remains respectably empirical. No doubt some pragmatic concepts of demonstration as between speakers, times, and objects will come into play. But such a concept is one we may hope to explain without appeal to notions like truth, meaning, synonymy, or translation. The same cannot be said for truth in a model. Convention *T*, even when bent to fit the awkward shapes of natural language, points the way to a radical theory of interpretation. (Davidson 1984 (1973): 75).

The work of reference is done by *T*-theoretic *axioms of indexicals*. It is often argued that a semantic theory cannot analyze demonstratives formally. A significant terminological feature is to mention here because there is a problematic ambiguity of the expressions *what a sentence refers to* and *what a sentence is about*. We stipulate that the use of the first is for relations between a patent singular term and what such terms refer to and of the second exclusively for relations between a sentence and what something is said about in a sentence. This is helpful to analyze indexicals within a truth theory because the axioms of singular terms work within this framework by compositionality, that is, when we know the logical form of sentences we also know the semantic role of their significant parts in the context of the theory. This is one of the main subjects within the history of the *unified theory* that emerges in continuation.

The truth-centered theory of meaning leads us to a recursive theory of so-called *absolute* truth, and it is to distinguish from theories that relativize the single-place truth predicate to "truth in an interpretation," "truth in a model," "valuation," or "possible worlds": "... Such theories cannot carry through the last step of the recursion on truth or satisfaction which is essential to the quotation-lifting feature of *T*-sentences." (Davidson 1984 (1973): 68) Yet absolute theories of truth are to apply to utterances and not to sentences only because compositionality works over all parts of linguistic behavior. If this could not be done, *RI* would be impossible. The truth-centered theory of meaning of *L* has the property that knowing what is stated by its *T-theorems* is enough to enable us to understand *L* (the knowledge what is stated by the axioms is not necessary).

1.3. The Task of *RI*

The *RI* of linguistic behavior of an individual speaker—in our own language and in alien ones—is the application of the truth-conditional theory of meaning:

> We interpret a bit of linguistic behavior when we say what a speaker's words mean on an occasion of use. The task may be seen as one of redescription. We know that the words 'Es schneit' have been uttered on a particular occasion and we want to redescribe this uttering as an act of saying that it is snowing. (Davidson 1984 (1974): 141)

Therefore the idiolect theory of language follows from *RI*: the truth-centered semantics is a theory of individual speakers because: "The only object required for the existence of a belief is a believer (as an individual, my completion)."(Davidson 2001(1997): 74)

RI begins at home, that is, "all understanding of the speech of other involves radical interpretation" (Davidson 1984 (1973): 126). *Radical* means that the interpreter does not assume or have any prior knowledge of the speaker's or agent's propositional attitudes. As interpreters we proceed through selecting the truth-conditions of single utterances via our successful theory. This *theory* starts from uninterpreted (natural) utterances. Therefore there is no foundation to make a distinction between the problem of interpretation of domestic and of foreign speech. It is not the point of theorizing to eliminate so-called vague and defective features in natural language but to show the logical grammar to grasp parts of a native tongue. The ascription of meaning to parts of linguistic behavior themselves results from *RI*. This explains why *RI* is a semantics of natural language. *RI* characterizes a zero-situation, that is, a situation where we do not suppose that there is any detailed knowledge of a speaker's belief and intentions and/or the utterance meaning. This situation is to compare with the basic situation of the theory of decision where, if we know the preferences of an agent with respect to his differing behavior, we can pick out his beliefs and desires. The theories of *interpretation, decision (action)* and *communication* work together because the ascription of desires and beliefs is connected with the interpretation of linguistic behavior and the individuation of the contents of attitudes (on an interpretation of the theory of decision with the assumption of supervenience, Preyer and Siebelt 2000 b). We identify an attitude by its propositional content. The task of a theory of meaning is to analyze the structure of sentences, not the meaning of single words. The meaning of words is to be stated as a result of the procedure of redescribing linguistic behavior. They derive from the truth-conditions of *all* sentences in which they are used. In this respect, a theory of language is holistic. It varies the Frege-principle: "A word has a meaning only in the context of a sentence", that is, we can only state the meaning of a sentence if we grasp the meaning of every sentence in a given language. It is the analysandum of a formal semantics that is often called literal meaning. The functionality principle of compositionality works together with the context principle (language holism). Davidson speaks of the *first meaning* of what was said, or of an utterance (2005 (1986): 91-93). The attitude of "meaning that" is added to the propositional attitudes, or the speaker means that *p* by uttering a sentence. The first meaning of an utterance is stated by the truth-condition applied to it.

The attitude of *holding sentences true* at a time, *wanting a sentence to be true*, or *preferring that one sentence rather than another be true* is to be distinguished from all other attitudes. The holism of attitudes has two features, an intra-attitudinal one and an inter-attitudinal one. The first one consists of relations within the categories of attitudes like beliefs or desires, the second consists of relations between the attitudes themselves like beliefs and desires with respect to, for example, intentions. (Davidson 2004 (1995): 13-17) In substance the connected theory of interpretation and action (decision) is holistic:

The Unified Theory is holistic through and through. It is designed to assign contents to beliefs, utterances, and values simultaneously because these basic attitudes are so interdependent that it would not be possible to determine them one at a time, or even two at a time. (Davidson 2004 (1995): 130)

The claim of *RI* is to develop a theory of beliefs and linguistic meaning in *one* step. The connection between belief and meaning cannot be eliminated in principle. Yet, if holding-true is evidence, we can understand what someone says without knowing his or her particular beliefs. When we hold a sentence true or accept a sentence as true constant, we have a means to solve the problem of the interdependence of belief and meaning. This leading propositional attitude is not affected by the interdependence of belief and meaning because such attitudes are to apply to all sentences and because the relation of holding true between a speaker and an utterance is extensional. We can know that without knowing what a sentence means. It is the essential feature of such attitudes like holding a sentence true relativized to time point, wanting a sentence to be true, or preferring that one sentence rather than another be true, that they are *non*individuative, that is, we do not distinguish their different propositional contents expressed by different utterances step by step. Therefore the radical theory of interpretation applies the principle of charity in an unlimited way. It optimizes coherence (consistence) and truth of attitudes. The step to externalism is taken if the content of attitudes is to individuate by distal stimuli. And this bridges the gap of the asymmetry of *RI*.

The most important assumption for *RI* is that a speaker normally *knows* what he *means,* therefore he knows the holding-true of a sentence, and in this respect he also knows the propositional content he believes. The function of Quine's observational statement with Davidson's account is taken over by the attitude of holding true. A language epistemic link to the world is no longer naturalized. It is formalized or rather semanticized in a form to be evolved now, so to speak. The authority of first person follows from the asymmetry of *RI*: a speaker does not interpret himself but an interpreter has, on the basis of evidence and inferences, to solve the task of interpretation (on the substantial role of the asymmetry of *RI*, Röska-Hardy 1997, on a critical evaluation of first person authority Lepore, Ludwig 2005: 343-72). Such an authority does not mean that our self-knowledge is total. It would not be *RI* if a speaker did not know the meaning of his uttered words. This is a general presupposition of understanding linguistic behavior: a speaker cannot be wrong about the meaning of his uttered words, and the interpreter has to interpret him in such a way that he is right. It is a requirement of *RI* that the radical interpreter assumes that the *speaker* knows his own understanding of his uttered words and the radical interpreter cannot make intelligible the propositional attitudes of any speaker *without* understanding his *utterances*. Therefore, from my point of view, interpretation in general applies the principle of epistemic justice (see capt. 2.1.3 in this book). But just this is substantiated by the third person attitude of *RI*, because a successful interpretation is not possible by a prior research of the speaker's particular beliefs and intentions. *RI* is the *inside* of the semantics of natural language but it is at the same time the *outside* because every intelligible redescription, be it linguistic or not, has to break in the circle of belief and meaning.

What is the overall ontological intent of the truth-centered theory of *RI*?

Firstly it is to mention that, in difference to Frege, the ontology we need for semantics is connected directly with a natural language. If it is the claim to conclude ontology from a theory of truth, we have to grasp language holistically, that is, such a theory has shown us the structure of natural language. In the truth-centered theory of meaning of linguistic behavior semantics, epistemology and ontology work together in a particular way. Compositionality is its basic theory.

1. I will call the ontology of the truth-centered theory of *RI* a *restricted one* because we assign to the interpretive theory only the standard referential devices (singular terms, including variables under assignment).

2. The ontology of the theory are *objects* and *events as particulars* to which singular terms refer. We may be free of the idea that predicates refer to properties and individual sentences are made true by individual facts, whatever the state of affairs, the situations, or circumstances may be like.

3. If we prefer facts to which true sentences refer, the slingshot argument shows that such entities collapse into the so-called Great Fact. But if there are no facts, the correspondence theory of truth is not right. In the end of the history of the truth-centered theory, Davidson gives up the talk on correspondence in general because it is a misleading expression. Distal meaning and reference connect language and the world.

4. Furthermore Davidson concludes that, if there are no facts as instances of the correspondence of sentences, the third dogma of empiricism, the epistemological distinction between *conceptual-scheme* and *empirical content* and the idea that propositional attitudes represent (stand for) something (facts, situations) are to give up. This is not the conception in Davidson's *On the Very Idea of a Conceptual Scheme* (1984 (1974), but he has emphasized that later:

If we give up facts as entities that make sentences true, we ought to give up representations at the same time, for the legitimacy of each depends on the legitimacy of the other. (2001 (1988): 184)

The epistemological claim is to give an alternative to realism as a radical nonepistemic correspondence of truth and to antirealism with a shrinking of truth into interpersonal verification without any objectivity. The objectivity of the ascription of attitudes ontologically links objective truth and the empirical content of knowledge, that is: sentences are understandable under the condition that the concept of objective truth is disposed about.

Explaining actions and linguistic behavior implies interpreting them, that is, ascribed attitudes are concluded from our interpretive theory of truth. The solution of the task of *RI* is holistic in nature. That is, we pick out *what* a speaker expresses in certain occasions of sentential use of language, that is, what he expresses in *his* language by uttering a sentence. A single speech-act can only be interpreted if—in a given situation—we take into account all dispositions to perform further speech acts. The linguistic behavior is to be described as a structured disposition. We interpret a speech act toward the background of a theory of a speaker's language, that is, an idiolect theory of language. But the empirical restrictions of the speaker's attitudes and behavior cannot be fixed for all cases because what an addressee understands through the words uttered by any speaker is not only determined by the meaning of the words but also by a speaker's beliefs of the world. In the fundamental understanding of this problem, Davidson's and Dummett's theories of language are different (on both B. Fultner 1998). This discrepancy is not a defect of *RI* but a logical consequence of all theories of meaning. This is in harmony with the fact that all ascription of attitudes is open to adjustments from the interpreter's point of view. So we move from *RI* to a "passing theory" conceived of as a bridge for intelligible redescription in general. It is a consequence of *RI* that rule-following, conventions of language, conditions of truthfulness or sincerity—shortly speaking: all intended purposes of utterances—cannot explain the concept of literal meaning but presuppose it; in the same way, lies and the use of metaphor cannot change the meaning of words. An expanded theory of meaning by *RI* aims at explaining how the concept of meaning is to apply to beliefs, intentions, and desires. It is a *total* theory of behavior. But for *RI* this is not a matter of conventions or rules: "Conventions and rules do not explain language; language explains them." (Davidson 1990: 316) The holistic truth-centered theory of *RI* in particular criticizes the nominalistic strategy of meaning of H. P. Grice, J. Bennett and others in principle. It is not the point here that we redescribe utterances as intentional actions, but intentions of speakers do not give meaning to (uttered) sentences. The contribution of a speaker's intention to the performance of illocutionary acts is that the action is to be interpreted in some way, for example, as an act of assertion (Davidson 1984 (1979): 114). Therefore it is to mention here that the *unified theory* will also give a particular answer to the so-called *Grice*-problem. Intentions and beliefs are essential to speak a language (on three semantic intentions, Davidson 2005 (1993): 170-71). The relationship between the two is to explain in such a way that in many cases intentions are dependent on beliefs. Or, in other words, intentions are dependent on meaning. For Grice, this is not the case. Davidson's applying *RI* to speaker intentions and other propositional attitudes is guided by the principle of autonomy of meaning. This principle says: it is the essence of linguistic behavior that a speaker can put all his purposes in his use of language. Language is cognitively neutral with regards to all purposes intended by speakers. This is exactly what is essential for a natural language. Contrary to Quine, observing physical facts and stating them is not at all fundamental. With this account, Davidson intends as well to solve the problem of ascribing attitudes by reported speech. The paratactical account of samesayer connects the autonomy of meaning with the ascription of thoughts and attitudes to solve the task of *RI* and also gives an analysis of illocutionary force. The semantic proposal of the paratactial account is also the key to understanding psychological sentences (sentences about propositional attitudes), and just this matter is epistemologically helpful to distinguish psychological concepts from others.

   The skeptical paradox (S. Kripke) and the debates on rule-platonism of the theory of meaning do not matter for *RI* (see also A. Bilgrami 1992). In the situation of *RI*, a fixed meaning or reference of expressions is not to explore. *RI*-approach itself criticizes any ontology of word-meaning. Reference is inscrutable, that is, we do not know what the singular terms of a language—on their own—refer to. The truth-centered theory of meaning does not theoretically eliminate reference, but the distal and satisfactional theory of meaning (reference) is no explanation of reference. For *RI* and radical translation, a semantic realism is hopelessly naive, that is, there is no objective semantic relationship between expressions and the world, no one and only correct semantic relation of reference (satisfaction). For *RI, fixing* meaning and reference are furthermore not depending on internal concepts (J. Fodor) or on a community of communication (Kripke).

1.4. Rationality

In analyzing utterance meaning, *RI* employs the principle of charity in an unlimited way, that is, to separate meaning and attitudes invokes the key principles of coherence and of correspondence. The first "endows the speaker with a modicum of logic, the other endows him with a degree of what the interpreter takes to be true belief about the world" (Davidson 2001 (1991): 211). Davidson calls these also the policy of rational accommodation or charity. Therefore making behavior intelligible plays together with so-called "basic rationality". This is the key to identify meaning, beliefs and other propositional attitudes, also values, simultaneously. I will re-systematize charity in continuation as the principle of natural epistemic justice.

Since the seventies, Davidson has argued more explicitly for an overall feature of a concept of rationality, taken to be "constitutive" or "normative", and since the beginning of the eighties he has moved on to an externalized epistemology. He considers this presupposition of ascribing attitudes including the understanding of linguistic and non-linguistic behavior. This step is not contingent. Rationality as a normative concept was first presented in *Psychology as Philosophy* (1980 (1974)) and was set out in *Paradoxes of Irrationality* (2004 (1982)), *Rational Animals* (2001 (1982)), *Incoherence and Irrationality* (2004 (1985)) and *Could there be a Science of Rationality?* (2004 (1995). Yet, "The question whether a creature "subscribe" to the principle of continence, or to the logic of the sentential calculus, or to the principle of total evidence for inductive reasoning, is not an empirical question." (Davidson 2004 (1985): 196). And furthermore: "… my word „subscribe" is misleading. Agent can't decide whether or not to accept the fundamental attributes of rationality: if they are in a position to decide anything, they have those attributes" (2004 (1985): 196-7). It is a consequence of *RI* — as an intelligible redescription of utterances — that we suppose a *connectivity* and *coherence* of beliefs, and we have to meet the requirement of individuating their propositional content. Irrationality is nothing but a disturbance within the coherence and connectivity of sets of beliefs. Irrationality is an *inner*-inconsistency of propositional attitudes. Therefore all intentional actions, though they may in some further way be irrational, have a rational element: this is the paradox of irrationality. Yet we have in mind that the assumption of rationality is introduced to grasp the quantificatory structure of beliefs.

The assumption has to explain to us why we could quantify in beliefs. We do not grasp beliefs one by one but by the logical relations that they have among each other and to other propositional attitudes. But there is a problem what it means that we count and quantify in attitudes and that our beliefs are largely true in essential.

The *unified theory* assumes that rationality is an *epistemic norm* linking the theories of language, action, decision, communication, and the mental. However, from the point of view of *RI* there is always a degree of rationality as a necessary condition, making behavior intelligible in any way. This is exactly what is born from our theory of interpretation, because in the network of attitudes of speakers we project logical and semantic features from our own point of view, and at the same time we individuate the content of attitudes by triangulation as well. Normative and causal properties of mental concepts play together and help us to be in a position where we can redescribe behavior intelligibly. Rationality is a social trait and only creatures that are able to communicate in the triangle are rational animals. The point is that intersubjectivity is not a matter of agreement among speakers about something, but it is dependent on causal interactions with the world. In the end, the *unified theory* and the triangulation of *RI* lead us to a methodological separatism between natural science and humanities. The cantus firmus of the *unified theory* is that all believers have to share rationality not only as an epistemic norm, but also for their self-identification as person. This is possible because the vocabulary we have to ascribe attitudes is equal in both directions, to myself and to others.

1.5. Externalism of Triangulation

From his theory of language, Davidson has concluded an epistemological approach of individuation of propositional attitudes. He develops his analytical ontology to an externalism of triangulation. This way of interpreting radically in terms of semantic truth allows for externalization—without naturalization in a Quinean way. I will call this externalism a *radical* externalism. For Quine, the criterion of ontology is: to be is to be the value of the variable that corresponds to the ontological standard: no entity without an identity. An analytic ontology exaggerated Quine's account with the motto: no identity without an entity. The linguistic counterpart is: no statement of identity without singular terms. The ontology of events argues that we have to accept events as entities and we could quantify over events like over entities. A radical externalism is the epistemological complement of an ontology of event and means: the perceptual beliefs we have are *directly* caused by events in the external world, and causal relations explain the content of those attitudes. Both his concept of rationality—the logical structure of propositional atti-tudes—and the epistemology externalized follows from *RI*:

Beliefs, intentions, and desires are *identified* ... by their relations to one another. A belief *that* it is about to rain would lose much of its claim to be just that belief if it did not have some tendency to *cause* someone who had it and wanted to say try to take appropriate action, such as carrying an umbrella. Nor would a belief that it is about to rain plausibly be *identified* as such if someone who was thought to have that belief also believed that if it rains it pours and did not believe it was about to pour. And so on: these *obvious* logical relations amongst beliefs; amongst beliefs, desires and intentions; between beliefs and the *world*, make beliefs the beliefs they are; therefore they cannot in general *lose* these rela-tions and remain the same beliefs. Such relations are *constitutive* of the proposi-tional attitudes. (Davidson 2004 (1985): 195-96, my italics)

The epistemological consequence of a radical externalism is that tradi-tional epistemology (the theory of sense data, phenomenalism, objects of thoughts as propositional in character) and the distinction between scheme and content as the third dogma of empiricism are to give up: there is no representation of reality by inner objects. Therefore all epistemic mediation of knowledge as its foundation is to reject. Perceptual beliefs are built directly and spontaneously, but the relation between stimuli and propositional beliefs is not tricked simply. The question "What is the role of external things and events determining the propositional con-tent of thoughts?" is one about language. Just this is the problem: "How do we give sentences connected with perception a content directly (an empirical content)?". Davidson calls such sentences *perceptual sentences*. (Davidson 2005 (1997):137) People have also unequal perceptual sen-tences. They may be different in many cases for everyone, and we can correct them according to the situation arising. This leads back to *RI* and the problem to learn new sentences. Solving the task of *RI* with the truth-centered theory is propositional in nature. The theory describes the propositional structure of linguistic behavior. This presupposes that speaker and interpreter classify objects, properties, events and situation similarly. Therefore it is assumed that *having a concept* is, at the same time, *having a propositional thought*. For that reason, Davidson concludes: "We perceive the world through language, this is, through having language". (141)

The task of a *unified theory* as a total theory of behavior is the redescription of utterances as actions. The ascriptions of attitudes as reasons are to justify in the triangulation between speaker, interpreter, and the external significant stimuli as a *pre-linguistic* and *pre-cognitive* situation. "The triangulation which is essential for thought requires that those in communication recognize that they occupy positions in a shared world." (Davidson 2001 (1991): 213) The triangulation is the frame of reference of a so-called semantic compatibility that makes a cross-cultural understanding of utterances in natural languages possible: that is, triangulation explains the individuation of propositional attitudes. The significance of redescriptions of linguistic behavior is concerned with non-lingual actions and events. It is the claim of the epistemological turn of the *unified theory* to clarify the internal connection between *objective truth* and interpersonal communication. That is where the triangulation of the subjective, the physical and the second person comes in—in such a way that no single dimension is to be reduced to the other. The triangulation explains the individuation of propositional attitudes and is the guarantee of attributing attitudes objectively:

The ultimate source of both objectivity and communication is the triangle that, by relating speaker, interpreter, and the world, determines the contents of thought and speech. Given this source, there is no room for a relativized concept of truth. (Davidson 1990: 325)

A radical externalism evolves from the critique of Burge's and M. Dummett's social (linguistic) externalism, but not from Burge's perceptual externalism. Davidson claims to connect both, the social with the perceptual externalism. The same holds for the critique of H. Putnam's sociolinguistic hypothesis of the universality of linguistic division of labor, his metaphysical externalism of natural kind words and his internal realism. Yet it is also a critique of the externalistic foundation of knowledge of D. C. Armstrong (1973) and of R. M. Chisholm's non-externalistic version of foundationalism (1966, 1977 rev. edn). Davidson criticizes the epistemology and semantics of social externalism by demonstrating the connection between the physical, a person's attitudes, and understanding other minds on the basis of causal relations caused by distal stimuli. Putnam's socio-linguistic hypothesis is criticized on the same footing. Davidson does not take the socio-linguistic division of labor to be the basis of understanding meaning. It is not the extension (sameness) of micro-structure that fixes the reference of words describing natural phe-nomena, for example, "water," but it is a result of evolutionary selections of classifications of reactions toward things and events that does so. The triangulation is to be characterized in a way that causal relations do not only fix the reference of some categories of words, but also of language and thinking *in general*, that is, our knowledge is not found thereby that our mind is within itself in contact with an object.

One of the issues of a radical externalism is the *explanation* of the sta-tus of first person authority. It was often stated but rarely explained by others. The explanation intends to clarify that all propositional thought requires the concept of objective truth, and this concept is valid only for creatures who are able to communicate. This is only possible if the com-municative exchange of speakers takes place in a common spatio-tempo-ral location. The first person authority, the social character of language, and the individuation of thoughts work together.

Davidson has already emphasized in *A Coherence Theory of Truth and Knowledge* (2001 (1983)) that the essential difference between the method of radical translation and *RI* is the nature of the sort of *causes* which determines interpretation, that is, the relation among the concepts of meaning, truth, belief and the causal individuation of propositional content (151; see also on this point the *Afterthoughts* 2001 (1987)). The claim is to close the chapter of epistemology from Descartes to Quine (2001 (1987): 157). In the following, the debate on externalism amounts to the opposition between the *proximal* (Quine) and the *distal* theory of meaning (reference) and evidence. For Quine, sentences have the same meaning if they are given rise by the same pattern of stimuli, and if prompted assent or dissent toward sentences is caused by these. In respect of our observation sentences, Quine is *no* holist. And, moreover, there is an epistemic, significant distinction between these and other sentences. Contrarily, a distal theory of meaning (reference) argues that the same meaning is caused by a common cause. Davidson asserts that Quine's epistemology is a Cartesian account leading to scepticism. We find the two accounts conflicting with respect to the priority of *evidence* or of *truth* building a theory of meaning. For the distal account, talking about the same meanings is based on common causes. Assent or dissent towards sentences are consequently caused by things, events, and situ-ations:

My approach is by contrast (to Quine, my completion) externalist: I suggest that interpretation depends (in the simplest and most basic situations) on the external objects and events salient to both speaker and interpreter, the very objects and events the speaker's words are then taken by the interpreter to have as subject matter. It is the distal stimulus that matters to interpretation. (Davidson 1990: 321)

The only intelligible or plausible *concept of evidence* is the relationship between sentences and beliefs. For the distal theory of meaning, reference and cognition are the same common causes significant for the individuation of thoughts and for understanding linguistic behavior. This is valid for both speakers and interpreters and, in the same way, for understanding the role of *second person* also in the framework of *RI*. The causal features of external events are the basis of all intelligible linguistic behavior, and this is a result of a triangulation. This link connects the knowledge of one's own mind, of other minds, and of a physical world. The causal chain between our ordinary beliefs and external events involves the sense organs, but for the distal theory of meaning (reference) the sensory experience has no epistemological priority. A causal connection between thoughts and events could also be brought about in any other way; for example, in our mind a chip is implanted and the causation is mediated by that.

Similarly it is common ground for Quine and Davidson that the ascription of the effects of stimuli is *obvious*. Quine argues that the truth of an observation sentence only depends on stimulus meaning (holophrastic meaning). For this "meaning", a principle of a bivalence is valid: stimuli take place or they do not. Some philosophers of language may doubt that. But the application of the principle of bivalence is also Davidson's account to identify belief and meaning:

Quine's suggestion, which I shall essentially follow, is to take prompted assent as basic, the causal relation between assenting to a sentence and the cause of such assent. This is a fair place to start the project of identifying beliefs and meanings, since a speaker's assent to a sentence depends both on what he means by the sentence and on what he believes about the world. (Davidson 2001 (1983): 147)

Truth — in this sense — is *obvious*, and meaning is really obvious if meaning is directly depending on observational truth. The ascription of attitudes in triangulation is *obvious* on the basis that linguistic behavior is triggered by the causal roles of things and events and by the communicational role of "second person" who is participating in the triangle. But attitudes are not to identify with behavior, because we have the first person authority to take into account. Otherwise, skepticism with respect to understanding other minds would not be rejected. From *RI,* a radical externalism follows by the two assumptions: beliefs are structured holistically, and the content of elementary beliefs is caused by events and things from the external world. But it must be mentioned that propositional attitudes (thoughts) are not to reduce to conditioning situations. The point is that the *same* response of the second apex (second person) is a necessary condition for speaking a language. Therefore this basic line to react to the same object as oneself reacts to is a guarantee that epistemologically different persons have the same object in mind.

RI leads us to restructuring epistemology in principle because the foundation of interpretation is not a foundation of knowledge. Triangulation makes distal causes the basis of individuation of propositional contents. Yet, causal relations are not relations of confirmation or disconfirmation and causes are not propositions, but events in the world or our sensory system. Events are not an evidence by themselves, but only as the cause of our believing something. Therefore, from the triangulation model of *RI* beliefs are essentially *veridical* in nature: they are caused by public things and events (on critiques McDowell 1994, see also the answer by Gibson 1999, on the dilemma of knowledge and its solution, see Davidson 2001 (1982): 168). The guarantee of this is that the simplest sentences we hold true are true. In sum: there is no epistemological foundation of our empirical knowledge. This is born from the nature of *RI* and the external individuation of the content of attitudes.

I will shortly comment on the triangulation model. Three models must be distinguished. Triangulation in a pre-cognitive (pre-linguistic) situation, triangulation by linguistic behavior, and its application to literary language (see Röska-Hardy 2005: 204-05, Davidson 2005 (1993): 176-77). The first describes also the communication between animals, the second is not only causal, but the ascription of attitudes is bound by propositional, linguistically expressed thoughts. Modifications of triangulation begin with language learning. The model is also applied to literary language (Davidson 2005 (1993): 177). The triangle of the writer, his audience, and the common background comes into play. Davidson argues, that without direct causal relation of linguistic behavior and world, the words have no content we can use. There would be no language without that. But what ties the writer and the audience if there are no direct causal and temporal connections between both? Understanding literary text cannot be a matter of a writer's intention or only the particular horizon of the audience like invention, education, taste and so on. Both is necessary but, from Davidson's point of view (181), this should not lead to a significant relativism. Literary understanding and criticism work only if there is a shared background of the writer and the audience.

It is to mention here that Davidson's total revision of traditional epistemology, concluded from his theory of meaning, is dependent on the validity of the triangulation model of *RI* and its assumption that the acquisition of knowledge is triangulated holistically and interpersonal from the beginning. Another point is that, for Davidson, there is an indeterminacy of interpretation because significant different theories of truth fit to the evidence of *RI* as well. This arises in case that a range of theories of interpretation are underdetermined by their evidence (on critique in detail, see Lepore, Ludwig 2005: 221-247). This leads to the evaluation of the project of *RI* and the question whether *RI* is possible in principle.

1.6. Events and Actions

Coarse-grained events are, in Davidson's philosophy, the key element in order to connect causation, human action and the mental. The descriptions of actions and the mental take no effect in our ontology. A total theory of beliefs and desires is a *unified theory* of thought, meaning, action and at the same time of decision and communication. Actions are events that we redescribe in a particular way. Davidson argued to adopt an ontology of events as *particular, unrepeatable, dated*, that is, *individual* events. The ontological commitment is given by the analysis 1. of the logical form of actions sentences, 2. of adverbial modifications, and 3. of singular causal statements. From the logical point form of view, events are to accept as individuals:

All this talk of descriptions and redescriptions makes sense, it would seem, only on the assumption that there are bona fide entities to be described and redescribed. (Davidson 1980 (1969): 165)

Davidson's option is: a Tarski-type theory of truth supplies the truth conditions of all utterances of sentences in a natural language that copes linguistic meaning meeting decision theory. Both are unified because, with the decision theory, we have at hand an extraction of cardinal utilities and subjective probabilities from simple preferences, and the subjective probabilities applied to sentences give the theory of meaning. The route is an interpretation of words, beliefs, and desires from simple preference toward sentences. But such a theory is possible on a structure dictated by the concept of rationality. From Davidson's point of view we have a powerful *theory* if all this works. And this *unified theory* is holistic in nature. But it is a static theory that gives us no information of the change of thoughts.

It is the claim of the logical form analysis of action sentences and singular causal statements to reason such ontology. This goes together with the slingshot argument. I call this the *Davidson*-argument. The relationship of identity between events is given by the truth-condition of sentences on the relationship of identity like "*a* = *b*" in that "*a*" and "*b*" are singular terms referring to events (on an analysis of identity statements, see R. Fingo and Robert May 2001). Events are identical if they are brought about by the same causes and effects. The nexus of causality is the general frame of reference for the identification and description of events. Yet the redescription of events by the instantiation of laws cannot change the effects of the events themselves. The unification of the theory of meaning, action and events ensues by the satisfactional (holistic) theory of truth. This is the unified frame of the logical form analysis and its application to actions, sentences, singular causal statements and the explanations of action. Also the individuation of desire and intentions is satisfied by events, for example, if someone has such attitudes of desire and intentions they are to fulfill by an event.

The framework of the analysis of beliefs, desires, intentions, and emotions is the semantic ascent (Quine). Therefore we do not understand actions from the radical interpreter's side directly, but only by redescription. It is the answer to the question of the nature of the relation that relates a *person* and an event and, in the same way, an *event* and a person. The semantic analysis of the descriptions of action has to show what our talk on action refers to. Therefore it is the claim of the logical form analysis of action sentences to give an answer to the classical problem in the theory of action:

How do we *immediately* relate an agent and his actions that we redescribe in different ways?

The logical form of action sentences gives an answer to the question why the assumption is justified that two or more sentences describe the *same action*. The magna charta of this account is:

As a first step toward straightening things out, we may try talking not of actions but of sentences and descriptions of actions instead. In the case of agency, my proposal might then be put: a person is the agent of an event if and only if there is a description of what he did that makes true a sentence that he did it intentionally. This formulation, with its quantification over linguistic entities, cannot be considered entirely satisfactory. But to do better would require a semantic analysis of sentences about propositional attitudes. (Davidson 1980 (1971): 46)

The semantic analysis of action sentences (descriptions) suggests to us the claim that things are like actions. Such sentences do not refer to individuals to whom the used singular terms refer, but to events as particulars and the semantic role of the verb, for example, "drives" in the sentence "Peter drives from Boston to New York" is to analyze as a predicate. Such sentences are true if and only if a respective event exists.

Yet, the step from *RI* to the theory of action (and decision) is not only taken by the solution of the task of intelligible redescription of behavior with its evidence of holding a sentence true, but also by the causal explanation of such a behavior as actions by pro attitudes and beliefs. Davidson calls this primary reasons (rationalization) or *explanation by redescription* in difference to non-explanatory redescriptions that do not state any purpose (Davidson 2004 (1987): 105). Prima vista the step from *RI* to the theory of action is not obvious because the task of *RI* is the intelligible redescription and not the explanation of speakers' doings. The interaction between the theory of interpretation and action is reasoned thereby that a theory of interpretation needs support because the evidence of *RI* — holding a sentence true — is connected with the ascription of desire and a description of action that are caused by our intentions. We find the transition from *RI* to the theory of action with Davidson's concept of reason and his ontology of events: actions are events and as such body movements that we redescribe with an intentional vocabulary and that we explain in the framework of quantified beliefs and desires. Davidson argues for a causal explanation of action by primary reasons and for the identity of body movements and primitive actions. Primary reasons have causal power, but it is not the ordinary event causation that explains agent causation. This sort of causation is explained by *primitive actions*. Such *actions* are events and as *events* mere movements of our body that we describe as intentional. The two acts in the act-pair A-A', for example, the moving of my hand and its result, such as the light being switched on, are identical: there is only one action $A \equiv A'$ that we describe in different ways (the identity thesis is already formulated in

Davidson 1980 (1963): 5-6). The identity symbol symbolizes an identity of content (Frege). This thesis goes back to G. E. M. Anscombe, and also D. S. Shwayder and others have argued for it. Following from that, the expression of agency is to interpret extensionally.

For an explanatory redescription of action we need nothing but *pro (con) attitudes*, *beliefs* and *primitive actions* themselves. The components are furthermore to analyze in respect of their causal relations. Given the ontological reduction to individual events, we find an answer to the puzzles of mind and body and can explain the freedom to act in the world of causality. A total theory is to develop that enables us to interpret sentences and to ascribe beliefs and desires to any agent: "This composite theory would explain all behavior, verbal and otherwise." (Davidson 1984 (1975): 163)

1.7. Explaining Actions, Anomalous Monism and the Unification

Normally we have accepted that causal relations are backed by laws that are based on induction. But the explanation of actions by primary reasons does not imply laws and inductive procedures basically. It is essential for the *unified theory* as a *total* (*composite*) theory of beliefs and desire (belief-desire account) that no system of ascription of attitudes, however good it may be, can give us predictions of actions. Davidson has already formulated the program of the unification in *Action, Reasons, and Causes* (1980 (1963)): "Any serious theory for predicting action on the basis of reason must find a way of evaluating the relative force of various desires and beliefs in the matrix decision; it cannot take as its starting point the refinement of what is to be expected from a single desire". (16) Ramsey's axiomatical description of preferences under uncertainty specified to individual agents is similar to an axiomatical theory of truth, because the theory gives us a separate theory for every agent just as the theory of truth is a theory of an individual speaker. But both theories say nothing about how their validity is established. In both cases the speaker or agent has satisfied certain conditions in principle. In the case of the theory of decision, all predictions imply quantitative descriptions with which we specify degrees of beliefs (subjective probabilities) and the relative strength of desire. Jeffrey's theory is helpful here because he has shown how subjective probabilities and

values are to extract from preferences that propositions are true. Davidson reinterprets Jeffrey's results with respect to the basic attitude that
is directed toward uninterpreted sentences, and he assumes as "basic
empirical primitive" that the (weak) basic agent's preference is that one
sentence rather than another be true. If we assume that we have these at
hand, this does not imply that we have any reason to assume also that
there is a strict law predicting what some individual will do next. If we
make the assumption that different systems of systematization of ascription lead us to different predictions, this shows nothing at all because,
nevertheless, the same system may lead us to different predictions also.
This shows that the *unified theory* is not a unification by strict explanatory laws as a hard core of unification.

Yet, the concept of coarse-grained events links the theory of action
and the mental. From this point of view, there is no dualism of causal
factors, causal systems or types of causation: the same event will have
the *same* cause, no matter whether it is described by primary reasons (as
an action) or as a physical event. Therefore, from the dualism of description it does not follow that there are two sorts of law. The step from the
mental to externalism is taken thereby because the mental is not a closed
system and the attitudes are to individuate by the external world shared
by speaker and interpreter.

Explaining action is the task of their explanatory redescription. The
leading question is:

What is the logical relationship between the description of any action
and the propositional content of the explained beliefs and other attitudes
if such attitudes stand in a certain logical relationship to the description
by which we explain the action?

It is the claim to give us a coherent understanding of moral conflicts,
weakness of will, and an intentional but irrational acting. We find the
logical relationship—not in the sense of the logical-connection argument—thereby:

A characteristic of teleological explanation not shared by explanation generally
is the way in that it appeals to the concept of *reasons*. The belief and desire that
explain an action must be such that anyone who had that belief and desire would
have a reason to act in that way. What's more, the descriptions we provide of
desire and belief must, in teleological explanation, exhibit the rationality of the
action in the light of the content of the belief and the object of the desire. (Davidson 1984 (1975): 159)

The word *because* in action explaining sentences takes logical and causal considerations into account (Davidson 2004 (1982): 173). Both are necessary but not sufficient. In *Action, Reasons, and Causes* (1980 (1963)) the causal analysis of *because* in 'He did it because...' is emphasized where we name a reason but not the logical/conceptual relation with respect to the content of the belief-desire pairs. This is modified explicitly in *Paradoxes of Irrationality* (2004 (1982)). Actions are to explain by desire-belief pairs in two different ways: 1. the content of these attitudes implies that something is desirable (valuable) about the action, and 2. their causal role in the occurrence of the action.

I reconstruct the development of Davidson's theory of action from *Action, Reasons, and Causes* (1980 (1963) to the final version in *Intending* (1980 (1978)) in 6.1., in this book). In *Problems in the Explanation of Action* (2004 (1987)), a sum of the theory of action with respect to the anomalous monism is given. In this context, his theory of practical reasoning in *How is Weakness of the Will Possible* (1980 (1970)) is also to discuss. A summary of his proposal and a historical overview are given in *Aristotle's Action* (2005 (2000)). The key element to explaining what *intentions* are is the distinction between *prima facie*, *unrestricted* and *all things considered judgements*. Pro attitudes themselves are prima facie judgements. The belief-desire explanation of action claims to show that intentions are not a genuine mental item (on a non-reductive conception of intention, see Mele 1992: part II). In *A Unified Theory of Thought, Meaning, and Action* (2004 (1980)) the formal picture of the unification is described.

The causal explanation of actions by primary reasons defines intentional actions by their causes: "A reason is a rational cause". (Davidson 1980 (1974): 233) By analytical considerations, such an analysis claims to find a law of behavior that, we would normally assume, is not a result of an empirical generalization. There is a coincidence: a *law* stating conditions under that agents perform intentional actions, an analysis of *freedom* to act that is not in any conflict with a causal power of primary reasons, and a *causal* analysis of intentional action (Davidson 1980 (1973): 76). Yet this account is considerably modified by Davidson in the same article *Freedom to Act* (1980 (1973) already. Laws of behavior or a general knowledge explain to us persistent and different preferences and beliefs, but the generalizations that are implied for an ascription of attitudes refer exclusively to individuals. Nomic wisdom concerning mankind can only be applied indirectly to explanation by primary reasons. This is exactly what limits the domain of the model of probabilistic explanation (on the relationship between explanations by our general scientific scheme and primary reasons and a modification of the role of laws in explaining action discussing Hempel's account, *Hempel on Explaining Action* (1980 (1976)). Davidson emphasizes that nomic wisdom concerning mankind informs us about the fact only that from a single action one cannot come to the conclusion of the existence of any disposition like a belief or a desire, but such a knowledge cannot be applied to explanatory redescriptions by primary reasons.

But why do both interpretation and the theory of action work together?

At first glance, *RI* seems not to be able to explain actions. Its task is the interpretation of linguistic behavior, not its explanation. It is unclear what it means that *RI* is a *unified theory* of thought, meaning, and *action*. But the solution of its task does not stand alone, because the ascription of beliefs and other propositional attitudes is connected with the interpretation of speech in principle. Behavior is redescribed as an action not only from the interpretive, but also from the explanatory route of an interpreter who takes into play the network of attitudes *and* their decision-theoretical strength. An event is an action if we redescribe it as a consequence of a decision-theoretical ordered network of attitudes. We redescribe the beliefs and desires by finding a relation between the speaker and his sentences (or utterances), that is, the ascription of attitudes depends on the interpretation of speech. It is hard to distinguish, for example, universal thoughts from their conjunctions, ascribe conditional thoughts or mixed quantifications like "he hopes that everyone is loved by someone" without having a language, and I cannot assign preferences without interpreting speech. Propositional attitudes are causal dispositions, and we acquire the elementary (empirical) cases from them by a causal interaction with the external world: *Communication begins where causes converge*. Explanation by primary reasons as rational causes are to characterize in a way that they connect causality with rationality as a normative concept. Normative and causal properties of mental concepts are related to a total theory of behavior. Therefore the theories of interpretation, decision and communication can only develop together. The hard core of this step is made within the truth-centered theory of *RI* because holding-true is extended to preferences as preferring-to-be-true directed toward sentences. This works within the assumption of charity (rationality) only as *policy of rational accommodation*. Therefore the theory of decision is prescriptive and at the same time descriptive. Beliefs and desires explain action by the process where an interpreter fits them into a pattern of behavior coherent by his *theory*. Beliefs are not behavior but beliefs and desires are supervenient on behavioral items. Therefore no ascription of attitudes is correct if we attribute them to objects that do not meet behavioral items.

Davidson's *philosophy of mental* and the individuation of a propositional content of attitudes is to distinguish from different versions of internalism (individualistic or physicalistic proposals; for example, J. Fodor, S. Stich) and classical externalist conceptions in the philosophy of mental (Burge), epistemology and metaphysics (Armstrong, Putnam). Explaining actions by primary reasons and the individuation of attitudes by the triangulation model of *RI* is a reasoning for an anomalous monism in the philosophy of mind. There is a particular relationship between the externalistic individuation of propositional attitudes and the ontology of events because externalism claims to discredit type-type identity theories, but not token-token theories of the mental. The anomalous monism is:

1. an *ontological monism,* but not a metaphysical materialism (there are no things and events that are not uniquely identified by definite descriptions of the physics and by such definite descriptions that are mental);

2. a *conceptual* and an *explanatory* dualism (the mental and the physical vocabulary are neither definitionally nor nomologically reducible in one or the other direction, and natural science cannot predict in principle any event under a mental description);

3. therefore it is to conclude that there are no *strict laws* that connect the mental and the physical, and

4. these points do not contradict the fact that there are *causal relations* between the mental and the physical, however they may be described (on the other hand, causal explanations are themselves dependent on a vocabulary we use to describe events and formulate laws). The conceptual and explanatory dualism will show that the semi-autonomy of the mental does not need to change our ontology.

5. Yet, in anomalous monism the fact that it is not disputed that the mental has a reality of its own is not sufficiently analyzed. Mental events and states are not merely projected from an attributer. Anomalous monism argues: mental events are as real as physical events as they are identical with them. Also Quine's "dramatic portrayals" understanding

of attitudes (the mental) does not imply that *nothing* is to portray (we have analyzed this problem in E. Rogler, Preyer 2002, 2003 a, 2003 b in detail).

Holism, externalism, and the normative features of the mental work together. Therefore psychology is not to reduce to, and not in competition with, any natural science. But the *unified theory* is not unscientific because an abstract structure is described and defined by it.

6. In this context, a further problem is to mention. Davidson focuses the analysis of mental states on propositional attitudes. Apparently qualia do not play a significant role for him: the causation of attitudes is not an epistemological foundation of knowledge. Sensations are not propositional. It is his claim to close the chapter of epistemology from Descartes till Quine. In contrast to that, he emphasizes that the awareness of objects and events — our causal interaction with them — is a prelinguistic (precognitive) basis of the objectivity of knowledge. Elementary perceptual beliefs are basically the exemplification of the individuation of propositional contents.

How are non-propositional mental states to integrate in the triangulation model?

Sensations and awarenesses run in the causal chain to the external world that caused them. But they are not any foundation of knowledge. For some philosophers, the problem of qualia is a dramatic one, for example for Kim (1998). Davidson distinguishes between the discrimination of the external world by beliefs as all animals do, and it is to distinguish between true and false beliefs as well, that is, we dispose of the concept of objective truth (2001 (1991): 209). Causal relations are no relations of confirmation or disconfirmation, because they are not beliefs or propositions. They are in existence between *events* in the world or in our sensory (organic) system. The link to sensations from the triangulation model is that they cause us to *believe* something. Among the commentators of Davidson's philosophy, Röska-Hardy (1997) has described how sensations or something made to happen in the mental as non-propositional in nature — Dilthey and Husserl talk about *Erlebnisse* — are conceptually linked with the individuation of propositional content in the triangulation model. I will not discuss this problem in detail in this book. In the evolution of mind — that is Davidson's view —, we can only distinguish between attitudes and have a shared world if we have the concept of coherence and truth at our disposal. And truth is at the same time a matter of evidence. Theoretically the formal semantic theory, in comparison to theories of fundamental measurement, is a powerful systematization. This is not a simple empirical question. We proceed on a way like theorizing in general: For making a test to give theories empirical content it is required that we have a set of axioms with which we specify the logical relations of the primitives (primitive expressions) and the entities we refer to (or we measure). Davidson makes a principal difference here between explaining *about* and *in the* theory.

The ascription of attitudes is not committed to an ontology of narrow mental states. It is the claim to show, in difference to Putnam and Burge, that mental states are *inner* as identical with the states of the body and at the same time to identify by causal relations to the objects and events *outside* the body. The ontology of individual events and their causal relations to one another is the key to showing this. The point is that mental states do not narrowly supervene on physical features in principle. Davidson has argued, in an answer to his critics, that *weak* supervenience explains us how mental states supervene on physical states (2005 (1993)). Therefore we see how the description of mental plays a particular role for explaining actions. Davidson emphasizes that his version of monism (identity theory) is not materialist. Yet it is a version of physicalism because all that exists has spatio-temporal locutions. The ontological commitment of unreducible entities (objects and events), concluded from the logical form analysis, connects his philosophy of language, the theory of action, and the philosophy of mental in the framework of a conceptual dualism in ontology.

But how do we describe that no event whatever has any direct consequences for the ontology we have?

It is Davidson's turn that causality itself is to explain from triangulation. Differences in causal history are to explain by the differences in the physical world. The common causes determine the content of utterances and thoughts. The pattern of causal relations caused in the triangle governs interpretation. The classification of patterns must take the different concepts, the vocabularies we use, into play. The anomalous monism implies ontological reduction, but not a conceptual one. This shows that the conceptual dualism is also given with the coarse-grained concept of events. When we describe an event with a physicalistic vocabulary this does not exclude that we describe the same event in another way as well. This leads us to the problem of mental causality within the framework of the *unified theory*.

This version of monism means that there are no strict laws of mental events or psycho-physical laws. Strict laws do *not* entail causally defined concepts. Such concepts are particularly typical of our normal explanation of propositional attitudes. The *autonomy* (freedom, self-rule) and *anomaly* (failure to fall under a law) of the mental is reasoned thereby that there is no systematic way to express a mental state in a physicalistic vocabulary. But this does not exclude the following also: every single mental event is a physiological event (token-identity). His argument derives from Quine's thesis of indeterminacy of translation (Davidson 1984 (1970): 222). The argument that there are no strict laws by which we explain the mental is motivated by the holistic feature of autonomy and anomaly of the mental: beliefs and other propositional attitudes are only manifest in behavior as modified and mediated by further beliefs and attitudes "without limits". The mental is no "closed system", that is, we individuate propositional attitudes externalistically. This holds for all cases. Davidson's anomalous monism implies in fact an ontology, but not as a "conceptual reduction"; that is why there is no law of the mind. In other words: supervenience implies monism but not a definitional or nomological reduction. For Davidson, the mental is a conceptual category, but not an ontological one. But different classifications and descriptions do not change our fundamental ontology of events and what they cause. The key element of Davidson's philosophy of mental is a coarse-grained concept of events (events themselves are neither mental nor physical).

Yet, the anomalous monism leads back to *RI* because the concepts of belief and meaning are not to reduce to physical, neurological and behavioral concepts and the attribution of mental is responsible for a background of reasons, attitudes, and intentions of the individual speaker. So there is no law of the mind. Putnam has argued that it is not possible that mental states are *inner* and, at the same time, to individuate by the *external* world (non-individualistically). The anomalous monism makes another turn. It follows from triangulation that ordinary mental states satisfy that they are inner as identical with states of the body (token identity), and at the same time they are to identify by causal relations to objects and events from outside.

It is the claim that, without any contradiction, we apply the first person authority to such relations. The conceptual connection between the first person authority (the knowledge of our own mind) and the knowledge of the world, the knowledge of behavior and our knowledge of other minds is not definitional but holistic. This is the ground why epistemic restrictions play no role to solve the task of *RI*.

The anomalous monism is critical of several views: *nomological monism* or materialism, that is, the correlated events are only one event actually, and there are correlated laws, of *nomological dualism*, that is, parallelism, interactionism, epiphenomenalism, and of *anomalous dualism*, that is, ontological dualism, Cartesianism, where there are no laws about the correlation of the mental and the physical. Yet, an anomalous monism also rejects strict relations between psychological concepts and psychological laws as well (R. Wilburn 1998: 143-144.) This is reasoned by the general norm of rationality, that is, the anomalous monism is the primary aspect of the mental as the counterpart of *RI* (on the weak supervenience with an answer to J. Kim, see Davidson 2005 (1993), on the contemporary philosophy of mind and the nomological reduction of the mental to the physical by bridge-laws—Nagel-model—, see Kim 1996, on the debate on anomalous monism in particular on the problem of mental causality and supervenience, see E. Rogler and Preyer 2001).

Explaining behavior as actions takes into play the agent's propositional attitudes, and such explanations are an irreducible causal concept. But the way of explaining and individuating actions is not a science of behavior that we find in physiology and physics. The *unification* of the theory of thought, meaning, and action, however, claims to be a powerful, attractive formal theory in harmony with many of our intuitions of the nature of rationality. Davidson gives a "conceptual exercise" of the unification of the basic propositional attitudes. The unified theory is described (defined) by an abstract structure. The structure of language and thought is given by the logic of quantification. This is not a description of what really happens in understanding each other or in acquisition of our first concepts and language. But we give the theory the empirical turn and its practicability by the structure of the normative features of propositional attitudes on their correct ascription in the procedure of interpretation of speech and explanation of action from the third person attitude of a radical interpreter. (Davidson 1984 (1974): 145-148), (1975): 162-63, 2004 (1980), (1984): 26-33)

The unified theory of thought, meaning and action coincides with the holism of attitudes, their normative features and the externalism of individuation of their content. Davidson claims to identify the place of a comprehensive theory of action and thought. The place is the basic attitude: *the agent prefers one sentence to be true rather than another,* therefore a degree of belief is not to be introspected. The theory of belief and meaning requires knowledge of the degree of belief in its truth and not only of what has caused it. From that, a *total* theory results for interpretation of sentences and at the same time ascribes beliefs, desires and other propositional attitudes. This *composite* theory claims to explain behavior in general. This is the hard core to unify the theory of interpretation and decision because the interpretation of linguistic behavior and ascription of attitudes play together in principle. The same *sentences* are objects of belief and desire. In this general line, Davidson takes in also evaluative attitudes. The key relation is what attitudes a speaker has toward sentences, not propositions like Jeffrey has assumed. The composite theory claims to relate concepts of beliefs, desire and linguistic meaning and to analyze belief in a quantified form (subjective probability, ratio scale) and measures desire in an interval scale, which is often called decision theory. In difference to Ramsey and Jeffrey and from Davidson's point of view, a theory of meaning is to take in. The distinction between the two scales goes back to Ramsey.

The unified theory is holistic in nature, the contents of beliefs, utterances and values are ascribed simultaneously. This is reasoned by the fact that the basic attitudes are also interdependent. They are not determined step by step. Rationality is one of degree. But rationality is not a policy, it is a basic rationality. The principle of charity is the normative feature that we read in the linguistic behavior and the attitudes. The interpreter discovers a degree of logical consistency in the speaker's attitudes and at the same time endows him with a degree of what the interpreter takes to be true belief about the world. Bayesian decision theory says nothing about the object of simple preferences that are extracted within its framework. The problem is:

How are preferences to describe without identifying their propositional content? The content itself, and also sentences, are not observable but utterances and inscription are. The interpreter has given the observable behavior a content. The objects of attitudes are objects which caused them. For Davidson, the only way is to identify the object share to speaker and interpreter by its common cause, that is, the same objects cause the content of their attitudes. This is the constraint: the theory of decision does not have to include a theory of interpretation only but also one of communication. This leads to a problem of understanding in principle also of moral values: it is a requirement of stating disagreement about objects, events and actions that we think and talk about the same of their aspects, and which is the guarantee that we identify and talk about the same things in our intercourse.

1.8. The Third Dogma of Empiricism

The reciprocal relationship between rationality, interpretation and the satisfactional theory of reference leads Davidson to a critique of T. Kuhn and P. Feyerabend and to an anti-representationalism as well. Yet, the radical externalism also warrants to give up the third dogma of empiricism, that is, the dualism between scheme and content. Revealing the third dogma of empiricism amounts to rejecting fundamentalist epistemology, such as the singling out of a neutral (epistemic) basic vocabulary. There are several versions of this that come into focus: the experience in general, stimuli as in Quine's neutral sensory input, and Kripke's rigid designators and also his metaphysical essentialism. Davidson classifies such accounts as "building block theories". Singular terms are not a privileged class of expressions that bridge the gap between language and the world; reference is inscrutable on the basis of behavioral items. In this respect, Quine's elimination of singular terms in his *Word and Object* (1960) is the right approach. But, on the other hand, the thesis of incommensurability, a conceptual relativism, seems unreasonable as it allows for different (theories of) truths. Davidson looks at relativistic theories in the perspective of Quine's indeterminacy of translation: relativism then amounts to a chance of pairing the same sentence with different truth values. Quine's classical question is what we are committed to by using bound variables in a theory. References of singular terms are theoretically ineliminable for the theory of natural language (speaker) because its axiomatization requires to treat them as *names* and *variables* (along to sequences and satisfaction). Such expressions designate objects and events (this problem is elaborated in detail by S. Neale 1999). They must accept the entities our singular terms refer to, but reference is *not* to explain behaviorally. By this, we see how semantics and ontology work hand in hand. We solve this problem of reference by distinguishing explanation *within* from explanation *of* a theory:

Within the theory, the conditions of truth of a sentence are specified by adverting to postulated structure and semantic concepts like that of satisfaction or reference. But when it comes to interpreting the theory as a whole, it is the notion of truth, as applied to closed sentences, which must be connected with human ends and activities. (Davidson 1984 (1977): 221-222)

The interrelation of belief and linguistic meaning hinges on the ascription of attitudes and the interpretation of sentences. It is because of the necessary translation of beliefs into linguistic meaning that Kuhn's and Feyerabend's dichotomy of concepts and content appears to be unreasonable. Conceptual schemes are translatable languages. Interpretation is translation in principle. If translation is successful, speaking of two conceptual schemes is not needed. This is the ground why a comparison of theories is always an open matter. In the same way this holds true even when there is a difference in meaning and reference amongst certain languages of theorizing about the world. This follows from *RI*. So it is not the *content* of attitudes itself but the things and events that make beliefs true or fulfill other propositional attitudes. But from the non-reducibility of psychological concepts one may conclude that it makes sense to speak of irreducible or semi-autonomous systems of concepts or schemes of description and explanation. This leads also back to *RI* because such concepts are a medium of understanding and communication. Davidson claims to demolish the scheme-content distinction in epistemology, that is, there is no representational system and no neutral empirical content outside it, but this does not mean that we do not believe in a (public) objective world we have not made.

Understanding and explaining something work together in the *unified theory*. But it is not disputed that our understanding (translation) is also a pre-theoretic skill. The ascription of attitudes is only possible by using language. Language is the medium with which we solve the task of *RI*. The conceptual dualism is saddled from *RI* because we make behavior intelligible without changing our ontology. This goes along with the distinction of *homonomic* and *heteronomic* generalizations as a theory of concepts. The homonomic generalization is such that we can find positive instances by adding further conditions stated in the "same general vocabulary". Such generalizations result in a law with perfect predictability and coherence with all the evidence we have. The measurement of length, weight, temperature and so on are examples here. Laws are valid only if we suppose an ideal theory, that is, a theory with powerful constitutive components. In this sense, homonomic generalizations are subject to correction. But if we assume that, in case of the heteronomic generalization, something like a law is at work, we have to shift in vocabulary. Both generalizations are not to be reduced to explanations as norms; rules and justifications are not to be reduced to facts. The assumption is that most of our practical knowledge and science also is heteronomic. The distinction between the two sorts of generalization is concluded from Quine's indeterminacy of translation. The linking of mental and physical statements (as an example for heteronomic statements) with the ascription of propositional attitudes is indeterminable and not to be eliminated—this leads back to *RI*. In general: there is a fundamental distinction between intrinsic properties of material entities including those of the brain processes and the content of attitudes. To sum up: no intelligible redescription of linguistic behavior and no ascriptions of attitudes go on without *RI* and both participate on the indeterminacy of translation.

1.9. Values

It is the claim of the unified theory also to give an answer of expressing evaluation, that is, some basic connections between evaluation and language are to show. Evaluation (evaluating attitudes) means something like wanting, desiring, cherishing, holding to be right and so on. (Davidson 2004 (1984), (1986), (1995), (2000))

How do the theory of interpretation and the partly external individuation of content of propositional attitudes play together with the claimed objectivity of evaluative judgements? What is the reasoning when we consider that values have the same objectivity like beliefs, without being ontologically real entities—values are pseudo-entities?

Davidson connects the theoretical assumptions of interpretation with the analyses of value judgements, because meaning, beliefs and desires conspire in principle. The unification of the theory of interpretation and decision assumes that the choices (decisions) show the speaker's preferences (experimental subject) that a subset of his uttered sentences are true. Therefore the total theory, concluded from that, gives an interpretation of particular sentences; we assign beliefs and also desires. Davidson is no Humean because he does not agree with Hume's theory of motivation (2004 (1984): 26). The basic relation for redescribing behavior is the attitude that the speaker has toward *sentences*. The point is that

The same sentences are the objects of both belief and desire. This reinforces the claim that the interpretation of the evaluative attitudes proceeds along the same general lines as the interpretation of cognitive attitudes. (Davidson 2004 (1986): 71)

The assumption is that we can make distinctions between beliefs, desires and evaluation in a shared frame of reference only.

How is the objectivity of value judgement given?

Davidson answers this question with respect to triangulation. The objects of beliefs and values are caused by the common object that speaker
and interpreter are caused to regard and to want as similar. Interpersonal
values are grounded on every interpreter's own values: that is, the value
of the principle of charity and what is valuable in itself. We do not choose
these values, we have them. But this is no fundamentalism, no fixed list
of standards or no external hierarchy of values, because the framework
within which we ascribe attitudes is introduced theoretically. This shows
us again the basic role of charity for the application of the interpretive
truth-theory within the procedure of *RI*. But the problem is whether
this requirement selects the correct behavioral items by the application
of the theoretical framework of re-interpretation of behavior in principle
(on a weaker assumption for the harmonization of cognitive and evaluative attitudes, the principle of tolerance, by ascription of evaluative attitudes, Preyer 2011 a).

1.10. On Debates

Since 1975, the debates on Davidson's philosophy were focused in particular on the question "What is a theory of meaning?". M. Dummett,
Putnam, Soames, Etchemendy, J. Forster, M. Platts, P. Horwich and
others are to mention here. The leading problem was whether the Davi-
son-program is successful, that is: is a theory of truth a theory of meaning?
Putnam, for example, has argued that Tarski's truth predicates are neither
to apply in semantics nor to our common conception of truth. The results
of this controversy lead to a modification and correction from Davidson's
side. In *The Structure and Content of Truth* (1990), Davidson has given
(more or less) a final result (see also 2005 (1994), (1995), (1996), (1997)).
With this modification, no knowledge of the interpreter is assumed that
the *T*-theory is an adequate theory, and the interpreter does not simply
ascribe true biconditionals to uttered sentences of a speaker's linguistic
behavior. The modification is to describe as follows: it is presupposed
that interpreters have an intuitive, not an explicit, knowledge of parts of
a *T*-theory, for example, they intuitively grasp logical truth. The theory
itself describes an intuitive knowledge of a competent interpreter— the
entire unlimited number of *T*-sentences—, and at the same time the
theory, by the evidence of *RI*, provides the strategy to know all this, that
is, "the theory specifies the conditions under which the utterance of a

sentence would be true if it were uttered." (310) The confirmation of the
theory itself, however, is not dependent on intuitions of their concepts,
because it is an empirical theory. Yet it is a general feature of theorizing
that we preserve entailment relations between sentences that eliminate a
vast number of *non-interpretive* theories. But the work of interpretation
can only be carried out on the condition that the speaker intends his utterance to have those truth-conditions: truth is a property of utterances.
Therefore the "ultimate *evidence*" of correctness of the theory is the
available token of how language is used (Davidsons 2001 (1988): 182). If
the interpreter knows the *T*-sentence of a speaker's truth *theory*, he can
understand him, but it is not required that the interpreter also knows in
addition that this is really an interpretive theory. Among commentators
it is an open question whether the last word has been said about these
modifications. Further philosophical research may be desirable.

This leads back to the treatment of indexicals to verify the interpretive
truth theory. Another point must be mentioned. If, following hypotheses
of Chomsky and Fodor, language is built into people by mechanism one
cannot conclude that language is not also learnt. And if this is the case,
the learnability of language leads us back to methods of *RI*. This could
be a further point of analysis.

Lepore, Ludwig (2005) have given a reconstruction of Davidson's
theory of meaning and language. They argue that, without the early history of Davidson's *initial project* (1984 (1965)) of a compositional theory
of the semantics of natural language, the followed continuation of his
philosophy cannot be understood. Davidson (1984 (1967)) has introduced the *extended project*, that is, the extensional theory of truth has the
power to give us the semantics of natural language. The step to the extended project and the continuation of Davidson's theory of language is
the clarification of the concept of meaning. The common interpretation
is that the theory of truth replaces the initial project: replacement theory.
Lepore's and Ludwig's critique is that the initial project is independent
of the extended project. In contrast to that, the extended project is a
proposal that explains the meaning of sentences within which primitive
and complex expressions occur. The replacement theory is to revise if
we go back to Davidson's initial project. Lepore and Ludwig show that
a compositional theory of meaning is developed by the application of a
recursive theory of truth. This makes the meaning of the sentences of the
object language available and is *interpretive*. It is their particular claim
to show that the reformulation of the extended project by *RI* leads to

a problem in Davidson's philosophy in principle. They make a distinction between the ambitious and the modest *version* of *RI*. The first is a
speaker who is radical to interpret by his nature; the second assumes that
whether a speaker is radically interpretable is an empirical question. A
principal problem of *RI* is identified by this. A long time ago I argued
that the epistemic restriction of interpretation is not eliminated by the
application of the principle of charity as a constraint of *RI*. Furthermore,
in the framework of Davidson's theory of language also they analyze
his epistemological and metaphysical conclusions (see also my reviews
2005 b, c).

Since 1970, the debate on Davidson's theory of action has begun regarding the role of body processes, the identity thesis, the logical form
of action sentences and the ontology of events (Goldman, Thalberg, J.
Hornsby, B. Aune, Mele, and others). Davidson has emphasized that
the theory of interpretation and Bayesian decision theory play together
(1990: 322). Here the problem emerges whether explanatory redescriptions by primary reasons are to interpret in a Bayesian way after all. J.
Nida-Rümelin, for example, has argued that agent relative beliefs are not
to explain by the classical decision theory in general and that they are not
incoherent (2002: 182-84). Explanatory redescription needs more than
a knowledge of consequences of actions. In Davidson's final version of
primary reasons, Bayesianism gains the upper hand. Yet it can also be re-
interpreted by agent relative reasons. Such reasons are not to evaluate by
the Bayesian (consequentialistic) strategy in principle. The interlocking
of the theory of interpretation, action and decision also claims to explain
the weakness of the will. Here, the writings of Mele must be mentioned,
for example his *Springs of Action* (1992, on Davidson's theory of action
see also Mele 2003, on intrinsically motivated actions, 73-75). Moreover
it is to mention that one must bring into play that weakness of will is
effected by weak intentions also. It is coherent in Davidson's theory of
action that the explanation of actions reduces intention to belief-desire
pairs, and intentions are no genuine mental item. Yet, our doings are not
only guided by relevant reasons (principle of continence), but to satisfy
intentions is their execution, and by this we evaluate what is done or not.
In this case the problem of the strength of motivation is to take into play.
Time after time there are cases where we decide about what we do from
particular interests and features, and this can be in conflict with relevant
beliefs we have. We would by no means say that in such cases people
have a weak will.

Since 1980 there has been a debate on externalism (Putnam, Burge) and internalism (Fodor, Stich) in the philosophy of the mental. In *Knowing One's Own Mind* (2001 (1987)), Davidson has responded to Burge and Putnam. The triangulation model of *RI* claims to show that ordinary mental states satisfy both: they are *inner* as identical with our body, and at the same time the content of such attitudes is to individuate *externalistically*. The meaning of words and the individuation of attitudes is acquired on the history of the causal interaction with objects, events and the social, that is, by interpretive triangulation. Fundamental events as non-abstract particulars claim to connect both the positions. This leads to criticism on epistemic mediators and the opposition between the proximal (Quine) and the distal theory of meaning (reference) and evidence. Another debate, partially connected with the foregoing, was on anomalous monism, supervenience and mental causation. Davidson has responded to his critics in *Thinking Causes* (2005 (1993)). The main topics were: the problem of epiphenomenalism in Davidson's philosophy of the mental that he rejects, the problem of consistency of the reasoning of the anomalous monism, and his conception of laws. One of the main questions was:

Can anomalous monism give us a convincing conception of the autonomy of the mental? Is the distinction between strict and non-strict laws right? Is a coarse-grained concept of event acceptable to explain causal relations?

Davidson has, for example, responded to Neale that he does not object to properties in ontology in general to explain sentences like "This is the same color as that", but the acceptable *T*-theory does not need any more conceptual resources to verify the right side *T*-sentence as given by the truth-condition of such sentences. There may be a problem to treat indexicals by such resources, but the theory works without positing properties as abstract entities (Davidson 1999 f.: 89, Neale 2001: 41-42).

Since 1990 there has been a turn to Davidson's critique of the correspondent theory of truth and his reasoning to give up facts. Neale (2001) has systemized that Davidson's anti-representationalism and his dismissal of the scheme-content distinction follow from the rejection of the modern correspondent theory of truth (Russell) stating that sentences stand for individual facts as non-linguistic entities to which representations correspond. If there are no facts, there is no representation of them: "If we give up facts as entities that make sentences true, we ought to give up representations at the same time, for the legitimacy of each depends on the legitimacy of the others." (Davidson 2001 (1988): 184, on the distinction between sentential (structural) correspondence (Russell) and non-structural correspondence theories of truth (Austin), see Neale 2001: 45). For Davidson, facts achieve nothing for the theory of meaning, and the formal slingshot (collapsing) argument undermines individual facts. This goes back in different forms to Frege and Gödel. Neale gives a detailed analysis of the argument, and he elaborates that if the slingshot is to succeed to reach the realm of facts it needs a precise theory of description.

Furthermore, from the holistic truth-centered theory of *RI*, the interpretive fulfillment theory of meaning of Lepore and Ludwig (2001, see also Ludwig 1997) and the account of mixed-quotation (H. Cappelen, Lepore) emerges. Their claim is "to specify in general the fulfillment condition of all types of sentences in terms of the conditions specifically required for each sentence type." (Ludwig 1997: 60-61) If the proposal is successful, it gives us an answer to how we incorporate non-assertoric sentences in an interpretive theory of meaning by a generalized fulfillment approach. This proposal is particularly helpful, because it shows that the traditional semantics-pragmatics distinction is misleading.

The post-empirical theory of meaning offers a specific account of linking language and the world. Ontological commitment of logical form and individuation of propositional attitudes in triangulation are paradigmatic now. The holistic truth-centered theory of *RI* and the individuation of propositional attitudes are not to separate in principle. The interpretation and redescription of linguistic behavior is indetermined by all attitudes. But by applying the principle of charity and the principle of autonomy of meaning one is enabled to separate beliefs from meaning while the interdependence is not eliminable. Here, the idiolect theory of language and the third dogma of empiricism merge. The indeterminacy of interpretation by all propositional attitudes and the requirement of individuation of propositional content lead to an epistemology externalized. This explains us the ascription of attitudes by redescription of linguistic behavior within the triangle. All these emerge from *RI*, because the interpretation of others is the basis of epistemology, the so-called basic theory.

Following Davidson, the analysis of logical form is of a structural matter, and it is also the hard core of a theory of meaning and language. We need to consider logic in the case of interpretation and analysis of sentences: without, for example, implications most of our sentences would be meaningless. Logical form and indexicality are parts of the theoretical frame of *RI*, and fixing reference is—following Quine—indeterminate. This is valid for ascribing attitudes as well. From an interpreter's point of view, a speaker is a black box, and ascribing attitudes is only possible on the basis of words uttered. In the case of non-linguistic behavior we inquire into the antecedent conditions of acting, and we expect similar reactions in case of similar antecedents. An interpreter uses sentences to ascribe attitudes. These sentences have a complex structure comparable to the attitudes themselves that we ascribe. And they do not per se indicate the content of the attitudes ascribed. All content is caused by distal stimuli.

Davidson's theory of language and meaning carries on Quine's postempirical semantics. In detail, in their epistemological and semantic investigations of linguistic behavior they assume:

Quine: Contrary to analytical accounts of linguistic meaning, understanding and talking of meaning is bound to empirical theories about using sentences. It is impossible to single out meaning by specifying sentential content by taking a route to reference, for example, a route from expressions to entities denoted. Talking about meaning is bound to sentence-meaning, and meaning and belief are interconnected. In this sense, intentionality is not reducible. Davidson shares these theoretical beliefs with Quine (on Quine and Davidson, see also R. F. Gibson 1994).

Davidson: 1. Speech-utterances—conceived of as actions—are the subject of understanding linguistic meaning. We aim at framing the ascription of propositional attitudes in a particular way, that is, on the sentential level. 2. This results in an expanded theory of understanding, that is, we switch the subject of the theory of meaning from the natural description of behavior to the intelligible redescription of speech acts and other actions. So we do not talk about actions in intentio recta, but of descriptions and sentences over propositional attitudes. 3. These attitudes as reasons are a part of understanding actions. 4. In each and every case, the principle of charity and its unlimited application is required for interpreting individual utterances and linguistic behavior of groups.

But what are the entities we deal with when we ascribe propositional attitudes?

The entities in question are speakers who believe something or who are in a certain mental state. For Davidson, the truth-condition of an ascription is to specify to a speaker to whom the interpreter applies the predication (sentence of ascription). But this is not enough—not for Davidson, either. We need to consider that contextual features of ascribing should be taken into account, such as, the same sentence could be heard and uttered in different idiolects and contexts.When ascribing, we also take the epistemic capacity of speakers more or less into account.

As *RI,* paradigmatically, moves along, the principle of charity has to be legitimated as not working epistemically (through interpreter's knowledge). In the seventies, Davidson developed his holistic theory of belief: evidence for interpreting an utterance is in general an evidence for redescribing the propositional content of sentences as a whole. In the same way, in the late eighties an externalist triangular theory of the mental emerged, dispositions to react differently to a whole of other speakers, objects and events causally interacting with natural speakers. Now the principle of charity is supplemented by the assumed causal interaction of communicating persons, objects and events. Charity, from my point of view, is to reconstruct as the principle of natural epistemic justice. This principle leads us to the constraints of interpretation and it bridges the gap between the asymmetry of interpretation—there is a reason as to the interpreter's knowledge—and a rationality of attitudes—a person has (good) reasons as to his or her causal history. The rationality of attitudes, or speaker's epistemic capacity, so to speak, is given a unifying triangle of externalist interpretation. But in the following it is to show that the externalistic model of *RI* borders on the epistemic capacity that limits the intelligible redescription.

Quine started from criticizing the myth of the ontologically given. In focusing on radical translation, he finds himself committed to at least two given schemes and one world. In contrast to that, Davidson puts more emphasis on the way in which we catch the meaning of utterances. He finds that process of interpreting is framed with reference not to stimulus meaning (proximal theory), but to the triangle (distal theory).

The strategy that originates from Quine's radical translation (situation of determining meaning) tries to catch up with its truth-conditional assumptions in a holistic fashion. This is done by not becoming physicalistic, relativistic or else naïvely realistic: it turns to the mental and social context in the triangle. So it is up to us to propose an account that deals with the restrictions of *RI.*

Davidson believes that our language implies ontology, but not as a theory about the world. He does not think that all philosophical problems are a matter of language. The *unified theory* and the externalism of triangulation are not committed to any theory about the world: "one true and complete description of 'the way the world is'" (Putnam 1981: 49), nor to metaphysical realism, but neither to the ontological relativity (Quine). What is the method of truth in metaphysics? To understand this, we have to distinguish metaphysics, for example, Kripke's and others' modern metaphysical essentialism, from ontology as ontic decisions. Ontological questions and assumptions of metaphysics are dispensable and not fruitful. What counts is just what we act upon linguistically, such is, rationally talk about, and are understood by others to be rationally talking about. We need to grasp that an analytical ontology is not an "ontology" in the traditional meaning of the word. Otherwise we do not understand a new paradigm in the philosophy of language, mind and action. It is to mention here that Davidson doesn't go along with Rorty's understanding of his philosophy in principle. Two points are relevant in this context. The logical form analysis settled our ontological commitments, and the attribution of propositional attitudes is an objective one: reality makes such attitudes true within triangulation. From Davidson's point of view, truth is furthermore no matter of utility that we have thereby and also no language game. This is not in harmony with any version of pragmatism in essential.

The hard core of Davidson's *unified theory* is of particular interest to me. Consequently this is a matter with which the following three leading themes will deal. From this *core*, Davidson has arrived at the externalism of triangulation, that is, the distal theory of reference and cognition. This is no contingent move.

1. In the first step I will discuss his theory of truth as a theory of meaning of natural language, that is, the application of Tarski's convention of truth to interpretation of linguistic behavior and its redescription. From here it is to conclude:

2. Davidson's critique on the intentionalistic theory of meaning (nominalistic theory), the so-called meaning nominalism going back to Grice,

3. the unlimited application of the principle of charity to the redescription of linguistic behavior and the distinction between the interdependence of beliefs and meaning as well as the principle of autonomy of meaning,

(a) the idiolect theory of language; this concept follows from *RI*, because the interdependence between belief and meaning is not eliminable,

(b) the critique on the third dogma of empiricism, the opposition between conceptual scheme and neutral content.

(c) This leads to the central question of Davidson's theory of meaning and truth, the problem of the conceptual relationship between the theory of truth and meaning and the theory of truth and belief.

4. In the second step I will discuss the ontological commitment of events that Davidson has elaborated in a logical analysis of action sentences and the singular causal statement. The claim of the analysis of logical form is to show a structural feature of linguistic behavior, and this is the hard core of his theory of language and meaning. Every interpretation and analysis of sentences presupposes logic. Without implications, for example, most of our sentences would be meaningless. Possible inferences (logical form) and indexicality (the convention T is to specify to speakers and time-points) are parts of the theoretical frame to interpret individual utterances. But all interpretations are indetermined in their fixing reference. This follows from Quine's radical translation.

5. In a further step I will discuss Davidson's concept of rationalization and the identity theory of action, that is, the identity between the two acts $A\text{-}A' = A \equiv A'$. The ontology of individual events is the link to connect the theory of action and of the mental. The concept of reason is the bridge to go from RI to his theory of action: the *unified theory* claims not only to redescribe behavior and assign attitudes but will also explain actions. The theory of interpretation and action is connected by this because the utterance of words is also an action and the teleological explanation is drawn from beliefs of desires. This way, making behavior intelligible by primary reasons leads us also back to RI and the connection between the theory of interpretation, communication and decision.

However, we will grasp Davidson's merits with respect to his concept of primary reasons only if we make reference to the three background theories of his proposal: the logical-connection argument, Hart's so-called ascriptivism, and also Danto's theory of basic acts. Davidson's identity thesis is criticized from different proposals. So I recall the two prominent objections from I. Thalberg and A. I. Goldman. Consequently I come to the result that the role of body movement and the body process is to find by the analysis as a component of actions, and the correct interpretation of the relationship of $A\text{-}A'$ is one of upshots or results.

It is the overall intent to show that the epistemology externalized, the causal interaction of communicating persons, objects and events in the triangulation is born from RI, and only if this interaction is successful we have an objective concept of truth at our disposal. So there is a semantic compatibility of making behavior intelligible. Without it there cannot be any comprehensibility of behavior, be it *linguistic or otherwise*, and no *RI*. This is not in conflict to the rich experience we have to the point that interpreters from different languages and cultures disagree over the truth and the meaning of utterances, but this is caused by the distinction they make in a world they share or are aware of. There is no further frame of reference that we bring ultimately into play, Davidson has argued. This is really a philosophical problem that also takes effect in our understanding of behavior and intercourse. It is an open question whether Davidson's philosophy is right about that because his arguments against different conceptual schemes are only successful if it is shown that his identification criterion of other conceptual schemes (non-inter-translatable languages) is justified. Just this leads us back to the problem of the priority of the third person attitude in the theory of meaning and psychology.

Outline of Donald Davidson's Philosophy

	Theoretical Basis	Independent Evidence	Theorizing on Sentential Level	Epistemological Concepts	Concepts of Communication	Surrounding of Speaker and Interpreter
Speaker	network of propositional attitudes	holding true of sentences	utterances token of sentences	first person authority (self-evident)		
Radical Interpreter	semantical knowledge, deducted by theory	principle of charity as a normative concept of rationality	redescription of linguistic behavior	third person attitude and shared world views[1] (distal event)	ascription and individuation of propositional content in triangulation[2]	time points, events, causal relations between events[3]
Theories	theory of mind	theory of interpretation and rationality	logical form, theory of deduction as back-ground theory (metalogic)	epistemology: externalism of triangulation, distal approach of cognition and meaning		

1 On the base of successful interpretation
2 Triangulation: things, events (relevant stimulus)

3 Davidson makes a difference between stating causal relations and explaining these

2. Truth, Meaning and Radical Interpretation

2.1 From Radical Interpretation to Radical Externalism

The theory of language that follows from *RI* is a continuation of Quine's post-empirical theory of meaning. It is its background theory. *RI* has evolved from radical translation as a redescription of the original problem with explicitly semantic means, that is, the truth-theoretic turn of radical translation. Both approaches agree in the assumption that understanding the meaning of utterances is supported by a relation to empirical theories of the use of sentences. The meaning of a sentence is not to single out in respect of an objective content of any expression: there is no property of an expression to refer to an entity. Reference of verbal behavior is inscrutable for radical translation and also for *RI*. Therefore meaning is tied to sentence meaning and conspires with propositional attitudes. Such attitudes and mental states are not to reduce to the physical. *RI* lines up the radical translation in a truth-theoretical way and leads us to semantics as an empirical theory of truth:

A satisfactory theory for interpreting the utterance of a language, our own included, will reveal significant semantic structure: the interpretation of utterance of complex sentences will systematically depend on the interpretation of utterance of simpler sentences. (Davidson 1984 (1973): 130)

Such structure should be given to us in a theory of truth in a Tarskian style. From this point of view, the step to radical externalism is taken:

We are interested in the concept of truth only because there are actual objects and states of the world to that to apply it: utterances, states of belief, inscriptions. If we did not understand what it was for such entities to be true, we wouldn't be able to characterize the contents of these states, objects and events. So in addition to the formal theory of truth we must indicate how truth is to be predicated of these empirical phenomena. (Davidson 2005 (1996): 35)

Davidson has elaborated the project of empirical semantics framed as an analytical ontology. The basic questions and decisions of his conception and the step to an externalism of triangulation as an epistemological turn are given in his concept of *RI* and its holistic truth-centered theorizing as a foundation of understanding one's language, thoughts and actions. The epistemological turn in Davidson's philosophy of language follows from the assumption that there is a conceptual link between language and the individuation of propositional content within the framework of an externalism of triangulation.

In the following I will show and reconstruct that the insertion triangulation model of *RI* joins together the different parts of Davidson's philosophy under the feature of an individuation of the content of propositional attitudes. The introduction of the first meaning and the autonomy of meaning is a consequence of a critique of an intentions-based theory of meaning, the so-called meaning nominalistic strategy (Grice, Schiffer, Bennett, Holdcroft, on first meaning Davidson 2005 (1986): 93-94, on Grice G. Meggle, M. Ulkan 1997, on a reconstruction of Grice's theory of meaning, Ulkan 1997, on semantic intentions as present in speech acts, Davidson 2005 (1993): 170-71). The solution of the task of *RI* leads also to a particular concept of language, the idiolect theory of language. The rejection of basic intentions that gives meaning to our uttered words follows from picking out the independent availability of the evidence of a theory of interpretation. The principle of autonomy of meaning is of general interest in the theory of language because it shows an essential feature of linguistic behavior and the ascription of attitudes. And this means that there is no logical relationship between external lingual purposes that speakers intend and the meaning of uttered sentences. This is a rejection of approaches that explain meaning by uses of words or sentences: all successful use of language presupposes the autonomy of meaning. The principle of the autonomy of meaning as a critique on Grice is not changed in Davidson's work. Yet it is to mention that the significance of intention in communication is accepted (Davidson 2001 (1992): 112). He distinguishes three sorts of intention: *ulterior intention*, that is, ends or intentions beyond the speech acts that can also be reached by non-linguistic means — "language is not a game: it is never an end in itself" —, the *intended force* of a linguistic utterance like, for example, to be an assertion, a command, a joke, whatever, and furthermore the *strictly semantic intention*, that is, it is necessary that a speaker performs a linguistic action with the intent that the uttered words (inscriptions) are to be interpreted with a certain meaning the utterance and inscriptions have. (Davidson 2004 (1993):170-71)

It is to explain why the principle of charity, the autonomy of meaning, the idiolect theory of language, the first-person authority, the third dogma of empiricism, but also the myth of the subjective follow from *RI* and why the step to an externalism is taken. To make these clear, I will analyze the intrinsic relationship between *interpretation (language)—rationality* (*charity*)—*triangulation* on the basis of the individuation of the content of propositional attitudes. Triangulation as the basic theory explains us how we conceptually link the mental (attitudes), language, the social and the rest of nature. It will be shown that there is a particular connection between the concept of language provided by *RI* and the distal theory of meaning (reference) and thoughts. In my view, this is not a contingent connection. But I will argue that, coming from *RI*, we require a broader frame of reference in order to interpret linguistic behavior. In particular the notion of rationality as an epistemic norm is at issue. To show all these, I will go on with taking the following steps: we can only grasp the *unified theory* to a sufficiently adequate degree if we realize why intentions and attitudes are not just an evidence for *RI*, and also what the task of *RI* is. A speaker does not interpret his utterances himself. Here, *RI* is to characterize by an asymmetry between a speaker and an interpreter. Only a radical interpreter has the task of interpretation. He constructs a theory about speakers' utterances on the basis of evidence. The asymmetry of *RI* explains us the authority of first person, the rejection of the myth of subjective, but also why the task of interpretation takes place in a third person attitude. This leads to the analysis of logical form as a significant structure in the frame of a truth-centered theory of meaning. It is the circle between belief and meaning as well as the asymmetry of *RI* that require a *theoretical* proposal of intelligible redescription. It is to show what makes the independent availability of evidence possible in order to cope with the circle between belief and meaning. But *RI* is only possible provided that its procedure has also an inner-lingual help, namely the autonomy of meaning. This autonomy plays a specific role for the explanation of first person authority and the paratactic analysis of imperatives of the interpretive theory of meaning and truth. It is the claim that the principle of charity gives us the necessary evidence of *RI*. To do this, the transition to the externalism of triangulation is shown from the individuation of the content of attitudes. I will resystematize this principle as a principle of the natural epistemic justice and make a move to take the Burge-problem, that is, the social frame of reference, into account. *RI* leads us to a version of an epistemology naturalized: the interpretive externalism of triangulation. The ontology of *RI* is answered by the analysis of logical form and the distal theory of meaning (reference).

2.1.1. The Circle between Belief and Meaning and the Asymmetry of Radical Interpretation

2.1.1.1. The Requirements of a Theory of Interpretation

A competent interpreter can, as a natural speaker, interpret any of a potential infinity of utterances and sentences including such that he has never heard or read before, but this knowledge is not generated by listing single cases. On one level, the explanation for this phenomenon of linguistic competence is obvious: our finite pool of words can be combined in an infinite number of ways. But from the fact that the meaning of sentences depends on the meaning of the words within which they occur it does not follow that the meaning of sentences is established out of word meaning. In modern semantics we find three accounts that also indicate word meaning: theories of word-meaning, sentence-meaning, and the communicative ascription of meaning (on that Preyer 1997). For Davidson, the meaning of sentences depends on their structure, and we cannot know parts of this structure if we do not know the meaning of all sentences within which these parts occur. So it is the aim of a theory of meaning to explain the semantic productivity, that is, the ability of generation and understanding of sentences that we have never heard before. If this claim is successful, we also explain the possibility of learning a language. This is the step to a holism in the theory of language.

Normally we make the assumption that the ability to master a language is that we are able to speak. In contrast to this, *RI* is the basic concept of a language for Davidson's theory of language. The essential feature of language is that a speaker himself is an interpreter of another speaker. Therefore the concept of language is analyzed from *RI* and its method. For *RI*, a detailed knowledge of a speaker's intentions and beliefs does not count as evidence. Therefore, the holistic truth-centered theory of *RI* is a refutation of an intentionalistic (nominalistic) theory of meaning. The nominalistic account makes the assumption that what an expression x means in a language L is logically connected with what a speaker means in general. So what a speaker means is the foundation of what x linguistically means. For *RI*, the ascription of intentions, beliefs and a speaker's meaning is the task of a theory of meaning making the assumption that each component of linguistic behavior is interpreted only if *all* components of such utterances are interpreted. From here it follows that intentions and beliefs are not the evidence of the theory of the content of language *saying that* ... as an empirical content, even though all illocutionary acts are intentional actions. It is impossible for an interpreter to verify beliefs and intentions without interpreting what a speaker's words mean. All strategies to define or explain linguistic meaning on the base of non-linguistic intentions, uses, purposes, functions, activities and the like are not only difficult but impossible, as has been pointed out, for example, by Wittgenstein or Grice. *Only by interpreting linguistic behavior are the speaker's attitudes to find out generally.* The interpretation of speech requires two levels: understanding what uttered words mean and what a speaker means by uttering them. The interpretation of speech and non-linguistic behavior is connected by our describing both of them in the light of a unified and intelligible scheme.

It is the requirement of a theory of interpretation that its application must be capable to interpret the infinite set of sentences to us that could be uttered by a natural speaker. Such a theory is to represent in a finite form. For Quine, the token of types of utterances in natural languages does not select between the net-meaning and the beliefs of speakers about the situations of utterances. This is the distinction between the meaning of uttered words, the indicated beliefs, and the consequences of the expressed beliefs in the words of speakers that they may communicate. Understanding linguistic behavior is confronted with the *circle* between *belief* and *meaning* that includes the dilemma of all interpretation: we cannot interpret linguistic activity without knowing what a speaker believes, and we cannot found a theory as to what his utterance $u(x)$ means on a prior subsentential discovery of his beliefs and intentions:

A central source of trouble is the way beliefs and meaning conspire to account for utterances. A speaker who holds a sentence to be true on an occasion does so in part because of what he means, or would mean, by an utterance of that sentence, and in part because of what he believes. If all we have to go on is the fact of honest utterance, we cannot infer the belief without knowing the meaning, and have no chance of inferring the meaning without the belief. (Davidson 1984 (1974): 142) Since we cannot hope to interpret linguistic activity without knowing what a speaker believes, and cannot found a theory of what he means on a prior discovery of his beliefs and intentions, I conclude that in interpreting utterances from scratch—in *radical* interpretation —we must somehow deliver simultaneously a theory of belief and a theory of meaning. How is this possible? (144)

The contribution of speaker intentions to *RI* is that we interpret the utterance, for example, as an *act* of assertion. But the meaning of saying that...—what x means—is not a result of such intentions. In his theory of action, Davidson analyzes the concept of intention with an *all-out judgement* or an unconditional judgement and the beliefs that correspond to such judgements (Davidson 1980 (1978): 98).

RI agrees with the radical translation in principal features. Both accounts make the assumption of the interdependence between belief and meaning. But *RI* begins "at home", that is,

All understanding of the speech of another involves radical interpretation. But it will help to keep assumptions from going unnoticed to focus on cases where interpretation is most clearly called for: interpretation in one idiom of talk in another. (Davidson 1984 (1973):125-6)

The difference between *RI* and the radical translation, as Davidson emphasized, is the explicitly *semantic* feature. Davidson agrees with the essence of Quine's *problem* of radical translation. But there are also some differences. Quine's procedure is to elaborate a translation manual, and as a result we are provided with a sentence in the language of the interpreter for each of the speaker's sentences. Translating utterances means: specifying a translation manual as a function that is recursively given. If the theory of logical form can formalize the contribution of expressions (sub-sentential aspect) to the meaning of sentences, the account shows the structural dependency of these expressions in a semantic way and goes beyond a translation manual.

2.1.1.2. The Evidence of *RI*

Interpretation is the task to translate one idiom of linguistic behavior into another. Davidson replaces the talk of translation by interpretation because his emphasis is an explicitly semantic turn.

How do we cope with the interdependence between belief and meaning of interpreting speech without having any knowledge of meanings or beliefs in advance?

Attitude as a way of entertaining a propositional content like *holding a sentence true, wanting a sentence to be true*, or *preferring that one sentence rather than another be true* seems to be an evidence of a theory of interpretation, because this attitude is to apply to *all* sentences and to *all* utterances even though each utterance is to interpret in a different way and is uttered from different motives and interests. Such evidential support allows us to build a theory of truth.

This method is intended to solve the problem of the interdependence of belief and meaning by holding belief constant as far as possible while solving for meaning. This is accomplished by assigning truth conditions to alien sentences that make native speakers right when plausibly possible, according, of course, to our own view of what is right. (Davidson 1984 (1973): 137)

Such attitudes, they may be true or not, are always the *same*. They correspond *immediately* to the beliefs of speakers. Yet, a speaker can only hold a sentence true if he has the *concept* of truth at his disposal. It is possible that a speaker has a false belief, but this does not mean that a radical interpreter makes the assumption that most of the speaker's beliefs are false and he is totally wrong. It is this pattern that fixes the truth or falsehood of a single belief (statement). Davidson makes a distinction between the *intra*-attitudinal and the *inter*-attitudinal feature of attitude-holism. The first are the relations within a category, like belief or desire; the second are relations between beliefs and desires, between both of these and intentions. The inter-attitudinal holism is significant, because all attitudes are connected by having a content. He called all propositional attitudes *thoughts* because true beliefs play a central role within them. These are a priori assumptions of an interpreter making behavior intelligible. (Davidson 2004 (1997): 13-17, 2001 (1982): 98-99). The problem is whether the requirement really selects the correct interpretation and the unique relations of the caused behavior. This leads to the epistemic restrictions of *RI*.

The attitude of holding a sentence true is a fundamental relation between a speaker's beliefs and the interpretation of his utterances. This explains us the particular role of truth-condition for *RI*, because the interpreter can *know* the holding true without having a knowledge about the meaning of the occasional utterances or the particular beliefs in a given case. But a theory of interpretation stands *not* alone, because holding true can only interpret an utterance in case we discover the speaker's intentions that are connected with our ascription of his desires and actions. It is to mention here that the problem of evidence goes back to radical translation. For Quine, such evidence reaching our surfaces is the neutral unconceptualized information that is the pattern of sensory stimulations (proximal stimulus) caused by physical receptors. Quine has called such information the *net-meaning* (evidence). This epistemology makes a fundamental distinction between a scheme and our content of knowledge. But what is the connection among beliefs, their truth and the linguistic expression?

With this connection we find the framework to link the mental, language and communication (the social) conceptually. This interaction among beliefs, their truth and linguistic expressions explains us why we apply the principle of compositionality on all levels of *RI*. But it leads us to the individuation of the content of propositional attitudes also by distal stimuli and consequently by individual events. At first we can clarify the mentioned connection by the circumstance that the concept of true belief is dependent on a true utterance. There are only such utterances if there is a common language. A belief may be idiosyncratic, but we cannot understand it as an only private state. We grasp what it means that someone has a belief if we recognize beliefs in their role for the interpretation of linguistic behavior. We can only have a belief if we also have a concept of belief at our disposal. This is possible only if a creature has a language. But this means that we also have a concept of error at our disposal and that we are familiar with objective truth. Now we can see why the epistemological step to a radical externalism follows from holding a sentence true as evidence of *RI*, because:

My point is that our basic methodology for interpreting the words of others necessarily makes it the case that most of the time the simplest sentences that speakers hold true *are* true . . . For the sentences that express beliefs, and the beliefs themselves, are correctly understood to be about the public things and events that cause them, and so must be mainly veridical. Each individual knows this, since he knows the nature of speech and belief." (Davidson 2001 (1982): 174, R. Wilburn 1998, on content externalism A. Bruecker 1998)

From my point of view this means that we have the concept of belief at our disposal only if we are a member in a community of common speakers. And we participate in such communities in case *we*, as individual speakers, have the same theories of interpretation at our disposal.

Yet this does not mean that a speaker does not also have wrong beliefs: "... the independence of belief and truth requires only that each of our beliefs may be false..." but not "...that all of them can be wrong." (Davidson 2001: 140). On the contrary: the distinction between holding a sentence true and its being true gives errors their point. A radical interpreter himself makes the assumption that most beliefs (statements) he ascribes to any speaker are true. And within this frame he fixes that single ones of the speaker's beliefs could be false. Holding a sentence true as the typical sort of evidence for *RI* is the fundamental relationship between the speaker's beliefs and the interpretation of his utterances. This explains us the particular role of truth conditions in the procedure of *RI* because an interpreter himself *knows* the holding true without knowing simultaneously what the speaker means factually or what belief he utters in given circumstances. However, the evidence of *RI* also explains us *why* all beliefs are a network and why they are not to evaluate as true or workable as single attitudes because:

...a correct understanding of the speech, beliefs, desires, intentions and other propositional attitudes of a person leads to the conclusion that most of a person's beliefs must be true, and so there is a legitimate presumption that any one of them, if it coheres with most of the rest, is true." (Davidson 2001 (1983): 146)

From my understanding of the role of evidence for *RI* and the unlimited application of the principle of charity it is a reasoning to grasp the quantificatory structure of attitudes. And it is not to conclude from the evidence that the beliefs of a speaker and his interpreter are correspondent. Neither is it to exclude that there is a change of beliefs. But a theory of interpretation "will (not) stand alone". Holding true enables us to interpret an utterance only if we can also ascribe intentions that are connected with desires. The *unified theory* born from *RI* links language and epistemology also: "Only a creature that can interpret speech can have the concept of thought." (Davidson 1984 (1975): 170) The evidence of attitude of holding true directed toward sentences gives the theory of interpretation its quantificatory form. And this is just the case: "... although most utterances are not concerned with truth, it is the pattern of sentences held true that gives sentences their meaning." (Davidson 1984 (1975): 162).

2.1.1.3. The Asymmetry of *RI*, the Causation of Attitudes and Communication

The theories of language, action (decision) and communication work together to solve the task of interpretation. For *RI*, linguistic utterances are the instances to attribute (identify) and to distinguish thoughts. The basis of *RI* is the assignment of holding a sentence true to the utterance of sentences. The redescription of linguistic behavior by a radical interpreter makes the assumption that the ascribed belief is coherent to the set of true beliefs of the speaker. But *RI* is to characterize by a foundational asymmetry: the speaker does not interpret himself. From his side there is no question of *RI*. Neither does he compare his uttered sentences with the external world to determine its empirical content. *RI* is a refutation of the myth of the sense data as also W. Sellars and J. L. Austin have held.

A speaker can express the truth or falsehood of his beliefs only with his uttered sentences: "...when we can express a thought, our own or that of another, we must fall back on the basic device of representing it in the fabric of our sentences. Our sentences provide the only measure of the mental." (Davidson 2001: 77) This does not mean that we eliminate the indeterminacy of translation of our interpretation of utterances. With this argument *RI* refutes the *myth of subjective*: "Beliefs are true or false, but they represent nothing." (Davidson 2001 (1988): 46). In the same way it is not possible to inspect our own mental in an introspective way.

Introspection offers no solution (for the explanation of the first person authority, the author), since it fails to explain why one's perceptions of one's own mental states should be any more reliable than one's perceptions of anything else. (Davidson 1994: 234)

We cannot inspect ourselves in the same way in which we look into a wardrobe to see how many suits there are in it. This was already emphasized by Wittgenstein and Ryle. But Davidson claims to explain the authority of first person (on Davidson and P. F. Strawson, A. Avramides 1999). The explanation follows from the asymmetry of *RI*, that is, only an *interpreter* who redescribes linguistic behavior is to confront with *RI*, not the speaker himself. Such a task is *theoretical*. It is to conclude from *evidence* what a speaker means and intends to tell and to do. Self-ascriptions are necessarily true and homophone in nature. But the first person authority is *not* a foundation of our empirical knowledge. This follows from *RI*.

RI, and also radical translation, takes place in the third person. This is something constantly misunderstood. The third person attitude of *RI* is reasoned thereby that a speaker does not have to know the sentences with which the interpreter redescribes his utterance. If this was a requirement of *RI*, linguistic communication could not be successful. It is an essential feature of language that this is simply not necessary. The first person authority is unavoidably a part of *RI*, because without such an authority the ascription of a belief of attitudes and its empirical content would be *empty*. If we ascribe a belief to a speaker on the basis of evidence, we cannot avoid making the assumption that the speaker *knows what* he says and *what* he believes. Nevertheless, the speaker knows his own thoughts in a way in which no interpreter can ever know it. He knows these without any evidence. Within the procedures of *RI* it is obvious *why* all ascription of attitudes is normally true. It shows us also how the authority of first person is connected with the principle of the autonomy of meaning. Moreover, the first person authority gives us an answer to the problem of self-deception. An absolute self-deception is not possible (on new research Mele 2001).

Basically, *RI* is an asymmetrical situation between a speaker and an interpreter, but it is symmetrical with respect to the truth conditions of sentences with which a speaker himself ascribes beliefs, and also the sentence with which an interpreter ascribes propositional attitudes to the speaker. This explains us the role of truth conditions of a semantics of natural language as a semantics of individual speaker utterances. It explains us also why the paratactical account of indirect discourse and the concept of samesayer is a part of *RI*. It is to conclude that the analysis of the semantic content of utterances *saying that* ...is connected with the ascription of beliefs. If a speaker said "I assert that snow is white", then the interpreter would ascribe a belief to him in his own language on the basis of the truth conditions of the sentences he uses for redescription of linguistic behavior. The ascription works by the paratactical account, that is, there are two sentences: "He believes that" and then "Snow is white", whereby the two sentences are logically independent. "that" plays a demonstrative role referring to the next utterance and not to a proposition. By the truth conditions of the sentences used in his own language (his semantic property) he attributes (identifies) the respective thought. We could call this a *redundancy* theory of beliefs, because the belief that *p* cannot be distinguished from the belief that *p* is true. But the concept of a true belief is dependent on a true utterance, and such utterances are there only for creatures that have a language. The attribution of beliefs is a result of the logical-semantic analysis of sentences on propositional attitudes like "Peter believes that...." by its truth conditions that are to complete with the individuation of the propositional contents of beliefs in triangulation: things, events, and situations cause *directly* that a speaker and an interpreter hold a sentence true. But the epistemic basic situation is symmetrical in principle. We have to select as speakers and interpret the evidence from which we conclude our interpretations and ascriptions. The epistemic frame of reference is the shared world that both of them have at their disposal. But the knowledge of the first person authority is basically different from the knowledge an interpreter has. In this respect there is an asymmetry. The speaker himself does not confront his beliefs and sentences with particulars and events to verify their truth thereby. No speaker is a radical interpreter. It is essential for *RI* that the interpreter assumes that the speaker knows what he says. This *explains* why all interpretations have to include first person authority (privileged self-ascription) in their procedures. If this was not the case, there would be nothing to interpret. And it is not possible to ascribe thoughts to creatures if the interpreter does not have his own thoughts. The autonomy of meaning is the link between self-ascription and the ascription of attitudes to other people, because it is essential for interpretation that sentences have a semantic property that we find by their truth-conditions. The first person authority that we have without having any evidence and the autonomy of meaning work together in interpretation: the interpreter takes first person attribution of attitudes as presumptively true. First person authority has its own right, but this is at the same time the end of the subjective, that is, of inner objects or mental representation to identify our states of mind. They are not *before the mind* as inner objects. Therefore the chapter of Cartesianism and empiricism in epistemology will be closed.

How can we bridge the gap that opens between the invisibility of attitudes and their non-locality from the interpreter's side to an intelligible relation between evidence and attitudes by which he can ascribe attitudes and utterances from the manifestation of behavior?

How far does the holistic truth-centered theory of meaning *revolutionize* our understanding of communication? What is the conceptual link between the semantics for natural language born from *RI* and communication?

Prima vista this is not obvious. The answer to this question leads us also back to the coping of the circle between belief and meaning and shows us the new role of interpreter that emerges from *RI* and the individuation of attitudes of someone else.

The distal theory of meaning (reference) leads us to the *new* role of an interpreter. The frame of ascription of meaning to utterances is our evidence to explain and understand the given behavioral items. It is not the *speaker*, but the *interpreter* who solves the task of interpretation by his taking into account the causal interaction between world and speaker in order to ascribe utterance meaning and propositional attitudes. The meaning of words, for Quine, is conditioned by our sensory stimuli, and the evidence is given in the description of conditions of utterances in a stimulus-response scheme. The understanding of attitudes, also the mental, is only possible by given linguistic behavior. But in difference to Quine, a distal theory of meaning (reference) characterizes the role of interpreter in a *new* way, because a radical interpreter concludes from his *own* reaction to the speaker's behavior. The new *active* role of the interpreter is the guarantee that both refer to the obvious causes that give his beliefs a content. Therefore, the distal causes explain the empirical content of saying that ... Only on this basic line of the *same* reactions of a speaker and an interpreter do communication and a higher level of systems of communication emerge. I will call this principle of *RI* — given by the new role of interpreter — the principle of *shared identity of reference of caused reactions*. Davidson speaks of a principle of correspondence. This principle is connected with the assumption that most of our beliefs are true: beliefs are veridical in nature. From Davidson's point of view, the role of interpreter is shown with the assumption:

We do not need to be omniscient to interpret, but there is nothing absurd in the idea of an *omniscient interpreter*; he attributes beliefs to others, and interprets their speech on the basis of his own beliefs, just as the rest of us do. (Davidson 1984 (1977): 201, my italics, on a critical analyse Lepore, Ludwig 2005: 326-27)

When the interpreter applies this procedure, he assumes that *other things are being equal.* The subject of a theory of interpretation is behaviorally given and the theory informs us what an utterance means, that is, it enables us to *ascribe* propositional attitudes. Nevertheless, we need an epistemological answer to the *individuation* of the content of these attitudes. This is the step *from* the theory of truth *to* a theory of interpretation and *from* the constraints of interpretation *to* the *distal* theory of meaning (reference) and cognition, that is, the ascription and individuation of propositional content in triangulation is the frame of reference for individuating the content of attitudes. Davidson speaks of the *attribution* of attitudes because a radical interpreter ascribes attitudes as a feature of utterances and caused behavior. Both beliefs and distal stimuli take effect in the process of *RI* in a way that they "take up the slack" between objective truth, holding true and communication. This leads us to another understanding of making behavior intelligible, epistemology and communication — without including triangulation: "The methodology of interpretation is, in this respect, nothing but epistemology seen in the mirror of meaning." (Davidson 1984 (1975): 169)

The revolution of our so-called understanding of communication is comprehensible, in case we realize that there are two points being fundamental for every communication: (a) systems of communication can exist only if, as participants, we are able to distinguish between holding true and being true; in general we must be able to evaluate propositional attitudes; (b) on the other hand, communication is possible only if the content of our beliefs is caused by distal stimuli and such causation has to be obvious in triangulation, that is, communications are to continue only by upshots of actions or communicative events that start from the individuation of propositional content. This is the basis of its recursion. A. Avramides has summarized the problem of the individuation of propositional attitudes with respect to the circle between belief and meaning in order to clarify why thoughts are dependent on communication:

... in communication one speaker understands the words and sentences of another; that is, in communication we find ourselves in the position of interpreters of the words and sentences of another. As interpreters we are faced with the following problem: what a person means is in part a function of their belief. Yet we have just been told that what persons believe is a function of what their words and sentences mean. Our dilemma is how to break into this circle of belief and meaning." (Avramides 1999: 146; Ludwig 1999: 41-44).

The revolution of our understanding of communication is that the first person authority, the social character of language and the external individuation of the content of attitudes work together. *Communication begins where causes converge.* (Davidson 2001 (1987): 151) Communication emerges only if the meaning and the semantic content of the utterances of speaker and interpreter are determined by the pattern of causal interaction between both and the external world. The meaning of linguistic behavior and of the content of thoughts is found by causal interactions that are a guarantee of the same response to external circumstances. Cum grano salis, this is a continuation of Quine's proposal. Philosophers may have a problem here, namely that the causation by the external world is directly observed in triangulation but not a semantic predicate instantiated by some vocabulary. The idea that we observe causation directly goes back to Anscombe.

From the triangulation model of *RI* and its truth-centered theory of meaning it emerges that our self-knowledge (first person authority), the ascription of attitudes and the intelligible redescription of behavior in a third person and also the semantic property (content) of language play together. This turn claims to demolish traditional epistemology. But this is the case only if the triangulation model is successful in attributing the content of attitudes.

2.1.2. Truth and Semantic Content

2.1.2.1. The Symmetry between Expression and Representation of Semantic Content

Davidson agrees with one of the essential breakthroughs in the study of language, coming from Quine: entities like meanings, propositions and objects of belief may not be meaningless, but they will be of no help when interpreting linguistic behavior. In this respect it cannot be an independent goal of the theory of language to identify such entities. Given the dilemma of understanding *meaning,* the problem of the independent availability of the evidence is resolved if a radical interpreter makes the assumption that the speaker holds most sentences he utters true. There are two holisms for an interpretive theory of truth and meaning, one of beliefs and the other of language. Both interact, and the verification of occasional sentences (perceptual beliefs) in the triangle is a basic feature of language.

The task of all interpretation of speech consisting of utterance meaning, attitudes, and uttering (behavior) is the intelligible redescription of linguistic behavior. We understand Wolfgang's sentence-utterance "Es schneit" by taking it, basically by redescription, as an act of *saying that* it is snowing. The task of *RI* is to give such redescriptions of utterances like saying that. We have to find an answer to the question what makes it possible to redescribe the sentence:

(1) someone utters the sentence *s*

as

(2) with the utterance of *s* someone said that *p*.

Thus, the question is:

In how far does the expression of the propositional content (language content) by that-clauses give us a significant structure as the subject of the theory of meaning?

It is to show that the structure of "content sentences", that is, the "that-clause", represents the propositional content of *saying that.* This is the claim of logical form analysis of sentences like, for example, "Galileo said that the earth moves".

For Davidson, theories of truths in Tarskian style give us a fruitful theoretical framework. His claim is to give a proof of a symmetry between the representation and the expression of propositional contents of sentences following saying that ... with the theoretical frame of logical form analysis. The theory about the structure of types of sentences in a given natural language is the logical form of the respective type. He calls the description of this structure the *logical form*. If we have such a theory, we can clarify our ordinary idiom mechanically with the means of canonical notations. This form is to construct in contrast to the surface of philologic grammatical form. The benefit of this form is to give us a *simple*, *powerful* and *coherent* description of the entailment-relation as a basic concept in semantics. The logical form as a deep structure is a theory of translation. The theory of truth is intended as an empirical theory that is a formal semantics of natural language. By fixing the logical form we get the information what entities exist. Moreover, the analysis of logical form is also to apply to non-assertoric utterances, and within this frame an answer between the relationship between the mode of sentences and the illocutionary force of utterances is to elaborate as well.

With the uncovering of the logical form of an uttered sentence as a deep structure we possess a theory of sentence-meaning that explains us the semantic role of significant expressions coextensive to the truth-condition of its parts. But this implies a second step to a holism as a basic feature of our theory of language; that is, the step from the holism of attitudes to the holism of language. Parts of sentences have meaning only in the way of making a contribution to the sentence in which such parts occur (compositional meaning theory). This leads us to a *holistic* view of meaning:

If sentences depend for their meaning on their structure, and we understand the meaning of each item in the structure only as an abstraction from the totality of sentences in which it features, then we can give the meaning of any sentence (or word) only by giving the meaning of every sentence (and word) in the language. Frege said that only in the context of a sentence does a word have meaning; in the same vein he might have added that only in the context of the language does a sentence (and therefore a word) have meaning. (1984 (1967): 22)

But for the truth-centered theory of *RI*, meaning is not defined by inferential roles (on these particular problems, Fodor and Lepore 2002: 14-20).

The arrangement of truth-functional sentences allows us a translation of all sentences in our own and into an alien language. This is Davidson's option. His claim is to show—with the logical form analysis— a symmetry of representation and expression of the propositional content of sentences following saying that. The theory of language-content and of understanding is an implementation of the scheme

(3) "s has the meaning p" (s = sentence)

requires as entailment sentences of the form

(4) "s means that p".

Understanding the meaning of individual utterances is dependent on the knowledge of speakers insofar as that Peter's knowing "snow is white" in the English language *means that* snow is white. This symmetry is reasoned by theories entailing sentences of the form

(5) "'s' is true iff p" (= T-sentence)

adding formal and empirical requirements as a guarantee that p is factually a correct interpretation of s resp. p is the condition that ensures the truth of the sentences. T-sentences are theorems for Davidson. The semantic content we express by "…means that…" is to substitute with "…is T". This is the proposal in *Truth and Meaning* (1984 (1967)). From here it is to conclude that p is an *extensional definiens of a semantic property*.

What we require of a theory of meaning for a language L is that without appeal to any (further) semantic notions it places enough restrictions on the predicate 'is T' to entail all sentences got from schema T when 's' is replaced by a structural description of a sentence of L and 'p' by that sentence. (Davidson 1984 (1967): 23)

In this respect, a theory of meaning has to entail all sentences of the form: s is T iff p. s is not a name of a sentence (Tarski) but a structural description. Otherwise the theory cannot explain how the structure and the elements of a sentence contribute to its meaning. In the scheme of such sentences, p is not only a translation in a metalanguage but it refers to both these instances, that is, "snow is white" is true as a possible utterance of any speaker at the time point t iff snow is white just at this time point t. The requirement of such a theory of truth is accordingly that the "theory" logically entails as theorems such biconditionals in that on the *left* side we apply the truth predicate to a sentence in an object language and on the *right* side there is a translation of this sentence (*interpretive* truth condition for an object language sentence). This modification of the Convention T requires only that the sentence on the right side of the biconditional is true. Therefore it is to substitute "…means that…" by ". …is true iff…". 's' is a structural description of a sentence that meaning is under study (object language) and p is a sentence of a language in which we express the theory, and in this language we state the meaning of the sentences (metalanguage) S^c^h^n^e^e^ ^i^s^t^ ^w^e^i^ß means that snow is white; ^ is a concatenation symbol; the left side of *means that* is a *definite description* to read as: the sentence consisting of the letter "S" concatenated to the letter "c" concatenated to a space concatenated to, and so on. Thereby the logical form (structure) of language content gives us a proof of the symmetry of representation and expression of the propositional content of sentences: *saying that* … A structural description of any expression means: it describes an expression as a concatenation of components we pick out from a fixed list, such is, of letters or words. If this was not the case, we could not explain how the structure and the components of a sentence contribute something to its meaning. This is what is to explain by the theory of meaning. The Convention T is the theoretical frame, that is, the "effective structure" to give us the analysis of meaning of sentences uttered in natural languages. The recursive characterization of the predicate „is T" has for its extension all (and only) true sentences of the given object language. A re-interpretation of the recursive characterization „can be treated as an implicit definition of the truth predicate for which it fixes an extension (i.e. the set of things it is true of). This implicit definition can, in turn, be turned into an explicit one (of sorts) by appeal to set theory." (Lepore, Ludwig 2005: 20, footnote 8, see also 76-77).

The intensional vocabulary, for example, "is significant", "is synonymous with", "analytical", "mean" is to be semantically eliminated. Because of this, the convention of truth is the theoretical frame, that is, an "effective structure" for ascertaining the meaning of sentences in a natural language. It does its job without any meanings. But it is to mention that the information we need to grasp the object language is not inferred from the truth theory itself. This leads us to the analysis of context-sensitive sentences (elements) in the theory of truth (Lepore, Ludwig 2003: 45-48).

The commentators of Davidson's interpretive truth-theoretic approach note that there are some difficulties with respect to established

T-theorems (-theory) as a semantics of natural language. I will not analyse all this in detail here but only mention some critical issues. One point among others is whether a *T*-theory for *L* states by *T*-theorems the acceptable knowledge to understand *L*. Another point is that a *T*-theory has to fulfill the requirement that the single *T*-theorems are to be interpreted as their corresponding *M*-theorems like (*M*) *S** means (in *L*) that *p*. But *M*-theorems (which are intensional) are more informative than *T*-theorems (which are extensional) to which they correspond. In the history of building a truth-centered theory of *RI*, Davidson has emphasized that the information of the extensional concept of truth like "*s* is true iff *p*" is to poor to grasp an intensional theorem like "*s* means that *p*". This is noted by many commentators, for example, Neale (2001: 32).

Davidson calls *T*-sentences "platitudes" and the fact how trivial this is displays us the general concept of truth (2001 (1988): 178-79). As a consequence, it is of more relevance for Davidson to take into play the canonical proof of the *T*-sentences. This is continued by Lepore and Ludwig (2002). Such proof shows us by a recursive analysis of satisfaction how we build *T*-sentences and how the truth conditions of a sentence are dependent on the semantic properties of the components. But a further feature is also to take into play, namely that the understanding of single sentences is dependent on the knowledge of the correct theory of truth of the whole language of which it is a member. Finally, the step from truth to meaning is the verification of *T*-sentences. This is a matter of the obvious relations between holding a sentence true and linguistic and non-linguistic behavior. These relations are not contingent in nature. This leads us to the epistemic restrictions of *RI*.

It is essential that Davidson reads in a *T*-theory the *ontology* of objects. The idea is that an adequate truth theory gives us axioms for singular terms and predicates and just these satisfaction axioms relate expressions to objects. There is a difference in principle between both the axioms. And this crucial feature shows us the nature of ontology of a *T*-theory. From a satisfactory account of truth condition it follows that we accept the objects to which the reference axioms refer as semantic values (particulars). Such axioms are not to eliminate. The constructed axioms of singular terms stand for (satisfied by) objects (*reference-rela-tive-to-a-sequence*), and at the same time the constructed sentences are satisfied by sequences of objects. By this, language is connected with the world we talk about. It is to emphasize that, for the truth-centered theory of meaning, quantification forces reference. For the descriptions of the reference axioms, I refer to Neale (1999: 80-83, see also Lepore, Ludwig 2003: 39-42, 43-48). But I will not analyze the semantics here when we determine the extensions to functions of interpretations of general concepts (predicates) leveling language on a higher level as M^1L (ML = metalanguage) with richer expressibility. This would lead us to classes of utterances. These do not refer to (individual) tokens of them.

We construct with the axioms of the truth theory of the form

(6) _____ is true iff …

Satisfaction is a *generalized form of reference*. It relates words and things (Davidson 2001 (1988): 180). The predicate and quantifier axioms are to construct

(7) $(\forall s)(s$ satisfied ___ iff … s …)

—'s' ranges over infinite sequences of objects. The axiom of the name "Peter" then is

(8) The referent of "Peter" = Peter
(9) $(\forall s)(Ref(\text{"Peter"}, s) = \text{Peter})$

—'s' ranges over sequences, Ref = reference relative to a sequence. With (9) we connect posits of language and entities (parts of the world). We construct axioms of individual variables with the scheme

(10) $(\forall s)(\forall k)(Ref(\ulcorner x_k \urcorner, s) = s_k)$

—'s' *ranges over sequences*, s_k *is* the k-th element of s; the Ref of a name is the same entity, Ref of a variable depends upon the given sequences. This analysis of reference does not need any reference relationship as property of expressions that connect words with entities in a right way. In this point Davidson agrees with Quine.

But predicate axioms introduce *new* entities. For the T-theory, such axioms work without positing properties in our ontology and the theory does not need an ontology of properties. For our ontological decision, we only need the notion of satisfaction, and all satisfiers are sequences of objects (the extensionalistic ontology of the T-theory is elaborated in detail by Neale 2001: 33-40, on singular terms and predicates capt. 10, in this book). The logical means to derive T-theorems from axioms of a T-theory is the extensional first-order logic with identity. The proposal is not accepted generally among philosophers of language, because it is well known that natural language quantification is richer than the expressibility of first-order language. A particular problem is, for example, to handle anaphoric relations between expressions by co-reference (standard variable-binding). I will not discuss this problem here. But I will analyze some problems of the used logical means in I 3., in this book. There is a further, deeper problem of the interpretive truth theory, namely that the employed semantic structure in the metalanguage works without any difference from the way in which the object language sentences work. If it does not, the theory is not interpretive. The essential point in the analysis of predicates is that Davidson does not accept semantic theories that treat predicates as referring or corresponding to something: predicate axioms have no semantic value (it may be that they still have satisfiers). The ground is that the verification of T-sentences (their right hand side) employs as the conceptual resources nothing but the truth conditions that are stated. This is emphasized by Davidson right from the beginning.

The language of quantification and its truth condition is available for an interpretive theory of meaning, the logical form of sentences and its logical power. Following this option, the arrangement of truth-functional sentences allows to translate all sentences of an alien language into our own. The particular relevance of the paraphrasing of event sentences with quantificatory means is, for Davidson, to show that their truth conditions are given in a successful theory of truth. The best explanation of the fact:

(1) "Ria runs quickly" entails
(2) "Ria runs"

is given by the logical form:

(3) $(\exists x)$ (x is running & x is by Ria & x is quickly,

and the logical form of (2) is:

(4) "$(\exists x)$ (x is running & x is by Ria)".

The logical form is to represent in Tarski's convention of truth:

(5) "Ria runs quickly' is true iff ($\exists x$) (x is running … and so on)" – the sentence is expressed in the metalanguage.

The application to adverbial modified action-sentences like "Peter goes into the bathroom at midnight intentionally" has the logical form:

(6) ($\exists e$) (goes (Peter, e) & (into the bathroom, e) & at (midnight, e)), e is the event, what makes the sentence true.

The modified verbs of action sentences are to analyze as an existential quantification. The modifiers themselves are predications of the respective bound event variables. The direct relation between action and an agent, that is, the property of an event to be an action, is therefore independent of our describing it in a particular way, such as "deliberately", "slowly", "voluntarily" and so on. Adverbial modifications cannot change the reference of the expression they modify, and we put this expression aside. This is a result of the discovered logical form (on the logical form of action sentences, I3.1, in this book).

2.1.2.2. The Modifications of Tarski

Davidson constructs the *RI* semantically as a theory of truth as Tarski does, notwithstanding with some modification. He became aware of these differences first in continuation (on Davidson and Tarski, Larson 1988, Kirkham 1992, on the definition of truth Essler 1999):

I. His goal is a theory of truth, but unlike Tarski's goal it is not an explicit definition. This is a point that refers to the question:

How rich is the ontology in a given language in which we construct the theory?

The ontology is given by Davidson's logical form analysis using Tarski's concept of *satisfaction* as a relation between predicates and objects to which axioms of the *T*-theory refer and the implementation of *RI* by triangulation. Satisfaction recursively defined is a generalized form of reference by which we relate expressions to objects.

Theories of absolute truth necessarily provide an analysis of structure relevant to truth and reference. Such theories yield a non-trivial answer to the question what counts as the logical form of a sentence. A theory of truth does not yield a definition of logical consequences or logical truth, but it will be evident from a theory of truth that certain sentences are true solely on the basis of the properties assigned to the logical constants. The logical constants may be identified as those iterative features of the language that require a recursive clause in the characterization of truth or satisfaction. Logical form, in this account, will of course be relative to the choice of a metalanguage (with its logic) and a theory of truth. (Davidson 1984 (1973): 71).

The step from truth to *RI* is taken by the instantiation of truth to properties of utterances, the next step to the implementation of *RI* is that the knowledge that we have of truth is consistent to the objectivity of the external individuation of the propositional content of attitudes. It is the pretension of a recursive theory of *absolute truth* to explain how the meaning of sentences depends on the meaning of its parts. Other accounts like truth in a model, truth with an interpretation, valuation, or possible worlds are to distinguish in a way because "they substitute a relational concept for the single-place truth predicate of *T*-sentences." (68). It is not possible for such accounts to take the last step in the recursion of *T*-sentences, such is, the step to truth or satisfaction—satisfaction always means satisfaction by the sequences of objects. This last step "is essential to the quotation-lifting feature of *T*-sentences." (68) The aim of *RI* is a *theory* of truth because an explicit definition "does widen the gap between the resources of the object language and of the metalanguage." (72) For a holistic truth-centered theory of *RI* it is essential that there is no difference between the ontology of the object-language and the metalanguage. Yet, absolute theories of truth are relative in a way because they are to apply to speakers, and this leads to *RI*.

2. A further modification is an essential feature. Tarski's Convention T requires that he gives conditions, such as for the predicate "is true", so that all sentences of a certain form are entailed. These are sentences of the well-known form: "'Schnee ist weiß' if and only if snow is white". For formalized languages, Tarski names these sentences *T*-sentences—Davidson calls them theorems—that are realized by their logical syntax. This is true even if the object-language and the metalanguage are different. For *RI*, the syntactic test of *T*-sentences is not informative, because it presupposes the understanding of object language that the interpreter intends to structure. All syntactic tests simply formalize the relationship of synonymy or translation, and that is not problematic in Tarski's account. But a Tarski-style theory is relative to a given language, and just this presupposes that sentences have a meaning before the theory

89

is constructed. The definition of truth must not be merely stipulative. Therefore the theory is viewed as an empirical one. Only a formal test does not decide about its empirical adequacy. This leads to the requirement that speakers mean the same by the sentences used by them. Just this is the problem of the *ultimate* evidence of a successful application of a truth-theory.

3. It follows from *RI* that the theory of truth is to specify to a speaker, time, and entities and events and their causal relations. Distal stimuli cause the content of attitudes, and the properties of entities and events have causal power (Davidson 1980 (1973): 64). In natural languages, demonstrative elements are given to us that are not to eliminate from our theorizing, because such expressions like demonstratives and tempora specify the truth-condition to a certain circumstance in which such utterances are made. From here it follows that, in the case of such application of *T*-sentences, the sentence on the right is *not* a translation of the sentence on the left. This is exactly what leads us to the question of evidence, the holding true of a sentence as the evidence of *RI*, a satisfactional theory of reference, and at the same time to the individuation of the content of attitudes.

The problem of interpretation of expressions like the words "that", "I", "this" and so on is: do we need a pragmatic or a semantic interpretation of demonstrative expressions? The ostentation by these words, not by gestures, includes a relationship between a speaker and a word in addition to a contextual reference between a word and an entity in the world. The so-called "pragmatic concept of demonstration" for the verification of *T*-sentences (Davidson 1984: 75) is to construct itself as *T*-theoretic axioms for "I", "we", "you", "he", "that", "yesterday" and so on (Neale 2001: 40-1). This contextual reference is a semantic feature, not only a pragmatical one (on the analysis of singular terms as semantic classes E. Tugendhat 1982, capt. 10, in this book). *RI* claims to handle reference of indexical expressions and speaker reference by the application of *T*-sentences to utterances as individual events, that is, to speaker and time point specified to the speaker's point of view.

The aim of *RI* is to explain meaning and translation by the concept of truth. The requirement is to judge acceptability of *T*-sentences not syntactically and not in order to use concepts, such as translation, meaning or synonymy, but given as factual interpretations of linguistic utterances by *T*-sentences that we accept. A theory of truth only generates interpretations if its *T*-sentences state truth-conditions in such a way that they may be treated as "giving the meaning" of object language sentences. The problem is to elaborate the constraints on this account. They have to be strong enough to guarantee acceptable interpretations. Taking this step, we have to take into consideration that interpretation is a matter of degree, of contextual reference and of background theories.

Translation is not a method applicable to *RI* (Davidson 1984 (1970): 129). It is not the intention of interpretation to translate one language into another—as the subject of radical translation—, but to interpret *one* language. Nevertheless, this is in fact an interpretation into another language because any theory is built in some language. Counting the language, we state the theory as part of the subject language. This leads to a confusion of object-language and metalanguage unless we have fixed it explicitly. In general, a theory of translation entails three languages: object language, subject language (the speaker language that is to translate), and metalanguage. Translating is a procedure that informs us which expressions of an object language are translated by which expressions of a subject language stated by the language of the theory. The latter informs us about the translation of expressions of the subject language into the object language. In this general case it is possible to know which sentences of the subject language translate which expressions of object language without knowing what any sentence in either language means; that is to say, interpreters who have the theory at their disposal could interpret sentences of an object language. In case that the speaker's language (subject language) is the same as the language of the theory, he can use a manual of translation interpreting alien utterances. This is possible because he knows the following—without its being stated by the theory itself —: 1. the speaker's language is his own and 2. he intuitively knows how to interpret utterances in his own language. Davidson exposes the theory of interpretation for an object language as a *result* of merging a structurally revealing theory of interpretation for a known language, and a system of translation from an unknown language into the known language. The so-called amalgamation leads to the result that reference to the known language can be dropped. With taking this step we get to a structurally revealing theory of interpretation (in particular on the topics of a method of translation and interpretation, Davidson 1984 (1973): 129-30). In general it is a requirement that the theory of translation reads some structure in linguistic behavior (sentences), but it is not to expect that it gives us information on how the meaning of sentences depends on their structure:

"A theory of interpretation for an object language may then be viewed
as the result of the merger of a structurally revealing theory of interpretation for a known language, and a system of translation from the unknown language into the known. The merger makes all reference to the
known language otiose; when this reference is dropped, what is left is a
structurally revealing theory of interpretation for the object language —
couched, of course, in familiar words. We have such theories, I suggest,
in theories of truth of the kind Tarski first showed how to give." (130)

So we have identified the initial problem in the theory of language that
leads from radical translation to *RI*. Yet it is to emphasize that radical
translation is the initiation of the holistic truth-centered theory of *RI*.
Consequently the same problem can be solved by other means, and this
leads to a redescription of the original problem.

2.1.2.3. The Method of Semantic Explanation
of Linguistic Meaning

It is to emphasize here that *RI* does not lead to a psychological theory
of meaning, but to a theory of truth. Stimulus meaning is not the basic
concept either. For Davidson, the truth-centered theory of *RI* is empirical theory, and the axioms of this theory have to be laws. The intelligible
redescription of linguistic behavior means that the semantic explanation
of linguistic meaning of uttered sentences follows in respect of the beliefs of speakers. But beliefs and meaning are connected in principle. The
holding true of sentences is the guarantee of the independency of the
evidence. The redescription proceeds in the following way:

1. Interpretation is effected by the application of a theory of truth.
The theory describes a structure of any language by the truth-conditions
of all sentences of a language. For that it is necessary to define the logical relations among the sentences. Davidson's view is that this theory is
comparable with the theory of fundamental measurement. Both are built
thereby that a set of axioms picks out the logical properties of primitives.
In interpretive semantics a particular primitive is truth.

2. Redescribing linguistic behavior intelligibly, we suppose that

(a) a speaker holds true his uttered sentences; this is not a single true
belief, but a single belief is true only if endless other beliefs are to be true;
a single statement as such is not to evaluate as true or false; and

(b) his holding-true is a behavioral item because the shared reactions
are immediately obvious in the triangle:

...most uses of language tell us *directly*, or shed light on the question, whether a speaker holds a sentence to be true." "There are obvious relations between holding a sentence true and linguistic (and other) behavior. If we could not often fathom from his linguistic behavior when a speaker held his sentence true, we could not interpret his speech. (Davidson 1984 (1975): 161, 2001 (1988): 190)

The attribution of beliefs is an exemplification of a property and its instantiation to an agent. But the behavioral evidence only counts before the background of the holism of propositional attitudes (mental) as a feature of intelligible behavior: "Beliefs and desires issue in behavior only as modified and mediated by further beliefs and desires, attitudes and attends, without a limit." (Davidson 1980 (1970): 217) This network is an indication of the autonomy and anomaly of the mental. We see why *RI* goes hand in hand with an anomaly of the mental.

3. *RI* gives Tarski's account an empirical turn.

Tarski's definitions make no mention of empirical matters, but we are free to ask of such a definition whether it fits the actual practice of some speaker or group of speakers—we may ask whether they speak the language for which truth has been defined. There is nothing about Tarski's definitions that prevents us from treating them in this way except the prejudice that if something is called a definition, the question of its "correctness" is moot. To put this prejudice to rest, I suggest that we omit the final step in Tarski's definitions, the step that turns his axiomatizations into explicit definitions. We can then in good conscience call the emasculated definition a theory, and accept the truth predicate as undefined. This undefined predicate expresses the general, intuitive, concept, applicable to any language, the concept against which we have always surreptitiously tested Tarski's definitions (as he invited us to do, of course). (Davidson 2005 (1996): 35-36)

An utterance is to construct "as an event or an event-object pair; and a context can be construed as some sort of *n*-tuple of objects or events" (Neale 2001: 40). In the meantime we name the application of *T*-sentences to utterances of natural speakers *Davidson's Convention T* to distinguish this new proposal from Tarski (Ludwig 1999: 30-31, Lepore, Ludwig 2002: 62). The truth-theoretical semantics is therefore an empirical theory.

4. In sum: the revision of Tarski's Convention T is its enlargement to context-sensitive issues. The turn is to show that the right side of the biconditional explains the meaning of the sentence denoted on the left, this is: *interprets* the object language sentence. Lepore and Ludwig have shown how the step is taken to the analog of Convention T for natural language (speaker) (2005: 83-84), I recall.

(T) s is T iff p

(M) s means that p

The assumption is that in Convention T replaced 'p' in (T) translates s, the corresponding M-sentence is true.

The requirement is made that we replace 'p' is related to s in (T) that the corresponding instances of (M) are true. Relativizing the truth predicate to speaker and time is at the same time the specification of the meaning predicate to such context. Therefore the meaning theory has theorems of the form:

(M') For any speaker S, time t, s for S at t means in L that p.

The truth theory as a theory of meaning requires that among its theorems, the instances of (T') whose correspondents M'-sentences are true.

(T') For any speaker S, time t, s for S at t is true in L iff p.

Call this T-sentences for context-insensitive language: a T-sentence is a sentence of the form T, applying to context-insensitive object language, that corresponding instance of (M) is true; for a context-sensitive object language of the sentences of the form (T') for the corresponding instance of (M') is true. The right side of the biconditional in a (T') form sentence is interpretive in case it is a T-sentence.

The *Davidson* Convention T is:

(D) An adequate truth theory for a context sensitive language L must entail every instance of (T') for which the corresponding instance of (M') is true.

The question whether a theory of truth is to apply to a language presupposes that the sentence has a meaning independent of the theory. An acceptable T-theory is to construct with a "generalized form of reference" and satisfaction is such a generalized form (Davidson 2001 (1988): 179). But this does not imply that "*any particular set of reference axioms* is ineliminable" (Neale 2001: 37). In the theory of truth, reference is not established by any empirical or intelligible mechanism like modes of presentations, causal chains, informational packages or intentionality that connect parts of language with reality. Predicate axioms themselves do not introduce new objects. The axiomatization within the truth theory "construes singular terms as standing for (or satisfied by) objects and construes sentences as satisfied by sequences of an object" that makes sentences and beliefs true or not (37-38). We see thereby *why* and *how* the truth-centered theory of *RI* (the logical form analysis with the background of an extensional, first-order logic—first-order inferential relations—with identity) is connected with ontology and the distal theory of meaning and cognition, that is, the ontological commitments of particulars and events as unrepeatable particulars.

5. It is a part of *RI* to individuate propositional attitudes (thoughts), and just this is essential for the semantic explanation of linguistic behavior. Yet this is beyond the framework of an analytical ontology. The logical form analysis leads us to an ontology, but not prima vista to a radical externalism. Such an analysis has reached its aim if the ontological decision of things and events as fundamental features of the world we have not made is reasoned. Yet the *inner*-theoretical step to a radical externalism from the holistic truth-centered theory of *RI* is not contingent.

But what is the inner-theoretical step from the *RI* of individual utterances to triangulation from the holistic truth-centered semantics of a radical interpreter? What are the necessary conditions for the application of a theory of truth in the style of Tarski in the process of *RI*?

On one hand, the answer to these questions explains us *why* a radical externalism follows from *RI* and its holistic truth-centered theory of meaning. Nevertheless this gives us a further reasoning for the autonomy of meaning, and it shows how the principle of charity makes *RI* possible. Charity is a bridge principle for the application of the holistic truth-centered theory of meaning. The particular role of *T*-sentences is: whatever operations were needed to create them and wherever ontology may help us in production, the *result* is that *T*-sentences state the truth-conditions on their own base. It means that the conditions are nothing else but what the sentence includes in itself. Insofar as the original sentence does not mention possible worlds, intensional entities, properties, or propositions, the statement of its truth-conditions does not do so, either. Tarski takes the concept of translation to be primitive and analyzes the concept of truth. Davidson, for his part, begins by taking truth as primitive and then goes on by analyzing translation and interpretation. In the homophone case, we confirm the theory on the deduction of *T*-theorems (*T*-sentences) basically from the axioms. The theorems have the form of biconditionals. In this case, the test seems simple because the interpreter can decide intuitively whether the theoretical description of sentences *s* is in the respective language. And by the substitution of these sentences with the *p*-place in a *T*-sentence the truth-conditions are generated. But this is not the case. We have to eliminate biconditionals that are true but *deviant*, such as, "snow is white" iff gras is green. The solution to this problem is: the sentences of the form

(1) "Schnee ist weiß" iff snow is white (*T*-sentence)

are to grasp as empirical generalizations of linguistic behavior and consequently they have to be true and also law-like. Some philosophers are not convinced of this clarification, for example G. Segal (1999). I think that Davidson's response to Segal goes along with my reconstruction of the relationship between truth, charity and externalism. He wrote on the theory he has in mind,

Being an empirical theory, it favors simplicity, like any other empirical theory. It also preserves entailment relations between sentences, which immediately eliminates a vast number of 'non-interpretive' theories. It also preserves, within reasons, relations of evidential support between sentences. (Davidson 1999e: 57)

In my view, the redemption of this claim is the transgression from applying charity as an epistemic norm of *RI* to a radical externalism: attitudes exist by truth and their contents are to individuate externally. At the end of the confirmation there is the evidence of the theory of interpretation, the assent or dissent of speakers to sentences on the base of distal stimuli in situations of awareness of the presence or absence of objects and events as the relevant stimuli. The holding true—forming a perceptual belief—is based on a causal connection with reality and the occasional sentences have a *direct* reference to the causal-relevant part of the awareness of this reality between both speaker and interpreter in the context of triangulation. This is Davidson's theory of ascription and individuation of the propositional content of saying *that*, and the answer to the question why the step is taken from *RI* to a radical externalism. So the adequate description of interpretation of one's utterances is to expand from a *T*-sentence to:

(2) "*s*" is true in *L* (*s*, *sp*, *t*, *c*) iff *p*

s = structural description of a sentence, *L* = language under study, *s* = sentence, *sp* = speaker, *t* = time point, *c* = causal relation of distal stimulus. The interpreter instances this quadruple to *utterances* as the focus of interpretation. This is the reason why we apply the primitive predicate of the core theory of interpretation not only to sentences but also to utterances. If this was not possible, there would be no *RI*. It is therefore not contingent that a speaker holds true sentences in a certain situation. This is not only a property of the logical structure of sentences, but it is caused by external circumstances.

The holistic truth-centered theory of meaning supposes a preanalyti-cal concept of truth, and it is its claim to explain translation (meaning). This modification by Tarski is reasoned through this because the sup-posed concept of truth has put us in the position to decide what counts as evidence of *T*-sentences. The modification is reasoned by the task of *RI*. The same is not valid for the concepts of satisfaction and reference. Its role is a theoretic one. This led to some misunderstandings, yet also to corrections (J. A. Forster 1976, Davidson's response to Forster 1984 (1976), Larson 1988, Fodor, Lepore (1994), Lepore, Ludwig 2005: 113-118).

Larson has rejected Forster's objection:

Forster's claim that the truth predicate must occur primitively in a Davidsonian theory falsely supposes that a theory of truth can be recognized as being about truth just in case the truth predicate occurs primitively. The supposition is false because *no* theory, of course, would count as being about truth simply because *it used a certain predicate*, regardless of *where that predicate occurred*; its use of that predicate must be correct, recognizable as giving a notion of truth. If what Foster actually means, when he says that the truth predicate must occur primi-tively, is that the theory must be *interpreted* by way of its *axioms*; then his claim, thought more defensible, is still wrong for all the *reasons* that the *Building Block* approach is *wrong*, that is, because it treats words rather than sentences as the units of meaning. (Larson, 1988: 12, my italics).

We can generalize this rejection with respect to the following: we do not directly confirm theories, but only sentences derived from them. This is a general feature of theorizing. *T*-sentences are theorems in an interpre-tive theory of truth and meaning. They are deducted from axioms. Both axioms and theorems have to be laws, because theories of truth are to understand as empirical theories.

Larson has put together the axioms, and he has emphasized the differ-ence to Tarski (1988, on Tarski: 5): 1. General logical axioms; 2. axioms that intuitively translate the axioms of theory of the object language. In accordance with Tarski, both the axioms have nothing to do with lin-guistics. They introduce a broad variety of normal terms that gives the axioms their necessary expressive power to interpret the object language. Quine's concept of observation sentences could also be counted among the axioms of the second sort; 3. axioms that describe the syntax of the object language. These are axioms that we find in Tarski's class calculi and that also give us the concepts of symbolic expression and concate-nation; 4. axioms that describe the semantics of the object language. This sort of axioms substitutes genuine definitions as in Tarski's theory. What counts among these axioms is an axiom of recursive characterization of satisfaction and truth and — not necessarily — an axiom that connects satisfaction and truth. These four axioms are sufficient for the following: each sentence of an object language entails a true T-sentence (Larson 1988: 13, on Quine's reception of Tarski, Davidson 2005 (1996); on the axioms of Davidson's satisfactional theory of reference, Neale 1999).

In *Truth and Meaning* (1984 (1967)), the proposal was that the T-sentences give us the truth-conditions for every sentence of the object language and such truth-conditions inform us about the meaning of the sentences under study. The modification is that the holism and the concluded T-theorems from axioms have to compensate that the meaning of a sentence (its semantic content) is not to give from simple biconditionals of the Convention T. The truth-predicate is to understand only if we presuppose it as a *general, indefinite, pre-analytic concept*. The step from truth to meaning is taken when T-sentences are verified. Therefore the theory of truth is a *theory* to ascribe utterance meaning under given circumstances.

For RI the compositionality works on every level. The basic theory of meaning is a semantic interpretation of the sentences in a given language building by a finite number of primitive expressions: "a theory of meaning for a language L shows 'how the meanings of sentences depend on the meanings of words' if it contains a (recursive) definition of truth-in-L" (1984 (1967): 23). The problem is how strong compositionality is assumed. For Davidson it is functional because the compositional requirement is to determine the complex expressions by the parts in the way they are put together. For Lepore and Ludwig (2005), compositionality is stronger assumed. The problem emerges because the question is how functionality of compositionality determines the semantic value of expressions in sentences we have never heard before. This leads to the problem of determination (109-112). For Davidson, the function principle works together with the context principle (language holism). For Lepore and Ludwig, compositionality works on the basis of the semantics of natural language. Davidson's replacement turn is connected with a weaker version of compositionality. Just this shows us the reason why Lepore and Ludwig argue for a stronger principle of compositionality. With the replacement turn, Davidson's concept of meaning as a disposition is connected in principle. The problem is how to fix the meaning (reference) of expression with this truth-centered theory. It is essential for this account that the choice among various languages of a speaker is not only the interpretation of their language, but at the same time the ascription of attitudes. Davidson argues that the evidence allows the interpreter a choice among the languages, because this choice is balanced by the appropriate choice of beliefs like holding true and other attitudes. If this is given, the language cannot be chosen freely and, at the same time, what a word refers to is to relativize to the leading attitudes. This is reasoned by the concept of meaning as dispositional in principle. But Lepore and Ludwig argue that the dispositional concept of meaning is not any guarantee for fixing the meaning of expressions, and compositionality is stronger to assume. If a truth theory with interpretive axioms (interpretive truth theory) specifies the meaning of the sentences in the given object language, the expressions (words) are not to fix by dispositions (attitudes). The problem is that the specification of T-sentences for a context-sensitive object language of the sentences of the form (T') requires fixing the role of singular terms. They have a meaning which is not given by a comprehensive account of attitudes. It is to note here that a single T-theorem does not give us any rich information of the meaning of an uttered sentence. We have to elaborate the logical relations of a sentence to the other sentences in a language.

2.1.2.4. The Paratactic Account of Reported Speech

It is of particular significance that the paratactic analysis of reported speech follows from the truth-centered setting of RI, because an interpreter's theory of interpretation has to select the truth-conditions of uttered sentences of any speaker in such a way that his theory enables him to ascribe attitudes. *That* has a demonstrative and a relational meaning. The phrasing "that p" in "x said/believes that p" does not refer to a proposition — in contrast to Frege's —; it requires no intensional entity and. in difference to an analysis that introduces said-that-p as a single predicate, this proposal allows us to take the step towards a semantic analysis of the sentence following "that". In so-called that-phrases: "saying that ..." the intensional connective "that" is semantically irrelevant (on Carnap's, Church's, Quine's, Scheffler's proposals, Davidson 1984 (1968)). The paratactic account claims to show that the demonstrative singular term *that* refers to an *utterance*, not to a proposition or a sentence. Davidson intends a new proposal of the semantic analysis of indirect discourse, belief sentences, sentences about commands, orders and the like, consequently of attitude-attributing locutions.

For *RI*, the required ordinary ascription of propositional attitudes has the logical form of *two* paratactically connected utterances, and the attribution of attitudes is to complete by the individuation of the content of such attitudes in the triangle. The paratactic analysis makes the assumption that the interpreter takes his own utterance as a starting point to ascribe propositional attitudes and thoughts to the speaker. Beliefs and propositional entities are a kind of things that make myself and other speakers to samesayers: "The idea ... is that of *samesaying*: when I say that Galileo said that the earth moves, I represent Galileo and myself as samesayers." (Davidson 1984 (1979): 104) This is the result of the paratactic analysis of samesaying. The ascription of beliefs is to carry out on the basis of the same truth-conditions of sentences that an interpreter uses for the redescription of the speaker's linguistic behavior. For this account the epistemic channel of a speaker to the samesayer is not significant. The semantic analysis of words like belief or desire is a result of logical form approach and its application to all components of linguistic behavior.

Sentences like:

* Galileo said that the earth moves.
* The earth moves. Galileo said that.
* Peter said that the earth moves.
* Peter moves his lips ...

are to interpret co-extensively for the paratactic account including the idioms of the reported speech. This analysis is:

* ($\exists x$) (Galileo's utterance x and my (or Peter's) last utterance "the earth moves" makes us (them) to samesayers)

Semantically the utterance of Galileo is to analyze in a way as the utterance of *two* sentences: "Galileo said that" and "The earth moves". The logical form of our normal ascription of attitudes is such of two paratactic connected utterances. What we redescribe with indirect discourse by the *that*-clause is the truth-conditions of those sentences. This is the solution of the problem of quantifying in the contained sentence of indirect discourse. Such discourse entails an indexical component, the demonstrative expression *that*. The "that" refers to the *second* utterance. The first utterance is true if and only if the content of the utterance of

Galileo is the same as the reference of the speaker's utterance: it is a translation of Galileo's utterance.

Finding right words of my own to communicate another's saying is a problem in translation. The words I use in the particular case may be viewed as products of my total theory (however vague and subject to correction) of what the originating speaker means by anything he says: such a theory is indistinguishable from a characterization of a truth predicate, with his language as object language and mine as metalanguage. The crucial point is that there will be equally acceptable alternative theories that differ in assigning clearly non-synonymous sentences of mine as translations of his same utterance. This is Quine's thesis of the indeterminacy of translation. (Davidson 1984 (1968): 100)

The sentences of indirect discourse

...consist of an expression referring to a speaker, the two-place predicate 'said', and a demonstrative referring to an utterance. Period. What follows gives the content of the subject's saying, but has no logical or semantic connection with the original attribution of a saying. This last point is no doubt the novel one, and upon it everything depends. From a semantic point of view the content-sentence in indirect discourse is not contained in the sentence whose truth counts, i.e. the sentence that ends with 'that'. (106)

RI means making behavior intelligible. The theory of truth claims to explain the first (literal) meaning of the uttered sentences. For such a redescription as attitudinal report, semanticists make two assumptions: 1. the report of propositional attitudes informs us on the relation between a speaker and the respectively propositional content, and also 2. the report of such attitudes is true only if the propositional content of the that-clause expresses the propositional content of the speaker's attitude. We can see now why the ascription of beliefs has no relationship to propositional entities.

How do we redescribe linguistic behavior in such a way that we report on both the *statement* (samesaying) and the *same token* of the utterance?

This leads us to the semantic analysis of the *mixed* quotation. The treatment is less discussed in the philosophical writings. It is the quotation we normally use in our ordinary talk.

Cappelen and Lepore (1999) have continued the paratactic proposal of quotation. Their claim is to give an analysis that does *not* refer to pragmatic factors of explanation of linguistic behavior. In a first step they underline the semantic features of:

(1) the *direct*, like, Clinton said, "I'll cut taxes",
(2) the *indirect*, like: Clinton said that he'd cut taxes,
(3) the *pure*, like: "'Lobster' is a word" and
(4) the *mixed* quotation, like Clinton said that he'd "cut taxes".

It is a semantic fact that a mixed quotation is not a report about words. This has to take its semantic analysis into account. Recall Davidson's construct in *Quotation* (1984 (1979)) the pure quotation of (3) as

* Lobster. The expression of which this is a token is a word.

Quotations are, on account of this, definite descriptions entailing demonstratives. Such expressions select the token within the quotation sign in such a way that definite descriptions denote an expression that is instantiated by the token the expression refers to. For the Lepore and Cappelen version of the paratactic account, quotation marks function as quantifiers that range over utterance-tokens, and the samesaying relation is a relation that holds between utterance-tokens rather than between speakers.

If we apply this to the paratactic account of indirect quotation, we will analyze (1) as

* Clinton said (produced) a token of the expression instantiated by that. I'll cut taxes.

The utterance of the *first* sentence is accompanied with a reference to the utterance of the *second* sentence (on the relevance of this proposal Lepore, Cappelen 1999: 95-96; R. Elugardo 1999: 118, note 19 calls this account a twin paratactic account of indirect quotation and pure quotation).

The utterances of (2) and (4) agree in *what* is said, and the mixed and indirect quotation have an overlapping semantic treatment. If we compare this with the utterances of (1) and (4), they both agree in another respect, because in these quotations a pure quotation occurs. So the direct and the mixed quotation also show us an overlapping semantic treatment. Yet it is not a semantic fact that the utterances (1) and (2) agree in any respect on what is said, also in case we ascribe to Clinton the full understanding of the English utterance. It might be that Clinton does not know any English and he utters "I'll cut taxes" to clear his throat. Consequently there is a different semantic treatment of the utterances (1) and (2). It is to note that (1) and (4) and "A token of 'I'll cut taxes' was uttered" (5) and corresponding "A token of 'cut taxes' was uttered" (6) implies a pure quotation. It seems reasonable to assume that a unified treatment of quotation is developed that expands Davidson's analysis in *On Saying that* (1984 (1968)) and *Quotation* (1984 (1979)). The unification just intends to avoid an assimilation of the single sorts of quotation, for example the indirect to the direct quotation (Carnap, Scheffler, Quine and others).

It is the claim of Cappelen and Lepore to analyze the direct and indirect quotation in such a way that they both satisfy the conditions (1) to (4). It is to emphasize that the given analysis of the pure, direct, and indirect quotations does not give us a successful semantic analysis of mixed quotation. Therefore, we have no means to integrate the quotations of (1) to (4) this way. With the indirect quotation we report about the same utterance token, and with the direct quotation we report about samesaying, that is, the complement clause refers to a statement (proposition) and we have samesaid such a statement respectively. The pure quotation is normally used as a singular term to refer to abstract entities or types of expressions (on pure quotation, Davidson *Quotation* 1984 (1979), Capplen, Lepore 1999: 95-97).

The mixed quotation leads us back to the semantic means of handling the report of (1) and (2). The problem of mixed quotation is that within the quotation "cut taxes" — together with other words — plays the role of a report about *what* Clinton *said* — that he will cut taxes and the uttered words also function to report about Clinton's utterance-token "cut taxes". The problem is:

How can the that-clause of (4) fix both: the statement by Clinton, that is, not any assertion about words, and reference to the words that Clinton uttered?

In other words:

How do we fix the extension of samesaying?

To grasp this, Cappelen and Lepore construct the mixed quotation in the following way:

*$\exists u$(Says(c,u) & $SS(u,$that) & $ST(u,$these). He'd cut taxes (ST = same token).

In this form the utterance of the first demonstrative refers to the complete utterance of "He'd cut taxes" and an utterance of the second demonstrative refers *only* to the sub-utterance "cut taxes". Therefore we have a unified account including a report about both: 1. the same utterance token (*ST*), that is, the relation between Clinton's utterance and the sub-utterance demonstrated in the mixed quotation, and 2. the samesaying (*SS*), that is, the relation between Clinton's utterance and the utterance we refer to.

From my point of view, this is the symmetry between the representation and expression of the propositional content of sentences (semantic property).

The paratactic account of sentences on attitudes makes a connection between the autonomy of meaning and the ascription of attitudes as the task of *RI*. If we did not apply the principle of autonomy of meaning to the translation and ascription of attitudes, no ascription of attitudes would be possible. The interpretation of a sentence is independent of its possible use, and this is the guarantee that we can describe attitudes at all. Our use of sentences cannot explain meaning. The ascription of beliefs to myself and to other persons in the frame of *RI* does not stand in a relationship to propositional entities. The semantic analysis of the structure of "that-sentences", so-called content sentences, leads to the result that the content of assertive utterances in the indirect discourse is *said* and not asserted.

2.1.2.5. The Autonomy of Meaning: Moods and illocutionary Forces

All methods to cope with the circle between belief and meaning are based on the application of the principle of charity. But, in this frame, *RI* and its truth-centered theory of meaning have to give us an answer to the relationship between *mood*, illocutionary *force*, and the *ascription* of attitudes also. This is to clarify by the paratactic analysis of imperatives. For both the authority of first person and the analysis of mood and force the principle of autonomy of meaning is important because it is an *inner*-lingual correspondence of *RI*. We have to give an answer to the question:

What is the relationship between the first person authority and the autonomy of meaning?

But also in a further step:

What is the relationship between the autonomy of meaning, the grammatical moods, the different illocutionary forces of speech acts, and the ascription of attitudes?

RI goes hand in hand with the interpretation of actions and the ascriptions of beliefs, intentions, and desires. A theory of meaning has to explain to us how we can conclude from a complete description of a language what an interpreter accepts as a meaningful utterance. *RI* makes the assumption that a competent speaker knows *what* he accepts as such utterances. But it is to explain *how* we apply our concept of meaning to propositional attitudes. We know already how this is to bring off. This explains us why this application is not grounded on linguistic conventions (Davidson 1984 (1982)). All linguistic utterances are intentional, and speakers' intentions are informative for the interpretation, but such attitudes do not inform us about the meaning of the uttered sentences. This is also valid if a speaker utters a sentence with an intention other than indicated by its linguistic meaning. All purposes and non-linguistic aims of speakers are not *logically* connected with the meaning of uttered sentences.

I conclude that it is not an accidental feature of language that the ulterior purpose of an utterance and its literal meaning are independent, in the sense that the latter cannot be derived from the former: it is of the essence of language. I call this feature of language the principle of *the autonomy of meaning*. We came across an application when discussing illocutionary force, where it took the form of the discovery that what is put into the literal meaning then becomes available for any ulterior (nonlinguistic) purpose and even any illocutionary performance. (Davidson 1984 (1982): 274-75, on illocutionary force, Davidson 1984 (1979))

The autonomy of meaning slightly tones down first person authority. It is not a feature of this authority that a speaker willfully determines the meaning of his uttered words. If this was the case, he would not have any such authority. Therefore it is to conclude that the truth-conditions of uttered sentences are fundamental for first person authority. A speaker can only say something with his utterances if certain conditions are satisfied. This is the guarantee for an interpreter that he will be able to understand a speaker. In this respect, there is a symmetrical relationship between both the speaker and the interpreter. The autonomy of meaning has to ensure that for *RI*. If this cannot be ensured, there is no understanding of linguistic behavior. The relationship between the first person authority and the principle of autonomy of meaning is to explain in the following way: If "I believe that snow is white" and "I" continue

to state the truth-conditions of my belief, "I" always state such conditions in my *own* language. This could not be possible if my authority or
my ulterior purposes changed the meaning of my uttered words. By this
we see the first person authority and the autonomy of meaning interact.
This interaction is also a ground for the anomalous monism as a conceptual dualism: *RI* has a mental counterpart, namely the network of propositional attitudes that the interpreter evaluates with his own standard of
rationality by the application of the principle of charity.

In single cases this may be an error. But it makes no sense to talk about
an error as an absolute one. If there was any such error, we could not
ascribe to a speaker a language that is a subject or *RI*. The autonomy of
meaning is a part of the first person authority. If both did not interact,
there could not be any language. On the other hand, the authority of
first person follows from *RI,* because it is a requirement that we interpret the speaker under study not only on the condition that he holds the
uttered sentence true, but also from the speaker's intent that he will be
interpreted in the right way. Davidson's theory of language is a version
of individualism of meaning. From this point of view, first person authority is the guarantee that a speaker does not use his words wrongly in
most cases. This is connected with the externalistic individuation of the
semantic content, because sensory stimuli are not an epistemic mediation
to determine the content of beliefs and sentences.

An interpretive theory of meaning would be incomplete if in its
framework it was not to elaborate also how non-assertive sentences are
to analyze. The leading question is:

Is there a conceptual relation between mood and illocutionary force?
The answer leads us back to the inevitability of the principle of autonomy of meaning.

In the theory of language we normally make a difference between
moods of sentences or syntactical modi and the correspondent illocutionary forces, such is, types of illocutions or semantic moods. The
moods of sentences are not to be mixed up with the moods of verbs like
indicative, conjunctive or imperative (on an overview about theories of
moods, G. Grewendorf, D. Zaefferer 1991). Davidson opposes Dummett's account that there is a convention governing the use of declarative
sentences. For Davidson, the mood is *no* conventional sign of assertions
and commands. Only for the grammatical mood is the theory of word-
meaning relevant but not for the multiplicity of illocutionary forces.
The analysis of non-indicative utterances does not leave the frame of

the theory of truth. The utterances of words like "Peter asserts that it is snowing" are to interpret as two sentences: "Peter asserts that", and: "it is snowing". We analyze all non-indicative sentences like indicative sentences by adding a further expression, the so-called "mood-setter". This setter syntactically indicates the relevant transformations. The paratactic inquiry of commands (imperatives) takes into account that the utterance of a non-indicative sentence has no truth-value. These utterances have a mood-setter and are to analyze as consisting of two utterances, for example: "Peter asserted that" and "it is snowing." Each of this utterances has a truth-value, but the whole utterance is no logical conjunction to which we ascribe truth-values. A mood-setter indicates the illocutionary forces, but these expressions do not assert the force of speech acts because only speakers make an assertion or give a command. This is the conceptual context between mood and force (K. Ludwig 1997). But his would not be possible if there was not an inner-lingual support, namely the autonomy of meaning.

The only form the mood-setter can have — the only function it can perform — is that of a sentence. It behaves like a sentence an utterance of which refers to an utterance of an indicative sentence. If we were to represent in linear form the utterance, say, the imperative sentence 'Put on your hat', it would come out as the utterance of a sentence like 'My next utterance is imperatival in force', followed by an utterance of 'You will put on your hat'. (Davidson 1984 (1979): 120)

The autonomy of meaning is the guarantee that uttered imperative sentences are self-declaring in their force, but they do not assert such forces. What such non-assertive utterances say can consequently be true or false.

It is to mention here that, in the controversy about the empirical adequacy of the truth-centered theory of *RI*, a gap is stated between truth-condition and the ascription of the intended meaning of utterances. For example, with the utterance "Brutus is an honorable man" Cassius intended to tell his audience that Brutus is a dishonorable man (on this gap Elugardo 1999). Davidson himself does not dispute that there is such a "gap" but he argues that the truth-centered theory of *RI* explains that the first meaning and the concept of samesaying are "flexible" enough to bridge it. (Davidson 1999c: 119-120) Davidson does not dispute that interpretation includes grabbing the force of an utterance, like, for example, as assertion, order, question, irony, whatever. This is something that the speaker intends toward his audience and we are successful in finding out the illocutionary force in many cases. But there are no conventions or rules to recognize the intended force. First of all it must be left open whether we are following this answer to bridge the gap between first meaning and the intended force of utterances (on this problem capt. 9, in this book).

With the logical form (structure) of an uttered sentence as a deep structure, we have a theory of linguistic meaning and of language content that explain the semantic role of lingual expression co-extensive to its truth-conditions. The Convention T is the theoretical frame for *RI* as an "effective structure" that shows us how we establish the meaning of uttered sentences in a natural language. This is the claim. Within this framework, a holism in the theory of language is introduced that claims to explain how we learn a natural language. The semantic productivity is to explain. It means the ability to generate and understand sentences we have never heard before.

A theory of truth describes the semantic productivity of linguistic behavior as a complex disposition and consequently as an essential feature of language in general.
A theory of truth does more than describe an aspect of speech behavior of an agent, for it not only gives the truth conditions of the actual utterance of the agent; it also specifies the conditions under which the utterance of a sentence would be true if it were uttered. This applies both to sentences actually uttered, by telling us what would have been the case if those sentences had been uttered at other times or under other circumstances, and to sentences never uttered. The theory thus describes a certain complex ability. (Davidson 1990: 310)

To sum up, the theory about the structure of types of sentences is a theory of the logical form of the respective sentences. Davidson calls the description of structure of all sentences its logical form. We find this form in difference to the surface grammatical properties, and it supplies a simple, powerful, and coherent description of the entailment-relation. But the theorizing makes the assumption that mastery of the theoretical structure is an idealization of our normal competence of the use of language. Finding the logical form as a deep structure is, for Davidson, a theory of translation. A theory of truth is an empirical theory and the axioms and theorems have to be the general status of laws. In this way we build a formal semantics of a natural language and the ontology we need for semantics is a matter of the ontology of natural language we filter out.

2.1.2.6. *T*-Sentences as Statements of Law

But how do we describe the evidence of truth-conditions of sentences uttered by an individual speaker?

The answer here is also the answer to the question:

Why are we able to grasp *T*-sentences as statements of a law?

A radical interpreter has made the assumption that the network of beliefs of any speaker is to a large degree coherent (consistent). This assumption is concluded directly from the holistic nature of beliefs. If one ascription of a belief to an individual speaker is successful, then it is also possible to ascribe beliefs to any speaker, presupposed the interpreter makes the assumption that the sets of beliefs are coherent (consistent). The solution of the task of *RI* cannot avoid adding "optimally fit evidence" to the theoretical framework. But this means interpreting a speaker in such a way that he is right in principle. The application of the principle of natural epistemic justice makes it possible "to take up the slake" between the ascription of holding true to an individual speaker and objective truth by public standards (Davidson 1984 (1974): 153-154). The indeterminacy of translation (meaning) does not take effect in such an ascription. In the framework of a *unified theory*, this leads Davidson to a radical externalism, *RI* of speech goes hand in hand with the ascription of desires and beliefs and "with the interpretation of action generally" (154).

Why are the entities of propositional attitudes to individuate in triangulation?

The application of the principle of natural epistemic justice and the perceiving of distal stimuli are the requirements for the selection of the truth-conditions of holding true. For *RI*, both is fundamental: a radical interpreter presupposes that a speaker holds true his utterance and the individuation of such utterances is obvious by distal stimuli in the triangle. Therefore we identify attitudes on the base of causal stimuli. The principle of natural epistemic justice and the distal theory of thoughts and meaning draw a borderline of a semantic interpretation of utterances in principle. Holding true and the individuation of propositional contents of utterances fix the restriction of understanding and the ascription of attitudes. This frame is *not* to offset for a holistic truth-centered theory of meaning.

However, the question is:

How can we ascribe a *single* attitude to someone? Can we count attitudes? What do we presuppose to grasp the quantificatory structure of attitudes?

The answer is:

* When we develop a theory of interpretation of linguistic and other behavior insofar as this behavior is sufficiently consistent and shows sufficient expressibility (structure), we have a basis to identify and distinguish attitudes.

Insofar as such conditions are satisfied, we can ascribe single attitudes. The ascription satisfied the quantificatory procedure to ascribe attitudes because:

... to the extent that we can see the actions of an agent as falling into a consistent (rational) pattern of a certain sort, we can explain those actions in terms of a system of quantified beliefs and desires. (Davidson 1984 (1975): 160)

Obviously the basis of expressibility or power is our language. It is a requirement of rationality that people have a language. Intelligible redescription is only possible if the interpreter makes the prior assumption that the network of propositional attitudes is structured so that the speaker appears to be a rational person. It seems reasonable to criticize the assumption that the interpreter projects his own standards of truth and consistency. The argument must be rejected partially, because the holistic nature of beliefs and propositional attitudes builds a network; an identification is only possible on this foundation, thus allowing a distinction of attitudes. If we assume an interdependence of beliefs and meaning, an interpreter can only grasp, distinguish and individuate parts of the network of attitudes by an application of the principle of natural epistemic justice. We are black boxes, and I can see no other way of doing this. Such attitudes and their correspondent behavior are caused by "objective situations and events". This reaction is itself directed to a sentence (utterance of a sentence):

... all the evidence for or against a theory of truth (interpretation, translation) comes in the form of facts about what events or situations in the world cause, or would cause, speakers to assent to, or dissent from, each sentence in the speaker's repertoire.... What matters is that what causes the response or attitude of the speaker is an objective situation or event, and that the response or attitude is directed to a sentence or the utterance of a sentence." (Davidson 1984 (1979): 230-31).

Therefore, Davidson does not agree with Quine's ontological relativity (in particular: 231-33).

This is, according to Davidson, the reason *why interpretation presupposes rationality* and why the identification of causal-relations in the triangulation between speaker-interpreter-external stimuli is the basis of ascription. The causal relations of parts of our beliefs and the external stimuli take effect in the semantic procedure of interpretation, and they are the relevant factor showing that *T*-theorems are statements of *law* at all. Belief as holding-true seems to be the qualification for elementary attitudes, that is, every attitude of this sort has a behavioral feature; it is also an instance of a behavioral rationality (someone-does-what-he-is-holding-true), and an extensional feature like the elementary predicate of the core theory qualifies to speaker, utterances, time points and causal stimuli. *T*-sentences are lawlike because the sentences that speakers hold true stand in a systematic correlation to certain circumstances. Causal relations are the conceptual resources to explain such correlations. Sentences and beliefs have a content only if there are causal relations to the external world.

Yet: if *T*-sentences are lawlike, are such laws strict or ceteris paribus laws?

T-sentences as laws could be ceteris paribus laws only because the individuation of the content of attitudes is effected in the triangle by observable distal stimuli and the reaction of individual speakers. If *T*-sentences were strict laws, this would contradict the anomalous monism and the explanations of actions by primary reasons (K. Ludwig 1999: 36-41).

The application of the principle of charity, including the principle of shared identity of reference of reactions caused by distal stimuli and the autonomy of meaning, are the guarantee for coping with the circle between belief and meaning and at the same time between the coherence of the ascription of attitudes and the understanding of the propositional-like content of the uttered sentences "that *p*". This is valid not only for assertions but also for other illocutionary acts, for example,

If a speaker's purpose is to give information, or to make an honest assertion, then normally the speaker believes he is uttering a sentence true under the circumstances. If he utters a command, we may usually take this as showing that he holds a certain sentence (closely related to the sentence uttered) to be false; similarly for many cases of deceit. When a question is asked, it generally indicates that the questioner does not know whether a certain sentence is true;

and so on. In order to infer from such evidence that a speaker holds a sentence true we need to know much about his desires and beliefs, but we do not have to know what his words mean.... But if we know he holds the sentence true *and* we know how to interpret it, then we can make a correct attribution of belief. Symmetrically, if we know what belief a sentence held true expresses, we know how to interpret it. (Davidson 1984 (1975): 161-62, 162)

We can see *why* the unlimited application of the principle of epistemic justice is the guarantee for ascribing beliefs and for picking out the meaning of uttered words.

By this procedure we do not make any distinction between homophony and the redescription of linguistic behavior as two methods of translation. Building a theory of *RI* is directed to:

Each interpretation and attribution of attitude is a move within a holistic theory, a theory necessarily governed by concern for consistency and general coherence with the truth, and it is this that sets these theories forever apart from those that describe mindless objects, or describe objects as mindless. (Davidson 1984 (1974): 154)

Thereby propositional attitudes are theoretical, and they are to conclude from our theory of interpretation. Every ascription must follow from the theory of attitudes of the interpreted speaker. The speaker himself can do no more than make his beliefs fit in a coherent system, but it cannot be excluded that he may be in an empirical situation where he is expecting too much of them. Our ascription is determined by these restrictions. This is exactly why it is presupposed that the sets of attitudes are not only consistent but also true and to individuate, that is, caused by external things and events. The irreducibility of the concepts of meaning and belief to physical, neurological and behavioristic concepts does not go back to indeterminacy of meaning and translation, but to the evidence that is the guarantee for coping the circle between belief and meaning. The indeterminacy is "only" significant to show us that *RI* goes "hand in hand with the interpretation of action generally." (154) It is the claim of the theory of behavior as a connected theory of belief and desire to enable us to move in this direction.

2.1.3. The Principle of Natural Epistemic Justice

The answer to the question:
   What is the guarantee of the independence of evidence of *RI*?
   is directed to answering the question for its so-called possibility. Or, in other words, the generalized presupposition of understanding linguistic behavior is to identify because listing cases gives us no generalized answer to our question. Without an assumption of unification, the solution of the task of *RI* could not begin. Holding true of sentences is introduced as the guarantee of the independent availability of evidence and makes a quantification in sets of belief possible. On this basis the interpreter constructs a theory about the beliefs of the respective speaker and his verbal behavior. This would not be possible if the interpreter imposed certain restrictions on his understanding. *RI* leads us, seemingly by itself, to elementary assumptions of rationality that cannot be evaded, that is, the so-called *policy of rational accommodation*. Yet, these are *our* own standards and it seems that they are not freely at our disposal. It follows that, in the context of *RI*, rationality is an epistemic norm, not in a moral or ethical sense. There are doubts toward this approach but only one objection against the reverting to such own standards is not convincing.

What would be the requirement of the priority of mutual standards over our own standards?

For a radical externalism, the application of the principle of correspondence is a guarantee of the objectivity of interpretation. This is a matter of mutual (similar) reactions that are caused by the external world in the triangle. The reactions among humans and the external causation of perceived shared stimuli are a necessary condition to apply the theory of truth. This epistemic complement is the reason for completing *RI* with the triangulation model of externalism. Therefore, the *second person* is to include in the solution of the task of interpretation. The assumption of mutual standards makes no sense, because there is only a reciprocal interpretation. The question should not be asked for a mutual standard but for the objectivity of interpretation as a guarantee of successful interpretation:

We should not despair because we cannot provide a standard by which to judge the standard, a test for whether the standard meter bar is actually a meter long. Our conclusion should rather be: if our judgements of the propositional attitudes of others are not objective no judgements are, and the concept of objectivity has no application (Davidson 2001 (1997): 84)

2.1.3.1. A Resystematization of Charity

For *RI*, the principle of charity is the answer to its possibility. Charity is the bridging principle of grasping objective truth and interpersonal understanding. The principle will be systematized by me in the next steps. It consists of some assumptions (principles) that are combined in *RI*. I will name my systematization the principle of *natural epistemic justice*, that is, the speaker is right if the opposite is not proven (therefore, I take the *Burge*-problem into account). Doing so, it is to show how the external individuation of empirical content or the contents of beliefs are connected with this principle respectively. At first glance this is not obvious from the evidence of *RI*, but a result of a resystematization of charity. By this we recognize *how* and *why* interpretation—rationality (charity)—externalism (and communication) take effect to solve the task of interpretation, and we can give an explanation why the triangulation model of *RI* leads to a particular concept of language. In this way we recognize *how* and *why* the individuation of the content of attitudes goes along with the solution of the task of *RI*. It must be emphasized that the principle of natural epistemic justice also gives the principle of charity another turn. Epistemic justice is a guarantee for a correspondence of the background theories between speaker and interpreter. Coping with the circle between belief and meaning always means breaking into the background theories of the speaker. Yet, from the line of communication and the role of the second person also the *social frame of reference* emerges within which we ascribe the local content of attitudes (on the local content Bilgrami 1992). This turn is in harmony with the inscrutability of reference and the indetermination of translation.

　1. *The principle of coherence*: The interpreter optimizes the speaker's self-consistency. If he did not do so, he could not understand him. This is an application of a two-value logic as a component of the theoretical framework of *RI*. Other versions of logic would not render a powerful instrument for the analysis of attitudes. Thoughts (propositional attitudes) like propositions stand in logical relations within a network of logical relations. There are no single thoughts which do not stand in a coherent relationship to others. The ascription of attitudes and the redescription of body movements as a certain behavior (action) could

not avoid making the assumption that the pattern of behavior which we fit in the beliefs and desires is consistent to a large degree. Consequently we assume a coherence (consistent) set of dispositions of the speaker and could only decide this way on the divergences in a given case. And emotions, too, have a propositional content and stand in a logical relationship to beliefs and values we have. Objective irrationality is an inner inconsistency. Therefore the composite theory of beliefs and desire, the total theory of behavior, applies the principle of coherence to make behavior intelligible in general. The first point is to complete with the following point.

2. *The principle of correspondence*: the interpreter assumes that there is a correspondence between the speaker's view of the world and his own, or, in other words, successful interpretations and communications are an evidence of these. The general features of language will be giving us the general features of reality. It is the claim of an interpretive theory of language to show this. The dependence of beliefs and meaning is concerned with three problems: the *ascription* of attitudes, the *interpretation* of sentences and the *individuation* of the content of attitudes. The guarantee of the independence of evidence and the individuation of the content of attitudes are given by the application of two principles: the optimization of true beliefs and the shared identity of reference of caused reactions. Both are connected: holding a sentence true and the causation of this attitude by distal stimuli.

(a) Holding a sentence true as an evidence of *RI* is a matter of the principle of optimizing true beliefs. *RI* applies a theory of interpretation in the style of Tarski, relativized to a speaker and a time point. Evidence is that the speaker holds true sentences in given circumstances. The formal feature is that the biconditionals are true and concluded from the axioms of the theory. It is a requirement of *RI* that the radical interpreter optimizes a correspondence with respect to true beliefs, and he identifies such beliefs only within a right sort of pattern of beliefs. If we did not make this assumption, speaking about *error* could not make sense.

Someone cannot have a belief unless he understands the possibility of being mistaken, and this requires grasping the contrast between truth and error—true belief and false. But this contrast, I have argued, can emerge only in the context of interpretation, which alone forces us to the idea of an objective, public truth. (Davidson 1984 (1975): 170)

The radical interpreter is forced to make the assumption:

We cannot intelligibly attribute the thought that a piece of ice is melting to someone who does not have *many* true beliefs about the nature of ice, its physical properties connected with water, cold, solidity, and so forth. The one attribution rests on the supposition of many more — *endlessly* more. And among the beliefs we suppose a man to have, many *must be true* (in our view) if any are to be *understood* by us. The clarity and cogency of our attributions of attitude, motive and belief are *proportionate*, then, to the extent to which we find others consistent and correct. (Davidson 2004 (1982): 183-84, my italics)

(b) The optimizing of true beliefs is to complete by the principle of similar reactions, that is, the interpreter presupposes that the speaker is disposed to respond in the same or in a comparable way toward things, events, properties as the interpreter does. The interpreter attributes true beliefs to the speaker. It is assumed that they are caused by individual events (distal simuli). This principle is the guarantee of the public channel of causation of beliefs, and the condition of objective truth that comes into play for the ascription of attitudes in the triangle. Such truth is about the content of beliefs that are caused by our objects of perceiving, such are "perceptual beliefs: the beliefs that are *directly* caused by what we *see* and *hear* and *otherwise sense*. These I hold to be in the main true because their *content* is, in effect, determined by what typically *causes* them" (Davidson 1999a: 18-19, my italics).

But what is the epistemological role of the causation of attitudes?

It is to emphasize that causal relations are not "relations" of confirmation or disconfirmation. Such relations do not build a block (building block theory). Causes are not propositions or beliefs, but events that cause us to believe something, that is, the belief itself is called the evidence and the event.

The principle formulates a shared identity of reference of caused reactions, be they verbal or not. Just this is presupposed for an application of truth conditions to linguistic behavior and ascription of attitudes. From triangulation, the existence of thoughts we have emerges. They have two features: their *objectivity* and their *empirical content* caused from prelinguistic surroundings. That means:

...I do have some suggestions about how we might approach the problem of saying something intelligible about the emergence of thought. There is a prelinguistic, pre-cognitive situation I can describe which seems to me to constitute a necessary condition for thought and language, a condition that can exist independent of thought, and can therefore precede it. Both in the case of non-human animals and in the case of small children, it is a condition that can be observed to obtain. The basic situation is one that involves two or more creatures simultaneously in interaction with each other and with the world they share; it is what I call *triangulation*. It is the result of a *threefold* interaction, an interaction which is *twofold* from the point of view of each of the two agents: each is interacting simultaneously with the world and with the other agent. To put this in a slightly different way, each creature learns to correlate the reactions of the other with changes or objects in the world to which it also reacts.... The triangle I have described stands for the simplest interpersonal situation. In it, two (or more) creatures each correlate their own reactions to external phenomena with the reactions of the others (or others). Once these correlations are set up, each creature is in a position to expect the external phenomenon when it perceives the associated reaction of the other. What introduces the possibility of error is the occasional failure of the expectation; the reactions do not correlate.... The point isn't that consensus defines the concept of truth but that it creates the space for its application. If this is right, then not only language, but thought itself, is necessary social. (Davidson 2001 (1997): 128-129, (1991): 212-213)

The entities of *RI*—the *un*interpreted utterances of natural speakers—are given us *directly* as intelligible behavioral items in this frame. Therefore, the theory of interpretation informs us what utterances of speakers mean. From such theories we derive the ascription of propositional attitudes and at the same time we individuate the content of such attitudes without researching such attitudes themselves. From here it follows that the distal theory of meaning (reference) and cognition does not need propositions as entities of propositional attitudes. Thought is composed by objectivity and the empirical content about the external circumstances. The truth and falsity of thought (objectivity) is not dependent on the existence of the thinker.

Davidson assumes that the pre-linguistic and pre-cognitive situation of triangulation works also among animals. The higher level of triangulation is given by language learning. In this situation the use of language builds a higher-structured description of things and events, for example, we master words in the absence of the words they refer to. From my point of view, on the level of mastering language the situational independency of reference emerges. Propositional truth is not only valid in a given situation. For Davidson, on the level of language learning the direct causal ties of language to the world do not disappear, but also give words their content: without such connections there is no language. But for him the triangle remains between writer, his audience and their background also when understanding literary language. Davidson concludes that interpretation of texts presupposes that in the hermeneutic circle a „broad basis of agreement" is established. Differences of taste, culture, periods, persons are a truism that does not reason a significant relativism of understanding (on the modification of the primal triangle 2005 (1993): 177-78; on triangulation and literature 178-81).

However, holding true and the principle of shared identity of reference of caused reactions increasingly take an epistemic effect in the procedure of *RI*. This is strengthened thereby because the interpreter constructs his theory of the speaker's beliefs on the basis of holding true and by the obvious reactions caused by distal stimuli. From my point of view, it is to conclude from here that it is essential to ascribe to the speaker not only a holding true of sentences but also a specific knowledge. This is the ground why all successful *RI* requires a convergence of background theories. If an interpreter makes these assumptions, we will have to consider an expanded frame of reference for *RI*. In confrontation with this approach, Davidson would draw back to the theory of truth as the hard core of *RI* in the following way because: "The theory describes conditions under which an utterance of a speaker is true, and so *says* nothing directly about what the speaker knows." (Davidson 1990: 312)

We can see how it followed from the holistic truth-centered theory that *RI* is *not* grounded by a particular knowledge about the meaning of the utterance and the beliefs of the speaker under study: the analysandum of *RI* are *un*interpreted (natural) utterances and also such utterances that a radical interpreter has never heard before. This is exactly what has to ensure the attitude of holding a sentence true because it is the *only* attitude that is to apply to all sentences without knowing anything about the speaker's particular beliefs. In my view, circumventing epistemic restrictions is an option of the theory of interpretation only if we presuppose the background theory as well known. Yet we do not get background theories completely out of our mind to solve the task of interpretation.

3. *The principle of continence*: The interpreter assumes a coherence between propositional attitudes and intentional actions. Actions are a consequence of a decision-theoretical structured network of attitudes, and the ascription of attitudes and the explanation of action is connectedly having a part in *RI*. We apply the following principle to practical reasoning: "One should prefer (act on) the judgement based on all considerations deemed relevant". (Davidson 2004 (1985): 194) or in other words: "perform the action judged best on the basis of all available relevant reasons" (Davidson 1980 (1970): 41), so-called "all things considered judgements". This is the motivational strength thesis (on that more

in detail, Mele 1992). Davidson compares this principle with Carnap's and Hempel's principle of justification of inductive (or statistical) reasoning that is not a part of inductive logic itself but a rational directive: "give your credence to the hypothesis supported by all available relevant evidence" (Davidson 1980 (1970): 41).

Objective irrationality is an inner-inconsistency of otherwise consistent sets of beliefs. Therefore all intentional actions — it may be that these are irrational in a further way — have a rational element: that is the paradox or irrationality. Ultimately we are unable to act against our strongest beliefs. Weakness of the will is in principle a borderline case, although in ordinary life we may often find evidence of weak-willed people. Practical thinking is an illusion, and this is exemplified by weakness of the will as a conflict to all things considered judgements. But this does not falsify the assumption of our standard of rationality because there is no genuine weakness of the will. This is the answer to the question *How is Weakness of the Will Possible?* (1980 (1970)). It is the claim of the constitutive (basic) standard of rationality to give a particular answer to the relationship between the intending and intentional actions. Forming an intention is an "all-out judgement" or "unconditional judgement" like "This action is desirable" followed from all things considered judgements. (Davidson 1980 (1978): 98). Such judgements do not refer to a will. "Self-deception", "overpowering desire", "lack of imagination" and so on are faults in the building of such judgements. Will-weaked people act with a reason and an unconditional judgement, but not in harmony with their best reasons. Wants, desires (both can be used interchangeably), principles, prejudices, felt duties, and obligations give us reasons for actions and intentions we express in prima facie judgements. Such judgements are desirable with respect to certain attributes of an action. Therefore they correspond to our pro attitudes. But intentions and the judgements that cause an intentional action are a result of an all-out judgement as a stronger judgement: pure intending is an intention as an all-out judgement that is a result of the relevant beliefs of an agent. This is Davidson's explanation of the relationship between intentions and intentional actions (capt. 6.1.1., in this book).

The interaction of the three principles in *RI* means: coherence (consistency), true beliefs, the shared identity of reference of caused reactions, and all things considered judgements are essential features of the network of our system of attitudes and their individuation (we are not successful to state attitudes one by one.) These are prerequisites of the emergence of each system of communication and its continuation and at the same time the condition for the formal structure of the unified theory. Such a system could not be without the interaction of these principles. With the second point the triangulation is introduced, because the content of beliefs is caused by surrounding things and events, and this is obvious in the triangle. This shows *how* and *why* the step to a radical externalism is taken when applying the principle of charity. But we also recognize *why* we are forced to systematize *RI* by the principle of epistemic justice: the intelligible redescription of speech and actions cannot avoid presupposing that the speaker (agent) is largely right with respect to the truth of his belief, the individuation of its content and his authority of first person. This is not a mere charity we allow him: "We must, if we are to interpret at all." (Davidson 1980 (1976): 290) This strategy allows us to pair the speaker's sentences and his reactions with ours that we also hold true in corresponding circumstances or when we react in a similar way. The restriction from the point of view of a radical interpreter is exactly the speaker's particular authority. We see how the authority of first person and the solution of the task of *RI* work together.

But why is the principle of epistemic justice in the procedure of interpretation introduced? What is the difference between the charity and its application and the principle of epistemic justice? What have we gained with this principle for the further constraints of interpretation? Is the asymmetry between the first person authority and the third person point of view of *RI* for the ascription of mental states to modify?

From the research on Davidson's philosophy it emerges that charity is not the ultimate guarantee for *RI,* and a full information about physical causal interaction between speaker and interpreter and their environment is not possible. Furthermore semanticists, unlike so-called semantic sneakers, ask for the meaning of linguistic expression, but just not for any causal interaction, social intercourse, background knowledge or whatever when understanding linguistic meaning.

The new role of interpreter in the procedure of *RI* and the introduction of the triangulation model of *RI* suppose the impossibility of massive error. Davidson said in conversation „he wished he had never mentioned the omniscient interpreter"(Lepore, Ludwig 2005: 232, footnote 241). This assumption is connected with his version of externalism and the rejection of social externalism because the triangulation model is a version of a naturalized epistemology: the externalism of triangulation is a form of *physical externalism.* Thoughts are not dependent on any other use of words, because from the third person point of view the dispositions of speakers respond toward changes in their environment, and the interpreter has to observe the interaction of the speaker with his environment. Methodologically this is a form of a synchronic externalism. Therefore, from Davidson's point of view social externalism is a wrong position. Most commentators agree that the impossibility of massive error is reasoned by two arguments: the *omniscient interpreter* and the application of the *principle of charity*. Consequently Davidson has concluded that global scepticism is wrong and the chapter in epistemology from Descartes till Quine is to close. Leibnizian monads would not be able to communicate because for them there is no shared extern world. For every interpreter, a spatial world which he and other speakers share by causal connections is a necessary condition to have a public behavioral given evidence for interpretation. The problem is that just this is introduced as an a priori assumption (truth) that the radical interpreter has to make without any empirical restriction. If we accept this a priori, *RI* is possible, as Davidson argues. It is to mention here that the Swampman thought experiment is not in harmony with the methodology of *RI* because I and my Swampman have different epistemic states. But this thought experiment is not the same as Putnam's Twin Earth. For him the distinction is to make between the meaning of our expressions standing in causal relation to our environment, and in the next step we suppose a Twin Earth within which we attribute attitudes, assumed the speaker uses terms with different meaning to our world.

The a priori method of *RI* is the distinction between holding true and being true. This gives errors their meaning. If we assume that this is true for *RI*: 1. the interpreter agrees largely with the speaker in respect of the awareness of the causal relations to the environment both have, and 2. the interpreter applies the principle of charity, then the question arises „What is shown by the largely true beliefs?". The problem is, if we assume we have an indefinitely large number of beliefs, then most could be true, even in case the beliefs and other attitudes about other minds, the external world, the future, theories (contingent general truth) are false (Lepore, Ludwig 2005: 324-25). This shows that the a priori pattern of beliefs is too weak for interpreting utterances and ascribing attitudes. If we would assign meaning to sentences, it is not enough to assume that the speaker is right in general beliefs, but also in a particular belief about his environment. A re-interpretation of linguistic behavior is required and the concept in our theory of interpretation could not be purely theoretical. I conclude: if the intelligible redescription, explanation and prediction of behavior, verbal or otherwise, by beliefs, purposes, motives and desires of people are connected by a unified (intelligible) scheme, we have evened out rationality and plausibility which lead us to the epistemic restrictions of interpretation. Therefore the principle of charity is to be rebuilt by the principle of epistemic justice. When we bring such restrictions into play, we modify the third person view of interpretation. From my point of view there is no conflict with the task of semanticists. Fixing meaning of linguistic expressions, sentences and also utterances take off with linguistic meaning firstly. Without such a concept, understanding of linguistic behavior would be impossible. Just this is the turn of the principle of autonomy of meaning. Yet, if we take into play the epistemic restrictions of interpretation, the first person authority is modified because we consider also conceptual errors in the procedure of re-interpretation. With epistemic restrictions as a limitation, the problem of understanding other minds emerges again, and at the same time we see that the self-ascription of mental states and the ascription from the third person point of view is not a criterion in principle. The problem of the procedure of *RI* is that the interpreter can identify speakers holding true toward sentences without any knowledge of what the sentences mean. This is reasoned by Davidson's concept of meaning as language disposition, following Quine in principle.

2.1.3.2. Triangulation, the Concept of Language and the Social Frame of Reference

The expansion of *RI* by triangulation leads to the epistemological result that the myth of subjective is refuted: thoughts have no mental objects. Davidson, Burge, Putnam, Dennett, Fodor, Stich, Kaplan and Evans and others agree on that: "propositions can't *both* determine the content of our thoughts *and* be subjectively assured ... It is not just proposition that can't do the job. No object could" (Davidson 2001 (1987): 37). Meaning is not a mental reality; and in the first person authority we have no (empirical) knowledge about ourselves.

What does this strategy imply for the concept of language?

When we apply this strategy, we find a basic property of linguistic behavior. The role of parts (words, sentences) is only to understand "in the context of the system (language)" within which their function is specified. To understand a language means "*translating* it into our own system of concepts". (Davidson 1980 (1974): 239) Beliefs and language are interconnected because "Beliefs cannot be ascertained in general without command of a man's language; and we cannot master a man's language without knowing much of what he believes." (Davidson 1980 (1974): 238) In the case of beliefs, desires, and action we proceed in the same way. The correspondence of true beliefs and the shared reactions among different individual speakers is the prerequisite for them to have a common language. If this was not the case, there would neither be a common language nor a public verification of the components of the principle of natural epistemic justice (coherence, truth (shared responses) and all things considered judgements).

But what does *common* mean in this context?

The idiolect theory of language leads back to the externalistic model of *RI*. *RI* applies the truth-conditions represented by *T*-sentences to the behavioral reactions of individual speakers. That is its fundamental procedure. For *RI* and its holistic truth-centered theorizing, language means always speaker language (idiolect theory). The correspondence in the use of language of individual speakers is a result of the development of similar reactions caused by stimulus-response in different situations. This is a concept of language that is reasoned by a theory of interpretation of natural speakers and an externalism of triangulation. A common language or a linguistic community exists only in case that the speakers have the same theory of interpretation. It is a basic feature of linguistic behavior that the participants of the triangle can verify their occasional sentences (perceptual beliefs). This is an essential feature of human language. It is to emphasize that triangulation fits the region of the social into *RI*.

Until a base line has been established by communication with someone else, there is no point in saying one's own thoughts or words have a determinate content.... Communication begins where causes converge: your utterance means what mine does if belief in its truth is systematically caused by the same events and objects. (Davidson 2001 (1991): 213, (1983): 151)

It is the prerequisite here that someone is right or wrong in his beliefs. But one must ask:

... why language is essential to thought. The reason, stated briefly, is that unless the base line of the triangle, the line between the two agents, is strengthened to the point where it can implement the communication of propositional contents, there is no way the agents can make use of the triangular situation to form judgements about the world. Only when language is in place can creatures appreciate the concept of objective truth. (Davidson 2001 (1997): 130)

Therefore, *RI* and the individuation of the content of attitudes presuppose language, or depend on language. We can only attribute thoughts on the basis of given languages, and no interpretation is language independent. But it may be that we have thoughts which remain solely our own, and we are unable to express them. Everyone knows a situation where he has a thought and it is difficult for him to express it in words. Thoughts and expressions in someone's language are factually interdependent, but there is *no* reduction of one to the other. This also holds in the case of reciprocal reinforcement. Consequently, understanding has also a *mental* counterpart. In this respect, the theory of interpretation leads to the theory of mind, Davidson's anomalous monism.

But how is anomalous monism connected with externalism as the causal nature of ordinary mental states?

It seems that mental states (or ordinary propositional attitudes) cannot be individuated by both: *inner* states and *external* facts (social or otherwise)—the *inner* is identified with neuronal processes that happen in our body. For the anomalous monism and the triangulation-model of *RI*, both conditions are satisfied: mental states are *inner* as being identical with states of the body and non-individualistic to individuate, because we identify such states by causal relations to objects and events *outside* the subject. Therefore, the hard core of Davidson's continuation of the truth-centered theory of *RI* to the externalistic model of *RI* is that the necessity of language for thought and triangulation plays together with communication. Communication is only possible by forming a triangle. (On the two arguments for triangulation, 1. the necessity of language for thoughts and 2. language as essential for communication that Davidson has not separated, Lepore, Ludwig 2005: 404-419)

The application of the principle of epistemic justice leads us to the peculiarity of the evidence of *RI*, that is, to the sentences and utterances directed to attitudes and actions that are not only the guarantee for interpreting sentences, but also for ascribing and individuating beliefs, desires, and intentions. But these are to modify by generalized fulfillment conditions of assertive and non-assertive illocutionary acts. In the continuation of the post-empirical theory of meaning (Quine) it is simply not possible to state at first what a speaker believes, desires, intends, and as a next step to give an answer to the question what uttered words refer to: *RI* states the inscrutability of reference in a new way, because if we have collected all evidence for our theory of interpretation, it is not possible to separate the contributions of beliefs, desires, thoughts and actions from *RI* step by step: we need "total theories" (Davidson 1984 (1979): 241). From the *RI* point of view, coping with the task of interpretation states once more the inscrutability of reference and gives us a theoretical revised version of it that is the non-eliminable combination of propositional attitudes. But this version is to modify by the epistemic restrictions and the social frame of reference, which works to solute the task of re-interpretation.

What is the connection between beliefs, their truth (objectivity) and their linguistic expressions?

With this connection we find the framework to link the mental, language and communication (the social). The interaction explains—that is the claim—, why we apply the principle of compositionality on all levels of *RI*. But from the triangulation model of *RI* it leads us also to the individuation of the content of propositional attitudes by distal stimuli, consequently by things and events. Yet the truth-centered theory of *RI* borders on the problem that the semantic redescription as an identification of truth-condition presupposes the so-called referential transparence of semantic context. The problem in Davidson's concept of *RI* is whether interpretation requires a third person point of view in principle.

This leads us to the *Burge-problem* (1979), because we need an answer to the problem—in Burge's counterfactual story—that the expression in a referential non-transparent position like, for example, "arthritis", does not allow us to ascribe individual propositional attitudes. This is the link to partially connect semantics and social science. The triangulation model of *RI* embeds the speaker in the causal relation with the environment he and the interpreter share. But the application of the principle of charity is not the ultimate guarantee to select a unique one among the causal relations. The problem is not only the causation of the content of our thoughts, but it is also to find the correct sort of causal ascription. The epistemic restrictions (background theories) are to be taken into play to re-interpret linguistic behavior. This leads us to a principal problem of the project of *RI*. Assumed this is correct, it does not demolish the project of *RI* in the theory of meaning. Finding the conditions under which understanding of speech and action is possible is a central question in epistemology, semantics, and ontology. The problem is whether the constraints of interpretation are focused as an a priori knowledge that we all have and whether the requirement of triangulation in communication and having the concept of objective truth is a justification of the third person attitude for *RI*. This also leads to the question whether the problem of other minds is solved in essential in Davidson's philosophy if we assume that behavior is the ultimate basis for the ascription of attitudes (mind) and their content. *RI* requires a *social frame of reference* of the ascription of attitudes that makes behavior comprehensible. The social frame of reference is introduced to continue *RI* as a feature of the ascription of comprehensible epistemic attitudes that take social considerations into account. And this leads us to the epistemic restrictions of *RI*, not only concerning individual speakers but also as a part of the social frame. *This is the link between meaning and the social* (on the epistemic restrictions, Burge, Putnam and the semantics of community, capt. 2.4., in this book).

2.1.3.3. The Ontology of *RI*

In the continuation of the history of the *unified theory*, its epistemological turn to an anti-foundationalism (the distal theory of meaning and reference) and also the relevance of logical argument against facts, the slingshot (collapsing) argument going back to Frege, is raised. Semantics, ontology and epistemology work together in the interpretive theory of truth.

How do the analytical ontology of the logical form analysis as the theoretical foundation of *RI* and the epistemic turn of the individuation of content in triangulation play together?

The analysis of logical form and the individuation of the content of propositional attitudes leads us to an epistemology in the mirror of the theory of meaning. Semantics as epistemology has left behind the third dogma of empiricism and also the myth of subjective. This is its claim. Yet a radical externalism is a version of an epistemology naturalized because the third person approached is embraced. Many philosophers are worried about that.

It is the claim of the truth-centered theory of *RI* to explain the individuation of the propositional content of attitudes. This is exactly what can be achieved by the triangulation model of *RI*. Distal stimuli are the basis of interpretation. The application of the principle of charity to solve the task of *RI* founds a *conceptual* and *explanatory* dualism and therefore a methodological separatism between (human) social science and also natural science, because the basis of intelligible redescription is coherence (consistency) and true-beliefs. The redescription of linguistic behavior has no "echo" in any natural science. Yet *RI* has a mental counterpart, namely the network of propositional attitudes. But there is no identity of type of the mental and the physical. Therefore the anomalous monism follows from *RI*. It is concluded from the evidence of *RI*. Let us now return to the ontology of *RI*.

What ontology stands behind the holistic truth-centered theory of interpretation?

Davidson, unlike Tarski, gives us no explicit definition of the predication of truth: for him, truth is an undefinable basic concept.

Convention T isn't a rough substitute for a general definition: it is a part of a successful attempt to persuade us that his (Tarski) formal definitions apply our single pre-theoretical concept of truth to certain languages. (Davidson 2005 (1996): 27: 5)

We are free to correlate a *T*-theory to all entities and events.

At first, Davidson's rejection of facts emerges from two contexts in the philosophy of language and ontology in principle: the compositionality semantics of natural language in *Truth and Meaning* (1984 (1968) and the assessment of theories of truth as correspondence-to-facts in *True to the Fact* (1984 (1969)). In the latter, Davidson raises an objection against Strawson's Austin-critics. For him, the correspondence theory is to give up. Davidson argues against this from the point of view of Austin's proposal, because it is his intent to elaborate a "purified version of the correspondence theory of truth" in a Tarski-style. In *A Coherence Theory of Truth and Knowledge* (2001 (1983)), he suggests a weak coherence theory, because correspondence follows from coherence:

First, truth is correspondence with the way things are ... So if a coherence theory of truth is acceptable, it must be consistent with a correspondence theory. Second, a theory of knowledge that allows that we can know the truth must be a nonrelativized, noninternal form of realism. So if a coherence theory of knowledge is acceptable, it must be consistent with such a form of realism. (139-40)

This version of realism is different to Putnam's internal realism and his metaphysical realism. Yet it must be mentioned that Putnam's natural realism stands epistemically near to a radical externalism, because both give up epistemic intermediaries. From an externalistic point of view, internal realism is strained with the third dogma of empiricism. Davidson regrets naming his view "coherence theory" (2001 (1987): 155) because, from his point of view, coherence doesn't have much to do with epistemology. Though he has given up this terminology, this was not a change of his epistemological re-interpretation of *RI*:

I called my view a coherence theory because I held (I still do) that there is a presumption that a belief that coheres with the rest of our belief is true. But obviously this doesn't make every such belief true, and so can't help define the notion of knowledge. Certain kinds of coherence among beliefs are related to the dim notion of justified belief, but otherwise coherence doesn't seem to me to have much to do with epistemology. There certainly are complicated, and important, connections between belief and truth, but coherence plays a minor role in spelling them out. (Davidson 1993a: 37; 2001 (1987)).

It is to mention, and Davidson has emphasized it, too, that "Coherence is nothing but consistency" (Davidson 2001 (1987): 155), and from a Tarskian point of view he rejects

Any further attempt to explain, define, analyze, or explicate the concept (of truth) will be empty or wrong: correspondence theories, coherence theories, pragmatist theories, theories that identify truth with warranted assertability (perhaps under 'ideal' or 'optimum' conditions), theories that ask truth to ex-plain the success of science, or serve as the ultimate outcome of science or the conversations of some élite, all such theories either add nothing to our under-standing of truth or have obvious counterexamples. Why on earth should we expect to be able to reduce truth to something clearer or more fundamental? (156)

Furthermore it is to mention that in *A Coherence Theory of Truth and Knowledge* (2001 (1983)) one of the leading themes is the key difference between Quine's radical translation and the method of *RI*.

Since 1990 there has been a turn to Davidson's critique of the cor-respondent theory of truth and his reasoning to give up facts. In *The Structure and Content of Truth* (1990) he argues rather for a middle course between a correspondence and a coherence theory. Truth as correspondence is interpreted as satisfaction in a Tarskian style (this is modified in Davidson 1993c: 37). Such instances are not states of affairs or facts. Therefore, Davidson claims to reject the modern correspon-dence theory, following in some point also C. I. Lewis (Davidson 2001: 183-4), that is, a true sentence stands for a fact (Russell). The argument that he used is called the *slingshot (collapsing) argument* following J. Barwise and J. Perry. It goes back to Frege. It claims to show with logi-cal means that all facts collapse into a Great Fact. This means that, if the reference of a sentence is its truth-value, all logical equivalent sentences correspond to the same thing. There is a coherence in Davidson's work on that since *True to the Facts* (1984 (1969), on modifications also made by Davidson of his own proposal of a Tarski-style theory of truth as a correspondence theory 2001 ((1988): 182-83, on the objection of correspondence theory 183-84). Neale (2001) has systemized the slingshot argument and has elaborated its validity in detail. I will not discuss his analysis here, because particular studies are needed of his elaborations (on a reconstruction of the slingshot with reference to Frege, R. Schantz 1996: 147-163, with reference to J. McDowells critique on Davidson, R. Manning 1998; on Rorty, Field, Dummett, Etchemendy, Putnam, Soames and the problem of a deflationary theory of truth, Davidson 1990, 2005 (1996)). Davidson concludes that facts do not play any role now in semantics, ontology and epistemology. He connects the slingshot with his rebuilding of epistemology: if we give up facts, we also give up mental representations (inner objects) distinct from an external object as an epistemological foundation of knowledge (Davidson 2001 (1988): 184). Yet it is to mention that, if we assume sentences to be singular terms, we have the real problem to presuppose entities such terms refer to.

During the progress of the 1990 years, Davidson has given up to speech on correspondence and coherence because these concepts lead to some misunderstandings. The differences, in Davidson's view, are only of a terminological nature. For him, a coherence theory is "absurd" and a correspondence theory is "trivial" (Davidson 1993c: 37).

But what does *trivial* mean in this context? Why does the interpretive theory of truth not explain Tarski's concept of satisfaction as correspondence?

I once argued that Tarski's truth definitions employed the notion of correspondence because they made use of the concept of satisfaction, which relates expressions with the subject matter of the language concerned ("subject matter" here means the entities over which the variables of quantification range). It is an important fact that you can't give a characterization of truth for a language with anything like the expressive power of a natural language without introducing such a relation. I also pointed out that Tarski defined truth in terms of satisfaction in a way that made it possible to speak of sentences being satisfied by certain objects (the satisfiers are not objects "in the world", but they are defined in terms of such objects). Call this "correspondence" if you please (I no longer do), but note the following: take some sequence that satisfies a given (closed) sentence. If such a sequence exists, the sentence is true. So let us for the moment say, the sentence "corresponds to" that sequence, and that is why the sentence is true. Correct, but utterly trivial, for that same sequence satisfies ("corresponds to") every true sentence, and to no false one. Indeed, every sequence satisfies (and so corresponds to) every true sentence, so absolutely nothing about the truth of particular sentences is explained by this notion of correspondence. (37)

Therefore, truth-centered theory of radical interpretation as a semantics of natural language does not explain Tarski's concept of satisfaction as correspondence, and this is explained by the Slingshot argument because "sequence satisfies (and so corresponds to) every true sentence, so absolutely nothing about the truth of particular sentences is explained by this notion of correspondence." (37) That is why Tarski's concept of satisfaction is not to be interpreted as correspondence. From the truth-centered theory of *RI* this is an *alternative* to the objectivist-realist understanding, that is, "the real and the true are 'independent of our beliefs'" and the antirealists views of truth. Davison calls his position a form of realism and at the same time truth of utterances is related to human context (concerns). (Davidson 2001 (1988): 185)

Davidson's *unified theory* rejects metaphysical questions that we know from metaphysical realism or a possible world semantics. It is not his claim to answer such questions: the theory of truth as a semantics of natural language is no theory about the world in any version of essentialism. This goes hand in hand with the rejection of a foundation of empirical knowledge. It shows again how the triangulation springs from the nature of interpretation: the mental or inferential bridge between external events and our ordinary beliefs is the causal interaction between distal causation and speakers' beliefs; this is just what the interpreter takes into account, that is, beliefs are veridical in principle. This is his final answer of understanding our concept of truth:

I make *shared* ("distal") causes the basis of interpretation, thus moving the relevant stimuli from the private world to the public. To vastly simplify the details, and to stick to the most primitive, but basic, cases: I ask myself what sentence of mine I am stimulated to assent to whenever you are stimulated to assent to a particular sentence of yours, and I use my sentence to give the truth conditions of yours. This is, of course, just a first, tentative step in interpreting a speaker, to be adjusted and corrected as further evidence accumulates. (Davidson 1993c: 39)

We see Davidson give up Platonism in semantics and an ontology of facts because 1. facts, for example, explain nothing in the theory of meaning, 2. the slingshot argument undermines the realm of facts, and 3. the explanation of the truth-conditions of particular sentences refers to the individuation of propositional attitudes (distal theory of meaning (reference) and cognition). 3. The restrictions making behavior intelligible—the speaker's subjective point of view and his arbitrary utterances—are to grasp in a theory of truth for that speaker's language. 4. The basis of the individuation of attitudes (empirical content) starts from distal stimuli and similar response in the triangle, that is, what people can learn about others in a world they share. Pragmatism is ultimately a wrong epistemology and theory of truth. Truth is connected with human concerns as pragmatism has argued, but reality itself makes our attitudes true or false.

Tugendhat has also drawn our attention to the giving up of an ontology of state of affairs and facts without using the slingshot (1982). The expression "that p" is to distinguish from the assertion p thereby that the expression has the same content, but the complement clause of p is no sentence: it is a singular term. This is reasoned thereby because we could complete "that is green", for example, by "is true", "is desirable", "is annoyed". Singular terms stand for an entity; we would say that the entities of such sentences are so-called states of affairs. Yet the problem is:

On what basis do we decide about the existence or non-existence of a state of affairs?

For Tugendhat and Davidson, the basis of this decision is the truth of the expression "that p".

We have the following range of equivalence: (1) the state of affair that p exists ≡ (2) that p is a fact ≡ (3) it is the case that p (objective truth) ≡ (4) that p is true ≡ (5) p. If the sense of (2) is not to explain by (1) but the sense of (2) and therefore also of (1) is to explain by (4) and (5), so we could not obviously explain the sense of (3), that is, the objective truth (of the entities of beliefs), by the equivalence with (2) and (1), but only by the equivalence with (4) and (5). (Tugendhat 1976: 64, my translation)

Tugendhat's and Davidson's view are in harmony with respect to giving up facts in the theory of truth. What is said with sentences like, for example, "That the cat has got the mange is a fact". Is it said that facthood is ascribed to entities? *Corresponds to fact* said nothing more than *is true*. The misleading understanding of what sentences refer to is caused when we analyze such sentences as being about a sentence. Facts are semantically not relevant. We may posit them, but they are of no benefit when analyzing the property of semantic content.

Tugendhat's view is also in harmony with Davidson that hoping, wanting, intending, being afraid have a propositional content. Brentano's account is valid in that the entities of such attitudes must not exist, for example, I can hope/I am afraid/I want that Peter agrees to my invitation without this really being the case. Yet in these cases we make the assumption of existence for the entities of such attitudes. And, in contrast to Brentano, this is not at all a relationship in our consciousness. It seems now that we have two universes for the entities of propositional attitudes: one with my wants, expectations, beliefs, and another one with the entities that motivate or make true my beliefs, intentions, desires, hopes. *RI* claims to solve this problem by the distal individuation of such entities by triangulation. "The simple fact is that we have the resources needed to identify states of mind, even if those states of mind are, as we like to say, directed to nonexistent objects, for we can do this without supposing there are any objects whatever before the mind." (Davidson 2001 (1989): 67).

To sum up, what does not come into play for the ontology of *RI* is *state of affairs* and *fact* (slingshot argument). The assumption of propositions as truth-bearer is not meaningless, for example as objects of propositional attitudes, but such entities are of no benefit and are untenable for a distal theory of meaning (reference). The ontological relativity is rejected by *RI*, but Davidson agrees with Quine that meaning is not to be modeled as an entity (myth of the museum). The claim of Davidson's *unified theory* is to explain the intelligible redescription of linguistic behavior and the attribution of attitudes in the triangle. Beliefs and truth are related. So the interpretive theory of truth is to apply to all components of linguistic behavior, for example, in the case of attribution and ascription of propositional attitudes and other speech acts. This step results from the consideration when the assent and dissent of sentences in the theory of language are taken into account. Interpretation is a result of both: it is composed of a redescription of behavior and the standard of a constitutive rationality as an epistemic norm. Constructing a theory of interpretation is orientated to that effect: *each interpretation and ascription of attitudes is a step in building a holistic theory, that is, we optimize coherence (consistency) and true beliefs, and we individuate their content by their external relations.* This leads us back to the problem how strong compositionality is assumed, because its strong version is not holistic in nature.

The solution of the task of *RI*, that is, coping the circle between belief and meaning by a holistic truth-centered theory, shows us: the authority of first person, the autonomy of meaning, the social function of language and the external causation of propositional contents go together. The step to these parts of a *unified theory*, its theory of the mental, of rationality and interpretation and the distal theory of thoughts, follows from the inner-theoretical requirements of *RI*. If there was no common language, there would not be any public verification of the attribution of attitudes as well. Therefore this verification plays a significant role for linguistic behavior and the individuation of the content of attitudes. Public verification means that the behavior and the causal interaction with the familiar objects of the environment are observable. But this is no normative concept. It is also the answer to the question *why* the myth of subjective and the third dogma of empiricism are rendered invalid. *All this springs from RI and its truth-centered theory*. The conceptual connections among the mental (attitudes), language, the social and the rest of nature are holistic, and we link these in the triangle from the line that beliefs and distal stimuli take effects in *RI*, Davidson has argued. Therefore triangulation brings the social together directly with perceptual externalism, that is, the second person (the social) is located within the causal nexus. Yet the problem is not only the causation of the content of our thoughts and the finding of the correct sort of causal ascription, but re-interpreting linguistic behavior by our epistemic restrictions (background theories) must also be taken into play. This is the challenge of a radical (physical) externalism of individuation of the contents of attitudes. Therefore the question "Is *RI* possible by the application of charity or is the gap between the ascription of content and the world by triangulation closed?" is not answered ultimately.

2.2. From the Idiolect Theory of Language to the Third Dogma of Empiricism

For a *unified theory*, the triangulation model of *RI* is the overall framework of making behavior intelligible, that is, the ascription and identification of attitudes on the base of causal stimuli as the "nature of speech and belief". On this basis we do not say which sentences and beliefs are true, but we saddle our view that the speaker's picture of the world perceived from his surroundings is like the picture we have ourselves. The essential feature of all interpretation in this frame is that a belief is *directly* expressed by a given individual utterance. Davidson's theory of language is therefore a theory of individual speakers, that is, of their linguistic behavior. On this matter he agrees with Quine. For both of them, language consists of a set of behavioral dispositions to assent to or dissent from sentences that we test by speakers in observable circumstances. Each sentence is a part of such a network (language, theory of language). So Quine's theory is a theory of linguistic behavior. *RI* and Quine's theory of language are not divided on this. In difference to radical translation, *RI* is explicitly outlined semanticly. But in the process of *RI*, the problem of a correspondence of background theory between speaker and interpreter emerges. In behavior, be it linguistic or not, education, biography, social status, whatever, take effect. For truth-centered semantics such things are obvious but the theory of meaning describes conditions under which a speaker's utterances are true. A speaker's theory of truth is a theory of meaning because the knowledge of the theory is sufficient to understand his linguistic behavior. Understanding is restricted to the literal (first) meaning of uttered words, independent of the further purpose and intentions the speaker has.

From my point of view Davidson, being faced with this question, makes a distinction between a prior theory and a passing theory. This leads us to an idiolect theory of language born from *RI*. The passing theory should help to solve the task of *RI* because the answer to the question "How do we evaluate that we successfully ascribe attitudes with our theory of interpretation?" is a matter of evidence. This cannot be decided only empirically or theoretically. The distinction of both theories is to explain by the circle between belief and meaning. *RI* does not only lead to a refutation of the myth of subjective, but also to a spectacular result, the third dogma of empiricism or the dogma of the conceptual scheme. When the third dogma is given up, a revision of the Cartesian paradigm in philosophy follows from there. *RI* does not only have to cope with the circle between belief and meaning, but we come upon the epistemic restriction of understanding.

2.2.1. Prior and Passing Theory of Interpretation

As a basic theory of linguistic behavior, the relationship between an individual speaker and the utterance of sentences to which we assign truth-conditions is introduced for *RI*. The intelligible redescription supposes that the ascription of beliefs fits in the scheme of the true beliefs the speaker has, and that is the reason why a shared world view is given between both the speaker and the interpreter. The empirical adequacy of the theory of truth is given by the generalization of holding true. This evidence requires no further interpretation. This is the ground why we do not describe the theoretical language of *RI* within the framework of linguistics.

In the tradition of the philosophy of language it is well known that language is governed by conventions as a medium of communication and understanding. Davidson will demolish this tradition (1984 (1984), 2005 (1986), (1994)).

I conclude that there are no such thing as a language, not if a language is anything like what many philosophers and linguists have supported. There is therefore no such thing as a language to be learned, mastered, or born with. We have to give up the idea of a clearly defined shared structure which language-users acquire and then apply to case. (Davidson 2005 (1986): 107)

He introduced the concept of *first meaning*, more or less the same as literal meaning, as distinct from conventional meaning. First meaning mirrored the truth-theoretical semantics applied to linguistic behavior of individuals.

(1) *First meaning is systematic.* A competent speaker or interpreter is able to interpret utterances, his own or those of others, on the basis of the semantic properties of the parts, or words, in the utterance, and the structure of the utterance. For this to be possible, there must be systematic relations between the meanings of utterances.

(2) *First meanings are shared.* For speaker and interpreter to communicate successfully and regularly, they must share a method of interpretation of the sort described in (1).

(3) *First meanings are governed by learned conventions or regularities.* The systematic knowledge or competence of the speaker or interpreter is learned in advance of occasions of interpretation and is conventional in character. (Davidson 2005 (1986): 93)

Davidson makes a note of some difficulties in the conditions, for example, the ambiguity of the word *same*. It has several semantic roles. For Davidson, linguistic conventions are not essential for linguistic behavior and communication.

The task of interpretation is to confront with the difficulty that in many cases there is no correspondence of the theories of interpretation between speaker and interpreter. It follows from here that one must distinguish between *a prior* and *a passing* theory of *RI*. This structure of *RI* shows that our understanding of utterances is *incomplete* and always open for *revisions* in general. The passing theories between speaker and interpreter do not have much to share, and in most cases correspondence is rare. Yet, both theories can be represented in a theory of truth. What an utterance means is a result of overlapping idiolects. But it is not a requirement of an intelligible redescription of linguistic behavior that the interpreter uses the same language the speaker uses for his report. This follows from *RI*. The interpreter brings his passing theory by adaption to individual cases into line with his prior theory.

As the speaker speaks his piece the interpreter *alters* his theory, *entering* hypotheses about new names, *altering* the interpretation of familiar predicates, and *revising* past interpretations of particular utterances in the light of *new* evidence. (Davidson 2005 (1986): 100, my italics)

An interpreter can understand a speaker if there is a correspondence of their passing theories. The conclusion is: social communication is successful only if there was such an occasion, and rules and conventions are not the foundation of linguistic communication. *RI* has two parts that we bring together in *one* step: the interpretation ascribes its meaning to the utterance, and the application of the principle of charity determines the degree of success of understanding. It is not successful to explore at first what a speaker believes, wants, hopes for, intends and then, in the next step, to give an answer to what his utterances or words mean or refer to. All interpretation requires that the utterance fits in a compositional scheme: not only sentences but also beliefs have such a structure.

2.2.2. The Idiolect Theory of Language

Davidson's truth-centered theory of meaning is a theory of individual speakers as the ultimate elements of the supposed universe of discourse, as he assumes them to be the instances of the theory of interpretation. The basic theory of *RI* is a dispositional determination of the meaning of their uttered words. Therefore, his step to an idiolect theory is coherent with his theoretical background. *The problem in principle is what role a public language plays for the description of our communicative abilities.*

This idiolect theory of language, derived from *RI*, was not accepted. N. Chomsky, for example, criticizes this account:

Davidson observes correctly that in an ordinary communication situation between (say) Smith and Jones, each will use any means to determine the intentions of the other. Thus in his terms, Smith will construct a "passing theory" to interpret what Jones is saying, employing any evidence available. From that correct observation he concludes that there is no such thing as language. This conclusion has two aspects. First: there is no need to postulate a "common language" shared by Jones and Smith to account for their communication. Second: there is no "portable interpreting machine set to grind out the meaning of an arbitrary utterance"—that is, no *I*-language. Three comments are in order. First, his argument is invalid in both cases. From the fact that Smith constructs a "passing theory", nothing follows about the basis on which he does so. It would be like concluding from the chaotic properties of weather systems that there is no jetstream. In particular, nothing follows about "common language" or *I*-language. Second, despite the invalidity of the argument, Davidson's first conclusion is correct, though understated. Not only is there no need to postulate a "common language," but there is no intelligible notion of "common language" to postulate. That is a truism that has always been assumed, virtually without comment, in the empirical study of language, which has no place for such notions as "Chinese" or "German", as is well known. Third, Davidson's conclusion about a "portable interpreting machine" (an *I*-language) is incorrect, as far as we know; he suggests no reason to assume otherwise. (Chomsky 1993: 299-300; *I* = internalized; the concept of *I*-language is introduced by Chomsky 1986 in difference to the *E*-language; *E* = externalized; it is the object of linguistic research.)

There are many misunderstandings in the criticism of Davidson's idiolect theory of language, in particular how this theory is explained. But it is to concede that Davidson invites them. He has answered his critics:

Kemmerling, like some of my other critics, enjoys quoting my words "There is no such thing as a language" while ignoring my careful explanation of how I am using the word "language" in this context. Of course I don't deny that there are languages like English, German and Basque or that, in some ordinary sense, people speak them. What is clear to almost everyone, however, is that no two speakers speak in exactly the same way; each speaker has, as Chomsky has maintained, a personal idiolect. In spite of the differences, both in practice and in implicit "theories" about what expressions mean, people who speak differently often understand each other. If it were not for this, we would have no way of defining the concept of language we appeal to when we call Russian or Amharic a language. (Davidson 1993a: 117)

RI rejects the philosophical concept of language in the following way: a language is a shared, learned system or set of linguistic (syntactic and semantic) rules and conventions. Yet Davidson has corrected his terminological distinction between prior and passing theory:

'A Nice Derangement of Epitaphs' (2005(1986)) is defective in a number of ways. It does not sufficiently stress the practical advantage that comes from a large degree of commonality among groups of speakers; the distinction between the prior and passing theories is clumsy, and makes a fairly simple point seem difficult; and there is, if not an actual confusion, a sort of fusion of two separable claims. The two claims are, first, that mutual understanding does not require that people speak the same language. It follows directly from this (obvious) point that shared 'rule' or 'convention', however convenient they might be, cannot illuminate what is essential to linguistic communication. And of course there is no conflict at all between this claim and an insistence on compositionality. The second, and trickier, claim is that speakers can deviate not only from other speakers, but from their own earlier regularities, and can still (often) be understood. This is an ability that on occasion engages all our intelligence, sympathy, sense of humor and knowledge of people and the world. (Davidson 1999: 73)

This leads us to the question:

What is the link between a speaker's idiolect and his linguistic community, that is, the sociolect he takes apart?

This interconnection is to discover as a connection between the triangulation of *RI* and a social frame of reference, *because such frames compass the ascription of different propositional content.* Yet the linguistic praxis in a linguistic community does not have any normative power, as Burge and others have argued, but we take background theories into account. This framework takes effect in our theory of interpretation as constitutive but not normative factors. This leads us to a sophisticated compromise between *RI* and linguistic externalism. In order to find this link, it is helpful to analyze the following features to find a regularity to link both *RI* and linguistic externalism. (On the reply to Dummett by Davidson 2005 (1994); on a re-evaluation of the debate on the idiolect theory with reference to Hacking, Dummett, D. Bar-On, M. Risjordand, see Lepore, Ludwig 2005: 263-97, they show that Davidson's individualistic concept of language is in harmony with his theory of meaning; on Davidson's and Dummett's concept of language and the idiolect theory as concluded from the meaning holism, B. Fultner 1998, on the idiolect theory and skills, D. Simpson 1998).

2.2.3. On the Modification of the Idiolect Theory
The Link between Idiolect and Sociolect: Semantical Regularities

It is the aim of radical externalism to show, in contrast to a semantics of social community (a social or linguistic externalism), that the individuation of propositional attitudes in the triangle and its objectivity is only possible if a creature is able to communicate. We know already how the concept of language—born from *RI*—goes hand in hand with the individuation of propositional attitudes: holding true and distal stimuli are the frame making behavior intelligible, and both are immediately given in the triangle. Just this is obvious in triangulation without any justification by a further particular knowledge of the speaker. We can only ascribe thoughts to creatures that are able to communicate. This is a result of the distal causation of behavioral reactions. Behavior is intelligible only if there are similar reactions of both speaker and interpreter. Davidson's answer to social externalism is that triangulation connects the social with perceptual externalism by the causal nexus. Causality connects the interaction of persons with the external surroundings.

Yet, the language that *I speak* is determined through *my* capacity to utter the same words (sentences) successfully in various circumstances, that is, I have beliefs about the successful use of words. Such use is determined by semantic regularities (P. Ziff 1960). Otherwise I cannot secure my uptake toward any audience. The principle of shared reference to similar reaction is such a regularity. From here it follows that an interpreter hunts for a pattern in given behavior. Successful utterances always mean that the addressee admits them to be successful. This supposes that speakers reciprocally concede not only that there are true beliefs, but also that there is an adjustment of their beliefs toward changing circumstances. This adjustment is to verify in an interpersonal way. Every communication always includes a regularity for its beginning and finishing. Successful understanding and communication cannot happen only *once*.

However, understanding what a speaker means is also dependent on his local linguistic community (sociolect).

How do we grasp the connection between idiolect and sociolect?

Success in *RI* is dependent on the knowledge of meaning. It is concluded from a theoretical structure: A theory of truth links speaker with interpreter: it at once describes the linguistic abilities and practices of the speaker and gives the substance of what a knowledgeable interpreter knows which enables him to grasp the meaning of the speaker's utterance. (Davidson 1990: 312)

Therefore, success in interpretation is dependent on the theoretical description of speakers' semantic competence (knowledge). Davidson speaks of a "linguistic ability" that I interpret in this way. Speech is a rational activity because such behavior is meaningful, and thereby we judge about such doings in a rational (successful) way; for example, we can make verifying tests about the successful use of words in a linguistic community, such is, toward utterances of a second person or within the social group in which we live. This way we find the regularities of linguistic behavior. Such regularities link idiolect and sociolect. In this procedure we always apply a passing theory with which we make our prior theory fit to individual cases. In respect of this situation the distinction between both theories is right. In such cases, for *RI*, we operate within the framework of a holistic truth-centered theory and the compositional structure of the theory of meaning respectively the semantic knowledge that is the basic for the *RI* and the ascription of attitudes, because we can read such compositional structure in sentences and attitudes.

It is obvious that there is no conflict between the compositionality and *RI*, because the guarantee of the ascription of attitudes is holding true. Yet, regularities as a link between idiolect and sociolect are a modification of the basic situation of *RI*, because we take into account that members of the linguistic group have sets of such regularities for intelligible redescription and its plausibility at their disposal. Davidson would argue here that a linguistic community, that is, *RI* in groups, begins with a correspondence of theories of interpretation of individual speakers. But insofar as we introduce the principle of shared reference to our reaction in the triangle between a radical interpreter and the second person, a semantic regularity ascribing the meaning of uttered words is born from such behavior. The interpretation of linguistic and non-linguistic behavior is principally connected.

The links between idiolect and sociolect are no norms of language, but semantic regularities for the adjustment of beliefs and the interpretation of linguistic behavior (see also Bennett 1976). Such regularities are to characterize by two features of linguistic behavior:

1. Regularities of understanding linguistic behavior; such pieces of advice are hypothetical imperatives like "If you want to use the term x in a regular way, you ought to use it under circumstances c". Such imperatives are necessarily grounded in another imperative: "And you ought to use term x in a regular way if you want to be easily understood." (Bilgrami 1992: 111-112) "Easily understood" and "understood without strain" are motivated by "extrinsic qualifications" and just *not* by any normativity. More and more it comes to our mind that, in this matter, categorical imperatives are philosophical obsessive ideas, in particular in the analysis of the language of morals, but also in ethics. In other words, the linguistic community semantics is not the framework of intelligible redescription in general. Regularities linking idiolect and sociolect are also reasoned by

2. regularities of shared reference followed from the radical externalism of the ascription of attitudes. The answer to the question:

Why could we assume that our reactions are the same (or similar)?

is given thereby that the individual distal stimulus and the response in comparable circumstances is the same, or similar, stimulus and response. This means that the participants of triangulation correlate the response of the second person with the token of single stimulus they are aware of from their point of view. Divergences can be recognized on this basis. The same (similar) response established a regularity of behavior in a shared world for the participants of the triangle. We need no research of the consciousness of speakers for individuating propositional attitudes. All successful individuation in the triangle is no falsification that we are black boxes.

A radical externalism is an individualistic account that claims to refute the theoretical alternative "individualism versus anti-individualism". Within this frame, individualism is not to understand as Burge has introduced it. For him, it is an account that explains behavior without reference to external circumstances. The step to an externalism in the frame of *RI* follows from its requirement of individuation of propositional contents of uttered sentences, because for intelligible redescription we suppose a tendency of regularity of reaction. This means that reactions are similar to one another, such is, we expect a stability of behavior. Interpretation always means to arrange utterances and sentences in a behavioral pattern:

We perceive a creature as rational in so far as we are able to view his movements as part of a rational pattern comprising also thoughts, desires, emotions, and vo-litions (In this we are much aided by the actions we conceive to be utterances.). (Davidson 1980 (1970): 42)

But what is the significance of the second person for the epistemological turn of *RI*?

We can ascribe meaning and attitudes only if we interpret the linguistic behavior of other people, and it is only possible that a person has a thought if there is a second person who interprets his speech. Yet, the problem is not only the causation of the content of our thoughts, but it is also to find the correct sort of causal ascription in a shared surrounding of different observers, and we have to explain the objective or different content of ascriptions. Therefore *RI* requires a *social frame* for the ascription of attitudes. Only in this frame there are objective thoughts. This goes together with the fact that all propositional attitudes and their confirmation imply a background theory that we intuitively handle for interpretation.

The asymmetry between knowing my own thought in the first person and the ascription of propositional attitudes to other persons in a third person is to explain by the basic relationship of *RI* that takes place between the participants in their shared surroundings. This account is to distinguish from the social externalism of Burge and Kripke (see also Bilgrami 1992). The expansion of *RI* by triangulation leads to the epistemological result of the refutation of the myth of subjective: thoughts have no mental objects. Yet, following Quine it leads to a new understanding of communication also. Communication is possible only if we make the assumption that the beliefs of its participants are caused by the same things and events. Success in communication presupposes "the existence of a shared, and largely true, view of the world." (Davidson 1984 (1977): 201), that is to say that communication can begin if causes convert. A semantics of community would undermine the first person authority and have a false concept of the social. Such semantics would be a third dogma of empiricism of second order, because a community would be the ordered force of the contents of our beliefs. The instances of individuation of contents would be social authorities, and the division of linguistic labor (Putnam: socio-linguistic hypothesis) would be the basic theory of interpretation. If this was right, there would be no *RI* because all interpretation would have to be relativized to an observation of linguistic authorities in a given community. Something is principally wrong with this account. Yet, if we expand *RI* with a social frame of reference, the problem emerges that pairing the referential transparence of an individual utterance with the evidence of holding a sentence true does not lead to a right translation/interpretation in general. This leads us back to Burge's problem and the epistemic restrictions of making behavior intelligible.

RI leads us to a radical externalism as a version of an epistemology naturalized. Yet it is a naturalism without reductionism. With the first person authority and the distal theory of meaning (reference) and thought, *RI* refutes the myth of subjective, sense data, and objects of thoughts. The epistemological distinction between a conceptual scheme and a neutral content is overcome by *RI*. Propositional attitudes are to analyze semanticly. All this follows from the truth-centered theory of intelligible redescription and the conceptual dualism in ontology. *RI* is a continuation of the classic analytic philosophy: thoughts are propositional in nature. Yet we grasp its propositional structure only if the uttered sentences have enough structure and expressibility, and this is exactly what is given by the compositional structure of propositional attitudes and sentences.

2.3. The Dismantling of a Myth

Demonstrating the third dogma of empiricism destructs and finishes up with the myth of framework. This does not exclude that within a language there are conceptual different and independent parts of vocabularies, for example, the different conceptual parts with which we describe and explain the mental, the physical and the social. This differentiation of classes of expressions is in itself not limited and vast. Nevertheless we have to give an answer for the order and the sorts of generalization of the use of such parts of language like the distinction between "homonomic" and "heteronomic" generalization (Davidson 1980: 219). If we distinguish these two sorts of generalizations, we are lead to a principal problem in the theory of science, that is, how far a law is deducted from an ideal theory ("a comprehensive closed theory") that determines its validity. In this respect, a conceptual dualism between the mental and the physical and different synthetic principles of these domains is not affected by the myth of the third dogma. But the end of the myth itself is not in any contradiction to a radical externalism of the individuation of the contents of attitudes, because the problem of such individuation is one of a radical interpreter and not of a speaker: the speaker does not compare the content of his utterance with the world if he gives his assertion a content. *This is to explain by the principal asymmetry of speaker and interpreter for RI and by the causal relation between beliefs, utterances and their causation from distal stimuli.* This causation is essentially veridical. If the contents of attitudes are caused in this way, we have to give up classical empiricism, phenomenalism in epistemology. The empirical content of our knowledge is therefore not constituted by inner objects and sense data.

2.3.1. The Quinean Picture of Epistemology

The third dogma of empiricism is directed against conceptual relativism, that is, "Reality itself is relative to a scheme: what counts as real in one system may not in another" (1984 (1974): 183). Yet it is also a critique of Quine's basic theory of epistemology. I will sketch the Quinean picture of epistemology as the particular context of the critique of the third dogma.

Quine's epistemology does not take off from any version of method-ological solipsism but from radical translation, that is, the function of the use of language within communication. This basic situation explains *both* the inscrutability of reference and the indetermination of transla-tion. If a speaker utters, for example, "rabbit", the reference cannot be discovered behaviorally by a radical translator (field linguist). Why is this the case? This problem is caused by the individuation of the terms in the situation of radical translation. It is a problem on the translator`s side, because the speaker does not individuate the terms, and he can also have particular theories of rabbits, for example, that they are spies of ex-traterrestrials. The translator proceeds in a third person attitude, because it is not a requirement that the speaker knows the sentence the translator has used for his translation. If this was a condition, no translation would be possible.

"Rabbit" can be an expression of classification (general concept) or a singular term (space-temporal part of the rabbit). The radical transla-tor draws up a translation manual (analytical hypothesis). Translation is indetermined on this basis, and reference is not to discover as an explanation of reference (a relationship of expressions to particulars), because it cannot be decided on this basis which analytical hypothesis should be definitely preferred. It is not a matter of facts to what expres-sions refer, that is, there is no absolute reference: reference is relative to a background theory or language (on the double relativity of reference and ontology: to a choice of manual of translation and to a background theory, see Davidson 1984 (1979): 232-33). Therefore it is to conclude: for radical translation, both the inscrutability of reference and the inde-termination of translation are connected. This picture of epistemology follows from Quine's post-empirical theory of meaning: all attitudes including our knowledge and meaning conspire and cannot be singled out on the level of linguistic behavior. If we are to solve the interdepen-dence between the two, this has to be done on the behavioral level, but just on this level this is not possible. Therefore, the concepts of stimulus meaning and stimulus synonymy do not coincide with the understand-ing of meaning in general. It could be a solution to assume meanings, but this is not in harmony with Quine's critique on distinction between analytic and synthetic sentences; both is not to delimit in principle. In the framework of the ontogenesis of reference, Quine claims to solve the circle between belief and meaning by filtering out the net-meaning by the stimulus meaning. For Quine, sentential truth is to grasp naturalistically. Natural truth under the particular circumstances of utterances means to give up a privileged class of sentences in the theory of meaning, like analytic or synthetic sentences. In his epistemology, sensorical stimulations are (the ontogenesis of reference) the causes of our scientific theories about the world we develop.

The commentators of Quine's work agree that the inscrutability of reference implies the indetermination of words, but not of sentences. Different interpretations of words are to even out within sentences. This may lead to a translation of sentences. We even out the differences by testing a speaker's disposition by its ascent and descent of sentences. However, this does not exclude that there are incompatible translations of sentences we even out in turn by their translation into other sentences. But the inscrutability is to conclude from the fact that there is no meaning of an expression in principle— independent of its stimulation in certain circumstances—that informs us on the meaning of sentences. The philosophical message is: the intension does not determine the extension.

But how is the indetermination of translation connected with the ontological relativity?

In Quine's epistemology one must distinguish between the inscrutability of reference (indetermination) and the holophrastic indetermination of translation. There is an indetermination at the bottom and an underdetermination from the top. The holophrastic meaning is non-theoretical, but the analytical differentiation of observation sentences is theoretical. The analytical qualification is relative to a background theory or language, that is, the relativity of reference in this language— the relational theory of entities of theories—is the ontological relativity. This is the first explanation why, in the continuation of the history of Quine's work, the inscrutability of reference and the ontological relativity coincide.

For Quine's epistemology and theory of sciences, there is an indetermination at the bottom (the inscrutability of reference) and an underdetermination from the top (the underdetermination of our theory of nature by observation sentences) in principle.

What is the difference?

Whether a theory of nature is true or not is a matter of fact, but one cannot decide by facts about the correctness of our analytical hypotheses. Different analytical hypotheses could fit to the dispositions of speakers, and we could more or less even them out by successful paraphrases. The extent to which we are successful in this process does not take any effect on our communication. It is a part of our everyday live. Therefore, radical translation is also involved in our linguistic behavior at home.

Quine's commentators also agree that, with the proxy function, he has given an argument for the ontological relativity that is independent of radical translation (1981). Proxy functions substitute the given (old) entities of a theory, and the general expressions (terms) become a new interpretation. That is a drastic change of a theory (permutation of our ontology). For Quine, following Russell, the following is valid: "Save the structure and you save all". It is the structure of the theory but not its entities that is significant.

Is this contradictory to Quine's realism?

This is not the case, because the proxy function and the permutation argument are not a part of ontology but of the "methodology of ontology" (on that, see Schantz 1996: 206-16). However, such a switch of our ontology does not change our behavior. Therefore, there are no collapses of communication because the logical relations of sentences are not changed, and the observation sentences are furthermore connected with our simulations. This is no wonder, because by permutation of our ontology no change of our physical, mental, social states and behavior will come about, that is, we modify neither our attitudes and behavior nor our use of language.

But in Quine's epistemology a conceptual relativism works that "seems to inspire . . . that reference, truth, and ontology must be relativized to a background theory or language" (Davidson 1984 (1979): 233). For Davidson, it is true what Quine says on cultural relativism: "someone 'cannot proclaim cultural relativism without rising above, and he cannot rise above it without giving it up'", and what he also says on ontological relativism and the relativism of reference to a background theory (234). Yet, Davidson also claims to give a version of relative reference, and he states once more the inscrutability of reference. The principal difference between both is that relativizing reference does not "fix ontology" (231-32). He does not accept Quine's "Save the structure and you save all" and, for him, the instructibility of reference means not to give up ontology. Therefore he does not agree with the step taken from the instructibility of reference to the ontological relativity. But both agree in the description of the situation by which the problem of instructibility of reference emerges:

There is no way to tell what the singular terms of a language refer to, or what its predicates are true of, at least no way to tell from the totality of behavioral evidence, actual or potential, and such evidence is all that matters to questions of meaning and communication. (Davidson 1984 (1979): 227)

2.3.2. The Third Dogma of Empiricism

In Kuhn's and Feyerabend's incommensurability thesis, the conceptual relativism also revealed that Davidson takes to relying on a distinction of scheme and content (on Kuhn, see Preyer 1998). He considers this distinction to be the third dogma in the tradition of Quine's dogmas of empiricism: 1. The distinction of analytic and synthetic truths, and 2. the assumption of an equivalence of meaningful statements with immediate experience. With the critique of Kuhn and Feyerabend, I will mention how Davidson backs Popper up against his critics. Kuhn considers the scientist to remain in the prison built by the puzzles. Only proselytizing can free him. With Popper's analysis of *Problemsituation,* we are considered to have a supervenient conception of a development of theories. Scientific hypotheses are not framed in a context empirically-zero. But they are viewed against background theories.

In order to find the steps of the critique on the third dogma as an application of *RI*, it is helpful to argue along the following lines:

How do we individuate conceptual schemes/theories? How do we know where schemes begin or end?

Making sense of words or thoughts of others relies on talking about the same thing, event, utterance and so on when applying the principle of epistemic justice. On our talk about different schemes, the same can be said as on our talk about different beliefs or differences of beliefs and other attitudes.

1. Identification/re-identification of the *same* depends on language. We must, for example, substitute singular terms. Identity is only given to us by language; that leads us to point (3). Examples for analyzing this are statements of the identity of events and the commitment of events that we individuate in the framework of causality. In this point Quine's criterion of ontology is valid.

2. Identification/re-identification, when using *several* languages, brings up the question how language/scheme and mind/content are related. This turns out to be the relation of linguistic theory to linguistic description. Davidson considers the clue to be:

The idea is then that something is a language, and associated with a conceptual scheme, whether we can translate it or not, if it stands in a certain relation (predicating, organizing, facing, or fitting) to experience (nature, reality, sensory prompting). The problem is to say what the relation is, and to be clearer about the entities related. (Davidson 1984 (1974): 191)

3. Language and theory are always tied together, content seems to be the entity opposed. Yet the problem is:

To give up the analytic-synthetic distinction as basic to the understanding of language is to give up the idea that we can clearly distinguish between theory and language. Meaning, as we might loosely use the word, is contaminated by theory, but what is held to be true. (187)

This argument shows us how the theory of language of *RI* and the idiolect theory lead to the refutation of the third dogma. For the solution of the task of *RI* it follows from the connection between belief and meaning that the ascription of beliefs and the assignment of truth-conditions to sentences and utterances construct a theory of a speaker's language. Davidson considers the ascription of knowledge itself to be independent of a linguistic theory considered plausible in the framework of triangulation by the assumption of holding true, and the external causations of beliefs are obvious in the triangle.

... if all we know is what sentences a speaker holds true, and we cannot assume that his language is our own, then we cannot take even a first step toward interpretation without knowing or assuming a great deal about the speaker's beliefs. Since knowledge of beliefs comes only with the ability to interpret words, the only possibility at the start is to assume general agreements on beliefs. We get a first approximation to a finished theory by assigning to sentences of a speaker conditions of truth that actually obtain (in our own opinion) just when the speaker holds those sentences true. (196)

4. Individuation, Davidson considers, is *impossible* without employing a concept of translation and truth-relation (interpretation). Truth and translation can simply not be separated. Davidson uses Tarski's convention *T* that does not rely on reference to facts, the world, experience or the like. Tarski's convention *T* itself is not independent of translation. So Davidson introduces holding a sentence true to a basis of the theory of interpretation, enabling us to ascribe propositional attitudes.

Since convention *T* embodies our best intuition as to how the concept of truth is used, there does not seem to be much hope for a test that a conceptual scheme is radically different from ours if that test depends on the assumption that we can divorce the notion of truth from that of translation. (195)

The semantics of natural language is a theory of linguistic behavior in terms of truth-conditions (a truth theory for the speaker language), and the distinction between scheme and content is to give up coping with the circle between belief and meaning for *RI*, because the question of interpretation is not to solve with different basic conceptual resources. However, from my point of view this leads us back to the background theory we have to presuppose or to pick out. Differences in the pre-theory make it possible that interpretation goes wrong.

The refutation of the third dogma assumes criteria of translation to be identified via the criteria of identifying conceptual schemes (theories). Speaking different languages has a conceptual scheme in common. It is this scheme that makes them translatable. Belief and meaning are interdependent. Ascribing a belief and interpreting sentences cannot be separated in principle. Yet, stating the interdependence between beliefs and meaning by *RI* is bound to the attributive ascription of beliefs and the interpretation of sentences. *RI* initiates a rebuilding of our epistemology in principle: "Nothing, however, no thing, makes sentences or theories true: not experience, not surface irritations, not the world, can make a sentence true." (194). *The point is that giving up the third dogma is born from RI and its holistic truth-centered theorizing, and with this step we also give up mental representation as inner objects as a foundation of epistemology.* Our beliefs are caused and correctly understood about the public things and events and are veridical in nature. Yet, this does not mean what sentences are. It is to mention here that, in his response to Neale, Davidson has modified his first view in *On the Very Idea of a Conceptual Scheme* (1984 (1974): "Maybe we can't locate a part of the world that makes an individual sentence true, but the world itself makes an individual sentence true, but the world itself makes the true sentences true ... those three little words ("not the world") were seriously misleading" (1999: 668-9, see also Neale 2001: 57-64, 63). Neale concludes from his review of the third dogma:

in order to demolish the schema-content distinction, Davidson needs (i) an argument against facts, and (ii) an argument showing that interestingly divergent schemes are not forthcoming on the view that true sentences are made true not by facts but by the world." (64)

An interpreter's translating of beliefs and of utterance-meaning or sentence-meaning shows that a dichotomy of scheme and content is impossible. Kuhn talks about a one-world universe potentially viewed from different points of view. Feyerabend considers conceptual schemes of ordinary languages as false theories. "Incommensurable" is their term for "not reciprocally intranslatable". The neutral content waiting for its being systematized is provided by nature. Feyerabend—and to some extent Quine—suggests to compare controversial schemes by "choosing a point of view outside the system or the language". He hopes that we are able to do so because "there is still human experience as an actually existing process." (Davidson 1984 (1974): 191)

What are the consequences of the translation of belief and meaning in the framework of a truth-centered theory of *RI* for the relativism on concepts and paradigms?

The answer is, I think, that we must say much the same thing about differences in conceptual scheme as we say about differences in belief: we improve the clarity and bite of declarations of differences, whether of scheme or opinion, by enlarging the basis of shared (translatable) language or of shared opinion. Indeed, no clear line between the cases can be made out. If we choose to translate some alien sentence rejected by its speakers by a sentence to which we are strangely attached on a community basis, we may be tempted to call this a difference in schemes; if we decide to accommodate the evidence in other ways, it may be more natural to speak of a difference of opinion. But when others think differently from us, no general principle, or appeal to evidence, can force us to decide that the difference lies in our beliefs rather than in our concepts. (197)

Davidson's arguments against Kuhn and Feyerabend are right: "complete" has to be distinguished from "partial mistakes" in interpretation. If there were complete mistakes in interpretation, there would be no significant strings of sentence in a language. Languages would be untranslatable. Talking about total mistakes does not make sense.

RI renders the following two views as implausible:

1. Each foreign language/culture equals another conceptual scheme

and

2. each foreign language/culture equals another world.

Davidson shows that talking about another conceptual scheme would assume that there is an alternative referential scheme, such as of a neutral (given) input, for example sensory stimuli (Quine). If understanding of an event of utterance itself is *theoretical*, assuming a neutral (given) content turns out to be implausible. Davidson shows that talking about another world would assume a referential semantics pairing terms from different languages with different objects in a certain manner. So a relation between language and world (a neutral content) is not a condition for understanding linguistic meaning. All such *pairing* is not successful because *RI* presupposes that in elementary cases most of our beliefs are true. Every justification always proceeds toward a background of beliefs that are without doubts.

Thus, the anti-foundationalist succeeds in making commitments to a mass of beliefs, in any particular case of justification, undogmatic, by showing that it is a condition of being able to speak meaningfully, or to express beliefs at all. It is not of course, that the anti-foundationalist is committed to a claim that there is some well-defined set of propositions that forms the invariable unquestioned background for all enquiry. Rather, the claim is that the justification of any given belief must always proceed against a background of beliefs that are not, in this context, currently in doubt. (M. McGinn 1981: 96)

In essential Davidson argues against different conceptual schemes that our understanding of a sentence to be true in a language is given by its translation in a language within which we have a truth-theory of the sentence. Therefore, to understand what makes a sentence true (or false) in a language requires translating the sentence into the interpreter's language. The impossibility of massive errors is the guarantee that translation is successful. Lepore and Ludwig have examined Davidson's arguments against radically different conceptual schemes in detail (2005: 305-21). They show that these are successful only if the identification criteria for different conceptual schemes are justified. From their point of view, this is obviously not the case (on the distinction of the individuation and the identification criteria, 305-06). For them, the first person authority is also inadequate (343-72). But they do *not* think that there are complete non-overlapping *conceptual* schemes for linguistic beings. For them, such schemes are to individuate by their concepts and this is fixed by the meaning of terms in the language. Thereby their truth-conditions are fixed. This is another theory that they do not develop from the *RI* point of view.

2.3.3. The Building Block Theory and the Paradox of Reference

When the third dogma of empiricism is given up, a conceptual relativism, but also the building block theory of an epistemological foundationalism, is untenable. The building block theory tries to grasp the semantic properties of, for example, names and simple predicates by their reference. It is at the "place where there is direct contact between linguistic theory and events, actions, or objects described in non-linguistic terms."

(Davidson 1984 (1977): 219). Names and predicates would directly assign their empirical content. We could characterize this epistemology in this way: some elementary propositions, beliefs or sentences are without doubt like statements on sensations, for example, "I have a headache", on emotions, for example, "I am in mourning", on sensory experience, for example, "it seems to me that I see an old man at the corner", analytic assertions, for example, "a bachelor is an unmarried man", or the Cartesian ego cogito; other statements are concluded from these basic propositions.

For a post-empiricism theory of meaning, the reference of expression as a semantic relationship of such propositions is no condition of understanding meaning. A generalized concept of reference is no condition of an adequate theory of linguistic behavior. A semantic relation of expressions is not to prove, and such relations are not needed for a theory of truth. The confirmation of the empirical content of a theory of meaning does not require any non-linguistic terms, neither any speaker reference. Coping with the circle between belief and meaning leads us to a refutation of subjectivity and of an epistemological foundationalism. It is the claim of the concept of truth and its implications for lingual communication to give us an objective reasoning of the ascription of attitudes. But a semantic relation of reference is not to prove, and it is not required "to complete an account of truth" (221): we do not need non-linguistic terms for the verification of the empirical content of utterances. The satisfactional theory of reference with respect to the posits that are required for the distal theory of meaning (reference) to individuate the contents of beliefs are described by the theory of truth (on an axiomatization, see Neale 1999).

In understanding the relationship between language and the world, a *paradox of reference* is given (Davidson 1984 (1977): 221). The building block theory has no chance to answer the question:

What is the reference of expression to non-linguistic characterizations?

In difference to that, the holistic method starts with sentences and tries to connect language to the description of non-linguistic behavior. Yet, this method leads us to some difficulties also.

But it seems incapable of giving a complete account of the semantic features of the parts of sentences, and without such an account we are apparently unable to explain truth?

Davidson argues

...to defend a version of the holistic approach, and urge that we must give up the concept of reference as basic to an empirical theory of language. (221)

How do we solve the paradox of reference with a holistic account?

To show that the concept of reference is to pose, Davidson introduces the distinction between the explanation "*within* a theory" and explanations "*of* the theory":

With the theory, the conditions of truth of a sentence are specified by advertising to postulated structure and semantic concepts like that of satisfaction or reference. But when it comes to interpreting the theory as a whole, it is the notion of truth, as applied to closed sentences, which must be connected with human ends and activities. ... I suggest that words, meanings of words, reference, and satisfaction are posits we need to implement a theory of truth. They serve this purpose without needing independent confirmation or empirical basis. (221-22)

Theory of reference is inapplicable, because *within* a theory we define truth with satisfaction, and in difference to that an explanation *of* a theory is its interpretation. This is called a satisfactional theory of reference. Terms of reference are consequently no class of expressions that connect language and the world. Reference is not to explore for *RI* (on a modified role of singular terms and the problem of indexicality, see capt 10, in this book).

It could be argued against a satisfactional theory of reference:

A Davidson theory of meaning explains the truth conditions of sentences in terms of the semantic properties—references, satisfaction conditions, etc.—of its parts, but it provides no explanation of the nature of these semantic properties. The axiom giving the reference of 'Ralph', for example, "Ralph" refers to Ralph, does not tell us what the reference relation is ...(R. L. Kirkham 1992: 245)

We could answer to this response: if we accept the inscrutability of reference, then this is the wrong question, because the test of a theory of interpretation is *not* to bear out on a prior empirical interpretation of reference. To fix the reference of "Feldberg", we have to find the role of this word in sentences. No non-linguistic terms are able to explain the reference of expressions. The evidence of *RI* is not to find in a separate procedure: *first* we state a speaker's belief, such as, there is a mountain at a particular degree of latitude and longitude; what he intends or wants, for example, to explain the geographical surroundings to a visitor of

Frankfurt am Main; and in a *second* step we are going on to pick out to what words refer, for example, a particular mountain in the Taunus, a place of the inhabitants of the town to go for an outing, and so on.

The critique on a semantic (empirical) relation of reference is a refutation of causal theories of names (Kripke, Putnam). Such accounts are versions of a building block theory (Berkeley, Hume, Mill). These theories make the assumption that a sentence has a rich content in a direct way by "non-semantic evidence". (Davidson 1984 (1977): 225; on the refutation of causal theories of reference in the context of Quine's assumption of ontological relativity 1984 (1979): 234-36). For *RI*, this evidence is the holding true of sentences and the obvious causation of beliefs in the triangle:

> ... all evidence for or against a theory of truth (interpretation, translation) comes in the form of facts about what events or situations in the world cause, or would cause, speakers to assent to, or dissent from, each sentence in the speaker's repertoire. (230)

In this point Davidson agrees with Quine. A building block theory is to compare with Quine's indeterminacy of translation in respect of different theories of truth that pair the same sentence with a different truth-condition because such building block means pairing each sentence directly with a content by non-semantic evidence:

> ... what Quine has shown is that if there is one way of mapping words onto objects that gives the right truth conditions of all sentences, there will be endless other mappings that yield the same truth conditions. There seems no good reason for calling one rather than another of these mappings "reference". Neither pointing nor appeal to causal relations can resolve this indeterminacy. (Davidson 1993c: 39)

RI leads us to an *anti-foundational* account that is grounded in the evidence of *RI* and the individuation of propositional content of beliefs in triangulation. The refutation of the third dogma is grounded by *RI* and its truth-centered theory. For *RI*, there is no separation of belief and meaning. The interconnection between the two is not to eliminate. This means modifying the epistemology of Wiener Circle, because we do not confirm single statements but sets of these, and every true statement presupposes that a set of other statements is true. We border on "the dilemma in the theory of knowledge" (Davidson 2001 (1982): 168). The dilemma emerges, if "self-certifying" as a private state is to connect with our public language. There is no foundation of our empirical knowledge from that we take off building block theories in epistemology. The triangulation model claims to answer in difference to any foundationalism in epistemology: "What needs explaining is why the beliefs that are formed in this way—by sensations, perturbations of the visual field, sense data and the like, my note—have the content they do, and why such beliefs are true as often as they are." (Davidson 1999d: 135). Therefore any neutral content as a basis of our knowledge is to give up. The anti-foundationalism closes the chapter of traditional epistemology: sensation and belief are not connected logically or epistemically, but causally. Beliefs are not causally arbitrary. But the cause is not proposition or belief. Beliefs themselves are veridical in nature. „There is, in other words, no philosophical purpose that the third dogma of empiricism is required to serve." (M. McGinn 1981: 98) The rebuilding of epistemology is born from *RI*, but the foundation of interpretation does not lead us to any foundation of empirical knowledge.

Why does *RI* give the inscrutability of reference a new turn without relativizing reference in a Quinean way to fix ontology?

The problem of interpretation is in general: if we have collected all the evidence for *RI*, it is not possible to single out the beliefs, desires, and intentions. For *RI* we need "total theories" and "many theories" may work well. Reference is relative to a language of an individual speaker. It is a fault to assume that there is only *one* language a speaker may speak to which an utterance fits. If we change the language, we change the reference scheme. If the same total evidence is given, we also change the ascription of attitudes with the interpretation of words. We have the option to even out the attitudes we ascribe or to adjust to other attitudes we assume. From here, ontological relativity does not follow. But if all evidence is collected for our theory of interpretation, we cannot single out the particular contributions of beliefs, desires, thoughts for intelligible redescription. We need total theories to solve the task of interpretation. Once more we see that we are confronted with the inscrutability of reference when coping with the circle between belief and meaning. Therefore, solving the task of *RI* "states once more the thesis of the inscrutability of reference, but it is also to hint at the reason for it." (Davidson 1984: 241)

2.4. On Epistemic Restrictions of Understanding

2.4.1. The Objectivity of Interpretation and the Principle of Rationality

The ascription of thoughts and beliefs to any speaker in the process of *RI* makes the assumption that the speaker has such concepts at his disposal. We all master the concept of truth, applying it to other speakers' linguistic behavior. But we dispose of concepts intuitively only if we are familiar with the concept of truth. So we can make the distinction between subjective attitudes and objectivity. This links the holistic truth-centered theory of *RI* with a version of an epistemology naturalized with a non-reductive naturalism of triangulation. The conceptual connections within the triangulation model of *RI* are holistic. Davidson emphasizes that by these holistic conceptual connections "There are ... no 'barriers', logical or epistemic, between the three varieties of knowledge" (2001 (1991): 214).

What is the compatibility between the so-called objectivity of understanding, the application of the principle of charity, and its implication of the ascription of rationality that an interpreter has to presuppose?

This leads us to the classical question of the dichotomy of *humanism* versus *scientivism*. But the assumption of rationality for *RI* itself forces on us the epistemic restrictions on which we border to solve the task of interpretation. From *RI*, we can describe the dichotomy between humanism and scientivism in the following way:

* could we translate our conceptual scheme of our ordinary language, that is our ordinary propositional attitudes in a scientific frame of reference or, rather, could we translate the terms of reference of common knowledge refraining from beliefs, intentions, and goal-attainments in a set of scientific propositions, for example, by neurophysiology?

We can give a tentative answer to this question. Firstly it is not the problem whether our common knowledge can be translated or whether it can't—it can be corrected, for example, by the result of scientific research and developments. The fact that we can change our minds supposes a capacity to learn. Secondly this is a matter that, in our procedures of interpretation and the ascription of attitudes, takes effect on the principle of epistemic justice. There may be a limitation on a high level of learning for us, but in elementary cases of recognition we make the assumption that we are able to make corrections and restackings in our attitude system.

In Quine's proposal the radical translation leads to two problems:

1. The truth of an utterance of an assertion or another illocutionary act in a foreign language/culture is not determined, and the translator cannot recognize the truth-conditions under study. The method of charity of interpretation of utterances supposes that there are true beliefs or the satisfaction of other fulfillment conditions. If this is not so, the utterances are not intelligible.

2. The translator is not sure that in a given case, for example, the assertion is false. The utterance can be untruthful in the case of individual or collective *deception*, and it can be false in the case of individual and collective *error*. Untruthfulness refers to the elimination of strategies of deception: if we cannot neutralize untruthfulness, we do not understand the *motives* of any speaker. Even if we know an agent's beliefs, it is not assured that we know his motives like "hate", "jealousy", "fear" and so on. Error, on the other hand, refers to the empirical-analytical knowledge about the speaker that the interpreter has. The objectivity of interpretation is born by the rational evaluation of attitudes and of the given regularities of behavior. We can follow Davidson in that, because this is only possible for creatures that have a shared world view and are able to communicate.

Are there objective grounds for choosing among conflicting hypotheses? Especially in this case we have to ask what makes grounds 'objective'. The only ultimate source of objectivity is, in my opinion, intersubjectivity. (Davidson 2001: 82-83)

The claim of objectivity and intersubjectivity of interpretation is guaranteed by the shared reactions of speaker and interpreter. Just this shows us *how RI* and a radical externalism are based reciprocally on our behavior. This supposes that massive error is impossible, and there are no any epistemic restrictions that limit *RI*.

2.4.2. The Epistemic Restrictions of RI

For *RI*, the empirical theory of a speaker's language is a part of a general theory including beliefs, desires, intentions and perhaps more. If we change our interpretation of a speaker's uttered words, given the same evidence, we change also the attitudes we attribute to him. Yet, all evidence for our theory of truth, interpretation and translation comes from the objective situations and events that cause assent and dissent to sentences.

However, what follows for the triangulation model of *RI* if successful interpretation is limited by the epistemic capacity of their participants?

Are we generally successful to cope with the circle between belief and meaning by holding a sentence true as evidence?

How do epistemic restrictions take effect in intelligible redescription?

The theory of meaning is conceived as a theory of constraints on understanding meaning we come upon to solve the task of intelligible redescription. These constraints go beyond the linguistic realm of reconstructing the sentential meaning depending on the meaning of single expressions (principle of compositionality applied on different levels of interpretations: sentences and attitudes). The next step to cope with the circle between belief and meaning is epistemic in character. It includes reference to propositional attitudes. But the problem arises with respect to the accessibility of knowledge ascribed. There are respective problems once we turn to the scientific constraints themselves: while the problem for the holistic truth-centered theory of meaning lies with the pairing of sentences between speaker and interpreter, the problem of the validation of theories lies with the grouping of sentences/statements from a given theory to the background theory. The radical interpreter has to epistemically limit his tendency of reading his beliefs into the speaker's mind. This problem runs parallel to discriminating theories, such is, only in the context of background theories we read one theory into others. The essential question is not what the theory is about, but rather what we can say about the functioning of the theory in the social role, that is, for interpretation of linguistic behavior. The point is that we are conditioned to hold sentences true on given occasions, and the use of other peoples' sentences as evidence implies in essential to interpret them. We are not to confront with relativism by this. The scientific process aligns statements in a general system of implications. Without implications most of our sentences would be meaningless. The objectivity of understanding is a question of the rational judgement of propositional attitudes only in the context of elaborating the background theories of a speaker. In this framework, objectivity and truth of understanding emerge in the procedures of interpretation, and I will give the inscrutability a *new* turn thereby .

But how do we describe the evidence of truth-conditions?

When following Davidson's theory of interpretation, it is necessary to presuppose that the network of beliefs of any speaker is coherent (consistent) in his belief-system. We identify the attitudes by their logical relations and on the base of the causal stimuli: this is an intrinsic relationship between *interpretation (language) — rationality* (charity) — *triangulation*. The principle of coherence (consistence) of propositional attitudes is directly deduced from the holistic nature of beliefs. If our ascription of beliefs is successful, it must be possible to redescribe utterances on the basis of the ascription of a consistent set of beliefs. This always means: we interpret the speaker in such a way that he is right in his beliefs and other propositional attitudes. The principle of charity and the distal-stimulus approach are a requirement for the selection of the truth-condition of sentences and utterances. *Both is constitutive*: an utterance $u(p)$ from abroad (which I have never heard before) can only be interpreted if the radical interpreter holds true $u(p)$ and individuates $u(p)$ in elementary cases by causal stimuli. The principle of charity and the distal approach of cognition and meaning draw a limitation for the semantic interpretation of $u(p)$ and therefore show us restrictions of intelligible redescription.

The fundamental question for the individuation of the propositional attitudes in the framework of a *unified theory* is:

In what way are beliefs to grasp as behavioral items without identifying simple beliefs with behavior, because the first person authority limits behaviorism?

This point was not to take into account in the debate of his philosophy, and it leads us back to the *Burge*-problem (1979). Burge's account is to characterize as follows: 1. his perceptual externalism does not argue for a metaphysical foundation of the causal explanation of reference; 2. he applies externalism not only to natural kind terms like Putnam, but also to terms like 'arthritis', 'contract' and so on, that is, all terms we could make a mistake about—there is no difference here to Davidson's version of externalism—; 3. his thought experiments deal with the individuation of contents of attitudes (mental states); from his point of view, de dicto attitudes are also to individuate externalistically; 4. propositional attitudes and also other mental states are to individuate partly by or within a social frame of reference. From my point of view, Burge's social externalism is to modify by the epistemic differentiation within the social frame of reference.

If beliefs were behavioral items, this would be enough for the redescription of any utterances in a natural language to describe the obvious behavior of speakers. But if beliefs were elementary attitudes for understanding linguistic behavior, they could not be mere behavioral tokens of utterances. Davidson does not argue that attitudes are to reduce to behavior, because there is a conceptual tie between attitudes and behavior (Davidson 2001 (1987): 23, (1982): 100). Yet, the fact that an interpreter states that a speaker holds true a sentence does not add an epistemic feature to the output of sentences of the theory of truth. The role of a speaker's belief for a theory of truth and the causation of elementary beliefs and their public discovery in the triangle tend to be a behavioral *Ersatz* for an epistemic requirement of a theory of meaning. A radical externalism is a naturalism by which our intentional behavior is naturalized by the observation of shared causal interaction with external objects and events. Yet, in contrast to that the epistemic modifications and means of interpretation are to specify to the speaker's knowledge in particular and the differentiation of epistemic procedures in a social community. All successful interpretation presupposes an implicit propositional knowledge on the speaker's side. Davidson evades this account. Epistemological qualifications of beliefs are not primary for *RI*, but the distal causation—obvious in triangulation—is the basis of signification of our linguistic behavior. But the externalism of triangulation leads us back to *RI* and its epistemic restrictions. He claims to show an alternative between realism (correspondence theory) and antirealism:

Realism, with its insistence on radically nonepistemic correspondence, asks more of truth than we can understand; antirealism, with its limitation of truth to what can be ascertained, unnecessarily deprives truth of its role as an intersubjective standard. If we want to speak the truth about truth, we should say no more than need be. (Davidson 2001 (1988): 191)

Epistemic considerations (background theories) play no significant role for the truth-centered theory of *RI* because: 1. there are obvious relations between holding true and our behavior, no matter whether they are linguistic or not, and 2. it is not the speaker's subjective perspective—his epistemic mental states—that is the guarantee that we can learn about others, but the distal stimulus and the social intercourse, 3. to sum up, for the triangulation model of *RI* it is the theory of truth of a speaker's language and an account why such a theory is true that make spare epistemic qualifications of beliefs.

The function of an epistemic qualification of beliefs and of all other propositional attitudes as a condition of success for all ascription of attitudes and consequently of interpretation entails more information like the immediate correlation of a speaker and his sentences. It is a matter of background theories that we bring into play. These are the frames to build hypotheses about speakers' beliefs, and interpretation means framing these theories toward linguistic behavior. Only in the framework of background theories are we able to identify and individuate beliefs and other propositional attitudes. Considering background theories, the situation of *RI* shows some other features. Here we also have a possible explanation why translations could fail.

In this context the restrictions of interpretation in general emerge, that is, we cannot understand speakers at all. Identifying these restrictions I refer to D. K. Henderson (2000) in some points and recall the Burge-problem. Henderson introduces a modified conception of interpretation: the *principle of explicability*. This is a bridge between "strict" and "reconstructive translations"(Henderson: 1994) as he called it. This means that we interpret the behavior of people to find explicable beliefs. Interpretation is a procedure to correlate such sets of beliefs with behavior, be it linguistically or not. The application of this principle does not presuppose that rationality is a normative concept. We only use descriptive psychological, sociological, and cultural generalizations as well as background theories as information for interpretation. Coping the circle between belief and meaning always means going native with these theories. The application of the principle of explicability is epistemic in nature, we make behavior intelligible when we redescribe the speaker's epistemic attitude. I think that the primary question in establishing a foundation of interpretation is:

Why are our redescriptions charity-conductive?

Why do all speakers or believers have to conform to a standard of epistemic norms, or why is charity the essential feature of all interpretive and epistemic rationality and the conduct of individuation of propositional content of $u(p)$, or why does charity solve the task of interpretation?

Lepore and Ludwig make a distinction between the *ambitious* and a *modest* project of *RI*. The first is that a speaker is radically interpretable in nature, in the second it is an empirical question whether he is or isn't radically interpretable (Lepore, Ludwig 2005: 148). Davidson argues for the ambitious project. The problem is whether the application of the principle of charity as an a priori assumption guarantees the selection of the correct theory of interpretation and the correct behaviorally caused relations by the environment to the speaker (agent). Lepore and Ludwig emphasize that the project of *RI* is grounded from behavioral evidence independent of what we assume a priori about the speaker. They argue that *RI* entails a stronger assumption. It is:

(Grace) Ceteris paribus, when we *p* replace '*p*' in (S)

(S) *S* believes at *t* that *p*

with the sentence that expresses the content of an environmentally prompted belief *S*'s, the sentence expresses also a condition in *S*'s environment that prompts that belief. (194)

This does not presuppose any omniscience but that the externally caused attitudes are determined by the condition that has caused them and that we read in the content of attitudes. The difference to charity is: charity makes the assumption that the speaker's belief is true about his environment, and there are direct causal ties of the content of attitude and the word; Grace, in contrast to that, correlates true beliefs with conditions, that is, the statements of such conditions and their verification ensure the ascription of the contents of attitudes. (On the assumption of Grace, 194-96). Lepore and Ludwig substitute charity by Grace. This lead us to the epistemic qualifications of interpretation.

Lepore and Ludwig have emphasized that the central difficulties arise from the distal theory of reference and cognition, because the epistemological turn of the truth-centered theory of *RI* assumes that the content of our thought and its individuation by the causal interaction with objects and events in the environment of speaker and interpreter that is perceived by both is underdetermined by behavioral evidence. Just this leads us back to the epistemic and conceptual resources of the interpreter; he has to solve the task of interpretation in the third person standpoint. Therefore we ask again for the *additional* requirements to solve the task of re-interpretation of behavior, be it linguistic or not.

In general, we agree with epistemic rationality if our theories are successful for our cognitive and other goal orientations. However, this is not an intrinsic property of our beliefs, but a selection, a natural or social one, of our confirmation of beliefs and successful doings — I think this is conform to externalism in general. The results are always open for descriptive and theoretical characterizations. From here it follows that the principle of charity would not be normative, but constitutive. Another point is: it may not be desirable, but inconsistency is often the price to pay for more and new information, and we gain this information by constructing alternative contextual features of redescription.

2.4.3. The Plausibility of Attitudes and the Social Frame of Reference

The question still is:

Why does the coherence between attitudes and truth-values of sentences define a significant interpretation?

In contrast to this, interpretation also refers to the *plausibility* of the ascription of attitudes, and in third-person theorizing such comprehensibility is given only by situational references, its history and background theories. Attitudes are plausible if they are self-evident and require no reasoning and justification in the communication process. They are the very attitudes which we also pair to the speaker's utterance as a possible intended meaning or speaker meaning. It is not the attitudes alone but also their plausibility which make utterances intelligible in a given case. Beliefs are only one possible case of attitudes. For a broader theory of interpretation, beliefs are the evidence only if we characterize the redescription also by the contextual reference of attitudes and its plausibility. This account introduces an expanded frame of reference to the correlation between speaker and sentences, uttered in given circumstances. I will explain this recalling Burge's problem that the autonomy of meaning does not correspond to an essential relationship between an individual belief and sentence meaning.

RI copes with the circle between belief and meaning by a holistic truth-centered theory of meaning and the observation of language behavior in triangulation. However, the questions are:

Can the speaker know what the interpreter knows? Are the perceptions of the situation of speaker and interpreter the same? Do they have the same disposal on comparable theories?

But the question also arises from the interpreter's side:

Does he possess the relevant knowledge of the attitudes that are expressed in the speaker's utterances?

I will introduce the problem I have in mind with asking the question:

What is the connection between beliefs, their truth and their linguistic expressions?

The holistic truth-centered theory of *RI* borders on the problem that the semantic redescription as an identification of truth-condition presupposes the so-called referential transparence of semantic context.

This is just what leads us to the Burge-problem because, we need an answer to the problem—in Burge's counterfactual story—that the expression in a referential intransparent position like, for example, "arthritis" does not allow us to ascribe individual propositional attitudes. Therefore we have to take social considerations in our interpretive procedure into account. Burge distinguishes between the causation of attitudes and their non-causal individuation. The role of the community is logical (conceptual) in nature for the social externalism. We can continue *RI* with the latter, because from the line of communication and the role of the second person the *social frame of reference* is given within which we ascribe the local content of attitudes. Therefore, the membership in a linguistic community and the participation in fixing reference is to take into play for the individuation of attitudes. Davidson could follow them. He criticizes Burge with respect to the normative role of the community. This is right. Yet, from my point of view the social frame of reference is *not* to characterize normatively *but* descriptively. The deeper difference between the two is that in Davidson's ontological framework the individuation of event token is explained by a causal pattern. The role of the Swampman example, which Davidson introduced in his critiques on Putnam and Burge (2001 (1998): 18-19), will show:

What I take Burge's and Putnam's imagined cases to show (and what I think the Swampman example shows more directly) is that people who are in all relevant physical respects similar (or 'identical' in a necktie sense) can differ in what they mean or think, just as they can differ in being grandfathers or being sunburned. But of course there is something different about them, even in the physical world; their causal histories are different, and they are discrete physical objects. (32-33)

The turn to the social frame of reference to individuate attitudes themselves is in harmony with the inscrutability of reference and the indetermination of translation at the bottom, because the reference of expressions cannot be discovered behaviorally, and the indetermination takes effect also on the top because the truth of translation does not decide about its ontological adequacy.

From my point of view, epistemic restrictions are to circumvent as an option of the theory of interpretation only if we presuppose the background theory as well known. For *RI*, this background is the theory of truth. *T*-sentences allow us testable predictions also. If we grasp the role of beliefs connecting meaning and truth, the background theory of *RI* seems to show "that truth is neither radically nonepistemic, nor radically epistemic" (Davidson 2001 (1988): 189) Davidson himself claims that giving empirical content to a structure of a truth theory in the Tarski-style is an alternative to realism and anti-realism, for example in the version of M. Dummett (see Davidson 2001 (1988): 190-91). But we border on the assumption that significant parts of our knowledge for translation and interpretation are only given outside the triangulation by a hypothetical construction of background theories. A restriction is, in general, that we do not completely find out the background theories; it is possible that such theories are difficult to explore; and it may be that we have no success in continuation to know these. This shows us that Davidson-charity leads us to restrictions of making behavior intelligible in principle, because the radical interpreter has to project his analytical-empirical knowledge to the speaker in essential. One option to handle this problem is given in accepting de re beliefs, as R. Schantz has argued in his version of externalism as a direct realism (1996: 139-146, 405-12). But if an interpreter does not know, for example, anything of psychological and social functions of religious beliefs, he cannot interpret religious attitudes that are manifest in behavior and actions. These are the restrictions of epistemic requirements of interpretation, and they cannot be compensated by de re beliefs. And furthermore it is not to exclude that there are cultural upper limits to that.

What we assign to an utterance as meaning must fit into the whole picture of attitudes that we ascribe to a speaker. And this picture is given by references within the background theory and the given circumstances. But this also presupposes that the ascription is dependent on the assumption of the speaker's cognitive structure and on the interpreter grasping the whole picture only in a hypothetical way. This information requires an expanded frame of reference of ascriptions. Thus we are confronted not only with the problem of understanding utterances but also with people, their culture and history. So the instances of confirmation of an expanded frame are given. The limitation of epistemic restrictions is a matter of deciding to limit our information. And so we find that a concept of rationality is possible only by conceptualizing it as bounded by logic, by contextual features and by the limitation of contextually given information. In general, the capability of setting limits is a basic feature of understanding and of rationality. And no more is known about meaning and rationality.

RI makes the assumption that there is a sufficient relationship between a correct translation or interpretation of linguistic behavior and the attitudes of individual speakers. The basic theory of *RI* and the ascription of attitudes—and thus of all successful interpretation—is that there is a referential transparency of individual utterance in triangulation. The intelligibility of the uttered words is born by holding-true, given by the assent and dissent to sentences. But the re-interpretation of utterances has to refer not only to sets of beliefs, but also to the social frame of reference. All redescription of linguistic behavior requires a partial referential transparency of this frame and also a particular knowledge about the background theories. This is presupposed for our successful ascription of attitudes. The opaqueness of reference gets a new turn by this.

Yet, every theory of meaning and attitudes has to start with the assumption that the justification of given beliefs always proceeds by regarding the background of beliefs. Or, in other words, it proceeds in respect of the background theories that are beyond questions. This is a non-foundational account. Here, background means nothing but sets of our propositional attitudes as a network. It guarantees that single beliefs are true or can be true. The attitudes stand in a logical relationship of coherence (consistence). In the context of speaker background we identify and individuate particular beliefs by applying our binary standard logic. When background theories are included, the situation of radical interpretation looks different: on this basis it is possible that not only translations but also understanding breaks down. If there are different background theories between speaker and interpreter, the translation is going to fail.

We start the redescription of semantic content of utterances $u(p)$ and the explanation of action with the assumption that we presuppose attitudes and background theories for an ascription of this content $u(p)$. Under this ascription, we describe utterances and actions as behaviorally comprehensible and rational in different respects. But it may be that theorizing on the propositional attitudes is wrong or not sufficiently elaborated. Many errors are made in such cases and no principle of interpretation can eliminate our misunderstandings and faults. A theory of interpretation presupposes a coherence between propositional attitudes and our intentional actions, in ordinary cases, also with the speaker intention (reference). In order to identify an utterance as an assertion, we presuppose that the speaker has the intention of stating something. But the utterance meaning is indetermined by all literal meaning.

For an analysis of utterance meaning there has to be a background of belief that is not put at stake again and again. Background stands for a network of beliefs (belief systems) guaranteeing for a single belief to be really true. The ascription of beliefs relies on a common view of speaker and interpreter. This perspective of the world has to be self-evident. The background is holistic. The set of beliefs can be modified without any limits. Beliefs can only be singled out against a background of theories as assigned to the social role of speaker. Partly, this is owed to classical logic. But it is also owed to a natural epistemic justice: I normally ascribe that the speaker is right if the opposite is not proven. This is not a falsification of the objectivity of understanding and neither of the restriction of all interpretation, namely that an interpreter has his own standards only. My understanding of this is that the ascription of single beliefs is concluded from our background *theory*. If we talk about a network of beliefs, it is structured by the logical relations as advised by the theory. It is not the task of semantics to ask where such theories come from; and I doubt whether this question would make sense at all.

To sum up: epistemic restrictions of the speaker or a group of speakers undermine the work of *RI* and the application of the a priori principle of charity. By this, both the a priori theory available to break into the circle between belief and meaning and speakers being radically interpretable in nature are limited. *RI* does not have *all relevant evidence* for intelligible redescription at its disposal. Interpretation requires a *social frame of reference* of the ascription of attitudes that makes behavior comprehensible. It cannot be excluded that there is an upper limit of understanding a speaker at all. I make a distinction of such a "frame" and a semantics of community, because it is *not* the autonomy of meaning which constrains us to introduce this frame, but the epistemic differentiations in the social universe of discourse. This is in harmony with meaning being always related to (empirical) evidence of the background theory/theoretical framework. This is exactly the paradigmatic inside of the theory of meaning beginning with Quine's radical translation.

3. The Logical Form of Action Sentences and Singular Causal Statements

The claim of a *unified theory* is to explain us how we ascribe actions and attitudes to other persons directly. It is a total theory of interpretation that explains linguistic and other behavior. *RI* makes the assumption that a speaker holds true a sentence and then explains how the truth of sentences depends on the knowledge of a speaker's truth-condition. Consequently these conditions come true for the ascription of propositional attitudes and understanding literal meaning. The principle of autonomy of meaning is the guarantee of the lingual expression of attitudes. Truth is a predicate that we apply to sentences and also to utterances. The application to behavior, be it linguistic or not, gives the theory of truth its empirical turn. The analysis of logical form gives us a theoretical contribution to the intelligible redescription of linguistic behavior, because it shows how the understanding of sentences is dependent on their structure, and this structure commits us to the ontological assumption of events.

Davidson's analysis of logical form of action sentences and singular causal statements in *The Logical Form of Action Sentences* (1980 (1967)), *Causal Relations* (1980 (1967)) and *The Individuation of Events* (1980 (1969)) claims to show with logical means that we are committed to the ontology of events. I call the extensional interpretation of logical form action sentences and causal relations the *Davidson-argument*. This analysis does not proceed linguistically in the narrow meaning of the word, because the claim is to introduce an ontological commitment in the theory of language that is of a structural matter. By the application of the analysis of logical form of singular causal statements it is to show furthermore that reasons and actions are to analyze as causes and their effects. But an explanation by primary reasons does not refer to general laws. Yet, not only for *RI* but also for the explanation of action a normative feature of understanding comes into play. It is the aim here to elaborate reasonable accounts of agency, explaining actions, and the relationship between the mental and the physical. It follows from the theory of interpretation that the aim of theorizing of natural science is to limit essentially:

168

...I do not see how even the most complete understanding of human psychology can avoid essential reference to the material forces that impinge on us. Nor do I see how psychology, as long as it deals with such concepts as those of action, intention, belief and desire, can either be reduced to the natural science or made as exact and self-contained as physics. As I suggested, we may even take Spinoza to have shown why such a psychology is impossible, the nomological irreducibility of the mental to the physical can be taken to point in this direction. (Davidson 2005 (1993): 312)

The leading question:

Are actions *mental* causes, *physical* effects, or a *connection* between both?

is motivated by the introduction of an ontological commitment in the theory of language, that is: the world consists of particular, unrepeatable, therefore dated, individual events.

When are two events identical? Or, when is one event identical with another? It seems only one answer is possible: no two events are identical, no event is ever identical with another. (Davidson 1980 (1969): 163)

This explains the theoretical account to analyze our descriptions of actions by singular terms and its reference. Actions are—following this proposal— concrete (individual) events that we describe in a particular way as "intentionally", "willingly", "quickly" and so on. An answer to the problem of reference is of general interest in the philosophy of language, because it is a test of our ontology (ontic decisions). Therefore we recognize clearly the connection between the logical form analysis (structure) of action sentences and its ontological commitment: we presuppose an ontology of events for the semantic analysis of action sentences, because actions are to individuate as concrete events.

Why is the analysis of logical form of action sentences of general interest in the philosophy of language and in ontology? This is the case because the analysis claims to show that we quantify over events in the same way as we do over things. Therefore, Quine's criterion of ontology is valid: to be is to be the value of the variable. This criterion corresponds to the ontological standard: no entity without identity. Davidson reformulates this standard with the motto: no identity without an entity. The linguistic counterpart is: no statements of identity without singular terms (Davidson 1980 (1969): 164). The ontology of events claims to show that we have to accept events as entities. Therefore the logical form analysis of sentences like "Peter has abused John" has to show that terms occur in such sentences that refer to events, that is, variables that have events as values. It is the result of the logical form analysis of action sentences that certain descriptions of actions and events refer to the same event-object. This means the syncategorematical account of action and event sentences. For this proposal, most adverbial modifications like "intentionally", "deliberately", "willingly", "slowly" and so on cannot modify the reference of verbs, but the events that are introduced by certain verbs. Yet, the individuation of events is not determined by logic in general because, for example, the effect of dying from having been given a fatal dose of poison can come about at an essential later time point. In such cases we need an empirical knowledge for the ascription of killing someone (177-178). But

> ... the causal nexus provides for events a 'comprehensive and continuously usable framework' for the identification and description of events analogous in many ways to the space-time coordinate system for material objects. (180)

Therefore we have an answer to the question how the logical form analysis of action sentences and singular causal statements are connected. The individuation of events that we redescribe as actions is given us with the help of causal nexus:

> It is a matter of the first importance that we may, and often do, describe actions and events in terms of their causal relations—their causes, their effects, or both. My poisoning of the victim must be an action that results in the victim being poisoned; my killing of the victim must be an action that results in the death of the victim and also an action that was caused, in part, by my desire for the victim's death. (178; on the account of causal conditions of individuation, see Quine 1985c and Davidson's answer 1985c; on an overview of the controversy of the individuation of events, R. Stoecker 1992).

The claim of the logical form analysis of action sentences is to show how an agent and his action stand in a direct relationship. Such an account makes the assumption that adverbial modifications are to analyze as dress-up predicates, that is, they are not predicate-modifying expressions, but they make up new predicates true of events. This is the presupposition if we want to apply the theory of truth to adverbial modifications (a). The analysis of singular causal statements is a further ground of the ontology of events. Both analyses apply the same principles of substitution (b). It is to show by what kind of arguments the ontic decision of events is reasoned in particular.

3.1. Logical Form and Adverbial Modification

3.1.1. Kenny's Problem and the Ontology of Action Sentences

The analysis of the logical form of action sentences begins with what A. Kenny (1963) has called the problem of the variable polyadicity of action verbs. For Kenny, actions are not to analyze logically as relations. Relations have a certain position, for example, "is higher than" as a two position predicate, "is angry" as a one position predicate. On the contrary, for action verbs the positions could be expanded, for example, Brutus killed Caesar at the point of time t, with a knife, and so on. Another feature of such sentences is that there is no limit to the input of further information in the sentences. The sentence like "Brutus killed ..." can be expanded with all the history of the Roman empire (on critics, see also N. Rescher 1967).

The logical form analysis gives us an answer to Kenny's problem, because the result is that there is no variable polyadicity of action verbs, but our speaking about events implies an ontological statement:

* There are events like entities, and we can state infinite things on such events.

Action sentences do not describe single events: their logical form is of general (structural) significance. But if these sentences are true, there is an event that makes such sentences true. The world consists of non-reducible and individual events:

But the assumption, ontological and metaphysical, that there are events, is one without which we cannot make sense of much of our most common talk; or so, at any rate, I have been arguing. I do not know any better, or further, way of showing what there is. (Davidson 1980 (1969): 162)

Events are to individuate in a coarse-grained manner (Quine: individual in sequences of time), not fine-grained (Kim: event, property, time point; Goldman), for example, "I phone" and "I phone hastily" are not to distinguish as events themselves. The difference is only a matter of description. If we individuate events fine-grained, we would state another cause for "I phone hastily". For the opponent of the coarse-grained proposal it is required to take into play the causal role of properties founding two-termed relations between concrete events (see also F. Siebelt 1994: 209-216).

Davidson's analysis of action sentences explains by the power of its

logical structure how the surface of action-ascribing sentences is structured. It is the task of elaborating the logical form to show us the underlying semantic elements of action verbs like "to kick", "to kill", and so
on. The adverbial clause does not modify the action verb but the events
that the verb introduces in the sentence position (Davidson 1980 (1969):
167). Action verbs and also other verbs of change are to put in with an
event position that corresponds to an event object. "'Sebastian strolled
through the streets of Bologna at 2 a.m.' then has the following form:
'There is an event x, such as, Sebastian strolled x, x took place in the
streets of Bologna, and x was going on at 2.a.m.'" (167) *Verbs of action
are to construct in a way that they contain a place for singular terms or a
variable that is not obvious on the surface grammar.* Adverbial modifiers
are of the same logical value as adjective modifiers. Such modifiers are
not significant for any semantic analysis of action sentences and are to
eliminate. The quantification in the event position as the variable of these
sentences gives us the answer to Kenny's question for the variable polyadicity. In this manner, action sentences are to analyze as generalized
and quantified sentences. The ontic decision for an ontology of events
is nowhere grounded by an empirical argument, but it is a conclusion
drawn from the framework of logical form.

There remains, however, a more direct consideration ... in favor of an ontology
of events, which is that without events it does not seem possible to give a natural
and acceptable account of the logical form of certain sentences of the most common sorts; it does not seem possible, that is, to show how the meaning of such
sentences depends upon their composition. (Davidson 1980 (1969): 166.)

3.1.2. Adverbial Modifications

Yet, is it really compelling to analyze adverbial modifications as modifications of predicates in general?
    The answer to this question decides over the application of a truth-
theoretical semantics to the modification of predicates. The analysis of
the semantics of adverbial modifications goes back to Austin (and Ryle).
Could we assert of actions, or negate it, that they are "intentional", "deliberate", "voluntary" and so on?
    Austin has argued that it is a linguistic fault to assert or negate that an
action is performed "intentionally", "deliberately", "voluntarily" and
so on (1956). This is correct only if the action departs from a normal
situation: no modification without aberration. A sentence like "Peter

paid his cigarettes intentionally" makes sense only in a situation where the seller is not the "seller" but a thief who disguises himself as a seller. The redescription with the modification would state that Peter paid his cigarettes assuming that the friendly seller was not a thief, or, in the example "Peter had a cup of coffee with the seller intentionally" would redescribe the situation in such a way that Peter was not forced to act as he did, but he did not know that the seller was a thief. In his chapter "6.3. The Assertion Fallacy" Searle (1969) has criticized Austin because he follows the slogan "meaning is use". For Searle, this is a methodological fault. He summarizes Austin's proposal: (1) There is a class of action-modifying expressions like, for example, "intentionally", "voluntarily", "deliberately" etc.; (2) the negations of such expressions are also action-modifying expressions; (3) modifications could be applied only if their conditions of application are satisfied; (4) such conditions are satisfied if there is an aberration from a normal situation of acting; (5) the aberration can factually concede or be fictive. For Searle, the first and the second assumption are false, and the third and the fourth assumption are vague. Against the first assumption he argues that the exemplified condition is not only to specify to the use of words, but it is of a generalized matter also. He argues against the second assumption that "no modification without aberration" is valid for a class of expressions and not only for the negation of an action sentence. For example, "I did not buy my bicycle intentionally, I was forced to do it" is not a linguistically false formulation but it is true or false. The utterance of sentences with action modified expressions is to justify by the reasons for or against the assertion. It follows from this that the assertion is not an assumption about the use of words or the use of sentences in certain situations respectively.

Searle gives the following reasons for his conclusion: it makes no sense to assert of a normal situation that such a situation is normal. This is correct only if there is a ground for the assumption that the situation is normal or it is not. If we assert toward a hearer that the given case is a normal situation, it is important that the speaker refers to this situation. The utterance "he did x" normally means "x is done intentionally", and therefore, it is a fault to add the adverb "intentionally" provided that the situation is not departed from normal cases. However, we have a deviant situation under study if we negate that x was done intentionally, for example, Peter did not have his coffee intentionally, he was drunk. Austin does not take into account that the condition for "x was done intentionally" is a reason for the assumption that "x was done non-intentionally" could be true, for example, Peter drank out of the cup of coffee in front of him intentionally, but he drank non-intentionally out of the cup of coffee of the person next to him at the table (he mixed up the cups). Austin shows that the two expressions like "he did x intentionally" and "he did x non-intentionally" are used for deviant cases, for example, Peter was forced to drink coffee, or Peter mixed up the two cups in front of him; yet it is not clear how both the formulations are to use only for deviant cases because with such expressions we redescribe actions. If Austin's analysis was right, then it would have to be explained how the two cases of description of "intentionally" and "non-intentionally" are to connect, because one and the same action, like drinking coffee, could be described as intentional and non-intentional. If we make this assumption, we would not be successful in ascribing actions because one cannot fix that items of behavior are to redescribe as actions. Therefore we have to find an answer to the question:

What modifies adverbial modifications? Are such modifications semanticly significant? How do we directly pair an action to an agent? Is this the right question, or do we pair actions to agents in an indirect way only?

If the logical form analysis were successful, then we would have an answer to the question how an agent and an action can be paired directly.

What is the problem of the logical form analysis of action sentences?

Many theorists have argued that claims to events like, for example, the basic ontology of events, are problematically related to our thinking about causation, space-time, ourselves, and the relationship to the external world we have (on the logical form of action sentences, the ontology of events, and actions as events, see, for example, P. Pietroski 2003: 137-62).

3.1.3. The Logical Form of Action Sentences

For Davidson, the analysis of action sentences applies to the theory of truth in the style of Tarski and the principle of extensionality. This means:

A context is extensional if its truth values cannot be changed by supplanting a component sentence by another of the same truth value, nor by supplanting a component predicate by another with all the same denotata, nor by supplanting a singular term by another with the same designatum. Succinctly, the three requirements are substitutivity of covalence, of coextensiveness, and of identity, salva veritate. A context is intensional if it is not extensional. (Quine 1995b: 90)

(1) Peter buttered the toast slowly, deliberately, in the bathroom, with a knife, at midnight.

Most analyses would characterize this sentence composed of five predicate positions:
(2) *a* buttered *b* in *c* with *d* at *t*.

But this shows a defect, because we make no difference between the relevant verbal components (verbs) of such sentences.
(3) Peter buttered the toast.
(4) Peter buttered the toast in the bathroom.
(5) Peter buttered the toast in the bathroom with a knife.

The sentences (3), (4), (5) are logical conclusions from the original sentence (1). This is reasoned by the logical form. If the original sentence (1) was composed of five unstructured predicates, the logical form would not justify this conclusion, the logical power of the inference could not be shown by the logical form. So it is another analysis that has to be correct. Davidson analyzes the sentence (1) as a statement about an event. It means: the event happens in a certain situation as an act where a toast is buttered by Peter, it happens in the bathroom, it is done with a knife, and it happens at midnight. Action sentences are a genuine subset of event sentences: this is the syncategorematic account of these sentences. The conclusion is: the correct analysis of action sentences includes a variable over an event about which it gives us a report. The ordinary sentence:
(6) Peter buttered the toast

is to describe formally:
(7) "$\exists x$ buttered (the toast, Peter x)".

The main theme of the logical form of action sentences is of a generalized matter, and it concerns the logic of adverbial modifier. The adverbial modifying is to represent by a conjunction:
(8) Peter buttered the toast at midnight (intentionally) = "$\exists x$ (buttered (Peter, toast x) & (x at midnight)".

In "x" we could only put in events. Actions sentences are of structural significance, because they have the logical form of existentially quantified sentences and "buttered" in our example is a *three* place predicate, that is, a theory of truth in the Tarski-style entails that such sentences are true if and only if the respective event exists. The unification of the theory of meaning of action is structured by the logical form, because the task of the truth theory is to identify a finite stock of truth-relevant elements, and thereby it makes explicit the truth-conditions of uttered sentences within which such elements figure. So-called action verbs are therefore translating (paraphrasing) in our quantificatory language by their semantic role. Such translating claims nothing but a systematization of the truth-conditions.

But how far can we represent the logical form of adverbial modified action sentences by conjunctions that do not include adverbs?

The problem is whether a simple action sentence like, for example,

(9) Peter buttered the toast slowly

is to interpret by the sentence:

(10) $(\exists x)$ (buttered the toast slowly) & (x by Peter).

Following the analysis of logical form, the adverbial modifications do not modify the verb but the event that is introduced in the position of action sentences. Therefore (8) is the right account but not (10). Yet the problem is that it is not simply possible to take the modification off the verb and transform it into a simple predicate about an event. The problem is in general:

If Jones buttered the toast slowly then, logically, we suppose, $(\exists x)$ (Buttered(Jones, toast, x) & Slowly(x)). But of course, if x is an event place to be filled by a singular term for an event, then "slowly" is the wrong modifier. The activity is done slowly, but the event at best is a slow one. "Jones' buttering the toast is slow" is nonsense, of course. Modifiers of acts are not modifiers of the actions which result from these acts. Or simply, these adverbs modify verbs and not nouns. (Clark 1970: 316)

The logical form account is to test by answering the question:

Is it really so that action sentences show us the three connected properties of extensionality: the substitution, the identity of reference, and also the generalization of existence of the singular terms?

The aim of the analysis of the logical form of action sentences is to show the deep structural property as purely extensional: the truth-value of composed sentences and the substitution of the singular terms—that we put in it—is dependent on the truth-value of the components of these sentences. If this is the case, we can put other statements into such sentences without changing their truth-value: first property of extensionality, the substitution of singular terms. Sentence

(11) "Peter buttered the toast in the bathroom"

shows as an essential property that the singular terms or names can be substituted by other expressions with the same reference without changing the truth-value: second property of extensionality, identity of reference of singular terms. We ascribe this property to sentence (11) because it seems that the expression "Peter" has the same reference like, for example, "the incumbent president of the university". Sentence (11) would be true iff the incumbent president of the university buttered the toast.

The second property of extensionality is dependent on a further, third property that we ascribe to sentence (11): the generalization of existence of the singular terms. If a statement that includes a singular term a is to interpret extensionally, we make a generalization in respect of the presupposition of existence of the position of the bound variable that occupies a. Sentence (11) consequently includes

(12) $\exists x$ (x buttered the toast).

Therefore we interpret the three properties of extensionality co-extensively: if a sentence s has one of the properties, we ascribe to it the other properties also. If it has no such property, we cannot conclude a valid inference from sentence (11) and

(13) Peter = the incumbent president of the university

to

(14) the incumbent president of the university buttered the toast.

because sentence (14) would not report anything about the person "Peter". The term "Peter" in the statement would not have its ordinary reference, and there would be no extentional interpretation of these sentences because the three properties of extensionality would not be given. The inference is valid only if the three properties are to interpret co-extensively. Everyone who accepts this assertion will vote for Davidson's theory of an adverbial modifier in the example of an extensional interpretation of the sentence (11). It has the form

(15) $\exists x$ (buttered the toast (Peter x) & (x in the bathroom)).

Without "$\exists x$", the sentence entails no complete sentence, but the formula includes two sentential functions that are bound by our standard of quantification. So we can find materially equivalent formulations, for example, if the statement

(16) $\exists x$ (buttered the toast (Peter)) & (x in the bathroom)) is true

then

(17) ($\exists x$) (buttered the toast (Peter x) & (x in the bathroom))

is also intuitively true. The statement in sentence (11) is exclusively to interpret extentionally. The surface structure may have a defect on extensionality, but if we have identified the logical form of the deep structure, sentence (11) is to interpret extensionally.

But there is another account to interpret an adverbial modifier. If we interpret sentences with such a modifier as functions (operators), they show a feature of non-extensionality. Sentences like sentence (11) do not have the first property of extensionality in every context. This is not a question of its referential features that we make transparent with ordinary tests, but a question of the substitution of new expressions. It is not necessary to assert that, if a complex predicate including its adverbial modifier is true with respect to an entity, other predicates we ascribe to that thing with or without any modification could also be true. If Peter butters the toast and spills the butter over himself, then the fact—the ascription of the complex predicate "butter quickly"—can be true, but "spills the butter over himself quickly" is false. It is furthermore not to exclude that the statement "Peter butters the toast quickly" does not refer to Peter but to Henry who is called by the affectionate name of "(poor) Peter". The speaker reference is not to establish by the principle of extensionality.

Here is another point: if we make the assumption that adverbial modifications have the same function as such modifications factually, that is, the predicate with a wider extension, for example, "butter" entails the predicate with the smaller extension "butter quickly", then we do not expect that the content of such statements like $\exists x(x$ buttered the toast (x is by Peter) & (x is quickly) shows us the first property of extensionality in all cases. The reason for this is: a modification may be meaningful if the modifier is connected with a predicate producing a nonsensical result. This is the case if the connection with another predicate is true. In the sentence

(18) Peter butters the toast with erotical power

both the following statements have the same truth-value and are materially equivalent if the presupposition is true:
(19) Peter butters and
(20) Peter's erotical power.

Sentence
(21) Peter butters the toast

represents a truthful proposition, but the sentence
(21) Peter butters the toast with erotical power

is meaningless. The defect is born with the presupposition that in sentence (18) the modification can be substituted by any material equivalent statement in the context of
(22) Peter butters the toast.

Adverbial modifications are not to analyze as extensional in every context (on further elaborations, see T. Parsons 1980, 1985, 1990).
   Davidson has emphasized that all events are physical events (spatiotemporal particulars). Events do not only occur at a certain place and time, typically they also have effects. Events are metaphysically primitive. But causes and effects are events themselves, and they are not to reduce to anything else. The problem of his analysis of logical form of action sentences leads us to the problem that he takes events as metaphysically primitive, or, in other words, the ontology of events into account.

3.1.4. R. Clark's Account

Clark has developed an alternative account for the analysis of adverbial modifications (1970). It does not interpret modifications of predicates as *predicates* or so-called "dressed up predicates", but as operators (functions) that generate new predicates. Therefore, the adverb "slowly" is to analyze as a modification of "travel" and it is to expand to the complex predicate "travel slowly". Furthermore, he makes a distinction between different types of predicate modification that are not connected by only one rule. The example in sentence (1) "Peter buttered the toast slowly, deliberately, in the bathroom, with a knife, at midnight." is to interpret for this account as a "simple relational statement" in which every modification introduces an individual term of varying degree like, for example, "slowly": degree *o*, "deliberately": degree *1*, "with a knife": degree *2*, and so on. "Rather, modifiers are operators which, attached to a predicate (of degree greater than zero), yield a predicate." (320, to a notational variation in that the „modifiers with their associated place for singular terms are prefixed to a predicate", see 321) The modifications then would have to represent as operators, and we would introduce first the simple and then the complex predicates.

Clark makes a distinction between core predicates and modifiers.

The natural view, which reflects the grammar of our native language, is to distinguish, as extant logical theories fail to distinguish, predicates from their modifiers. Modifiers cannot, alone, in general be ascribed to subjects. This is marked most clearly with adverbs: "John is drunkenly" is nonsense. (320)

Core predicates are such predicates that contain no predicates as parts, for example, "spill *xy*". Attributive modifiers, like, for example, "is red" or "is famous" are no core predicates. But with such expressions we can build a core predicate by inserting a prefix, for example, "famous tennis player". Clark enlarges the core predicates in such a way that certain modifications could also be predicates in particular sentences, for example in "*x* is a Japanese pilot" "Japanese" is a modifier, but it can also occur as a core predicate, for example, "*x* is a Japanese" (see on the redefinition: 330-32). Clark distinguishes two sorts of pred mods (predicate mods), the "classifiers" (grammatical ordinary nouns)—that could be core predicates—and attributive mods (grammatical adjectives).

There are various ways to do so, but perhaps the simplest is simply to syntactically distinguish core predicates from other modifiers and to bar attributives from the class of core predicates. (333).

The distinction is reasoned as follows:

What we can infer from the fact that this is a large, red ball is that it is a large ball, and that it is a red ball. We do not want it to follow from the fact that this is a large chigger, that this is large. So, too, I believe, we should not want it to follow from the fact that this is a very red chigger, that this is very red. A very red chigger need not be very red at all. (334).

Modifiers are operators to generate new predicates. Predicates are to apply to individuals. If we apply predicates to predicates, we have higher order predicates that are to apply to lower order predicates, but they are no modifications, for example, "red" is a property of a zero level and the sentence "Red is a color" is a property on the first level. Yet, in the case of modifier it is different. Modifiers can, rather, be compared with sentential operators (junctors) like "not" or "and" because we build new sentences with them. Clark makes a difference between syncategorematic operators for predicates, normally coinciding with sentential operators that do not signify anything, and categorematic operators for predicates. With the latter, we generate predicates of a larger degree if the modification is not of degree o, for example, "slowly", or we generate new predicates that have the same degree as the original if the modifiers are of the degree o, for example, "buttered slowly".

Davidson and Clark develop a theory of adverbial modifications that claims to allow us to infer from the sentence like "Peter buttered the toast slowly, deliberately, in the bathroom, with a knife, at midnight" to "Peter buttered the toast". This is the goal of the analysis of sentences over events (Davidson) and the predicate modifiers (Clark). Davidson applies the standard logic. We find the deep structure of action sentences by the introduction of the event position. The surface structure may be defect. Nevertheless, if we have the deep structure, the different surface structure is no hindrance for the analysis. By way of contrast, Clark gives an account for the surface structure of ordinary sentences. Therefore it is a requirement to introduce further inferential principles: 1. The permutation principle for modifiers (operators) and 2. the detachment principle for predicates (321-322) The first principle means that pred mods are to substitute. The principle is only valid for pred mods but not for modifiers of modifiers (mod-mod) like "powerful" in "powerful compelling performance" (328).

The detachment principle is introduced by an initial segment: any predicate implies any initial segment of itself. An initial segment is a core predicate, that is, a predicate that has no predicates as parts like, for example, butter xy — predicates without modifiers — or predicates that are generated by the application of core predicates or already generated initial segments like, for example, "butters slowly in the bathroom" (321). The detachment principle is a reverse of the generation of more and more complex predicates by the application of modifiers (operators) to the core predicate, for example, "butters xy". Clark applies the detachment principle to the predicates in general, that is, to predicates that do not entail modifiers or by prefixing of pred mods: the classifiers (class terms that could be pre mods but also autonomous predicates) and attributive mods (no autonomous predicates).

For Clark, a large class of modifiers belongs to modifiers only. But there are also borderline cases where predicates have the function of a pred mod in a sentence, for example, "Yamamoto was a Japanese admiral". In this case "Japanese" is a pred mod. In the example "Yamamoto was a Japanese" "Japanese" seems to be a core predicate. Clark gives three solutions to this problem: 1. "Japanese" is a core predicate, therefore, in certain cases, a core predicate can have the function of a pred mod. 2. The logical form is not explicitly given by grammar, for example, the sentence is to interpret as "Yamamoto is an admiral who was born in Japan". 3. "A Japanese" is no core predicate. However, with regard to the third solution we could ask "Why could 'Japanese' not just be a core predicate?"

Aune gives the following summary of Clark's proposal:

Largely in response to Davidson's remarks on action sentences, theories of adverbial modification have recently been developed that do not involve quantification over events, states, conditions, and the like. Romane Clark's theory is a case in point. His theory, unlike Davidson's, provides a thoroughly general account of predicate modifiers. His key idea is that predicate modifiers are not themselves predicates, or even predicates in disguise: they are operators, which make big predicates out of little ones. The adverb 'slowly' thus occurs as a modifier of 'travels', yielding the complex predicate 'travels slowly'. Since there are significantly different types of predicate modifier (apart from standard ones, Clark recognizes fictionalizers like 'mythical', enlargers like 'possible addict', negators like 'fake', and neutralizers like 'alleged') no single rule holds for all of them. According to the rule for a standard modifier like 'slowly', the sentence 'John traveled slowly' logically entails 'John traveled'; according to the rules for a nonstandard modifier like 'possible', there is no entailment relation between 'John was a possible addict' and 'John was an addict'. In Clark's system the statement Davidson discusses, 'Jones buttered the toast in the bathroom with a knife at midnight', is interpreted as having the form of a simple relational statement with a core predicate complicated by three modifiers. Each modifier introduces a singular term, and if, in line with the usual logical practice, we collect these terms at the end of the formula, we can represent Davidson's specimen sentence as follow:

[In [At [With [Buttered (Jones, the toast)] (a knife)] (midnight)] (the bathroom)].

Clark's basic idea, that predicate modifiers function as operators that generate complex predicate from simpler ones, is extremely plausible, but it appears to have the consequence that statements involving such modifiers are non-extensional. Although, as I shall argue in a later section, this consequence may actually be avoided, we can grant it for the time being.

The argument is:

According to Clark, the modifier, 'with...' functions as an operator that generates a complex two-place predicate '...does A with...' when applied to the one-place predicate '...does A'. If we adopt this view of the modifier 'with...' we can say

(3) Jones hit Smith with the intention of hitting Smith

(Aune argues that 'Jones hit Smith intentionally' is an elliptical formulation of the longer statement (3), my note)

has the form of

(5) *WHjsi,*

where the predicate '... hits ... with ...' is abbreviated as '*WH*'. Also, as we pointed out, statements with the form of (5) seem to be referentially transparent, they also seem to lack an important mark of extensionality: evidently, materially equivalent formulas cannot be validly interchanged within them. Thus, if Jones hit Smith and thereby angered Mary, we cannot infer that if Jones hit Smith with a stick, he thereby angered Mary with a stick.

I said that sentences with the form of (5) seem to lack an important mark of extensionality, not that they actually do lack such a mark. I put the point in this guarded way, because if we accept Clark's approach to predicate modification, we can say that sentences like (5) only appear to contain sentences within them. The idea is that when we uncover their logical form we can see that they contain a single complex predicate generated by an operation of adverbial modification. Of course, the symbols '*Hjs*' occur in the formula '*WHjsi*', but the letter '*H*' does not function as a predicate there and '*Hjs*' does not function as a core sentence there. Thus, although the formula ,*WHjsi*' may appear to consist of a core sentence ,*Hjs*' modified by an adverbial phrase '*Wi*', it actually consists of a single, syntactically complex predicate '*WH*' flanked by three singular terms, '*j*', '*s*' and '*i*'. Since '*WHjsi*' contains no core sentence and no predicate other than '*WH*', the rule permitting the interchange of equivalent formulas is simply inapplicable to it (except in the trivial sense that the whole formula '*WHjsi*' can be interchanged for itself) as is the rule permitting the substitution of predicates coextensive with '*Hxy*'. Since these rules are inapplicable to '*WHjsi*', they cannot be violated or falsified by that formula. Consequently, the formula can be regarded as extensional. (Aune 1977: 32-34, 93-94.)

To sum up, it is the merit of Clark that there is a class of expressions which are modifiers. But the borderline between such expressions that play the role of modifiers only and expressions that could play a role as modifiers and as core predicates as well seems not to be fixed. The consequence of Clark's account is that action sentences do not entail a quantification over events or states. The adverb "slowly" is to interpret

as a modification of "butter", and it is to expand to the complex predicate "butters slowly". We structure the statement in Davidson's sentence
(1) "Peter buttered the toast slowly, deliberately, in the bathroom, with a
knife, at midnight" as a "simple relational statement" in that the domain
of the application of predicate includes three modifications. Each modification introduces a singular term. This account does not commit us to
an ontology of events. Here is the problem in principle. This is valid for
the whole inclusion of modifications of any predicate.

A handling of adverbial modifications as "dressed-up predicates" is
the presupposition of the application of the truth-conditional account to
modifications of predicates. Davidson's proposal is that if we know the
logical form of a sentence, we also know the semantic roles of all significant properties of the sentence in the context of an overall theory. But
adverbial modifications like "deliberately", "intentionally", "wilfully",
are intensional and intentional:

> The second point to notice about Davidson's proposal is that it is unclear how
> it is to be applied to adverbial modifiers like 'slowly' and 'deliberately'. The
> problem with 'slowly' is that it is attributive; under one description, an action,
> or sets of actions, can be done slowly, under another quickly: 'She crossed the
> Channel in eight hours'; 'God, that was slow'; 'She was swimming'; 'God, that
> was quick!'. The problem with 'deliberately' is that it is both intensional and
> intentional, ultimately making reference to the agent's mental state. (M. Platts
> 1979: 196).

3.2. Causal Relations

3.2.1. The Problem of Logical Form of Singular Causal Statements

The Davidson-argument of the logical form of singular causal statements
provides a further argument for an ontology of events. The application
of the logical form analysis to the concept of causality is also a reasoning
that reasons and actions stand in causal relationship. The assumption
is: if descriptions of actions and events refer to something, they refer to
the same. This shows us again the significance of individual events for
the *unified theory*. Actions are body movements (physical events) that
are identical with desires and cognitive states. Therefore the adverbial
modifications cannot change the reference of expressions. The substitution of a singular term of the descriptions of actions and events does not
modify its reference.

It is to mention here that in contemporary philosophy there are two accounts to analyze events. I can see no bridge connecting them. They are the *coarse-grained* (Davidson, Quine) and the *property* (fine-grained) conception (Goldman, Kim, Bennett and others) of events. The first makes a principal distinction between stating causal relations and explaining them, the second argues that causal relations and their explanation are not to distinguish because properties figure in both and explain us causation.

The Davidson-argument claims to show that the logical form of singular causal statements commits us to an ontology of space-temporal events as particulars. It is not the strategy to argue for the logical form of causal relations directly, but to defend this account with a critique of a possible alternative proposal (1980: 151-52). This proposal makes the assumption that

(1) The short circuit caused the fire.

has the logical form

(2) *The fact that* there was a short circuit *caused it to be the case that* there was a fire.

The alternative form is distinguished from Davidson's account, because the word "caused" is to construct as elliptical for the connective statement (the italicized words are to interpret as connective like 'and' or 'if. .., then...'). A complex connective is expressed by the words:

 * The fact that ... caused it to be the case that ...

If we use such connective statements, we select fine-grained events, for example, in case we suppose "The fire was caused by a short circuit and not just by striking a match". Both would be different from their explanation. In difference to that, Davidson analyzes singular causal statements as extensional, that is, their logical form is expressed by a two-place relation between events. The hard core of the Davidson-argument follows along the line:

It is obvious that the connective in (2) is not truth-functional, since (2) may change from true to false if the contained sentences are switched. Nevertheless, substitution of singular terms for others with the same extension in sentences like (1) and (2) does not touch their truth-value. If Smith's death was caused by the fall from the ladder and Smith was the first man to land on the moon, then the fall from the ladder was the cause of the death of the first man to land on the moon. And if the fact that there was a fire in Jones's house caused it to be the case that the pig was roasted, and Jones's house is the oldest building on Elm Street, then the fact that there was a fire in the oldest building on Elm street caused it to be the case that the pig was roasted. We must accept the principle of extensional substitution, then. Surely also we cannot change the truth value of the likes of (2) by substituting logically equivalent sentences for sentences in it. Thus (2) retains is truth if for 'there was a fire' we substitute the logically equivalent '($\hat{x}$ =x & there was a fire) = $\hat{x}$ (x = x)'; retains it still if for the left side of this identity we write the coextensive singular term '$\hat{x}$ (x = x & Nero fiddled)'; and still retains it if we replace '$\hat{x}$ (x = x & Nero fiddled) = $\hat{x}$ (x = x)' by the logically equivalent 'Nero fiddled.' Since the only aspect of 'there was a fire' and 'Nero fiddled' that matters to this chain of reasoning is the fact of their material equivalence, it appears that our assumed principles have led to the conclusion that the main connective of (2) is, contrary to what we supposed, truth-functional. (see also the note to the argument, Davidson 1980: 152-153).

Davidson's strategy to show that the connective in (2) is not truth-functional is "…we may reject the hypothesis that (2) gives the logical form of (1), and with it the ideas that the 'cause' of (1) is more or less concealed sentential connective, and that causes are fully expressed only by sentences." (153) We can see (again) how putting causal statements into a quantificational form goes together with ontology that claims to give sense to "our most common talk" (162). The key element is the coarse-grained concept of events.

3.2.2. The Davidson-Argument

The Davidson-argument is: singular causal sentences are to interpret extensionally. They express a two-place relation between events as unrepeatable particulars to those singular terms used like definite descriptions or others they refer to. Both the sentences (1) and (2) express relations between events and have the logical form: $\exists x$(fire x & y(short-circuit y & y caused x)). We have to distinguish between causal statements and explanations, in principle (for other proposals like, for example, Goldman, Kim, Shoemaker properties exemplify the relata of causal relations, and they explain the causation of events to us; therefore, the role of properties of events is significant for causing events expressed in two-termed causal relations).

This argument shows:

(3) There are logically valid equivalent formulations in the context of sentence (2),

(4) it can also be valid to substitute co-extensive singular terms in such context, and

(5) also materially equivalent formulations in such context could be substituted.

But if there is an obvious counterexample, we are concluding that (5) is false and so (3) and (4) are also false. Provided that we draw this inference, I have my doubts about the premise of Davidson's argument. This is the problem of the logical form of (3) in question.

The commentators of Davidson's work (Aune, Lepore, Ludwig, Manning, Neale and others) agree that his claim that there are valid inferences to the materially equivalent formulations of sentences of the sort "(2) *The fact that ...caused it to be the case that...*" will show

(6) For any statement P and Q

    (1) if P is materially equivalent with Q

    (2) then is $S(P)$ materially equivalent with $S(Q)$

    (3) a sentence $S(P)$ of the sort

        (a) "The fact that ...caused it to be the case that..." is

        (b) only different from $S(Q)$ in the content P in the case where $S(Q)$ entails the statement Q.

The inference (proof) that *(3)*—the substitution of materially equivalent formulations in a given context—is inferred from *(1)*—the logical validity of *(2)* and *(2)*—the occurrence of valid co-extensional substitute terms—then asserts:

(7) *(1)* and *(2)* and the antecedence condition *(3)*.

For Davidson, it is a sufficient condition for the assertion of the implication

(8) $S(P)$ implies $S(Q)$.

For this assertion we need a radical translation of the sort:

(9) assert $S(P)$ then find out that P is logically equivalent to

(*) $(x = x \& P) = (x = x)$.

(10) $(x = x \& P) = (x = x)$ is substituted for P in $S(P)$ and find out

(*) that P is materially equivalent with Q, so consequently both the singular terms are equivalent and are to interpret co-extensively:

(*) $(x = x \& Q) = (x = x \& P)$.

In accordance to the premise *(2)* it is to substitute then
(11) (x = x & Q) = (x = x & P) in the formulation:
(12) ((x = x & Q) = (x = x & P))

and we have the form
* S ((x = x & Q) = (x = x))

The formulation
(13) (x = x & Q) = (x = x)

is logically equivalent with Q, consequently it is to conclude within the premise *(1)* to S(Q).

The critical point of the Davidson-argument is that it presupposes: there is a logical equivalence between logically valid inferences and the substitution of logically equivalent formulations and materially equivalent terms in a given context (their logical equivalence), also in case we could not substitute materially equivalent formulations in it, for example, "Nero" does not refer to a Roman imperator but to another person with the name "Nero" who fiddled. Davidson's argument of the logical form of singular causal statements and action sentences in general is reasoned by this presupposition (on the Davidson-argument, see Neal 2001: 210-216, on "Facts and Causes": 216-220)

What we conclude from the argument is: sentences with the form (2) have a problematic logical form because the Davidson-argument claims to show that causal statements are not intensional connectives. If there is a counterexample, no valid substitution of the material equivalent formulations is possible in the context of such sentences. This is the problem of the overall application of the principle of extensional substitution. Neale has shown in detail that the Davidson-argument uses the slingshot argument against a non-extensional interpretation of causal connectives (2001). Yet the problem is "Are causal contexts extensional?"

Davidson (1980: 161) further introduces another sort of singular causal statements like

(6) "The failure of the sprinkling system caused the fire."

(7) "The slowness with which the controls were applied caused the rapidity with which the inflation developed."

(8) "The collapse was not caused by the fact that the bolt gave way but by the fact that it gave way so suddenly and unexpectedly."

(9) "The fact that the dam did not hold caused the flood."

Some of these sentences may yield to the methods I have prescribed, especially if failures are counted among events, but others remain recalcitrant. What we must say in such cases is that in addition to, or in place of, giving what Mill calls the 'producing cause', such sentences tell, or suggest, a causal story. They are, in other words, rudimentary causal explanations. Explanations typically relate statements, not events. I suggest therefore that the 'caused' of the sample sentences in this paragraph is not the 'caused' of straightforward singular causal statements, but is best expressed by the word 'causally explains'. (Davidson 1980 (1969)161-162, see also the note to the argument)

But the alternative interpretation of the examples (6) – (9) with "causally explains" is also to apply to the normal cases or ordinary singular causal statements. So instead of

(10) "The short circuit caused the fire"

we can say

(11) "the fire is causally explained by the fact that there was a short circuit."

The example shows that Davidson takes an alternative proposal of interpretation of singular causal statements into consideration. This explanation does not state relations between events but sentences and is not committed to an ontology of unreducible events (basic events).

3.2.3. Causal Relations and Causal Explanations

For Davidson, the distinction between *stating simple causal relations and explaining these by linguistic means* is valid in his writings. This is the problem of the epistemological role of the causal law-theses and also the role of singular causal statements constructing the general scheme of scientific explanation. I will give some evidence of this problem with the following citation. It shows us also the ontological role of unreducible events stated by singular causal statements for understanding causal relations.

But it is an error to think no explanation has been given until a law has been produced. Linked with these errors is the idea that singular causal statements necessarily indicate, by the concepts they employ, the concepts that will occur in the entailed law. (Davidson 1980 (1963): 17)

Causality and identity are relations between individual events no matter how described. But laws are linguistic; and so events can instantiate laws, only as those events are described in one or another way.... The principle of the nomological character of causality must be read carefully: it says that when events are related as cause and effect, they have descriptions that instantiate a law. It does not say that every true statement of causality instantiates a law. (1980 (1970): 215)

The main source of confusion, I think, is the fact that when it comes to events people find it hard to keep in mind the distinction between types and particulars. This in turn makes it easy to conflate singular causal connections with causal laws, and invites neglect of the difference between explaining an event and simply stating that a causal relation holds (Davidson 2005 (1993): 1998)

In sum: for laws *classifications* of events are required which are *types* of events. The entities we deal with are satisfied by specific concepts. In difference to that, causal relations are independent of their description and classification.

Discussing the accounts of Burge, N. Goodman, J. McDowell, C. J. Ducasse, M. Margenau, R. Cummins, and Anscombe, Davidson argues that the reasoning for the causal law-thesis is in some respect of an a priori matter (Burge), and we do not justify the "thesis" with our normal logic or empirical issues (2005 (1995). The causal law-thesis does not have the meaning that any particular causal laws are a priori. He interprets the causal law-thesis in this respect so that the thesis is consistent with the extensional interpretation of singular causal statements. The truth-values of these statements are invariant with respect to the substitution of names or descriptions of events and do not change by the substitution with other names or descriptions of the same event. But this interpretation has taken precautions with which we guarantee the projectibility of the status of individual predicates from the past to the future (on Goodman's new riddle of induction, Davidson 1980 (1966 Appendix, 2005 (1995: 206-08)). The guarantee is given with the following interpretation of the causal law-thesis:

* if the causal law-thesis is true, we make the assumption in the case of the adequacy of an extensional interpretation of singular causal statements, that we can in principle give a law and it explains the individual case. We could know this without knowing at the same time the explanatory law. The epistemic justification of this knowledge is the best reasoning of the explanation of causal relations that are at one's disposal: we explain these relations with a certainty of the truth of given laws or the singular causal statement is covered by a law (on a contrafactual analysis of singular statements, see J. Woodward 1986, on an interpretation of causal statements with Lewis-contrafactual conditionals, see E. Lepore, B. Loewer 1987, on singular causal statements, Rogler, Preyer 2001).

This may be a plausible version of the causal law-thesis.

But is it a justification of an ontology of events?

I have doubts here, because in the reversed case it is not events that have to be specified but only prognoses, that is, sentences deducted from laws. Davidson recognizes this point. He criticizes Ducasse's interpretation of the existence of general laws with the argument: he has confused particular events with events of the same type and the application of the idea of sufficient conditions to events and also to sentences and descriptions of events. For Davidson, the singular causal statement (explanation)—to state an individual event as cause—is extensional, but the explanation by a deduction from general laws—referring to descriptions of events—is intensional.

A theory of singular causal explanations has to give us an answer to the following questions:

First, an acceptable theory of singular causal explanation ought to make it clear (that is, identify the structure feature in virtue of which) such explanations explain and it presumably must do this by setting such explanations within the context of a *general theory of why-explanations*.... Second, the feature in virtue of which singular causal explanations explain must satisfy *certain epistemological requirements*. Users of singular causal explanations must be able to recognize and appreciate these features and to readily ascertain whether preferred explanations provide them. Third, an acceptable theory of singular causal explanation must provide a basis for distinguishing *what such explanations explain from what they merely presuppose*.... Fourth, (and this is a closely related point), an adequate theory of singular causal explanation ought to reflect, if possible, the intuition that sometimes *what such an explanation explains is the occurrence of an individual event, rather than why an individual event has certain properties*. (J. Woodward 1986: 276-278, my italics.)

It is the claim of the ontology of particular, unrepeatable, dated, that is, individual events to give us an interpretation of action sentences and explain us the ascription of propositional attitudes. We have in mind that this is linked with the conceptual dualism, but that is monism between the physical and the mental. How we describe events does not take effect on the fundamental ontology of events as particulars and what they cause. It is the claim of this ontology to give us a plausibility how we ascribe actions to an agent directly. The logical form of singular causal statements and their truth-theoretical interpretation is a further ground for the ontology of events, because the individuation of events is given to us by the nexus of causal relations: "... events are identical if and only if they have exactly the same causes." (Davidson 1980 (1969): 179) Events are on this account to accept as individuals. The analysis proceeds in such a way that we "substitute for questions about identities about questions about sentences about identities" (Davidson 1980 (1974): 163).

Davidson replies to the critique of Quine:

I may also have made the mistake of thinking that if objects and events are both individuated by spatiotemporal location, we must identify events with objects. But Quine makes us see that this is a separate matter. For events and objects may be related to locations in space-time in different ways; it may be, for example, that events occur at a time in a place while objects occupy places at times. It is easy, though, to question distinction. If a wave crosses an ocean, that is an event from the point of view, so to speak, of the ocean. But the wave is also an object in its own right, keeping to a general shape while rapidly exchanging waters. Examples like this are easy to multiply.... These difficulties in deciding between objects and events are, however, generated by identifying space-time content with space-time content. Grammar allows no such confusion.... Occupying the same portion of space-time, event and object differ. One is an object which remains the same object through changes, the other a change in an object or objects. Spatiotemporal areas do not distinguish them, but our predicates, our basic grammar, our ways of sorting do. Given my interest in the metaphysics implicit in our language, this is a distinction I do not want to give up. (Davidson 1985a: 176)

Philosophers may argue that the criteria of the individuations of identity-sentences where the terms refer to events are far from clear. But it is more obvious that the criteria are given when the sentences are true.

The theory of primary reasons and the identity thesis between the acts A-A' is a further ground for the ontology of events. We redescribe and explain action without leaving the framework of the ontological interpretation of logical form. Actions as intentional body movements are individual events that are different from other events in a particular type of explanation: the explanatory redescription by primary reasons. The ontology of individual events also claims to explain what actions are and how we fit such events in a causal ordered world. The step from the theory of interpretation to the theory of action does not compel us to change our ontology. Actions are events and as events part of the world. Such events are not less real than other matters, but we redescribe them under certain features as intentional, willing, purposeful, deliberate and so on. This shows us again how the mental, physical and the social are connected in the unified theory.

Part II
Primary Reasons, Body Movements and Actions

4. The Logical-Connection Argument

Only then do we understand Davidson's theory of primary reasons, primitive actions, the semantic analysis of sentences on propositional attitudes to an appropriate degree if we bring into play the background theories against which he has argued.

1. The question "How do we describe action?" was answered by the so-called "two language" argument, that is, a reply of the logical (conceptual) connection argument was given by an anti-Humean answer. This problem was put in the context of a further question:

Are reasons for actions—like beliefs, motives, intentions, or wills—causes?

The word *because* in sentences like "...did ...because..." is interpreted as logical (not causal), causal or in a particular way logical and causal. G. Ryle (1949), Anscombe (1957), R.S. Peters (1958), H.L.A. Hart, A.M. Honore (1959), A.I. Melden (1960, 1961), N. Malcolm, C. Taylor (1964), G.H. Wright (1971), Strawson and others have argued that the explanations by reasons and a causal explanation are logically different accounts in nature. There is a logical (conceptual) relationship between an agent's propositional attitudes to do something *A* and his *A*-doing. Danto (1973), Davidson (1980 (1963)), A.C. MacIntyre (1962), A.J. Ayer (1964), S.E. Toulmin and others reject this, and they bring the explanation with reasons closer to a modified causal explanation. The Elster-Davidson Version (J. Elster 1985) and Mele's proposal (1992) are mixed accounts between both (on the Elster-Davidson Version, R. Bhargava 1992: 134-141, on the two different ways (logical and causal relations) in which belief-desire pairs are related to actions, see Davidson 2004 (1982): 173). Wright's theory of action is a version of a more mixed account, a so-called Verstehens-account: explaining actions by reasons is an understanding of action (1994). But for him, desires and needs have also a causal effect on our behavior.

It was the result of these debates that we have to distinguish between the explanation of actions and of other *human events* like, for example, "to flush", "to fluster", "to be confused", *states* like, for example, "to be stupid", *expectations* like, for example," to hold a promise", *feelings* like, for example, "fear", "pleasure", *faults*, and *omissions*. It is Davidson's merit in particular that he has shown the following: the fact that we begin the explanation of action from its redescription does not imply a decision about the type of explanation. Therefore, the explanatory situation within which we solve the task of explanatory redescription does not fix that the relation between reasons and action is only logical (conceptual) and not causal. At the same time he gives a particular answer to the logical relationship between the explained propositional attitudes and the description of actions. Following D. S. Shwayder (1965), the distinction between reasons and the knowledge of reasons is significant. Reasons alone explain nothing, but the knowledge of reasons has an explanatory force.

Yet: are actions always caused by reasons?

The question "Why do you go to the station?" could be answered by "Just for fun". In such cases we have no further reasons for the explanation of a given behavior.

A specific question of a semantic analysis of the description of actions was introduced with the so-called "accordion-effect" (Austin, J. Feinberg). It means that an action can "be squeezed down to a minimum" or "else stretched out" like the musical instrument. "Because of the accordion effect we can usually replace any ascription to a person of causal responsibility by an ascription of agency or authorship" (Feinberg 1968: 106), but this property is only a feature of description of actions and not of actions themselves. The description of action further leads us to the question:

How does an interpreter identify intentions?

The accordion-effect gives us no answer whether the action we ascribe was done intentionally.

Are actions and intentions items that differ *really* or *logically*?

How can we explain that the same movement of my hand has different actions and occasions as consequences?

The latter question leads us to the distinctions of act-constitutive principles act-generation (Goldman).

2. Hart has argued in his classic article *The Ascription of Responsibility and Rights* (1949: 132-45) that we do *not* use the description of actions descriptively, but ascriptively. The account is well known under the name "ascriptivism" (see also P. T. Geach 1960: 221-5, on critiques of the logical-connection argument, F. Stoutland 1970). It is the aim of Davidson's analysis of sentences on propositional attitudes to show on the contrary that the individuation of actions is a matter of an attributive ascription, such is, the agent has certain features we ascribe. Yet, this is caused by the ontological and analytical question of analysis of descrip-

tion of action in different vernaculars with the example of reference of singular terms. Following Davidson, the ascription of action is to justify together with the individuation of propositional attitudes by distal stimuli in the triangulation. In this respect the ascription of actions leads us back to *RI* and its ontology, because the questions:

"What are actions?" "Are actions mental causes, physical effects, or a connection between both?" "How do actions differ from other events?" "How do we individuate actions?"

are motivated by an introduction of an ontological commitment in the theory of language: the world consists of events as particulars, they are not to reduce.

3. There are two more questions we must ask:

Are actions body movements? Are they identical with the normal physiological process? And which role do intentional body movements play for the analysis of actions?

The answer to this question is of particular significance because thereby we assign ontological decisions in the theory of language and action. This is just the case if we are concerned to analyze the reference to descriptions of action along the *individuation* of acts.

This is the hard core of Davidson's analysis of the logical form of action sentences because of the claim to show how we immediately instantiate an action to an agent. The criterion of agency is intentional but the expression of agency itself is *extensional*. Actions are intentional body movements, and the relation between the agent and the event that is performed is not dependent on the descriptions of the items. His concept of primitive action is a critique of Danto's distinctions between basic and non-basic actions and his causal interpretation of the act-pair *A-A'*.

4. For the theory of action, the presupposed concept of events is of main importance. There are three views from which the problem of act individuation can be answered: the *coarse-grained* view (Davidson), the *fine-grained* view (Goldman) and the *componential* view (Thalberg). I have discussed these views in my writings on analytical theory of action between 1975-80 (see also Mele 2003: 64-67).

Davidson has paradigmatically introduced the leading question of the individuation of action. "Peter flips the switch, turns on the light, and illuminates the room."

How many acts have been carried out?

In Davidson's view, there is only *one* action, but in our example three descriptions are given. This follows from the coarse-grained individuation of actions. The analysis of logical form of action sentences and the interpretation of singular causal statements claim to commit us to the ontology of coarse-grained events, and it is at the same time connected with his rejection of the logical connection argument. His conception of primary reasons gives us an answer to the question: what does a causal explanation of action mean? For his theory of belief and meaning, the concept of reason plays a particular role: pro attitudes and beliefs are the causes of action; they have causal power. The logical relation is only a matter of redescription of behavior in the light of the rationality of attitudes, and this is not relative to individual agents.

Goldman, in difference to the coarse-grained view, has a fine-grained view. The alternative to a coarse-grained individuation of action token is that in our example "Peter" has performed *three* acts with distinct act-properties. Another view is Thalberg's componential view arguing that the action of "Peter" has various components like, for example, moving his arm, flipping the switch, and so on. I will discuss both proposals in continuation.

To sum up, we have to distinguish three accounts of explanatory redescriptions of behavior as a *causal* relationship of belief-desire pairs and actions, the *logical* (conceptual) connection argument, and a *mixed* version that takes into play both logical *and* causal considerations (see also Bhargava 1992: 134-141). The problem is whether there is something like a theory of action and whether descriptions of action are to analyse as singular terms in principle. In order to grasp Davidson's syncategorematic account of intention it is instructive to recall the background of his theory. (Preyer 2011b, on the reference of action description 33-52, on explaining action 52-89, on practical thinking 91-108)

4.1. H. L. A. Hart: Ascriptivism

Hart (1949) has argued that we do not use sentences of the form "he did it" in a descriptive way, but we ascribe something by its usage. If I am obliged to do something, for example, by my father or by the law, then someone or something has obliged me to perform certain actions. On the other hand, if I am obliged to someone to do something or was obliged to do something, for example, something for a friend of mine, then I am obliged to him *by* the doing of something. It is an essential feature that there is a difference in the meaning of obligation in the two cases. The person who obliged me to do something, for example, had helped me, but the person I was obliged by did not give me any help. If someone is under an obligation, we have some evidence for a necessary obligation.

Hart makes the distinction between "being obliged" and "having" or "being under an obligation". The latter refers to legal and moral obligations. These cases are to specify within the context of institutionalized rules and expectations. Legal and moral obligations imply social obligations, like, for example, within the family, among friends and so on. In such cases there are actions that are expected, are demanded or are moral imperatives. This is the difference between "being obliged" as a legal or a moral obligation and being obliged by certain circumstances. Hart argues: moral and legal obligations to do something imply that a person is affected by "being under an obligation", but being obliged by a terrorist does not imply that. So there are two sorts of being obliged. Yet, in Hart's analysis there is no distinction between the cases "he was forced legally..." respective "he was forced by the terrorist". In that way we can explain the difference in the implication between the two cases "he was obliged legally" and "he was obliged by certain circumstances" with the instance that obliges us to something, for example, in case we use the words "forced" and "required".

The second argument for the two sorts of being obliged is to find in the strictness of the premises in both cases. The sentence "he was obliged by the terrorist" implies the premise "he did x" but with "he was obliged to do x by the contract" this is not the case. It is more obvious that the use of "obliged" is dependent on "being obliged by something". The two uses of being obliged and their application to the ascription of actions do not distinguish far enough between actions that are *undertaken* and deeds that are *done*. With the consideration of this distinction we can make a difference between the responsibility for an action and the responsibility for an action I have done.

The expressions "Peter did x" and "Peter is responsible for x" do not mean the same, because the "doing a" asks for the agent causality and the ascription of responsibility presupposes contexts, value orientations, social norms, and so on. Furthermore we have to make a distinction between obligations and commitments if we ascribe a responsibility. Another point is that we do not use action sentences in an exclusively ascriptive way, but we could use these sentences ascriptively as well as descriptively (Feinberg 1968, on Feinberg and the accordion effect, see Davidson 1980 (1971): 53-56, 57).

If we begin to describe an item of behavior in continuation as an action, our description is essentially incomplete, and it is always an uncertainty to fix the positive values of such descriptions, such is, the ends and doings are not determined under certain conditions. We are confronted with the incompleteness of such descriptions. The best principle to limit these descriptions is the propositional expression, that is, it is the case that … We describe action if we answer the question "what was done?" or "what has he done?". We ascribe actions if we have—metaphorically speaking—an action in our hand and want to know whom it is to fasten on. We use simple action sentences like "Peter laughs" only to ascribe elementary acts like in cases where we ask for the personal identity of an agent, for example, "Who was that man who laughed?". The generalized feature of the ascription of actions is that one must presuppose that the redescription of it is reasoned from the agent's point of view. We ascribe action in the context of a theory about the propositional attitudes of the agent. Many philosophers agree on that. This assumption is conform to Hart in that all ascriptions of actions are defeasible. Ascriptive sentences are not wholly theoretical or factual, but their use shows us a feature of our own discretion and estimation. We also bear in mind that all ascription has contextual features. We could ascribe to James, for example, a, b or c; whether we ascribe to James something in a justified way like, for example, "a violation in traffic" (a), or "he makes Mary angry" (b), or "he turns on the light" (c) is a matter of different factors like our knowledge, practical goal-orientations, the sort of contexts, rules and so on. (on Hart, see P. T. Geach 1960, A. R. White 1975, P. M. S. Hacker, J. Raz 1977, Preyer 1996).

But how do we answer the Hart-problem?

It is to show that we take into account that the ascription of actions is not ascriptive in nature, as Hart has assumed, but also the attribution of actions does not work generally (capt. 7.3. in this book).

4.2. A. I. Melden's Anti-Humeanism

The logical connection-argument means that there are two sorts of vocabulary (universes of discourse or systems of concepts) within which we describe events, body movements and actions. R. S. Peters has argued that it is not possible to find a set of statements to describe movements that is equivalent to such statements like "he signs the contract" (1958). He has spoken of the "logical gulf" between nature and convention.

What is the relation between the event *e* and a further event *e'* that can be described, for example, as "a muscle movement of the arm", "rising the arm" and "giving a sign"? We could not explain actions causally because there is a logical gulf. But there is a requirement to explain the relationship between the body process and its description and the action of "raising one's arm". The logical gulf means that two classes of ontological entities exist. But this is not a conclusion from the premise of the non-reducibility of descriptions of action to body processes. The concept of logical gulf implies that there is no systematic connection between a conventional act like signing a contract and a body movement like moving my hand. Another proposal is to classify body movements as dependent components of actions. This entails, also in case we accept the logical non-equivalence of statements about actions and body movement, that the two acts like, for example, moving my hand and signing the contract, can stand in a certain connection.

The priority reason of the two-language argument is not that merely our reasoning is "good" or "bad", "significant" or not, but that actions are not to explain with Hume's concept of causation, that is, causes and effects are logically independent. Our explanations are not to distinguish logically from the redescription of actions, and mental causes could not be classes of Hume-causes. The logical-connection argument introduces a significant problem, but we need to consider an answer different from the one the logical-connection argument has given. The problem is: what are beliefs and intentions, and how does the connection of both make an intentional action happen?

It is Melden's claim to show that in the relation of *A-A'* there are no congruent events. Giving a sign in traffic is the example chosen here. Signaling describes an event at a certain point of time. First of all it seems not plausible to assume that there are two events in the relation *A-A'*. If a road-user gives a sign, he raises his arm, but "raising the arm" is not the cause for giving a sign. The body movement and giving a sign are not two successive actions that we could describe as "raising one's arm" and signaling. If a road-user gives a sign, his behavior is to describe in different ways.

How does a road-user give a sign?

It is to show that the relation *A-A'* consists of two distinct tokens whose descriptions are not synonymous.

In what way does the occurrence of the two events constitute the same relation?

"I signal by raising my arm—that is how I do it, and similarly, I raise my arm by moving certain muscles in such-and-such a manner—that is how I do that." (Melden 1961: 63) The question:

How does one raise one's arm?

entails two problems: 1. The answer describes an action in a way that by the doing of A someone performs A'. 2. Whatever the relation between A-A' may be, the descriptions of A-A' are not synonymous. If someone raises his arm, he performs some action. But in the case of "I raise my arm" we do not conclude from the fact of *raising the arm* that there is an event E which would be distinct from the event *raising the arm*. Melden has argued that it is a commitment for all causal explanations to find an event E that is common and individualized in all such cases, for example, giving a sign in traffic (87; on criticism of this concept of causal explanation, see Davidson 1963: 12-14).

How do we describe "raising the arm"? What is the difference in principle between my arm rising and my raising my arm, between my muscle moving and my moving my muscles, that is, between a physical movement (happening) and an action? And how do we place the relationship between the description of the event of the movement of muscles, raising the arm, and giving a sign?

If we distinguish the movement of muscles as a cause of raising the arm, it is not clear which role the "movement" plays as a cause of "my raising my arm". The criterion for the Humean causality is that the cause is logically independent of its effect. There is a difference between a description of the rising arm as a body movement and "raising one's arm" as an action. The reference of both descriptions is not the same.

Melden introduces a tentative formulation: an action is a body movement with an inner mental event—a motive. So we have two cases here: 1. raising the arm, and 2. raising the arm and a motive. Melden identifies a circle in this definition, because the motive is already supposed: the motive is a "motive" for raising the arm. It is a fault to define action as a physical event and, at the same time, as any other congruent mental or corporal event. The reasoning of the logical-connection argument is: a motive or reason for actions cannot be any event that causes an action. The characterization "the reason is a cause for an action" is self-defeating, because the cause cannot be an action at the same time. If the motive or will were a Humean cause—this is emphasized by Melden—such a cause would, as an inner event, be logically independent of its alleged effect. Reasons for actions give us information about what an action "does", "leaves", "prevents" or what an agent "carries out", for example, a redescription of a movement of the hand toward another road-user as a warning of danger. What is done is logically or conceptually dependent on the intent that is satisfied. Giving reasons is an extensive information for us like, for example, that the agent believes that there will be a concert in the evening, he is annoyed with his wife and has decided to go out, and so on. Hume-causes could not achieve these relations. Reasons are not to connect with deeds causally but logically. In the case of a conventional signaling, for example in traffic, we establish a necessary logical connection between motives or attitudes (reason) and actions.

How is the connection to be described?

For Melden, we have to find a connection in the following way:

For our concept of an action is the concept of an action for which the agent may have a reason and a reason of the kind that relates to the social intercourse of agents. (Melden 1961: 191)

Following the logical-connection argument there are no synonymous descriptions of A-A'.

But is this a reasoning for the complete distinction of body movements and actions? Is the description of actions by finding reasons why something is done an evidence for a structural difference between body movements and actions?

The movement of my lips is a part of my laughing, and it is not necessary to order the two items as numerically different issues. My laughing entails a body movement, but it is not a result of it. There is no conclusive proof of postulating two realms or structural discrete items as ontological commitment of an ascription of actions.

Wright (1971: 92, 89-93) has reconstructed the logical-connection argument in the following way:

How do we verify that an agent has a certain intention, or how does a particular behavior show the correspondent intention of an agent?

Wright argues that the ascription of attitudes is logically dependent on the verification of the circumstances that have to be available to us so that we could ascribe attitudes. Exactly this dependency is the argument showing that attitudes cannot be Humean causes. The logical-connection argument introduces a significant problem in the theory of action:

What are beliefs and intentions, and how do we explain that the connection between both brings about an intentional action? Is there a logical or conceptual relation between such attitudes and their content? What is to conclude from the premises of practical inferences?

This leads us to the act-constitutive principles and the radical theory of agency. However, it leads us also to Davidson's answer to what this logical relation is.

5. Basic Acts

5.1. Properties of Basic Acts

The theory of primary reasons and the syncategorematic account of intentions are not only a critique of the logical-connection argument and Hart's concept of ascription. The concept of primitive actions is an objection to the distinction between basic and non-basic acts and its causal interpretation of the relation between A-A' of Danto's theory of action. It was Danto's claim to show that the components of actions consist of basic and non-basic actions. This was an innovation in the theory of action and an impetus to further clarifications of what actions are. A basic act is an action that cannot be reduced to another action. For Davidson, the two acts, such as the movement of the hand and the switching on the light, are identical. Yet, we can describe actions in different ways. The concept of agency is extensional and actions are intentional body movements. Therefore, one must object against a causal interpretation of the pairs of acts A-A' because the single items are not different in a numeric sense.

Basic actions have the following properties (Danto 1973):

1. Basic actions are to analyze without any reference to intentions.
2. Every mediated action entails a basic action as a component.
3. A basic action is a basic action only if it is not caused from outside.
4. Basic actions could be caused — concept of response.

But how do we explain their reference with the set of descriptions of actions, the class of all non-basic and basic descriptions?

Therefore, for Danto, this question of identity, the reference of descriptions, is not only to explain with an analysis of the semantic properties of these descriptions. (42-44.) He answers this question with a concept of identity, such is, an identity of basic actions with the normal physiological process = n-series. (63) It is the claim that with the assumption of identity the meaning of both expressions

1. "the raising of an arm: mDa" and
2. "what happens, if someone raises the arm"

is compatible. In a first step, Danto exemplifies the thesis of identity with the meaning of our talk on doing. (74-75.) The expression '*mDa*' means: *m* = an agent brings about *a*, for example, that his arm is raised by doing *a*, that is, by the raising of the arm. *D* is a sign for an assertion that *a*, that is, the raising of the arm is done; therefore, *a* is an event that is to redescribe as an action. In the first step, the thesis of identity is explained by the doing (74-75).

5.2. Immanent and Transeunt Causation

Danto goes back to the distinction between an immanent causation between complex types of events and an transeunt causation between compound types of events (Chisholm: 1966). The compound type of event has the form of external related, logical different events. The two leading questions to explain causation are:

1. How can we connect a basic action as an example of an immanent causation with a transeunt causation?

2. How could complex events or basic actions be an integral component of compound events and hold a relation of cause and effect?

Types of Events	Causation	Relation between Events	Interpretation
complex	immanent	internal	intensional
compound	transeunt	external	extensional

An extensional interpretation of *mDa* means: the truth-value of the expression is dependent on its parts. In difference to that, the intensional interpretation of *mDa* refers to an internal relationship between *m* and *a*. But the relationship between *mDa* and *a* is not of a logical nature. So Danto analyzes the concept of causation and the application of its results to basic actions (104-115.)

5.3. The Causal Explanation of Action

Danto has argued that the cardinal dependency of action is causal in nature, that is,

1. b is a basic action of x if and only if 1. b is an action and 2. whenever x performs b, so there is no other action a that is performed by x in the respect that b was caused by a.

2. b is no basic action of x if there are one or more actions a that were performed by x in the respect that b was caused by a'.

But how is the class of descriptions of the event b ("the arm has risen"= determinated) to connect in both descriptions, for example, m raises the arm and m's arm has risen = b? What is the descriptive meaning of doing in the expression "m causes the event b" that describes a basic action?

We grasp the direct (immediate) relationship between m and b with the doing. It describes no separate event that stands in a transeunt relation to another event. In the sentences we use for the ascription of basic actions, the descriptive meaning of doing is that m causes the event b, for example, "the arm is raised". If we give a causal analysis of ARA', it is to explain how m directly causes an event. Davidson explains this causation with primitive actions. Yet, these are no basic actions in the sense of Danto. If e and f are events (e = event, it is entailed in mDb as a complex event, for example, the throwing of a stone, f = the flexing of a triceps) and mDb is a complex event, then in this case there are two episodes, one of a transeunt and another of an immanent causation, such as, m raises his arm and b: the event that is entailed in mDb and b = determinated. The throwing of a stone (= e) causes the raising of the arm, but it does not cause the raising of the arm *itself*. The raising of the arm (= b) is caused by the flexing of a triceps (= f), but f was not caused by m raising his arm (= mDb). m causes b directly and so in b it crosses an immanent and a transeunt causation. mDb has different causes and this is not the case for b, for example, "the arm has risen" = determinate (Danto 1963: 59).

Both events are distinct if they have different causes, and they are identical if they have the same cause. This is to explain with the non-identity between mDb and b — m raises his arm in the respect of doing and m's arm has risen. A basic action is not a case of a transeunt causation, such as, b was not caused in a transeunt way if we redescribe f itself as an action. This comes to the conclusion: If b, such as, "the arm has risen"

= determinate was caused by f—"the contracting of the muscle"—, and mDf, then mDf can be a component of mDb if b, such as, the arm has risen = determinate is a basic action: basic actions have no components that are actions.

What is the relation between the event f—"the contracting of the muscle"—and b—"the arm has risen"—as a case of a transeunt causation, if mDb is a basic action?

This is the question of the relationship between m and f—"the contracting of the muscle".

5.4. The Role of the n-Series and the Concept of Identity

Danto introduces the normal physiological process = n-series to solve the problem to instantiate f to m. b is caused by n, but n is not caused by b. Therefore, the causation is effected in the lawlike relationship between mDb and n in the relevant direction as well as for b and for n. mDb happens only if b happens, therefore n is a temporally earlier event compared with b.

But how is the relationship to describe or to interpret if we predicate it to m as a mental entity? Do the two expressions "mDb causes n" and "n causes b" have a different meaning?

Danto answers these questions by the concept of identity.

If we make the assumption that a series of events begins with the event n and terminates in b, then we assert that a complex event—the basic action mDb—is identical with the n-series: therefore, there is one and the same event. The concept of identity has to solve the following problems:

1. How do we make use of the expression "to make something happen"? The answer is that we explain the use of the expression in the following way: an agent makes an event happen e in a direct way, that is, event e is the cause of something he does in so far as it is case that the cause is a part of a compound event. His action is identical with this event e: people are identical with their deeds and their body: "we are our deeds", as Danto, inspired by Nietzsche, says. I am not sure whether this is right.

2. The concept of identity claims to explain the sort of causation in the expression "to make something happen", that is, the concept covers an immanent and a transeunt causation.

3. With the concept of identity, the reference to the relevant type of event = n-series is also to explain: so the basic action is identical with the n-series.

4. All causes outside the n-series are no normal cases: a basic action is a basic action only if the action is not given having arisen from outside.

With the concept of identity, Danto has found a solution of the reference of descriptions of basic actions. The description of the n-series and basic actions are co-reference descriptions, and this is the criterion to describe basic actions with basic sentences. Basic actions and n-series have the same properties, therefore the talk of "the raising of the arm (mDb)" and "what happens if the arm is raised" are compatible. In a further step Danto explains the concept of identity with the doing: by doing b of m "the arm has risen" m causes something (= doing). A basic action is an episode of a doing: doing b can be the cause of b. Doing is an episode without any reference to something—for example, the difference between preterite and present infinitive. The compound event is sufficient to classify a body movement as a basic action. So we have a theory of basic actions with which we refer to a compound event e: on the one hand we have a doing of b and on the other hand we have a b. The pair is connected with an episode of a transeunt causation and a complex event—the basic action—is an integral component of a compound event as a relationship between cause and effect.

5.5. On Critiques

Danto's analysis of the role of the normal physiological process and a causal theory of basic actions has initiated a debate on the causal explanation of action and what elementary actions are (in particular on actions, body movements and muscle contractions with reference to Danto: Hornsby 1980, on critiques of Danto's theory of basic actions, M. Brand 1968, Davidson 1980: 56, F. Stoutland 1968 and others). Problems of prime importance were:

What is the role of the body process in the performance of actions? What is the reference of descriptions of actions? What is the causal role of elementary actions? How are acts to individuate?

Strictly speaking, the problem of the role of the physiological process, in general, is this: if someone clenches his fist, his body movement is that he closes his fingers: but a causal explanation asserts that the forearm muscle had moved before he closed his fingers. This is the problem of Danto's interpretation of the relevant direction of causation in the relationship between mDb and n—the complex event—it is the basic action "m raises his arm" and b is the event that is involved in mDb "the arm has risen"(b = determinate).

Davidson rejects the concept of causation of basic acts with the following three arguments: *firstly*,

It seems to me that this conception of actions and their consequences contains several closely related but quite fundamental confusions. It is a mistake to think that when I close the door of my own free will anyone normally causes me to do it, even myself, or that any prior or other action of mine causes me to close the door. So the *second* error is to confuse what my action of moving my hand does cause—the closing of the door—with something utterly different—my action of closing the door. And the *third* mistake, which is forced by the others, is to suppose that when I close the door by moving my hand, I perform two numerically distinct actions (as I would have to if one were needed to cause the other)." (1980 (1971): 56, my italics).

So the distinction between basic acts and mediated actions is wrong, but there are primitive actions that I simply perform. It is connected with the concept of primitive actions that *trying* to do something has no significant role in the analysis of action (60).

The assumption that in the event b ("the arm has risen") an immanent and a transeunt causation have crossed leads to a dilemma: either we deny that by the clenching of the fist a contraction of the forearm muscle is caused, or we deny the temporal priority of the cause to the effect.

In what way does the causal interpretation of ARA' confuse the act of clenching the fist with the body movement of closing the fingers?

The two episodes in the relation mDb and b that the expression "make happen" has to cover with the concept of identity can be reformulated by us in the following way:

1. m makes happen the event e, for example, the closing of the fingers at the time-point $t_{1...n}$ and therefore, it seems that he has also made happen the earlier event.

2. It seems to be true, for example, that the contracting of the forearm muscle at the time-point t_1 causes the closing of the fingers.

But these formulations do not give us a complete account of the causation in the relationship between mDb and b: we only specify with

Danto's proposal of the concept of identity: m effects to the time-point t_{n+1} an earlier event and also an event having happened simultaneously because the later event b "the arm has risen" = determinated specifies that also an earlier event was made happen.

In chapt. 7.3., in this book, I will, in difference to Danto's account, give a reclassification of the component of body movement like, for example, "clenching the fist" also as a causal factor.

6. Primary Reasons
and the Identity-Thesis

In a first step we have identified the principal problems of the logical-connection argument, of Hart's ascriptivism and Danto's causal analysis of basic acts. Now we dispose about the background of Davidson's proposal of primary reasons. The *unified theory* is a total theory of behavior. Consequently, it is a composite theory of beliefs and desires (desire is an umbrella term for any so-called conative attitude). From the analysis of the logical form of action sentences a syncategorematic account of action and event sentences follows. Therefore, the identity thesis of actions is reasoned by a logical argument. The unification of the theory of meaning and action (decision) claims by theoretical grounds to take the step to so-called explanations by redescription that explain us in difference to non-explanatory redescriptions the purpose of an action, that is, an intention. If we have settled to ascribe actions to agents directly by the logical-form analysis of action sentences, an answer must be given to the question:

What is the relationship between intentions and intentional actions?

Therefore it is not enough to ensure that the action is intentional or performed with a certain intention, it must be explained that the action was caused by that intention. The final answer to this problem is,

…for intentions depend on the belief that one can do what one intends, and this requires that one believe nothing will prevent the intended action. Thus intention would seem to have just the properties needed to make sense of the idea that a speaker has failed to go on as before" (Davidson 2001 (1992): 112).

The logical form of action sentences gives us a particular analysis of adverbial modification. An adverbially modified action sentence, such as, "Peter went into the bathroom at midnight intentionally" has the logical form: $\exists(e)$ (went (Peter, e) & (into the bathroom) & (intentionally, e)), e is the event that verifies the sentence. Following this theory, most adverbial modifications like "slowly", "intentionally", "deliberately" and so on cannot change the reference to the expressions that they modify. They are of no importance to the semantic analysis of action sentences. An agent doing something intentionally cannot be considered as a feature of his acting, but as the description of his respective action. Adverbial and attributive modifications must be analyzed on the same level. Davidson's critique of the logical-connection argument is a consequence of the analysis of logical form of action sentences and singular causal statements. The result is the theory of primary reasons. In the relation between the two acts A-A', there is only one action, that is, an event with a certain property, that we can describe in different ways: $A \equiv A'$. Hence, it is necessary to give an answer to the following question:

What is the logical relation between the description of actions and the propositional content of explained attitudes, provided that these attitudes stand in a logical relation to such descriptions, and, how can we explain actions with these attitudes?

The answer to this question is given with the primary reasons and the syncategorematic account of action sentences and intentions. They both go together. This account reduces intentions, as a mental item, to beliefs and desires. Actions are a consequence of decision-theoretical structured nets of attitudes. We have found the logical (conceptual) relation between the description of an action and the propositional attitudes, provided that such attitudes explain the performance of an action, that is, in the light of their rationality, that is, the coherence and truth of attitudes together with all things considered and all-out judgements. Such relations are to generalize and are not *only* valid for an individual agent. But, as dispositions, the attitudes themselves have a causal power. Also this conception is to understand from a conceptual (linguistic) dualism in ontology, because such explanatory redescription is found by an interpreter being interested in applying an (intentionalistic) explanatory redescription. In this conceptual way, actions go along to the mental. It is the claim that primary reasons will give us an answer to the "mysterious connection" (S. Hampshire) between reasons and actions.

It is the claim of the ontology of individual *coarse-grained events* to understand actions, their explanation, causality, and the relationship between the mental and the physical. The *unified theory* as a total theory of behavior has argued for a monistic ontology that should be compatible with an anomaly and autonomy of the mental: "The mental and the physical share ontology, but not ... classificatory concepts." (Davidson 2004 (1990): 92) The presupposed monism—the "shared ontology"—leads us to a substantial problem with this proposal in the philosophy of the mental. To make this clear, I will proceed with taking the following steps. Firstly, it will be shown how the explanation of action by primary reasons is connected with the syncategorematic account of intentions, and how we analyze the causal relations between the components of actions: pro attitudes, beliefs, and primitive actions. Primary reasons define intentional actions by their causes.

Do we, when having a causal theory of actions, at the same time have a law of behavior at hand, based on analytical considerations, where we would normally assume that it is an empirical generalization?

In this context we are faced with the problem of the right sort of *external* and *lunatic internal* causal chains. The latter has a particular significance because it makes us realize that we are black boxes for radical interpreters in principle (a). Secondly, the thesis of the anomalous monism of the mental is as follows: there are no strict laws of mental events or psycho-physical laws. This version of a monism detects the autonomy (freedom, self-rule) and anomaly (failure to fall under a law) of the mental by arguing that there is no systematic way to express a description of mental states in a physicalistic vocabulary. This argument is derived from Quine's thesis of indeterminacy of translation. In the same way it is assumed: every single mental event is a physiological event (token-identity). But from anomalous monism the problem of mental causality emerges in the elaboration of debates on Davidson's philosophy of mind. Yet, from my point of view the evidence of *RI* advises us to make a turn to a pure anomalism of the mental (b).

6.1. Pro Attitudes, Beliefs, Primitive Actions and their Causal Relations

6.1.1. A Resystematization of Explanatory Redescription by Primary Reasons

The distinction between *intention*, *intentional actions* and *intending* goes back to Anscombe. In *Actions, Reasons, and Causes* (1980 (1963)) Davidson emphasizes that intentional actions are an *acting with an intention*. Therefore the concept of intention is the basic concept. An action is performed with an intention if such doings are caused by primary reasons. In the further development of this account, intentions are equated with all-out judgement, and they are no longer the basic concept. It is to find out which role pro attitudes, beliefs (intentions) and primitive actions and their causal relations play. Yet, the question for the right way causing the upshot of acting must be answered, that is, the question for the external causal chains, and for what follows from the problem of lunatic internal causal chains for our explanation of actions.

For Davidson, our explanation of actions is an *explanation by rede-scription*, that is, we state a purpose with it, that is, an intention, and such explanations are to distinguish from explanations in natural science in principle (2004 (1987): 105, 112). We (often) identify actions by their consequences. But Davidson does not argue for an utilitarian conse-quentialism in general (2001 (1995): 41).

What does a syncategorematic account of intentions and the explana-tion of actions by primary reasons mean?

The expression 'the intention with which James went to church' has the out-ward form of a description, but, in fact, it is syncategorematic and cannot be taken as a reference to an entity, state, disposition or event. Its function in this context is to generate new descriptions of actions in terms of their reasons; ... (Davidson 1980 (1963): 8)

"The intention with which James went to church", is *no* state or does not *refer* to anything (on the modification, it is reported in Davidson 2004 (1987): 106, I discuss this in the following in this chapter). "James" is the agent of an event, if and only if there is a description of what he has done that makes a sentence true, and this sentence states that "James" did something intentionally. In accordance with this theory, the statement "James did *A* intentionally" is equivalent to the assertion that an action is caused by a sort of primary reason. These reasons are given by the ana-lysis of the word "because" in sentences with which we explain actions:

If we interpret this 'because' as implying (among other things) a causal rela-tion—and I believe we must—then in describing an action as performed with a certain intention, we have described it as an action with a certain causal history. So in identifying the action with a physical event, we must at the same time be sure that the causal history of the physical event includes events or states identi-cal with the desires and cognitive states that yield a psychological explanation of the action." (Davidson 1980 (1973): 254)

This citation is good evidence for giving the reason why the unification of the theory of meaning and action is based on an ontology of individual events.

The claim that an agent does something intentionally is to redescribe in the following way by *primary reasons*:

(*) The act of doing something intentionally is caused by primary reasons, that is, by a complex mental state. Such states are composed of

   1. pro attitudes toward an action *a* with a particular property *p* that we express in prima facie judgements, and

2. the belief that this action *a* has, under a given description, the desirable property *p*.

The antecedence (pro attitudes and beliefs) is to distinguish from the action *h* and precedes *h*. Therefore, attitudes and beliefs are candidates for causes. *h* is caused by primary reasons, and we redescribe *h* as intentional. By redescription with primary reasons we get an interpretation, that is, a new description of what someone did, that we fit into a familiar picture including agents' beliefs and other attitudes, goals, ends, principles, general character traits, virtues or vices. The description of primary reasons is not essentially connected with the individuation of actions by coarse-grained events, because we can take '*A*' as an action variable for both, the actions themselves or actions under *A*-description (Mele 2003: 71). Therefore, and in order to give a reasoning, the description of action is to specify to corse-grained events.

It is to mention that the pair of pro attitudes and beliefs explains actions only if it is connected with other beliefs, desires, assumptions and so on, and *not* if it is merely a single pair. Primary reasons are a pair of such attitudes that are stronger in confrontation with others and thereby cause the action. Such attitudes are desires and subjective probabilities: beliefs resulting in hierarchies (a transitive order) of alternative options for actions (on a response to well-known criticism of the descriptive coherence decision theory with our commonsense explanation, Davidson 2001 (1997): 126-27). The interplay between rationalization and making decisions is the key for Davidson's answer of *How is Weakness of the Will possible?* (1980 (1970)) because a weak will acts against our strongest beliefs (principle of continence). This shows how explaining actions is connected with the theory of decision: an agent is to redescribe in such a way that he fixes consequences by a matrix of preferences that taxes probabilities of such consequences, and he acts so that the results are to the highest expected benefit. Therefore choices, beliefs, desires cohere with Bayesian decision theory (consequentialism).

To Davidson, causal explanations by primary reasons are not in any conflict with our freedom to act: "...what an agent does do intentionally is what he is free to do *and* has adequate reasons for doing." (Davidson 1980 (1973): 74) The role of such beliefs can be explained by the distinction between prima facie judgements—pro attitudes—and all-out judgements. The mental states themselves are no actions or events.

The only hope for the causal analysis is to find states or events which are causal conditions of intentional actions, but which are not themselves actions or events about which the question whether the agent can perform them can intelligibly be raised. The most eligible such states or events are the beliefs and desires of an agent that *rationalize* an action, in the sense that their propositional expressions put the action in a favorable light, provide an account of the reasons the agent had in acting, and allow us to reconstruct the intention with which he acted. (72)

Therefore "To know a primary reason why someone acted as he did is to know an intention with which the action was done" (Davidson 1980 (1963): 7). Such reasons are rationalized causes and Davidson assumes that primary reasons have causal power. Yet, knowing the intention does not mean that we know all primary reasons of an agent, for example, the intention that rationalizes my slow driving on the road to Wiesbaden does not state my primary reason why I drive to this town; and from our given interest we are free to describe actions in endless ways. But a causal theory has to give us a solution of the problem that our action can be contrary to our strongest reasoning.

Examples for pro attitudes are desires, economic preferences, aesthetic evaluations, social conventions, private and public goal orientations, which reveal attitudes of an agent toward his actions. Therefore these are original mental states or dispositions, for example, the statement "James goes to church intentionally" is true just in case that his behavior is caused by the complex of pro attitudes and beliefs. Yet, the pro attitudes are not events or episodes or anything else of what "James" intends. The statement "James did *a* intentionally" is therefore equivalent to the statement "James did *a* as a result of his primary reasons *R*". James is an agent who caused an event *e* by the antecedent of a complex state. This state consists of a pro attitude toward the event *e* with a certain property and the belief that the event *e*, under a certain description *d*, has that property *e*. The pro attitude toward the event *e* and the belief directly cause such a complex state of the agent: this state—that is not an event or an action—is a primary reason. Actions are physical upshots of a mental state and merely body movements of an agent. If an agent moves his hand, he brings about an event *e* by his doing: he is an agent of this event. It is the aim to construct a *class* of events that are actions. Causation is a relation between events and not a feature of their descriptions.

If we can say, as I am urging, that a person does, as agent, whatever he does intentionally under some description, then, although the criterion of agency is, in the semantic sense, intentional, the expression of agency is itself purely extensional. The relation held between a person and an event, when the event is an action performed by the person, holds regardless of how the terms are described. Therefore, we can speak without confusion of the class of events that are actions which we cannot do with intentional actions. (Davidson 1980 (1971): 47)

Thereby our classification imposes restrictions of the object language we use for the identification and ascription of actions on us. If we make the assumption that an action is a property of an event that is just not dependent on its description, then knowing this property, for example, "to run over my neighbor", "to fall down the stairs", "to spill the coffee" and so on, we are not in the position to state that the event is an action. The analysis of the logical form of action sentences and the explanation of action by primary reasons apply to the principle of extensionality. This is a further reasoning for the ontology of events: actions are intentional body movements. These are events we distinguish from other events thereby that they are caused by primary reasons we redescribe in an intentional vocabulary. Actions themselves are to be ascribed to agents *directly*.

The theory of primary reasons is an objection of the intentionalists' proposal in the action theory (on conceptual and causal relations for redescribing the causal relevance of the mental, see Mele 1992: 21-28).

1. Knowing the intention does not mean to know the cause, and therefore the primary reasons in detail, for example, if someone knew my intention of visiting my mother's friend in hospital; one does not know whether I do my duty only, or whether I take it as a chance to buy a new suit in the shop near the hospital, and so on.

2. *Descriptions* of intended results of behavior could give us a better explanation of actions

. . . than stating that the result was intended or desired. 'It will soothe your nerves' explains why I pour you a shot as efficiently as 'I want to do something to soothe your nerves', since the first in the context of explanation implies the second; but the first does better, because, if it is true, the facts will justify my choice of action. (Davidson 1980 (1963): 8)

This leads us to the question why the assumption of a class of intentional actions is going wrong.

3. The logical-connection argument gives us no analysis of the word *because* in sentences that explain actions by attributing details about desires and beliefs to an agent:

If, as Melden claims, causal explanations are 'wholly irrelevant to the under-standing we seek' of human action then we are without an analysis of the 'be-cause' in 'He did it because...', where we go on to name a reason. (11)

We have to distinguish that there are two meanings of *because*. We dis-tinguish acting *with* a reason from acting *for* it. For the latter, beliefs and desires have a causal power. The word *because* in statements like "he did x because y" — as I have already mentioned — is interpreted in three ways: as a causal relationship, as only logical (conceptual), that is, not causal (logical connection argument), and as both logical and causal. In his critique of Melden, Davidson emphasizes the causal meaning of *be-cause*. Many commentators of Davidson's theory have overlooked that the cause that explains actions is, for him, a *rational cause*, that is, *because* is to interpret *causally* and *logically* (Davidson 2004 (1982): 173).

The logical relation is shown by the particular relationship between the redescription of actions and the content of attitudes that explain them, that is, this content is intelligible by being conceptually structured by coherence and truth. *The doctrine of the causal explanation of action is that primary reasons as causes satisfy the demand for rationality.*

The logical-connection argument has argued that the explained reasons cannot be causes for actions, because there is no logical or conceptual tie between causes and effects, and this is just to assume for explanations of action by reasons. Davidson's objection is that there is no logical and conceptual relation between reasons and actions as there isn't between causes and effects: from my preferences and beliefs, the performance of any action can neither logically nor conceptually be concluded (this is modified with respect to the desirability of the content of attitudes, Da-vidson 2004 (1982): 173). This argument is relevant to the interpretation of practical syllogism, because such syllogisms are no helpful model for evaluative reasoning (1980 (1963): 16). The idea of a causal explanation of actions by primary reasons is: we talk about such explanations without referring to statements of laws. We name laws only when we justify our statements.

In brief, laws are involved essentially in ordinary causal explanations, but not in rationalization. (1980 (1963): 15)

Yet, the explanation of primary reasons follows the logical-connection argument in two points: 1. we explain action starting from intelligible redescription, and 2. primary reasons themselves are no Humean-events or actions. However, in *Hempel on Explaining Action* (1980 (1976)) Davidson gives a slightly modified version of the role of laws for explaining actions. He integrates explanations by primary reasons into deductive nomological explanations. Such laws concerning mankind are generalizations for the ascriptions of attitudes, but they are exclusively valid for individuals, that is, they are not to apply directly to primary reasons but make them informative.

In *Agency* (1980 (1971)), it is distinguished between *intention* and *intentional actions*. The following is emphasized however: not all intentional actions can be reduced to intentions. The ascription of actions shows us a semantic opacity:

Hamlet intentionally kills the man behind the arras, but he does not intentionally kill Polonius. Yet, Polonius is the man behind the arras, and so Hamlet's killing of the man behind the arras is identical with his killing of Polonius. It is a mistake to suppose that there is a class of intentional actions: if we took this tack, we should be compelled to say that one and the same action was both intentional and not intentional. (46)

Just this "opacity" makes the solution of ascribing intentions possible by analysis of "Someone is the agent of the event", that is, the action is caused by primary reasons. The rejection of a class of intentional action is concluded from the syncategorematic account of intention and the logical form analysis of action sentences. There is a class of events that are actions, because the relations between an agent and an event of action itself is not dependent on its descriptions. The agency is *more basic* than the intention of the agent.

The agent causality (I. Thalberg) must be distinguished from the ordinary causality of events in the following way:

What distinguishes agent causation from ordinary causation is that no expansion into a tale of two events is possible, and no law lurks. By the same token, nothing is explained. Therefore, it seems unreasonable using such expressions as 'cause', 'bring about', 'make the case' to *illuminate* the relation between an agent and his act." Yet: "Causality is central to the concept of agency, but it is ordinary causality between events that is relevant, and it concerns the effects and not the causes of actions (discounting, as before, the possibility of analyzing intention in terms of causality). (Davidson 1980 (1971): 53)

It is the body movement as a sequence of primitive actions that causes the action directly. Actions are a physical upshot of a mental state and consequently mere body movements of the agent:

We must conclude, perhaps with a shock of surprise, that our primitive actions, the ones we do not do by doing something else, mere movements of the body — these are all the actions there are. We never do more than move our bodies: the rest is up to nature. (59)

The picture of an agent, comparable to Danto in this respect, is that we, as agents, are identical with our body.

The theory of primary reasons is also an objection to a causal interpretation of the relation between A-A' (Chisholm, D. Bennett, A. Kenny, R. Taylor, and others) because the intentional action and the body movement are not causally distinct items. The ordinary event-causality can be useful if we want to explain how the primitive action transfers itself to other described actions, but it does not explain the agent causation. In this sense, we have to classify some actions as primitive, because they are not standing in a causal relation to any other of the agent's actions. In this respect, it is not the case "…that if I do A by doing B my doing A and my doing B must be numerically distinct"(Davidson 1980 (1971): 57, note 16). If an event is an action, we classify it on the level of its description as primitive or intentional. But we cannot "stretch" these primitive actions — by means of the accordion effect (Austin, Feinberg) — and transfer actions to other actions, because there are no further actions but only other descriptions of these doings. Following this account, intentions are no basic concept for understanding agency.

The logical form of action sentences has shown that the concept of agency is purely extensional. In a further step, this logical argument to attribute an action to an agent directly is completed by analysis of the agent causation. There is only one action A in the relation ARA': $A{\equiv}A'$ that we can describe in different ways. That is the reason why the distinction between basic and non-basic action (Danto) is rendered invalid.

Doing something that causes a death is identical with causing a death. But there is no distinction to be made between causing the death of a person and killing him. (Davidson 1980 (1971): 58)
But what is the relation between my pointing the gun and pulling the trigger, and my shooting the victim? The natural and, I think, correct answer is that the relation is that of identity. (Davidson 1980 (1967): 109)
Excuses provide endless examples of cases where we seem compelled to talk about 'alternative descriptions of the same action' seriously, i.e., literally. But there are plenty of other contexts in which the same need presses. *Explaining* an action by giving an intention with that it is done provides new descriptions of the action: I am writing my name on a piece of paper with the intention of writing a cheque, with the intention of paying my gambling debt. List all the

different descriptions of my action. Here are a few for a start: I am writing my name. I am writing my name on a piece of paper. I am writing my name on a piece of paper with the intention of writing a cheque. I am writing the cheque. I am paying my gambling debt. It is hard to imagine how we can have a coherent theory of action unless we are allowed to say that each of these sentences is verified by the same action. Redescription may supply the motive ('I was getting my revenge'), place the action in the context of a rule ('I am castling'), give the outcome ('I killed him'), or provide evaluation ('I did the right thing'). (Davidson 1980 (1967): 110)

However, there is also an alternative analysis of the act-pairs A-A' to the identity thesis, for example, of Goldman (1970) who has found a transitive relation between the pairs of acts and who gives a reconstruction of the identity thesis on a level-generation of act-tokens.

Davidson makes the assumption that we individuate events with the principle: "... if events are identical, they consume identical stretches of time" (Davidson 1980 (1969): 177), whereby the caused effect of an action is its *end*. All primitive acts are body movements and in connection with such acts a production of body movement. Actions described in causal items must be analyzed with such elementary activities and events. This follows from the ontology of coarse-grained events that links at the same time the mental, actions and the individuation of the content of attitudes.

How do we explain the paradox that the effect of an action will happen at a later time, such as, the poisoning of water in a water pipe that would kill the inhabitants, even though their death would occur three months later?

For Davidson, this problem is not a dramatic one. If it took a long sequence of time for something to take effect, like, for example, between the poisoning of the water in a water pipe and the deaths of the inhabitants, the action of poisoning could also be unsuccessful, and other events could cause their deaths. Finding the cause of the end of an action is an empirical question; and the empirical knowledge of an agent makes his actions more or less paradox and fixes the understanding of a statement like "You have killed the inhabitants" (Davidson 1980 (1969): 177-78). In *Agency* (1980 (1971)) the identity thesis gives us an explanation of agent causality. If an event is an action, we describe it in one respect as primitive and in another as intentional. Yet, we find no answer to the question of the relationship between intentions and intentional actions, that is, a general concept explaining that an agent is caused to do something.

In *Paradoxes of Irrationality* (2004 (1982)), the distinction is made of two relations between actions and desire-belief pairs: firstly, a logical relation between the content of the attitudes and the desirability about the action, and secondly, the causal role of primary reasons. Both conditions are necessary, but not sufficient. If we interpret the word *because* in actions explained sentences like "*x* did *y* because…", the relation between reasons we name and actions is not only causal, but also *logical*. The logical relation is that the content of beliefs and desires implies the *desirability* of the action (see in particular Davidson 2004 (1982): 173, (1987): 110, on the desirability-axiom (1980) 162, 161-164).

This is a modification of the analysis of the word *because* in action explained sentences in Davidson (1980 (1963)). Yet, in this article no solution to the relation between intentions and intentional actions in principle is given. Logic cannot tell us what we have to do, but the mental is structured by logical and semantic relations, that is, the interlocking propositional attitudes with which we make behavior intelligible. The paradox of irrationality

from which no theory can entirely escape, is this: if we explain it too well, we turn it into a concealed form of rationality; while if we assign incoherence too glibly, we merely compromise our ability to diagnose irrationality by withdrawing the background or rationality needed to justified any diagnosis at all. (Davidson 2004 (1982): 184).

In *How is Weakness of the Will possible* (1980 (1970)) the principle of continence is introduced: perform the action judged best on the basis of all available relevant reasons (Davidson 1980 (1970): 41). Such judgements are formed by all things considered judgements, that is, prima facie judgements in respect to all relevant properties of the action known by the agent. Prima facie judgements are "judgements that actions are desirable in so far as they have a certain attribute." (1980 (1978): 98). All considered judgements are conditional because their content is: it would be best to do y, or better to do y than x. Therefore, practical thinking is to form a decision from all things considered judgements. But it is an illusion that such thinking leads to an action as a consequence from our deliberation as such. Practical thinking does not take any effect in our acting by itself. It is dependent on the strength of our desire of the flesh, customs, training, the disposition to listen to the voice of reasoning, and so on. Incontinent actions are an error in a set of the most part true belief. Single beliefs and actions as such are not to evaluate as irrational. The judgement "dogs can fly" as such is irrational only in view of the background of our knowledge about this animal. Therefore, the feature of irrationality of an action is shown if an interpreter takes into play the background of other beliefs and actions of the speaker under study. Davidson calls the sum of his relevant principles, opinions, attitudes, and desires itself (also) a reason (inclusive reasons). There are reasons to do weak-willed actions, and the agent's failure is not his unconditional judgement: but such reasons are not the best ones the agent may have. He does not act in conformity with an all things considered judgement. (on the problem of a right characterization of akratic action Mele 2003: 76-79)

What is it that stops the conditional judgements?

This leads to the concept of forming an intention as an unconditional judgement.

In *Intending* (1980 (1978)), *pure intending* in difference to intentions and intentional actions is the foundation for our explaining of action. It shows us how intending and intentional actions are connected. This is a modification of his earlier account of *acting with an intention* (Davidson 1980 (1963)). Pure intending is a kind of intending that occurs without practical reasoning, action, or consequences. It is possible that I intend to go to the movies this evening, but I have not decided to do it, deliberated about it, formed an intention, and so on. But it might happen that, despite my intention, I do not do so nor even try to do so. Intending of this kind is a problem if we claim to analyze the concept of intention without mysterious acts of the will or other sorts of causation that are not usual in science. It seems that pure intending is a particular case of unfulfilled intentions, but the subject is intending in general, that is, "intending abstracted from a context which may include any degree of deliberation and any degree of success in execution" (Davidson 1980 (1978): 89), that is, we have to abstract something to grasp what intending is.

How is the relation between pure intending, intentions and intentional actions to analyze?

To intend performing an action is, on my account, holding that it is desirable to perform an action of a certain sort in the light of what one believes is and will be the case. But, if one believes no such action is possible, there can be no judgement that such an action consistent with one's belief is desirable. There can be no such intention. (100-01).

But forming an intention does not mean anything in itself. Therefore, a performative theory of intending is not argued for. "Forming an intention may be an action but it is not a performance and having an intention is not generally the aftermath of one." (90).

To answer the question of the relationship among intending, intentions and intentional actions, Davidson introduces—in contrast to prima facie judgements—so-called all-out or unconditional judgements like "this action is desirable". Prima facie judgements cannot be connected directly to actions because: "We can hardly expect to learn whether an action ought to be performed simply from the fact that it is both prima facie right and prima facie wrong." (37) Therefore, an *all-out judgement* is to introduce by which we decide on the desirable property of an action as a sufficient reason to do something or not.

For a judgement that something I think I can do, and that I think I see my way clear to doing, a judgement that such an action is desirable not only for one or another reason but in the light of all my reasons; a judgement like this is not a mere wish. It *is* an intention. (This is not to deny that there are borderline cases.). (101)

Pure intending is a sub-class of all-out judgements that are directed to future actions built from the beliefs of an agent. Pure intending means nothing else but: an intention is an all-out judgement. That is concluded from an all things considered judgement, that is, the action has all relevant and desirable properties (principle of continence). Such judgements are directly connected with intentional actions. In this *new* version of primary reasons they possess a conative feature therefore, but they have no representational inner objects. Wishes, desires, principles, felt duties and so on are reasons and also intentions for actions we express by prima facie judgements. The relation between an intention and an intentional action cannot be connected with prima facie judgements, because the desirable property does not make an action reasonable. The problem is that pure intending is not an action that is a good or desirable one. It is a judgement with respect to the desirability of particular actions, and such actions are generally judged whether they have the desirable property or not. Yet, it is not the case that these judgements lead to a reasonable action. If we have accepted pure intending, we could also allow that an intention of the same sort is present at the same time when the intentional action is done. We find a plausible explanation of intending that is in harmony with intentional action by the introduction of a *new* element for the analysis of intentional actions. It is the all-out judgement and the belief that the judgement is seen about future affairs. The judgement takes into play all my relevant reasons: it "*is* the intention" (101). All-out judgements that stop conditional judgements are "practical only in the subject, not in its issue" (Davidson 1980 (1970): 39). But this does not exclude that the action done was a weak-willed one because the agent has not enough virtue. Davidson has reaffirmed his proposal of practical thinking and incontinence:

I am committed to the view that an agent is incontinent only if he fails to reason from a conditional 'all things considered judgement' that a certain course of action is best to the unconditional conclusion that course of action is best. (Davidson 1985b: 206, see also Mele 2003: 77-79)

The problem here is that Davidson has noted how people make the virtue of continence their own and he thinks that such behavior is not any more difficult than being brave. (Davidson 1970 (1980: 41)

6.1.2. Davidson's Version of the Desire and Belief-Thesis

Humeanism was a dominant tradition criticized by moral realism. The problem for Humeans is: Are actions only motivated by desires in principle?

A Humean theory of motivation is:

The dogma from philosophical psychology is that any complete specification of even a prima facie reason for action must make reference to the potential agent's desires or possible desires. The idea, crudely, is that even any prima facie reason for doing something will make reference, in the antecedent of a conditional, to the potential agent's actual or possible desires — 'if you desire that...', then, prima facie, you have a reason to make it the case that...'. Such a reason becomes the potential agent's own reason, a motivating reason for him, if he has, and recognizes himself to have, the desire specified in the antecedent of the conditional. If, then, the agent performs the appropriate action, and does so for that reason, then he does so because he has, and recognizes himself to have, that desire. It is just that the prima facie motivating reason was, in the circumstances (including his other desires), a sufficient reason for acting; it sufficed for action. (Platts 1980: 73)

For Hume, our reasoning itself is unable to motivate our actions in essence. It can cause our actions only indirectly. Our motivation to do anything is only caused by desire (a passion) as a necessary condition. He insists on the general distinction between desires and beliefs as reasons and intentions or other attitudes as motives. For this account, descriptions of actions show us desires that are of original existence. In the case of conflicting desires, the stronger desire is going to win and causes the action. But if someone brings about something, we presuppose that he has also beliefs about how he might put his desire into effect. Desires take effect in our actions only if they instruct the causation to our deliberation about the performance of acts. Conventionally we name this deliberation that ends in a decision *practical thinking.* I think that a decision is always founded on an estimation of a situation and is required by a solution of its inherent requirements. We can induce to do something by beliefs and desires.

For Davidson, primary reasons have causal power. His explanation of actions by primary reasons is not a Humeanism. The desirability of the semantic content of beliefs and desires rationalizing the action is a modification of the Humean view. There is no doubt that, for him, Hume's theory is not right.

According to Hume, 'reason is, and ought only to be the slave of the passions'. By this he seems to have meant that the passions (desires) supply the force that moves us to act, while reason (belief) merely directs this force. I doubt that desire can be distinguished from belief in this way; belief and desire seem equally to be causal conditions of action. But there is a sense in which desire can be said to be more basic conceptually. Desire is more basic in that if we know enough about a person's desire, we can work out what he believes, while the reverse does not hold. (Davidson 2004 (1984): 26)

For Davidson's concept of desire, no simple non-relative (undirected) desire works basically. A desire is a fundamental relation between *an agent and two alternatives of which one is stronger than the other* (26). The key to the understanding of the causal power of primary reasons is the distinction between prima facie judgements and unrestricted ones.

What role do pro attitudes play for the causal explanation of action?

The suggestion is made that belief alone is often adequate to spark off an action. Thus, someone may perform a disagreeable task simply because he promised to, while finding nothing desirable or attractive about it. It is true that in explaining an action there is usually no need to mention both the belief and the pro-attitude. If it is asked why someone lowered his foot, the answer may be that he believed that by putting his foot down he would crush a snail; if this is the answer, it is obviously assumed that he wanted to crush the snail. But in the same way one could mention only the desire; the belief would then be obvious. A more important issue is involved, for to deny the need for a pro-attitude in the aetiology of action is to lose an important explanatory aid. If a person is constituted in such a way that, if he believes that by action in a certain way he will crush a snail then he has a tendency to act in that way, then in this respect he differs from most other people, and this difference will help explain why he acts as he does. The special fact about how he is constituted is one of his causal powers, a disposition to act under specified conditions in specific ways. Such a disposition is what I mean by a pro-attitude.

Intentional actions are, then, by their most common descriptions seen as sandwiched between cause and effect. If we know that someone intentionally crushed a snail, we know some action of his was caused by a desire to crush a snail, and a belief that by performing the action he would promote the crushing of a snail; and we also know that the action so caused itself caused a snail to be crushed. (Davidson 2004 (1987: 107-08)

We see that, for Davidson, desires and beliefs have causal power and the causation of actions is *obvious* and *directly* noticeable. Davidson emphasizes that for our explanation of action we cannot avoid taking into account that the semantic contents of the beliefs and desires that rationalize actions "imply the desirability of the action as seen by the agent" (43). But desirability seen by the agent is not compelling Bayesian, I think, if we introduce desire of second, third order and so on. It may be there are some basic desires. But this is an empirical psychological question. (On desires of higher order in continuation and also modifications of H. Frankfurt, see Nida-Rümelin 2005: 79-87, on a critique of the Humean standard-theory Nida-Rümelin 2001: 21-38)

In sum: Humeans give no answer to the question:

Why is a desire necessary for an intentional action?

Conditionalization is surely no justification of the power of desire only. Contrary to Hume, my assumption is that our deciding and intending are caused only by the requirements of a given situation. Reasons can motivate our actions. Intentional actions may be projected by the system of attitudes and the complex of desire, but they are only born by *decisions*.

6.1.3. On Modifications

With this proposal, Davidson has modified his concept of primary reasons in *Action, Reasons, and Causes* (1980 (1963)). These refer to the following issues:

1. *The meaning of because and the knowledge of laws explaining actions:* (a) In Davidson (1980 (1963)) he has argued that the word *because* in action-explaining sentences is to interpret causally: primary reasons are causes. Yet, this is modified in Davidson (2004 (1974): 173): the belief-desire pair gives us the reasons to explain action also by the logical relation to the content of attitudes implying that something is valuable or desirable to do, and reasons cause the occurrence of the action. There-

fore "because" is to interpret causally and logically. (b) Laws on mankind are a general knowledge that makes our explanatory redescription informative, and thereby we fit the explanation by primary reasons into a larger scheme of scientific explanation. Such knowledge is helpful to ascribe attitudes, beliefs, and traits, but it is not directly connected with primary reasons and is exclusively valid for individuals.

2. *The desirability of the semantic content:* Stating that the action was done intentionally by the redescription of actions by primary reasons does *not* allow the conclusion that the action is simply desirable to perform. We can only deduce that the action has such a property. This helps us to ascribe the intention that has caused the action by primary reasons. But the reasons we take into account when we explain actions are not constituted by all of the agent's reasons. Therefore, our explanatory redescription does *not* show his actual reasoning. An action may be prima facie right or wrong. From this fact we cannot conclude that the action ought to be performed. But it is a requirement that reason-explanation takes into account the redescription of belief and desire by its semantic content that implies the desirability of the action from the agent's point of view.

3. *The syncategorematic account:* Davidson (1980 (1963)) first assumed that the syncategorematic account of intentions is: intending — the intention by which something is done — is no state and does not refer to anything. He changes that, because intending can occur before the intentional action is factually carried out, and an intending action may never be performed (Davidson 2004 (1987): 106). From his point of view, intentions are all-out judgements as the key element to explaining the relation among pure intending, intentions and intentional actions, but they are *no* part of an action. This explains us why his earlier account of "acting with the intention" is to modify (Davidson 1980 (1963)). From my point of view, this is in harmony with the syncategorematic account of actions sentences and intentions, because actions are coarse-grained events that we redescribe in different respects, and all-out judgements assimilate intentions to beliefs. The belief-desire explanation of action is not given up.

4. *The unrestricted judgements:* We may equate an action with a conclusion of practical inferences, and this means that an action is born by an all-out judgement. This causes us to do the specific action. In the first proposal of primary reasons in *Actions, Reasons, and Causes* (1980 (1963), it was not clear *how* intending and intentional actions can be

connected. It was assumed that intentional actions are caused by primary reasons as intentions, because something was done intentionally under a certain description (see, on this modification, Davidson 1980 (1978): 98-99, 2004 (1987): 106). This is answered by the concept of unrestricted judgements.

5. *The causes of actions*: If we express the manner in which beliefs and desires cause an action in a practical syllogism, we can *never* exclude that this action could be caused in a way differing from what was assumed. This leads us to the problem of the right external causal chains and the lunatic internal causal chains. I will discuss this later. Therefore, it is not to recognize in particular *how* attitudes cause actions that we redescribe by primary reasons (Davidson 1980 (1973): 79). But normally we identify most actions by their consequences.

For this account, the difference between intended or non-intended effects of action is *only* concerned with the description of the upshots as in the case of torpedoing the Bismarck instead of the Tirpitz where it refers to a description of the result of an action as not being intentional. The analysis of intending is coherent with acting with an intention—the unconditional beliefs are equal to an intention—but the prior intention is not the basic concept. A present intention is like an "interim report", that is, "…given what I now know and believe, here is my judgement of what kind of action is desirable" (100).

6. *The power of practical inferences:* To sum up, it is to emphasize that the explanatory redescription is to give in the third person. It is a part of an explanatory strategy taking off from *RI*. From prima facie judgements one cannot conclude whether an action ought to be performed or whether it oughtn't. Our practical reasoning does not lead to a forced conclusion to do something or not to do it. Therefore, actions are *not* to systemize by practical inferences in general, because there are no premises to deduct a right action. But if we would challenge inferences between prima facie judgements and all-out judgements in general, our practical thinking would be a mere illusion (Stoecker has analyzed this problem in particular, 1994: 313- 338). Davidson solves this problem by a comparison with our probabilistic reasoning (2004 (1981): 154-165). A coherent theory of practical reasoning has to explain why we cannot "*detach* conclusions about what is desirable (or better) or obligatory from the principles that lend those conclusions color" (Davidson 1980 (1970): 37). It is to argue: the solution is that our practical reasoning often arrives at unconditional judgements that are practical not only

in their subjects (39), but also in the strength of their motivation. And the last is just a modification of Davidson's theory, because for him the correct theory of practical reasoning shows that practical thinking is an epiphenomenon: it is a matter of its subject only, not of its issue.

It is to be emphasized that, for the theory of belief and meaning, the concept of reason is of prime importance. If we explained actions by beliefs—but also desires—, we would make the assumption that the agent to whom we ascribe such beliefs has a reason to fulfil his beliefs also. Such beliefs are not restricted to an individual agent. Primary reasons that consist of pro attitudes expressed in prima facie judgements and unconditional beliefs are causes of actions. But a causal explanation of reasons must also satisfy the demand for rationality, that is, the description of action has to clarify the rationality of the content of beliefs. This is the difference to non-explanatory redescriptions. Intentional actions are performed by reasons, and the agent has an answer to the question: why have you done that? It is usual to distinguish three sorts of reasons: *cognitive* reasons like beliefs, *conative* reasons like values, goals and orientations, and *artificial* reasons like competencies of different sorts and professional experiences. The causation of an action, in connection with our intentions and pro or con attitudes, is the *decisive* factor of beliefs. Yet, it is to emphasize that there is no absolute principle of evaluating our reasons: "Principles, or reasons for acting, are irreducibly multiple" (34; on the plurality of good reasons see J. Nida-Rümelin 2000). Therefore, there is no absolute reasoning. The redescription of actions and their explanations by primary reasons leads us back to *RI* and the principle of charity, because the task of interpretation is to redescribe linguistic behavior, not only as saying that ... but also as a doing (on the connection of the theory of interpretation, propositional attitudes and the causal explanation by primary reasons, Heil 1996). Charity as the constraint of *RI* as a bridge to unify the theory of interpretation and decision leads to the problem in general, whether this a priori principle of charity is a guarantee for a successful interpretation and the ascription of attitude.

The result of Davidson's theory of action is: in order to understand an action with an intention we require *pro attitudes*, *beliefs* and the *primitive action* itself. The analysis of the causal relations of these components has to be added to it. Davidson has argued that, if an ontological reduction is given at our disposal—the ontic decision of individual events—, it "is enough to answer many puzzles about the relation between the mind and the body, and to explain the possibility of autonomous action in the world of causality." (Davidson 1980 (1978): 88). *From my point of view, the problem of this account is that the concept of primitive actions as mere body movements is reasoned by the ontological commitments of individual events: the coarse-grained concept of events is essential for his theory of action.*

6.1.4. The Law of Behavior as to be Concluded from Analytical Considerations

It is the claim that by analytical considerations the causal theory of intentional actions should give us a law of behavior, a law—we would normally assume—that is a result of an empirical generalization (Davidson 1980 (1973): 76; on the exposition: 76-81).

These things, then, stand together: a law stating conditions under that agents perform intentional actions; an analysis of freedom to act that makes it a causal power; and a causal analysis of intentional action. They stand together, or they fall together. In my opinion they coincide if we want explicit, non-question begging analyses, or laws without generous caveats and ceteris paribus clauses. (76)

Nevertheless, this account is a problematic one for Davidson also because we cannot use it to find a solution of the problem of ascribing attitudes. This is really a matter of an explanatory role of such laws of behavior in their relation to the explanation by primary reasons.

Why are such analytical defined laws of behavior falsified by the evidence of *RI*?

1. The central problem is:

How does the causal condition of intentional action provide us with an empirical law of prognosticating behavior?

This law of causality would not mention any concepts of causality. The use of causal concepts is a "cloak for ignorance". In ordinary life we normally use rules of thumb for the prediction of events and the explanation of action, because we do not know any sufficient and exact law. If we had such laws, we would often not have the knowledge of the particular events from whose descriptions we conclude such laws.

If we grasped the antecedent's condition of the attribution of propositional attitudes with physical and behavioral concepts, the empirical character of this law would be clear. Yet, this is not successful if we accept the anomalous monism of the mental, a radical externalism of the individuation of propositional attitudes, and the evidence of *RI* holding a sentence true.

2. The ascription of propositional attitudes by oblique or direct considerations of empirical laws, the way we take laws into account by explained reasons, has individual agents as its explanandum only. Such laws do not improve our explanations by primary reasons. The explanation of actions also requires a general knowledge of the agent, because a single action in itself is not evidence enough to decide whether it is right to ascribe any attitude. Therefore, a general knowledge is informative to our explanations of actions. It tells us something about permanent preferences and beliefs, but we do not apply it in explaining primary reasons (Davidson 1980 (1976): 273-74). We may argue that such general knowledge consists of assumptions to make our behavior comprehensible, but we cannot conclude anything about the primary reasons, in particular why, for example, "James" makes a promise to his colleague; maybe he wants to curry favor with him.

3. There is an open question however:

What gives an explanation by primary reasons its empirical thrust?

For Davidson, the explanatory power of primary reasons is due to the ascription of attitudes and preferences and is not given from the axioms of decision theory or from rationality as a human trait, as Hempel has argued (1980 (1976): 266-67, 273-74; on rational patterns of preferences: 268-69). However, if we connected general laws of behavior with the explanation by primary reasons, Davidson's answer would lead us to the problem of making behavior intelligible in principle. There is a conflict between the two points of view: grasping the action from the inside and describing it from the outside. Every description of action from the outside as a happening seems to ignore the *performance* of actions (T. Nagel 1986, on Nagel see Hornsby 1993). This problem leads us to the role of decision from which our doings are born and also to our responsibility for actions. Yet, the perspective from the inside is taken into account by *RI,* because every ascription of attitudes has to ensue from the belief system of the agent under study. If this is right, all mental events (states), the network of propositional attitudes, are to be explained in a frame of reference that has no echo in physical laws.

Such accounts of intentional behavior (the explanation by primary reasons) operate in a conceptual framework removed from the direct reach of a physical law by describing both cause and effect, reason and action, as aspects of a portrait of a human agent. (Davidson 1980 (1970): 225)

Possibly we may get explanations for single mental events from natural science insofar as we know the particular identities (225), but natural science itself cannot explain such states as a *class*. Precisely this matter is clarified by the anomalous monism of the mental. It is an essential feature of the conceptual framework within which we ascribe attitudes that we cannot *detach* its exemplification from the framework itself.

6.1.5. Anomalous External and Lunatic Internal Causal Chains

Now, how do we answer the question of the right way of causation, insofar as we explain actions by primary reasons?

For the explanation by primary reasons the *because* in "…he did it because…" leads us to the concept of causality. In principle, it cannot be excluded that the causal chains show an anomaly. An agent may have pro or con attitudes and beliefs that rationalize and cause his action without which we attribute the described action as intentional. Such cases are anomalous *external causal* chains like in the example of the man who wants to kill someone by shooting him, misses the victim, but the shot stampedes a herd of wild pigs that trample him to death (the example goes back to D. Bennett 1965). This anomalous causal chain leads to the question of the responsibility of the deed. If the "wild pigs" trample the victim to death, we would not ascribe to the marksman that he had killed someone intentionally. Another case that is connected with this example are *lunatic internal* causal chains like the well-known example of the climber (Davidson 1980 (1973): 78-79). The example is:

A climber might want to rid himself off the weight and danger of holding another man on a rope, and he might know that by loosening his hold on the rope, he could rid himself of the weight and danger. This way, this belief and wish might unnerve him to cause him to loosen his hold, and yet, it might be the case that he never chose to loosen his hold, nor did he do it intentionally. I think that it will not help to add that the belief and the wish must be combined to cause him wanting to loosen his hold, for there will remain the two questions of how the belief and the wish caused the second wish, and how wanting to loosen his hold caused him to loosen his hold. (79)

Lunatic internal causal chains, such as the example of the climber, show us that the desired effects are not only caused by the intended effect we redescribe by primary reasons. In the example of the herd of wild pigs that trample the victim to death we may ask whether the marksman has killed the victim intentionally or not. In doing so, we are asking for the right causal chain at the same time. From lunatic internal causal chains arises another problem in principle. It shows that if the primary reasons have caused the actions in the right way, such actions could also be caused in a different way. Therefore, Davidson concludes that we could not extract in particular cases how attitudes factually have caused actions in order to redescribe actions as rationalized by primary reasons: we are black boxes, and this cannot be smoothed out (to solve this problem, Wright makes the distinction between internal reasons (states) as a part of the motivational background of agents and their effective reasons, 1994, 148-49).

This leads us to the following question:

How do we grasp the relationship between intentional and non-intentional effects of action?

The identity thesis states that there is only one action in the relation between A-A' that could have different effects and consequences. These are no parts of action, but there is only *one* deed we redescribe in different ways.

The analysis of the concept of an action comes, then, if I am right, in two stages, the first bringing in intention directly, and the second extending the concept to action in the first sense, redescribed in terms of unintended consequences or other unintended characteristics. (Davidson 1980 (1973): 71)

6.1.6. Is the Syncategorematic Account of Intentions to Generalize?

Yet: how far can the expression "x makes happen y" be interpreted in general as "x is the agent of the event" in the sense of Davidson's syncategorematic account of intentions?

Davidson's theory of action argues: a person who moves his hand brings about a movement, he is the agent of the event. Hence, someone is the agent of an event if there is a description of his doing that makes the sentence "true", saying that it was an intentional action. The statement "James brings about something" has two different readings:

1. "James" does something a that causes c or
2. "James" is the agent.

"x brings about c" usually means: x does something a that brings about c, such as, he pours gas onto the ground, lights it with the result: (that) there is a fire. The second interpretation refers to Davidson's theory because, in case someone did something that caused the fire—in correspondence with the accordion-effect (Austin, Feinberg)—we would describe the doing as an act of making a fire. But the ordinary use of the expression does not mean: x is the agent in the sense of Davidson's view, because with the expression we ascribe intentions. For Davidson, this is not the case. Intentions are no sufficient conditions of any ascription of action because g, the action x, for example, the spilling of the coffee, may be the case if non-p, for example, "James" does not have the intention of doing it.

Yet, it is certainly not absurd to explicate the expression "x brings about c" in Davidson's view. In this case, explication means finding a technical equivalence for a vernacular talk. If we interpreted the expression this way, we could ask the question to this account: how do we ascribe propositional attitudes with these expressions? The ascription of attitudes has to be handled on this basis: normally we use the expression "x brings about c", in the respect of doing c, to ascribe intentions. If a speaker uttered in a given situation s "James did x with the intention to do a", we interpreted the expression in such a way that, by using his words, the speaker s refers to the same state that conventionally corresponds to "I want to (shall) do a". But "doing something wilfully" is the case only if I do it intentionally. When interpreting the utterance "I want to (shall) do something, now" we interpret the word "want to" as an expression of an attitude. But we do not need any mysterious acts of will. If we make the assumption that the series of acts overlap (Anscombe)—though I think it is a misleading assumption—, the answer to the question of the identity of actions presupposes that all parts of actions refer to the performed action, and all tells about the same entity. The question:

1. Why does James give a piano concerto?

must be distinguished from the question:

2. Why does James play the piano?

The questions (1) and (2) may refer to the same event, but (1) gives us no answer to the question of the intention of playing the piano; the answer could be, for example, "James was invited to do it". Only then, provided that we know the intention, could we answer (2), for example, James plays the piano because he wants to show his artistic playing. Therefore intentions, also as mental items, play a role for explaining action. We do not explain the real happening of events, but *why* a certain event happens or not. This is a further reasoning for the notion that the semantic analysis of action verbs cannot provide for instances of designated expressions.

In the expression "I shall (want to) do something now" we interpret the word "shall (want)" as an expression of an attitude. Anscombe (1959) wrote: "The primitive sign of wanting is trying to get." For Davidson, Hampshire's (1965) proposal becomes clearer when he argues

'A wants to do X' is equivalent to 'other things being equal, he would do X, if he could'. Here I take (possibly contrary to Hampshire's intent) 'other things being equal' to mean, or anyway to allow, the interpretation 'provided that there is not anything he wants more'. (Davidson 1980 (1970): 23-24)

This interpretation of "I shall (want to) do something now" connects intentions with a desire or a motivation with an unconditional judgement: pure intending is such a judgement. To move from a judgement means moving by a want. Davidson concedes that "to do something is wanting to do it", but intending itself is not a wanting. Wishes and desires "are best viewed as corresponding to, or constituting, prima facie judgements." (Davidson 1980 (1970): 102). We make the given behavior intelligible by explaining it with the assumption that the agent realizes his strongest beliefs, such as, why an agent wants to do x more than he wants to do y, and this causes his intentional actions. This is a judgement that expresses that one's beliefs are desirable. Such judgements are *no* wishes *but* intentions.

The syncategorematic account of intentions does not argue that mental descriptions (concepts) do not refer to events, states or dispositions. We can also not exclude cases like, for example, a person having an intention or a disposition, but not acting this way; for example, he intends to sink the Tirpitz, but torpedoes the Bismarck, or he has a disposition to drink ink, but he does not do it. The first case is of principal interest, because the semantic opacity shows that it is mistaken to suppose a *class* of intentional actions. If we made this assumption, the same action would be to name as intentional and non-intentional. Actions are coarse-grained events that we redescribe as intentional or not.

However, how do decisions and choices enter explaining actions?

Intention does not cause intentional actions like, for example, moving the switch and turning on the light. The word *"intending"* stands in a relation to *choice* and *decide* (Austin). But it is not to assume that all actions may be born this way. Both refer to a mental activity that implies a deliberation. I conclude from the explanation by redescription from primary reasons that the logical re-interpretation of "because" indicates to us that we distinguish between actions and mere behavior. The logical relation between the description of an action and the propositional attitudes explains the performance of an action. The analysis of the word "because" in action-explaining sentences then requires a modified answer to the relation between an intention and an intentional action. Thus we find a way to analyze intentions with a non-Davidson account (see Preyer 2002b: 306-10). The logical relation is to re-interpret as a practical syllogism (on this problem, see in detail: 324-340). But the re-interpretation of an explanatory redescription by practical syllogism does not show us that the action is desirable to do, and it is not a redescription of the actual reasoning of an agent. It is not determined whether a practical syllogism leads us to a prima facie judgement or to an action. It is also to mention that practical syllogisms are no normative accounts of evaluative reasoning; such inferences are hypothetical and do not commit the agent to anything. The entailment of beliefs and desires of such reasoning does not commit us to do anything. Therefore:

We can hardly expect to learn whether an action ought to be performed simply from the fact that it is both prima facie right and prima facie wrong. (Davidson 1980 (1970): 37)

Concluded from practical reasoning, this reasoning is hypothetical in nature. The analysis of intending by all-out judgements is to develop in such a direction that the realization of an intention will happen only by our decision to do something: when deciding in favor of something we form our intention to do something. In this context the prior intention is significant, because intending is forming a decision by our strongest beliefs as exclusionary reasons (on the desire-belief reductionism about intention, see Mele 1992:163-170). Decisions and intentions are executive in nature (the former are deeds, but not the latter, they are satisfied or they are not). From here the problem emerges whether the desire-belief pair captures this executive feature. I doubt that this is the case. Therefore I have introduced the principle of execution of intention and making true of beliefs (Preyer 2002b: 329-32). It is to mention here that Mele has also emphasized the executive dimension of intention (1992: 154-171). I have already put forward this principle in my first work on analytical theory of action, written between 1976 and 1979. For Davidson, however, we could also come to all-out judgements without such modes as deciding, choosing, and deliberating to arrive at them (Davidson 1980 (1978): 99). Yet, we cannot eliminate the problem of lunatic internal causal chains, that is, we cannot rationalize in particular how attitudes factually have caused any action. Moreover, it is to emphasize for the pattern explaining actions that in order to explain our doings we take into play not only our prior intention(-s), desires and beliefs, but also the agents' practice and the social background also including attitudes of other people. Many philosophers of the philosophy of action have directed our attention to this matter. In the following I will distinguish between two problems, the problem of mental causality explained by supervenience, and the re-classification of body processes as a causal factor also (capt. II 7.3., in this book).

6.2. From Anomalism of the Mental to the Unified Theory

6.2.1. Anomalous Monism and Supervenience

For Davidson, actions are intentional body movements that we describe as intentional, and we explain such events that we redescribe as actions by primary reasons that have causal power. Most interpreters of Davidson's philosophy of the mental agree that, in the framework of the identity theory, the primary reasons cannot have causal power (properties). In the answer to his critics, Davidson has introduced the concept of *weak* supervenience (Davidson 2005 (1993)). The overall problem, pointed out by these critics, is whether the mental is in any way to reduce to any lower-level physical features. On the other hand, it is not to dispute that it is Davidson's intent to harmonize the mental and the physical and that, at the same time, he wants to give the mental its own domain, that is, he rejects a type-type identity of both. Nor is it to dispute that, for Davidson's philosophy of the mental, coarse-grained events are the key element.

Does Davidson's version of supervenience explain us mental causality? How far did the holistic truth-centered theory of *RI* reason an anomalous monism, and why does *RI* lead us to a pure anomalism?

RI has a mental counterpart that is the network of propositional attitudes. For *RI* it is required that an interpreter makes the assumption that this network is extensively coherent and consistent. Therefore, the speaker is endowed with a modicum of logic. This is a necessary condition for every interpretation and ascription of attitudes. Irrationality is an inner-inconsistency as a deviation from a belief from a set of otherwise consistent beliefs of the speaker. The application of *RI* is not only the ascription of beliefs and actions, but also of intentions, desires and passions. Also passions have a propositional content, such as, pride is pride to something that causes the passion. Causality and rationality have to go hand in hand when interpreting behavior. But the attribution of the mental and the ascriptions of action, on the other hand, lead us back to *RI:*

It is a feature of the mental that the attribution of mental phenomena must be responsible to the background of reasons, beliefs, and intentions of the individual. There cannot be tight connections between the realms if each is to retain allegiance to its proper source of evidence. (Davidson 1980 (1970): 222)

For an anomalous monism and the assumption of supervenience of the mental over the physical, we should be committed to a monism between both, but not to a conceptual reduction of the mental to the physical. There are no psycho-physical laws that could motivate us to bring about such a reduction by reasons of ontological economizing. Since the mid-eighties, Davidson's account has initiated an extensive debate. Kim has argued, for example, that a non-reductive materialism is a myth (Kim 1993a, b, c, 1993c: 265-284, on Davidson: 267-271, 275-277; on the anomalous monism in general, Heil and Mele 1993; on a defense of the anomalism, N. Melchert 1986; on Kim's concept of supervenience causality, the problem of mental causality and the concept of causality, in particular an analysis with contrafactual conditionals, see E. Lepore, B. Loewer 1987, 1989; on the debate on anomal monism and on Davidson's concept of supervenience, see Rogler and Preyer 2001, 2003 a, b; on the autonomy of the mental, see L. M. Antony 1994; on a study of Davidson's *Knowing One's Own Mind* 2001 (1987), see Röska-Hardy 1994). In a first step I will recall what an anomalous monism is. It is helpful to recognize why, from here, we will proceed to a pure anomalism:

1. *The principle of causal interaction* (*CI*): there are causal relations between mental events and physical events.

For this assumption, an ontology of particular, unrepeatable and dated events is presupposed. Therefore, there is an identity of tokens between the mental and the physical, but not an identity of type. For all events it is valid that their descriptions (or properties, as we characterize them) cannot change the causal power of such events, that is, what they cause. Causality and identity are relations between individual events. Such relations are extensional. But the principle of the anomalism is:

Mental objects and events are at the same time physical, physiological, bio-logical, and chemical objects and events. To say of an event, for example, an intentional action, that it is mental is simply to say that we can describe it in a certain vocabulary — and the mark of that vocabulary is semantic intentional-ity. Reason-explanations differ from physical explanations because they are couched (in part) in an intentional vocabulary, and the basic concepts of this vocabulary cannot be reduced, or related by strict laws, to the vocabularies of the physical science. (Davidson 2004 (1987): 114)

2. *The principle of the nomological character of causality (NC)*: the causal relations of events are necessarily governed by strict laws.

But there is a difference between singular causal statements referring to individual events and causal explanations that refer to statements. *Covering by law* means: a law is expressed in a language that entails a statement (sentence) about the corresponding (described) event and a statement (sentence) about the happening of the corresponding effect. A generalization is not only lawlike if it is true, it also has to be deter-ministic, and its validity is to state without ceteris paribus restrictions. Therefore, the universe of a closed system has to be presupposed. Such explanations are complete physical explanations of a finished physics. It is an open question whether this model of explanation is adequate for natural science in general. Yet, this is not my subject in this context. Generalizations that do not fulfil this condition are so-called non-strict laws. It is to mention here that not all philosophers of science have ac-cepted the concept of the closed system as basic in physics.

In accordance with Davidson's account, the distinction between state-ments on simple causal relations between events and their explanation is the essential point. The confusion between the two emerges from our everyday understanding of events. In our ordinary reasoning, often we do not distinguish between causal relations of particulars, such is, the short-circuit in the electric wiring that sets a house on fire, and types of events that are lawlike (Davidson 1993e: 15-16). The latter have to be suf-ficient. Therefore, the proposal given in *Mental Events* (1980 (1970)) is valid: not every true singular causal statement is covered by law (213).

3. *The principle of mental anomalism (MA)*: mental events cannot be subsumed under strict laws.

The mental counterpart of *RI* is the network of propositional atti-tudes. The holism of this network is the evidence for the autonomy and the anomaly of the mental. It follows from the holistic truth-centered and holistic theoretical framework of *RI* that the concepts with which we (re-)describe mental events must be distinguished in principle from concepts we use to describe physical events. For Davidson, this argument is not reasoned by the objection of psycho-physical laws, because if the mental and the physical are connected by a causal relation, a shared ontology between both is given. The extent to which we make a reduction is the degree of anomaly (2005 (1993): 194). He has, for example, also sympathized with Kim's local reduction.

With the further assumption that all mental events stand in causal relations and these are only founded by strict physical laws, AM follows: all mental events are physical events.

Yet, the first principle is in harmony with the other two. Prima vista we would say, "This is not the case." But it is the point of Davidson's theory that the principles are consistent. I assume that he thinks that mental events have also physical properties beside their mental ones. Therefore, they are covered by strict physical causal laws and stand in the relation of causes and effects. An anomalous monism is not an epiphenomenalism. Some critics have argued that, from the second and the third principle, the property-*epi*phenomenalism follows. Therefore, the problem emerges whether that is in harmony with the first principle (on critiques, and a detailed elaboration also on the concepts of supervenience, see Rogler, Preyer 2001).

4. Davidson (2005 (1993)) has answered his critics. Adding the (weak) supervenience thesis (WS) as a fourth principle, he claims to justify mental causality and thereby rejects the critiques of property-epiphenomenalism.

Denote the conjunction of the three premises as P, the core of Davidson's theory as $AM+P$ and together with the thesis of weak supervenience as $AM+P+WS$. Propositional attitudes are supervenient on different things like behavioral, neurophysiological, biological, and physical issues.

What is supervenience?

There are different concepts of this. In our context, a general characterization is sufficient. We may assume that there are families of properties, for example, mental and physical properties. Supervenience then means that the mental properties supervene over the physical properties thereby: if any two objects have the same physical properties, then they also have the same mental properties. Therefore: physical similarity implies mental similarity. Mental causality is reasoned from Davidson's point of view by the following:

1. Mental differences imply physical differences (by contraposition from the supervenience thesis).

2. Physical differences imply causal differences, that is, two events with different physical properties cover under different strict causal laws and, therefore, stand in different causal relations; for example, they cause different neuronal processes directly and, by this, different behavior indirectly. Therefore: mental differences of two given events imply that they stand in different causal relations.

Yet, this does not show that there is mental causality. This would be the case only if it were shown that two events cause physical events from their different mental properties. But this is not Davidson`s intent. He also argues that physical events "matter to causal relations". The causal efficiency is not to reason by supervenience. It is to mention here that supervenience is in harmony with different psycho-physical theories like, for example, identity theory, psycho-physical parallelism, epiphenomenalism, and also emergentism. However this is not my subject here (see on that Rogler, Preyer 2001).

Anomalous monism is a monism and a conceptual (linguistic) dualism. Such dualism is found thereby:

Explanations require classifying concepts, a vocabulary that has the resources for sorting objects and events in ways that allow the formulation of useful generalizations. (Davidson 2004 (1990): 91)

The anomalism is "a necessary condition for viewing action as autonomous" (Davidson 1980 (1973): 225). The mental is conceptual in nature. How we describe events does not lead us to changing our ontology and the causal power of events. We can see how the philosophy of the mental and the ontology of fundamental events play together in Davidson's philosophy. Concepts like belief, desire, intention, and so on are not suited to physical science, and mental states are partly to identify by causes and effects from the interpreter's point of view. This is reasoned in difference to a description of objects, states, and events that instance a strict law that does not contain causal concepts. But it is to emphasize that propositional attitudes are not fictions, they are subjective states and the attribution of them is objective. This leads us back to *RI* and the conceptual dualism because of the following:

But if mental concepts are not reducible to physical concepts, there is no reason to suppose we would lose interest in explanations in mental terms just because we had a complete physical explanation. What is true, of course, is that psycho-logical explanations are never full and sufficient; like most explanations, they are interest-sensitive, and simply assume that a vast number of (unspecified and unspecifiable) factors that might have intervened between cause and effect did not. (2005 (1993): 199)

From my point of view, the conceptual (linguistic) dualism is: what men-tal states (attitudes) are is found by their non-locality, that is, we have to interpret speakers' words to ascribe attitudes. Therefore, interpreting attitudes is relative to a scheme of translation: what we know of attitudes is concluded from our theory of interpretation as a formal framework; at the same time, their ascriptions are objective from the triangulation point of view. This tends to cause tensions between an instrumentalistic and an objective interpretation of the ascriptions of attitudes. Davidson claims to bridge this gap by similar reactions as the basic of objectivity born from the triangulation turn of *RI*.

5. The anomalous monism of the mental is therefore not only rea-soned by *RI*, but also by a radical externalism. The distal individua-tion of the content of propositional attitudes in triangulation between speaker, interpreter and the external world itself discredits type-type identity theories; therefore it has no echo in neuronal processes. For the individuation of attitudes we presuppose a shared picture of the world. But mental-physical identity theories are not rejected by this (Davidson 2001 (1987): 33). If we identify propositional attitudes in the situation where we acquire them, that is, by their causes *outside* of the body, the "monism" of the anomalous monism claims to show also that the states of mind are *inner*, that is, physical states of a speaker. Like the ontology of coarse-grained events this shows us again how the authority of the first person, the social character of language, and the distal individuation of thoughts and meaning belong together.

To sum up from Davidson's point of view: firstly, mental events are physical events, but "this makes them no more physical than mental. Identity is a symmetric relation". Not all identity theories are to call *materialist* (33). Secondly, definitional reduction is out of the question. Thirdly, strict law could not combine normative with non-normative vo-cabularies (concepts). The latter is grounded thereby that strict laws do not employ causal concepts, but mental concepts are irreducibly causal and are related by normative and at the same time by causal properties.

We have accepted to a large degree that the essential feature of the mental—refraining from unconscious motives—is its intentionality

(Brentano). We normally distinguish sensations like pain, visual awareness, and propositional attitudes as mental states (beliefs, intentions, desires, hopes, pride). Davidson calls all propositional attitudes *thoughts*,
because true belief plays an essential role among such attitudes (2001
(1982): 99). This kind of attitudes has a content that we grasp semanticly. The feature of all mental states is the authority of the first person.
Yet, the conceptual dualism leads to an essential distinction between the
physical and the propositional attitudes. This shows again how conceptual dualism, interpretation and language work together: *intentionality
(intentional states) of propositional attitudes is dependent on concepts: we
have a belief, and only then do we have a concept of belief (that is the difference between mental states and beliefs), and the concepts are acquired
only linguistically by creatures that have a language.*

From my point of view, the problem of anomalous monism is the acceptance of an identity of the token in principle and the claim to analyze
the relation between the mental and the physical with the paradigm of
strict or non-strict laws. Burge argues, for example, to give up token-
identity by the introduction of a contrafactual situation (1993). As long
as we do not give up an identity of the token, the philosophy of the
mental poses us problems we cannot solve, and it is also impossible to
form an understanding of our self-knowledge. Davidson wants to give
a solution to *The Irreducibility of the Concept of the Self* (2001 (1998)),
but monism (and externalism) blocks his intention. It is not a matter of
the consistency of anomalous monism if we accept their premises, but a
substantial issue.

Therefore I will give up the idea of the identity of the token between
the mental and the physical, and I will argue for a pure anomalism. This
follows from the principle of charity and from the fact that the ascription
of attitudes is dependent on *our* theory of interpretation. Such anomalism is reasoned by the evidence of *RI*. To summarize, the well-known
problems within the philosophy of the mental, such as the problem of
epiphenomalism, the different versions of supervenience, or the problem
causal-explanatory exclusion are a result of handling the metaphysical
framework of monism (materialism).

6.2.2. The Pure Anomalism of the Mental

From my point of view, Davidson goes into the right direction. For the now following passages one should bear in mind that "concepts like those of meaning and belief are, in a fundamental way, not reducible to physical, neurological, or even behavioristic concepts" (Davidson 1984 (1974): 154). A pure anomalism is reasoned by the following arguments:

1. The mental is holistic in nature, because propositional attitudes are not single attitudes in nature, that is: „no beliefs without many related beliefs, no belief without desires, no desires without beliefs, no intentions without both beliefs and desires." (Davidson 2001 (1997): 126) The relationship between attitudes is logical in nature. The holism of the mental has *no* echo in the network of brain processes. Yet, I do not argue for an ontological dualism of properties between the mental and the physical, because from *RI* it is concluded that the restrictions of the ascriptions of attitudes are not fixed eventually.

2. We can only ascribe propositional attitudes to creatures who have rationality at their disposal. This follows by the application of the principle of charity or, respectively, by the principle of natural epistemic justice, as I call it. This means for *RI*: only creatures who are able to communicate meet the concept of an objective world. It is a dimension of the triangle.

Beliefs and other attitudes can only be ascribed to by the procedure of *RI*. Such ascriptions have to cope with the difficulties of the circle between belief and meaning. This is only possible in case a radical interpreter makes the assumption that most of the speaker's beliefs are true, and the interpreter presupposes in the triangulation model of *RI* that similar reactions are caused by the external world. Therefore we conclude that attitudes cannot be ascribed to by neuroscience, whatever the development of such a science might be. The principle of charity does not only have no echo whatsoever in natural science, but its knowledge is also not instructive for the ascription of attitudes. This is reasoned by the background of *RI,* that is, the network of propositional attitudes. We conclude from here: if we are required to make the assumption of rationality or to apply the principle of natural epistemic justice to make behavior intelligible, we assume the existence of *both* domains of different synthetic constitutive principles:

Hence, if each domain is to retain its own integrity, there cannot be laws connecting them.... I have always thought that the power of the Davidson argument for mental anomalism is seen in fact that, if it works at all, it should work against laws of all kind ...(Kim 1993a: 25, see on this problem also Hornsby 1993).

This is a correct conclusion from Davidson's philosophy of the mental, because we are not forced by *RI* to make the anomaly coherent with an ontological monism between the mental and the physical:

The heteronomic character of general statements linking the mental and the physical traces back to this central role of translation in the description of all propositional attitudes, and to the indeterminacy of translation. There are no strict psychophysical laws because of the disparate commitments of the mental and physical schemes. (Davidson 1980 (1970): 222).

The commitment we bring into play characterizes the primary feature of the intentional states. If propositional attitudes are dependent on concepts and such attitudes are acquired semantically (linguistically), we have taken the step to a pure anomalism of the mental.

3. The ascription of action is a result of the causal explanations of primary reasons, and mental concepts have a causal origin. The mental does not "constitute a closed system" (Davidson 1980 (1974): 239). It is connected with the external world and not excluded from the outside. Mental phenomena are not an instance of explanations with strict deterministic laws. The externalistic individuation of the content of attitudes is concluded from the holistic truth-centered theory of *RI*, and truth has to play the role that is essential if we want to understand linguistic behavior: "belief is in its nature veridical" (2001 (1983): 146). The theory of interpretation has its place "within a more comprehensive theory of action and thought" (Davidson 1984 (1975): 162) with its *own* constitutive principles. If this were not the case, "the notion of a true belief" could not be dependent on the "notion of a true utterance" and "this in turn there cannot be without shared language." (170) Yet, this is exactly what has no echo in the physical.

4. Davidson's monism is a weaker version of materialism. Therefore, it seems to be more obvious to take the step to a pure anomalism that is reasoned by the evidence of *RI* and triangulation. The anomalous monism is no eliminativism, because the ascription of mental states is of an attributive matter: people are in such states. Such ascriptions are not rendered invalid by any scientific progress. The ontology of individual events is supported by a monism that means: there is no psychological

phenomenon without the physical. But anomalism of the mental is also no dualism of properties of the mental and the physical, because from the radical interpreter's side the empirical restrictions of the speaker's attitudes and behavior cannot be fixed for all cases. What an addressee understands about the words uttered by any speaker is not only determined by the meaning of the words, but also by the speaker's beliefs about the world (background theory). In this respect, all understanding is indeterminated by the network of propositional attitudes.

5. Monism (and externalism) blocks an adequate understanding of self-knowledge (self-consciousness). Davidson has actually integrated the *Irreducibility of the Concept of the Self* (2001 (1998) in a response to Dieter Henrich in his epistemology, but he understands the concept of oneself in a restricted way, that is, "as an independent entity depends on the realization of the existence of others, a realization that comes into its own with communication" (90). It is restricted because the vocabulary we use to ascribe attitudes to oneself and others is equal, and its content is conceptually expressed in the public domain. His concept of the self is motivated by his rejection of introspective investigations. This may be right, but conceptually it is not the only version of self-knowledge.

It is to emphasize that, for Davidson, the origin of self-ascription is not a fictive intentionality or authority: I know my attitudes because I have them myself. Mental properties are no less real than physical properties and are therefore not only components of a merely fictive superstructure. These varieties of knowledge cannot be reduced to one another but condition each other mutually. Because self-knowledge and knowledge of other minds presuppose the reality of mental properties, their denial would mean an annihilation of all knowledge and communication. There are convincing reasons for the acceptance of mental properties in Davidson's theory of the mental. Its usual characterization as an ontological monism and a conceptual (ideological) dualism is therefore at least misleading. It would be conclusive to characterize his theory as an ontological monism of events (respectively things) and a psychophysical dualism of properties that corresponds epistemologically to a dualism of concepts and descriptions. But such an interpretation is confronted with the problem of mental causality. And it is to ask what it really means that "A reason is a rational cause" (Davidson 1980 (1970): 233).

Bearing these issues in mind, we give up monism (materialism) and argue in favor of a pure anomalism of the mental. In this point, philosophers like Putnam, McDowell, Burge and others come together. Recalling, for example, Burge, it is not hard to sympathize with this.

The flood of projects over the last two decades that attempt to fit mental causation or mental ontology into a ,naturalistic picture of the world' strike me as having more in common with political or religious ideology than with a philosophy that maintains perspective on the difference between what is known and what is speculated. Materialism is not established, or even clearly supported, by science. Metaphysics should venture beyond science with an acute sense of its liabilities. (1993: 117)

6.2.3. The Unification

Explaining behavior as actions takes into play the agent's propositional attitudes, and such explanations are an irreducible causal concept. But the way of explaining and individuating actions is not a science of behavior that we find in physiology and physics. The unification of the *unified theory*, however, is a powerful, attractive formal theory in harmony with many of our intuitions of the nature of rationality, Davidson argues. He gives a "conceptual exercise" of the unification of the basic propositional attitudes. The unified theory is described (defined) by an abstract structure. The structure of language and thought is given by the logic of quantification. This is not a description of what really happens in understanding each other or in acquisition of our first concepts and language. But we give the theory an empirical turn, and the task of its practicability is the structure of the normative features of propositional attitudes on which we impose their correct ascription when interpreting speech and explaining actions. (Davidson 1984 (1974): 145-148), (1975): 162-63, 2004 (1980), (1984): 26-33)

The result of unification is a *redescription of RI*. The new procedure runs through the sequences of interpretation (Lepore, Ludwig 2005: 257-260):

* Sequence 1: The interpreter uses the pattern of normative features among preferences for the identification of truth-functional connectives. Logical truths are assumed as intuitively given.

* Sequence 2: He ascribes subjective probabilities and desirabilities to sentences with Jeffrey's technique.

* Sequence 3: Holding truth is to relate to degrees of beliefs that are to identify toward occasion sentences. We take in information about the conditions under which such sentences are held true and their degree, such as:

(L_R) For times t, speaker S, ceteris paribus, S holds true (to degree R) is at t iff p.

* Sequence 4: Lepore and Ludwig modify the principle of charity by *Grace* leading to a redescription of the framework within which the data for the truth theory are given (on *Grace,* Lepore, Ludwig 2005: 194-196, see 162, in this book). The triangulation model of *RI* assumed for the identification of the caused true beliefs is replaced by the resulting *degrees* from the application of L_R. Just this limits the ascription of attitudes to the relationship between the evidence of interpretation and to the data that the interpreter has at his disposal.

* Sequence 5: The interpreter applies *T*-sentences in the sequence 4 that he had found to discover the initial truth theory of interpretation which entails such sentences.

* Sequence 6: He finds information about subjective probabilities to find out hypotheses about the axioms for theoretical terms and utterances of sentences in the given language under study.

* Sequence 7: At the end of the procedure he makes predictions about the speaker's actions and the situations within which he holds true untested sentences related with different degrees, until the theory about behavior meets the interpreter's observations.

The unified theory of thought, meaning and action falls together with the holism of attitudes, their normative features and the externalism of individuation of their content. Davidson claims to identify the place of a comprehensive theory of action and thoughts. The place is the basic attitude: *the agent prefers one sentence true rather than another,* therefore a degree of belief is not to be introspected. The theory of belief and meaning requires knowledge of the degree of belief in its truth and not only of what has caused it. From that, a *total* theory results for interpretation of sentences, and at the same time it ascribes beliefs, desires and other propositional attitudes. This *composite* theory claims to explain behavior in general. This is the hard core to unify the theory of interpretation and decision, because the interpretation of linguistic behavior and ascription of attitudes play together in principle. The same *sentences* are objects of belief and desire. In this general line Davidson takes in also evaluative attitudes. The key relation is the speaker's attitude toward sentences, not propositions like Jeffrey has assumed. The composite theory claims to relate concepts of beliefs, desire and linguistic meaning and to analyze belief in a quantity form (subjective probability, ratio scale), and it measures desire in an interval scale, which is often called decision theory. In difference to Ramsey and Jeffrey and from Davidson's point of view, a theory of meaning is to take in. The distinction between the two scales goes back to Ramsey. The unified theory is holistic in nature, the content of beliefs, utterances and values are ascribed simultaneously. This is reasoned by the holistic nature of attitudes. They are not determined step by step. Rationality is a matter of degrees. But rationality is not a policy, it is a basic rationality. The principle of charity is the normative feature we read in the linguistic behavior and the attitudes. The interpreter discovers a degree of logical consistency in the attitudes of the speaker and at the same time endows him with a degree of what the interpreter takes to be a true belief about the world. Bayesian decision theory says nothing about the object of simple preferences that are extracted within its framework. The problem is:

How are preferences to describe without identifying their propositional content?

The content itself, and also sentences, are not observable, but utterances and inscription are. The interpreter has given the observable behavior a content. The objects of attitudes are the same kind which caused them. For Davidson, the only way of individuating attitudes is to identify the object share to speaker and interpreter by its common cause, that is, the same objects cause the content of their attitudes. This is the constraint, that the theory of decision has to include not only a theory of interpretation but also one of communication. This leads to a problem of understanding also moral values in principle: it is a requirement of stating disagreement about objects, events and actions that we think and talk about the same of their aspects.

7. Flight from Body Movements

7.1. I. Thalberg's Theory of Action and the Accordion Effect

7.1.1. Doing versus Undergoing

The two prominent critiques of Davidson's thesis of identity between *A* and *A'* are given by I. Thalberg (1972) and A. I. Goldman (1970); on both, Hornsby (1980: 16-19, 29-32). Thalberg has argued that in the act-pair *ARA'* there is a *replenishing* of acts. One must distinguish between human and natural events. Therefore we have to distinguish between *doing* versus *undergoing*. So we conclude: there is a difference of type between body movements and actions. Yet, Thalberg's theory leads back to Davidson because the question of identity of action arises in the sequences of replenishing. In difference to Thalberg, my account is that the relation between *ARA'* is *not one between single acts but between upshots of acts*. Goldman has argued that the two acts in *A-A'* show distinct properties. He gives a rejection of the identity theory, and he introduces basic acts of a higher level of generation of *A-A'*. I will argue that Goldman's theory leads to a theory of agent redescribing action in terms of constitutive principles of actions. This theory takes different principles of generation acts into account, and I conclude that we do not immediately instantiate action to an agent. The leading question is:

What are beliefs and intentions, and *how* does the connection between both generate an action?

"James changes a wheel of his car on a cold winter day. He gets frozen to the marrow, he drops the tool, and in the course of this he hurts his hand however much that he begins to bleed. He almost has a shock. His clumsiness makes him enraged, and he feels the desire to run amok."

Are all his body movements and events actions? Can the description of "what happens to James" be brought into line with the description of his doing? Do the comments of his doing under features of his own control, like "deliberately", "overhastily", "carelessly", "rashly" and so forth, give us a classification of action verbs?

The answer to these questions is the main theme of Thalberg's theory of action. He develops his theory starting with a critique of Davidson's identity thesis of the pairs of act *ARA'*. Thalberg begins with the question of finding linguistic facts to construct the class of general action verbs. But he argues that the linguistic feature is not sufficient to build these verbs. This is also the argument of Davidson (1971: 44-45). The essential feature of action verbs is its qualification by control. This is the difference to verbs of a sort that report about an "undergoing" (Thalberg 1972, 1967). In a first step, the feature of control allows us to distinguish between actions and body processes. It is useful to distinguish the action verbs as opposed to verbs of "undergoing". But the distinction between "doing" and "undergoing" does not primarily mean the question of reference to descriptions of actions. The feature can be introduced first of all without any analysis of verbs because actions are deeds that we ascribe to people, and we characterize the ascription with a specification of intentions, desires, goals, decisions. If "Peter", for example, greets the president of the university, goes on holidays, gives a sign in traffic, "his" doing can, should the situation arise, be described as "intentional", "deliberate", "appropriate", "unintentional", "doing something in a situation where someone exerts pressure on me". There is a wide scale of expressions that inform us of the extension of control about actions. The feature of control consists of the capacity to do something or to leave it, and it also entails the responsibility for actions. So the asymmetry between having control or not having control gives us a restrictive feature for all so-called action verbs, like "killing" in the relation to "murder".

7.1.2. The Component View of Actions

Thalberg makes a further distinction between action verbs of three other groups:

1. Body process verbs, like "to bleed", "to get cold" and so on. With these verbs we do not describe any doing, as processes that happen to us are no "doing" on our side.

2. Reaction verbs like "to flush", "to be shocked", "to pant", "to vomit" and so on. We ascribe these verbs to people like deeds but do not apply any expression of control.

In the case of reference to certain situations, body processes and reactions, verbs could certainly be brought into line with action verbs. With these verbs we describe the body process as a component of actions, for example, getting cold when changing a tire of a car in winter, blushing if someone makes a mistake in the heat of the moment.

3. Accident verbs like (a) "to stutter", "to run amok", "to stumble" and so on, (b) "to snore", "to die", "to have no energy" and so on. They are to distinguish from reaction verbs, as there is no situation that they modify. With these verbs we do not ascribe actions.

For Thalberg, there is an action of replenishing in the relation *ARA'*. He makes a distinction between actions that we make happen by a doing and events that are not a result of this: doing contrary to undergoing. *Therefore, actions are assembled of doings and events the agent has not done, that is, the component view is that actions have smaller actions among its components (parts).*

What does a person do who pumps poisoned water into a water pipe?

This example goes back to Anscombe. In this case, we suppose a doing on the side of this person if a poisoning of house occupants has taken place. The answer cannot be: "He operated the pump." But Thalberg's answer "the poisoning of house occupants" is also not convincing, because the action of poisoning does not happen until the house occupants will drink the water at a later point of time. Moving the pump is a part of the performance of an action that is added onto his replenishing to the poisoning, but the pumping is to distinguish from the poisoning.

Thalberg's claim is also to give a solution to the climber-example. He gives us the following solution: there are actions that are brought about by doings which are to distinguish from events where this is not the case. Some effects of the movement, such as James's arm which pumps, are replenished to the movement of pumping as an action. Therefore, some effects of his operation of pumping that are replenished to the work of pumping bring off the action of replenishing: the water running in the house, and some further events that are added onto the replenishing of running of water, bring about the poisoning of house occupants in this way. So the actions are such of *replenishing*, there are *no* numerically distinct tokens in the series.

How is the theory reasoned that there is an identity between "the pumping of James" and "the poisoning of house occupants" in the way that "James" does nothing else but operating the pump? Which actions take up the new *parts* in the temporal succession?

In this respect we have a question of identity of acts in *ARA'*.

7.1.3. Are Actions Movements?

The problem of the relationship between *both* events A-A' leads back to Davidson's theory. He also claims to give a solution to the well-known and much discussed riddle: if James kills Henry by doing—he poisoned him—so it is a killing. Killing implies a death. But the death can happen a long time after the deed was done.

How it is possible that the killing is identical with the poisoning?

We look for an event that both events make true. It is to explain how something that is "true" of an action would be "true" of any other event. We construct a relative clause like "that causes the death" in relation to the sentence phrase, and describe, for example, the movement of "killing" as "there is a movement of the finger x against the trigger x that causes the death". Thalberg excludes this construction (in particular, see Hornsby 1980: 31). Following his theory, the body movement that causes the death is the killing, but he disputes that killing is a movement because, in this case and in correspondence with such movement, everyone would kill. This is a real problem: no movement is a part of the death, such as the poisoning of house occupants. The description of poisoning that causes the death is not to specify to a movement. Therefore, a movement itself cannot cause the death.

If we start out that the event a, for example, "turn the light switch" causes the event b, for example, "the light is burning", it may be that an act or the activity of the first event a stands in a transitive relation to the second event b. But this interpretation of "by turning the light switch James turns on the light" is to compare with the conception: James's act of turning the light switch is identical with the act of turning on the light. It is not a relation between acts *but* between upshots (results) of it that must be explained:

My poisoning of the victim must be an action that results in the victim being poisoned; my killing of the victim must be an action that results in the death of the victim; my murdering of the victim must be an action that results in the death of the victim and also an action that was caused, in part, by my desire for the victim's death. (Davidson 1980 (1970): 178)

Yet, my account is different from Davidson's because, for his theory, everything that causes the end of the action does not add a new event. This is to conclude from the thesis of identity of acts.

7.1.4. *The Accordion Effect*

Austin and Feinberg have shown an important property of our use of description of action that Feinberg has called the accordion effect.

Apart from the more general and obvious problem of the use of 'tendentious' descriptive terms, there are many special problems in the particular case of 'action'. Should we say, are we saying, that he took her money, or that he robbed her? That he knocked a ball into a hole, or that he sank a putt? That he said 'Done', or that he accepted an offer? How far, that is, are motives, intentions and conventions to be part of the description of actions? And more especially here, what is *an* or *one* or *the* action? For we can generally split up what might be named as one action in several distinct ways, into different *stretches* or *phases* or *stages*. Stages have already been mentioned: we can dismantle the machinery of the act, and describe (and excuse) separately the intelligence, the appreciation, the planning, the decision, the execution and so forth. Phases are rather different: we can say that he painted a picture or fought a campaign, or else we can say that first he laid on this stroke of paint and then that one, first he fought this action and then that one. Stretches are different again: a single term descriptive of what he did may be made to cover either a smaller or a larger stretch of events, those excluded by the narrower description being then called 'consequences' or 'results' or 'effects' or the like of his act. So here we can describe Finney's act *either* as turning on the hot tap, which he did by mistake, with the result that Watkins was scalded, *or* as scalding Watkins, which he did *not* do by mistake. (Austin (1956-57) 1968: 40)

Thus we can say that Jones opened the door and thereby caused Smith (who was inside) to be startled, in this way treating Jones's act as the cause of a subsequent effect; or we can say (simply) 'Jones startled Smith' (by opening the door), and thus incorporate the consequence into the complex action. If Smith suffered a heart attack and died, we can say that Jones's opening the door caused his death, or that Jones's startling him caused his death, or simply that Jones killed him (by doing those things). "This well-known feature of our language, whereby a man's action can be described as narrowly or broadly as we please, I propose to call the 'accordion effect', because an act, like the folding musical instrument, can be squeezed down to a minimum or else stretched out. He turned the key, he opened the door, he startled Smith, he killed Smith—all of these are things we might say that Jones did with one identical set of bodily movements. Because of the accordion effect we can usually replace any ascription to a person of causal responsibility by an ascription of agency or authorship. We can, if we wish, puff out an action to include an effect, and more often than not our language obliges us by providing a relatively complex action word for the purpose. Instead of saying Smith did *A* (a relative simple act) and thereby caused *X* in *Y*, we might say something of the form 'Smith *X*-ed *Y*; instead of 'Smith opened the door causing Jones to be startled', 'Smith startled Jones'. (Feinberg 1968: 106-107)

From Austin's and Feinberg's point of view, the accordion effect is not only a property of descriptions but also a feature of actions: that is, it is not possible to describe actions that we make go on, stretch or pull together ourselves, but the actions themselves have such properties. Yet, these properties show the descriptions only but *not* the acts we describe, as Austin and Feinberg assume. The accordion effect "In brief, once he has done one thing (move a finger), each consequence presents us with a deed; an agent causes what his actions cause" does not show how far the action can be called intentional (Davidson 1980 (1971): 53). But with this effect we grasp that the consequences of actions are to distinguish from natural events.

When we describe an action, for example, "the killing of Peter by James", a reference to "Peter" must be involved (entailed) if we describe the action of "James". But the death of "Peter" was no part of "James's" doing like raising his arm, moving his fingers, pulling the trigger, firing the gun and so on. The death of "Peter" was a causal consequence of his act and not a part of it, that is, of the action that was done by "James": "James shot Peter dead" and the consequence was that his friend died. When describing the doing of "James" it may be that the description was stretched and pulled and we refer to the "death of Peter". But stretching and pulling together is not a property of any act itself. "James's" act is to describe as an activity, and "Peter's" death was an upshot of this doing but no part of this act. An action and its causal consequences are to characterize as two distinct items. The significant point — in difference to Thalberg's theory — is that the relation in *ARA'* is not a matter between acts but between results of acts, which is to explain.

7.2. A. I. Goldman's Critique of Davidson's Identity-Thesis

7.2.1. The Identity-Thesis

The fundamental problem of the theory of action in A. I. Goldman's proposal is the examination of act-individuation and the reference of description of actions (1970: 1-10). He begins his investigation with a critique of the identity-thesis of Davidson and Anscombe. James (1) moves his finger (that causes that...), (2) pulls the trigger, (3) fires the gun, and (4) kills Peter.

Has Peter performed *four* different acts or are these acts *one* and the *same* act?

This is the question of the nature of acts. In Davidson's theory, the action of "pulling the trigger"is identical with "the killing of Peter". For the identity-thesis the assumption is valid in general that if $A \equiv A'$, then it is obligatory for A to have all, and the same, properties like A'. Goldman shows that the identity-thesis is not to generalize, because some pairs of act that are putatively identical do not have the same properties.

Which relation holds between the act of "killing Peter" and the event *e,* for example, "Firing the gun"? Does this act cause the event *e,* for example, "James kills Peter" causes that the gun fires?

Surely this is not the case. "James kills Peter" causes that the gun fires would be a strange description. In fact it is the case that James's act of pulling the trigger, namely the event *e* in question, has caused, for example, the firing of the gun: James pulling the trigger has the property of causation of firing the gun, but James kills Peter does not have the property of causation of firing the gun!

The acts in the relation ARA' show us different properties. Each of these acts has a property that is missing with the other act, and that is why the acts could not be one and the same. So it is a fault to identify both the acts of James with each other. The identity-thesis refers to effects and/or consequences of alleged identical actions. A further problem of the identity-thesis is the examination of causes and causal factors of actions. If A and A' are one and the same action, then there is one and the same event. Provided that the two acts are one and the same event e, we could expect—if the event was caused—that it was caused by the same set of events or state of affairs. But A and A' show different causal factors against it. That is why the two acts are not identical in general.

Goldman argues that the relation between A-A' has the following properties (5):

1. It is *asymmetrical*: if A' was performed by A, then A is not performed by A', for example, James turns on the light by flipping the light switch, but he does not flip the light switch by turning on the light.

2. It is *irreflexive*: it is not possible that James turns on the light by turning it on.

3. But it is *transitive*: the relation is to examine in the way that the act A' was performed by another act A.

In a given context the term *by* refers to the relationship that holds between the two acts A-A'.

We often say of a person that he performs one act "by" performing another. We say, for example, that John turns on the light "by" flipping the switch, of that he checkmates his opponent "by" moving his queen to king-knight-seven. As used in these contexts, the term "by" expresses a relationship that holds between acts, between John's act of flipping the switch and his act of turning on the light, and between John's act of moving his queen to king-knight-seven and his act of checkmating his opponent. The relationship in question might be expressed by saying that the one act is a "way" or "method" by that the other act is performed. Typically, when act A is the "way" by that act A' is performed, we can explain how act A' has been performed by citing act A. For example, if John checkmates his opponent by moving his queen to king-knight-seven, we can explain how he checkmated his opponent by referring to his act of moving his queen to king-knight-seven." (5)

The by-relation is asymmetrical and irreflexive: if James did A by the doing of B, then it is false: 1. that James did B by the doing of A and 2. that James did A by the doing of A. A possible answer to Goldman's problem is: James's particular act may be called by us "his relational property": "the killing of…" can cause the "firing of the gun". This is strange talk because we tend to confuse the causal relation between events with the explanatory relation between statements or propositions. The fact that the gun fires is not causal to explain by the fact that James killed Peter. The action that James performed by doing makes happen the death of Peter—we describe it as the "killing of Peter"—, and it may be caused by the "firing of the gun":

* James's act of killing Peter is the very activity which caused that Peter died, and this activity may be of such a kind that it has caused the pulling of the trigger.

Davidson could argue against Goldman that he does not take two features into account: the causal relation between events and the explanatory relation between statements or propositions. Another point is that we cannot consistently interpret the causal relation as a transitive one, if, for example, $a_1 \rightarrow b_2$ and $b_2 \rightarrow c_3$ we cannot always conclude that there is a causal relation between $a_1 \rightarrow c_3$. The inference is only valid in the case of the identity of contexts.

But there is just another point for analyzing the by-relation. If we use singular terms to specify the relationship of relevant acts, we could not say meaningfully:

(1) James turns on the light by James's flipping the switch.

The word *by* is not a clear example to characterize a relation (on the meaning of "by", Hornsby 1980: 6-8, 27-8). It can be used to connect the two sentences:

(2) James turns on the light by flipping the switch.

We read this statement in the sense:

(3) James flips the switch and thereby he turns on the light.

H. A. Prichard has analyzed this reading as (1965; on Prichard see Melden 1960: 75-77):

(4) James caused: the switch was flipped, and he caused thereby the turning on of the light.

The agent causality would this way be reduced to a causality of events:

(5) ∃A (A is an activity by James with respect to the fact that A causes the flipping of the switch and therefore causes turning on the light).

The word *thereby* may connote a *by*-relation in these statements, but in the given reading the relation does not hold between acts but between upshots of acts. The event of the flipping of the switch therefore causes the event of turning on the light. The act or the activity of the first event may then hold in a transitive relation or causation respectively to the second event, but this interpretation of "James turns on the light by flipping the switch" is comparable with the account that James's act of flipping the switch is identical with his act of turning on the light.

7.2.2. Act-Types and Act-Tokens

Following N. Rescher (1967), Goldman (1970: 10-19) has analyzed the individuation of acts with the principal distinction between both:

1. Act-*types:* the act-properties like "running", "killing", "holding a lecture" and so on. If we ascribe an act to an agent, then we exemplify an act-property.

2. Act-*token:* the performance of an act like holding a lecture at a given time-point.

An act-token is not a property, but an exemplification of an act-type by an agent at a given time-point. So the natural way to individuate act-tokens is: two act-tokens are identical if and only if they were exemplified by the same agent, the same property, and the same time-point (10). Goldman does not assert that the identity-thesis of Davidson is irrelevant. From his point of view, it is a requirement to find identity-conditions of actions to give an answer to the question:

What do we mean to say with statements about act-types?

For this purpose, Goldman makes the distinction between act-types and act-tokens:

The heart of my position is that act-token A and act-token A' are identical only if they are tokens of the same type (property)'. But since killing Smith and moving one's finger are distinct types, John's killing Smith (at t) and John's moving his finger (at t) are distinct act-tokens. (11)

Statements about act-types mean:

(When) we say 'John signaled for a turn'... we ascribe an act property or (what is to say the same thing) act type to John: the property of signaling for a turn ... to ascribe an act type to someone is to say that he exemplified it. If John and Oscar perform the same act (i.e. do the same thing), they exemplify the same act type. (1971: 769)

The semantic content of action sentences are types or properties, and we use these sentences to ascribe these properties by a nominalization of this content.

Since an act token is standardly designated by a nominalized form of action sentence and since an action sentence associated with such a nominalization asserts that a person exemplifies a certain act property, it is natural to view the designatum of such a nominalization as an exemplifying of an act property by a person. Thus John's (signaling for a turn) is an exemplifying by John of the property of (signaling for a turn). (770)

From this account, Goldman takes the theoretical step leading to the assertion that these expressions designate events that we distinguish as act-types:

Moreover since the act type of (signalling for a turn) is distinct from the act type of (extending his arm out of the car window), it seems natural to say that (John's) exemplifying of the act type of (signalling for a turn) is distinct from (John's) exemplifying of the act type of (extending his arm out of the car window). (771, on Goldman, to this point in particular, see Hornsby 1980: 16-19).

For Goldman, action sentences designate act-tokens by their nominalized form, and their truth is to verify by the reference to such tokens. Without any theoretical risk he can make the assumption that the expressions

(1) "I did the same that you did" and
(2) "he did the same that you did"

do not require the identity of particular events. For his theory, the talk of

(3) bringing about a movement,
(4) bringing about the movement of my hand,
(5) causing the attentiveness of the waiter

exemplifies three distinct act-properties (types). But none of these properties are one and the same action.

How far do the nominalizations of action sentences designate act-tokens? Is it the case that action sentences are true by virtue of their specification to particular actions?

Goldman's universal quantification said:

(*) the act-type of giving a sign is to distinguish from the act-type of moving the hand.

Normally we would make the assumption that any exemplification of the act-type of giving a sign is different from every exemplification of the act-type of moving the hand. But the quantification is presumably not valid without a particular context-reference. It is possible that we have reasons to say that the property of being an "author of a book" is different from the property of being an "author of an article", and these properties are to distinguish from other properties of a person. If we suppose

* "…is an exemplification of James's property…"
and
* "…has the property…"

has the same logical form, so the argument about the authorship picks out the same form that is necessary for Goldman's theory. But on the basis of this argument about authorship we could conclude that the author "James" is not James (see on that also Hornsby 1980: 17-19).

The problem of Goldman's theory is in general that we do not explain the *real* happening of events but *why* events happen or not.

7.2.3. Levels of Generation of Act-Tokens

Goldman analyzes the relation between pairs of act-tokens A-A' of the same agent as a level-generation of act-tokens: AR_gA', and diagrams the structural relationship of these tokens. The claim is to give a recursive definition of an act-token. The structural feature of the leveling is that on the lowest level we find basic-acts tokens as an instance of a basic-act type, whereas on a higher level we find non-basic act-type exemplifications. Leveling the act-individuation does not mean a sequentialization of action. This would be misleading: an agent generates the levels uno actu. Between these levels no causal relations exist as, for example, between a body movement and switching on the light. Goldman distinguishes four categories of level-generation. They are based on the description:

* if it is true that a person performs P -> A(B) by doing of A(B) then the generation can be leveled as a "causal", a "conventional", a "simple" or an "augmentation" generation (1970: 22-30.)

1. The difference between *causation* and *causal* generation is reasoned thereby that two acts could not be leveled at the same time by causation and causal generation, for example, Peter takes his sleeping pill at 10'clock. Peter does something by his taking the pill: 1. he takes the sleeping pill (act), he falls asleep (not an act), and he causes himself to fall asleep (act). Taking the sleeping pill causes him to fall asleep, but it is not causally generated. Making himself fall asleep A' was causally generated but it is not caused by A.

Distinction between causation and causal generation

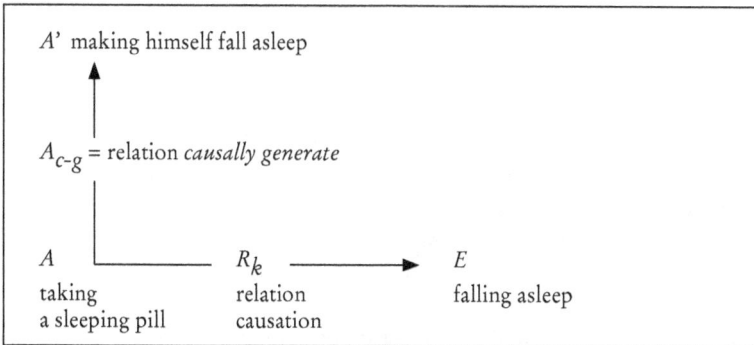

A' making himself fall asleep

A_{c-g} = relation *causally generate*

A
taking
a sleeping pill

R_k
relation
causation

E
falling asleep

2. The *conventional* generation is to characterize in such a way that there are rules, conventions, norms, and/or any social praxis that makes it possible to ascribe the act A' to a person, for example, P extends his arm out of the car window = $A \rightarrow P$ signals for a turn = A', P breaks his promise = $A - > P$ does what he ought not to do = A'. We analyze the conventional generation on the basis that there is a relevant situation as an instance and, for example, a rule, and in this context the agent performs the act A' by A.

3. The *simple* generation is introduced in contrast to the causal and conventional generation. It is a feature of this generation that there are no causal relationships and no rules but a situation, and in this context we level the act-pair A-A', for example, P jumps 6 feet high = $A \rightarrow P$ out jumping James = A', P asserts that p = $A \rightarrow P$ contradicting his other statement etc.

4. The *augmentation* generation is a distinctive case. It means that the generated act A' entails the performance of the generated act A, that is, there is augmentation in the act-pair A-A' in the significant situation, for example, P extends his arm = $\rightarrow P$ extending his arm out of the car window, P says "hello" = $A \rightarrow P$ saying "hello" loudly, and so on.

The exemplifications of basic act-types are the foundation for the analysis of higher level actions. Goldman analyzes the act pairs A-A' that A is an exemplification of a basic act-type from which a hierarchy of actions arises (38-48). Consequently the body movements can be instances of different actions and plans.

7.2.4. Basic Act-Types

These action plans consist of desires and sets of beliefs (56-57). The concept of basic acts is essential for Goldman's analysis of intentional action and the recursive definition of act-token. He makes the assumption that, for example in the case of a conventional generation, the act of signaling is determined by the act of moving a hand. The act is to specify directly to an agent: P does A' by the doing of A. This instantiation is to understand with an ascription that implies the talk of act-tokens as a result of wanting. Goldman uses "want" in a broad sense (48). Basic-act tokens are intentional acts and indicate wants and sets of beliefs. Firstly, Goldman formulates the standard condition of basic-act types:

* S (= agent) is in standard condition with respect to property A at just in case

1. there are no external forces at t making it physically impossible for S to exemplify A at t, and

2. if exemplifying A involves a change into state Z, then S is not already in Z.

In the next step he reformulates the necessary condition for basic act-types

* A is a basic act-type for S at t only if:

if S were in standard conditions with respect to A at t, then if S wanted to exemplify A at t, S's exemplifying A at t would result from this want. (65, on the complete definition: 67)

Goldman introduces a concept of basic act-types—in difference to properties that are not basic—with reference to the dependency of these acts on *level-generational knowledge or belief*. The explanation of action is, in this account, a species of causal explanation, and we analyze an agent's reason for action in terms of action plans that cause his doing. (78) This way, agent-causation is to explicate by wants and beliefs-causation. (80-81)

7.2.5. Is a Theory of Action possible?

An alternative account to Goldman's level-generation is:

* If a person does A, then we assume that the same person thereby performs $A(A')$ with respect to different types of primary reasons.

In correspondence to Goldman's principle of act-generation, we redescribe and explain the performance of action with reference to different principles of act-constitution.

But what theory of action is possible if we suppose the individuation of acts as explanandum of the theory of action?

If Goldman develops his theory of action under the feature of individuating acts, then the same questions as in the ontology of events proposal arise. We recognize a problem to individuate actions ontologically to unreducible events in principle:

In many discussions of action identities, there is a presumption that all of the parties are agreed about what actions are, and all would be talking about the same things, but that somehow in any particular case a dispute has emerged over whether the same thing is being talked about. It is as if Goldman and Thalberg and Davidson all shared a conception of events, and that Goldman chose to discriminate them finely, Davidson coarsely, and that Thalberg, a trimmer, elected to compromise. The picture of the controversy has prompted one recent writer to say that 'perhaps no position on these matters is "the" correct one', even if in practice we have to pick one view and talk as if it were correct. But if we believe that, in speaking about what people do, we talk about actions, and that what we say about actions is true or false according to how actions are, then the only possible view is the one that makes the same sense as we make in narrating what is done. The philosophy of action does not need to invent or to stipulate its subject matter. (Hornsby 1980: 31-2).

In a strict sense no theory of action is possible, but there is a theory that corresponds to the theory of action (Aune 1977). Let us call that a radical theory of agency. Its theme is not simply a rational individual agent, but agents within a social frame, and we suppose acts they perform. One may call such agents "rational" if their behavior is made intelligible, that is, we can ascribe epistemic attitudes and apply act-constitutive principles to them. And this is the task of re-interpretation. The different feature of this theory is that the analysandum consists of act-predicates (as classificatory expressions) and their ascriptions, whereas, in contrast to that, a theory of action asks for the individuation of acts and the reference of singular terms (action sentences, – description as singular terms). Instead of

* James slaps Peter and Mary is angry

the radical theory of agency makes the assumption:
* that Mary is angry because James slaps Peter.

From here it follows that we analyze the ascription of actions on the main connecting thread from epistemic attitudes that are connected with the network of attitudes. But we are not committed to speak of the reference of such sentences to fundamental events.

The radical theory of agency is to introduce as a theory not only of translation but also of *re*-interpretation, because there are no requirements of counterparts to it in a plausible theory of action. On the other hand, we might expect such counterparts. If Goldman asserts that the act of "signaling in traffic" is generated by the different act of "raising the arm", then Prichard would argue that signaling is determined by the act of moving the arm. If we make the assumption that there are corresponding counterparts between a radical theory of agency and the theory of action in the sense of Goldman, then the instantiation of acts is *indirect* in principle. For Goldman, the concept of generation instantiates acts directly. In correspondence with his argument, the ascription of action makes the assumption:

* If an agent is extending his arm in a certain way, then he is signaling a coming turn, because in a specific domain there is an interconnection between both.

For all ascriptions of action there is the requirement of satisfaction of contextual presuppositions that take effect in the analysis of the word "because" in sentences like "…did …because…". I call this the *principle of constitution for instantiation* of act-tokens. So we explain agent causation in the following way:

* if James fires a torpedo and the Bismarck goes down because he fires the torpedo, then he sends the Bismarck to the sea bottom.

However, if James had done this as an actor in a movie we would not say that he sent the ship down, because what happened has a particular contextual presupposition. This account corresponds surely to Goldman's principle of causal generation. The problem of the satisfaction of act-constitutive principles to ascribe an action can be compared to Hart's ascriptivism (capt. 4.1., in this book).

7.3. Body Movement, Events as Actions and their Causation

7.3.1. Body Movements as a Component of Actions

The analysis of the logical form of action sentences and the syncategorematic account of intentions has claimed to show that our primitive actions are „mere movements of the body" (Davidson 1980: 59, on this, see Hornsby 1980: 1-15). Davidson's solution to the puzzle of agency is:

If an event is an action, then under some description(s) it is primitive, and under some description(s) it is intentional. This explains why we were frustrated in the attempt to assume a basic concept of agency as applied to primitive actions and extend it to further actions defined in terms of the consequences of primitive actions: the attempt fails because there are no further actions, only further descriptions. (Davidson 1980: 61)

What alternative reclassification is to put forward on the status of body movements like "contracting the muscles", also as a causal factor, and the physiological process?

We could make the assumption that the body movement that happens if, for example, a fist is clenched, is closing the fingers. The later movement is a result of another movement that was before it and we can disregard it. The analysis of the role of the body and muscle movements in action theory shows us two properties:

1. If we begin with the assumption that body movements are dependent components of actions, the analysis of muscle contraction of "clenching the fist" does not lead to the conclusion that an action begins before the fingers were closed, namely at the time point of "bracing the muscles". The temporally earlier events, and also the prior items of behavior and body movements, are ultimately unknown, and they are to compare with the discovering of an initiated movement of throwing a ball (on the role of body movement as a component of the infra-structural substrate of actions, Wright 1994: 237-253, J. Habermas 1984; this is in harmony with parts of Thalberg's account in principle; for Wright, the reasons to act step up from the motivational background, and the physical aspect of this activity consists of innervations of the body process (the robust substrate)).

2. But do we conclude from body movements as dependent components that someone who "is clenching his fist" is *doing* "the bracing of his muscles"?

I do not think that this is the case. Shwayder, for example, has argued that if the context within which body movements are to describe as actions is changed, then the same movements are actions no longer. It is an empirical question which act was performed while the muscles were braced. Whatever may be the case, the contraction happens, but such an event is not brought about.

Therefore we conclude: whatever role the physiological process may play, such events are to distinguish from our reasons for actions. The puzzles of agency cannot be solved if we describe the causal explanation of action in the picture of two parallel chains of independent, but temporal coordinated components, one from the primary reasons and another from the body process whereby both flow together in an action (Wright

1994: 246). In this case we are confronted with the downward causation, and Descartes's revenge comes into play (Kim 1998).

7.3.2. The Individuation of Action by Events

There are a number of difficulties that pertain to handling ontological strategies or reductive theories in the philosophy of mind.

Is the narrow content of beliefs to reduce to physico-chemical processes?

These processes certainly influence mental states: I am depressive. I take some pills and feel better. Attitudes come to mind, and we are not always aware of their causes in their aetiology.

But to what degree do we have an available method for the selection of events or states that we classify as attitudes, provided that we assume for the statement about states as attitudes that all relevant (neurological) events that happened earlier are well known?

The answer to this question concerns the correlation of neurological descriptions of events to mental states as well as to behavioral items. The well-known theories of propositional attitudes are "too coarse, or too fine-grained, or in some other respect less apt than intentionalistic successor notions" (Mele 1992: 40, this was also brought into play by Hornsby 1980: 31-32). The neurophysiologist classifies an event independent of any ascription of attitudes. This is no cause for criticism. But following this path we do not find a reasoning for the assumption that the neurophysiological events—which the neurophysiologist selects—are the same as the specification of the semantic content of the ascription of attitudes. Whatever the role of physio-chemical processes may be, it is not instructive for the ascription of propositional attitudes. Intentional psychology and the theory of action are not physics or neurophysics. This is also the case if we accept that attitudes of biologically basic needs are caused by neurophysiological processes. We distinguish two universes for the ontological strategy when we interpret descriptions of physiological events and sentences about attitudes. For an ascription we need no causal knowledge about physical events making behavior intelligible, but we outline a comprehensible picture of the agent. In this framework supervenience is irrelevant—whatever we may know about this (C. Preti 1998). Physical states do not tell us anything about the interpretation of speech acts and the ascription of attitudes, because all attempts to make behavior intelligible is (partially) holistic, and self-understanding and the understanding of other people like ourselves is a part of the comprehensible picture of the agent. That is to say, we optimize the coherence and truth of the attitudes we ascribe, and we grasp human behavior not as a listing of individual cases but within a greater framework of behavioral patterns. There is a difference of types between body processes in general and all attitudes or the whole system of belief. In other words, we have to distinguish classificatory concepts when understanding the mental and the physical (linguistic/conceptual dualism). Philosophers like, for example, Strawson, Warnock, Pears, Melden, Shwayder have argued in this direction. This is best explained by a paradigmatic example: the ascription of attitudes.

If we make the assumption that there is a cardinal dependency to characterize primitive acts in the following way: the doing of "James" x is a primitive action if and only if

1. x is a primitive action and
2. if "James" performs x, then there is no other action y that is performed by x in the sense that x is caused by y.

So we conclude from this dependency: every action of "James" is either a primitive action or another event in a causal chain under a certain description, and some earlier links in this chain are also to describe as actions performed by him. If "James", for example, "moves his finger", "turns on the light switch", "switches on the light", "lights up the room", we could describe his body movements as different actions, and every action is the cause of the one that follows. The general problem of individuating action, that is, the reference of descriptions, lies in this proposal: if we redescribe the series from "moving the hand" to "lighting up the room" as a singular action in a chain of more or less direct effects, then the descriptions like, for example, "moving the finger", "switching on the light", "lighting up the room" denote causal relations between events, but none of this items is a description of an action. If we demand to specify the descriptions and properties to primitive actions, then it is to conclude that all instances that satisfy a singular term are to classify as primitive actions, but others are not.

However, in an object language describing items of behavior we cannot determine whether a certain description of an action is a description of a primitive action or not. If James, for example, raises his right arm, so the "raising of his right arm now" may for some observers be a basic description of James's action. But James can raise his right arm by his left arm also if, for example, his right arm lies in a loop. In this case "James raises his arm" specifies an action, but the description is not one of a primitive action. If something is right with the concept of primitive action, we could expect to find a basic description of any particular action of "James", but we do not expect that an exemplification of basic descriptions like, for example, "James moves his finger" describes actions. For the ascription of actions we do not require a causal knowledge about causal basic properties of behavior.

For ascription we need no causal knowledge about physical events making behavior intelligible. There is a difference of *type* between body processes in general and all attitudes or the whole system of them. So we arrive at a generalized conclusion. No matter which role the physiological process may play, it is to distinguish from the beliefs and pro attitudes to do something. We suppose two distinguished universes of discourse for the ontological strategy when interpreting descriptions of physiological events and sentences on attitudes or actions. So there is a difference of types between physiological processes, body movements on one hand and actions and their descriptions on the other hand.

Certainly we know that no one moves her finger unless her finger moves; and we know that we can tell by observation what people do, and that we could not observe someone move her finger unless we saw her finger move. But we also know that these considerations alone could not suffice to show that her finger's moving is a part of her action—no more that similar considerations could suffice to show that Jones's death was a part of Smith's killing him. Again we know that typically when there is an action, an agent moves her body and thereby initiates a series of events, so that something the agent wants comes to happen. But this consideration does not circumscribe an action, beyond showing it to be where the agent is. It is not at all clear what would definitively settle the question as to which things are parts of actions. This will not seem worrying if we are aware that there need be no more plain truths about the events that are actions than there are plain truths about action (about agency, and things people do).

The events that are actions are understandably a focus of philosophical debate; but they are not ordinary objects of scrutiny." (Hornsby 1993: 176-177; see also Wright 1994:150).

So we know now what the essential problem of a theory of action is that claims to individuate actions as events by movement of our body or of attributing actions in the framework of a basic ontology of events.

7.3.3. The Causation of Actions

We describe the action, for example "Peter turns on the light by the movement of his finger" referring to "Peter", if we describe "the movement of his finger". But turning on the light is itself no part of what "Peter" has done, for example "his contraction of his muscles, his movement of the fingers, his concentration" and so on. Turning on the light is a causal consequence and *not* a part of any act. "Peter turns on the light" and as a result the light is burning. The occurrence of the light burning itself was a causal consequence but *no* part of an action, that is, the act that was done by "Peter". It may be that in describing Peter's doings the description is stretched and pulled (accordion effect) and a planful reference to the light burning now is included. But we could stretch and pull only the descriptions but not the actions themselves. The accordion effect shows us that the consequences of actions are not to redescribe like the ordinary effects of natural events. "Peter's" act is to describe as his activity and "the light is burning" is an upshot of such doings, but the upshot is not a part of the act itself. Actions and their causal consequences are two distinct items. If we make the assumption that, for example, the event *a*, for example, moving the finger, causes *b*, for example, the light is burning, then it may be that the act or the activity of the first event *a* stands in transitive relation to the second event *b*, but the interpretation of "Peter turns on the light by moving his finger" is comparable with the re-interpretation: Peter's act of flipping the switch is *identical* with his act of turning on the light. In the relation between *ARA'*, for example, the moving of the hand *A* and turning on the light *A'*, a relation between acts themselves is consequently *not* to explain, but one between upshots of acts. This is in harmony that the re-identification of these upshots is itself dependent on act-constitutive principles. I have called this the *principle of constitution for instantiation* of act-tokens that are presupposed from an interpreter for his redescription and identification of actions, for example, for the identification of the behavioral item of raising the arm as a traffic sign. From here it is to conclude that all ascriptions of action, though it may be unlikely in many cases, are defeasible by re-interpretation.

We *de*scribe actions if we answer the question: "What was done?" or "What has he done?", we *a*scribe action, if an action is given and we ask for the authorship, for example, "Who laughed?". If the ascription of action begins with its description, then the interpreter makes the given behavior intelligible by the ascriptions of beliefs, that is, he assumes: x assumes/believes that a is required for z in y. If in a given situation we use "Peter did x with the intent to do a", we interpret the use of this expression in such a way that we refer to the same state that we conventionally express by the utterance of "I shall do a". Both have the same truth-conditions. But "to do something willingly" is the case only if it is done intentionally. Forming an intention is to explain by our beliefs, but also by intentions as a mental item, and therefore we interpret the word "shall" as the expression of such attitudes.

Attitude-theorists agree more or less that attitudes may change in time, but they are dispositions that cause judgements and actions under certain conditions. All attitudes are connected and do not stand alone. In the pattern of attitudes, the truth of beliefs "coheres with a significant mass of beliefs" and our beliefs are intelligible "in the light of this presumption, much as every intentional action taken by a rational agent (one whose choices, beliefs, and desires cohere in the sense of Bayesian decision theory) is justified" (Davidson 2001 (1983): 139). The truth of beliefs determines their existence and contents and is supervenient on different sorts of domains (behavioral, neurophysiological, biological, physical, social). Actions are upshots that are caused by the strength of primary reasons. The explanation of action is a theoretical construction by the theory of decision that coheres with the consistence and truth of propositional attitudes. Behavior is an action if it is a consequence of the decision-theoretical ordered network of attitudes, and reversed the ascription of intentional attitudes is a part of the explanatory action-theoretical strategy of *RI*, that is, the unification of the theory of meaning, action, decision and communication.

But how far do our strongest beliefs that we express in all-out judgements cause our intentional actions?

The answer to this question leads us to the explanation of action as an interplay among desires, beliefs and intentions with respect to the desirable content of an action in respect of an "all things considered judgement", that is:

When an intention is formed we go from a stage in which we perceive, or imagine that we perceive, the attraction and drawbacks of a course of action to a stage in which we commit ourselves to act. This may be just another pro-attitude, but an intention, unlike other desires or pro-attitudes, is not merely conditional or prima facie. If it is to produce an action, it can't be simply an appreciation that some good would come of acting in a certain way. (Davidson 2004 (1987): 107)

From such strongest beliefs as premises, an interpreter redescribes the intention (explanatory redescription) of purposive behavior. Yet, an interpreter is *not* successful to discover in particular *how* an agent comes *from* his prima facie reasons *to* the conclusion that an action is desirable. I doubt that from the Davidson-view we will find an answer to the question:

What are beliefs and intentions, and *how* does the connection between both generate an action?

Davidson eliminates intentions as genuinely mental items. But we need a re-analysis of his answer to the question what intentions are in order to show how beliefs and intentions are interconnected when explaining actions (on an answer Preyer 2002 b: part III).

7.4. On Hempel's Account

7.4.1. How do we integrate Explaining Actions in Scientific Explanations?

Mental anomalism means, on one hand, that mental events cannot be subsumed under strict laws. On the other hand, Davidson does not give up the unification of scientific explanation.

What are the difficulties to integrate the pattern of explaining action in the general scientific explanation?

This question leads us to the role of statements of laws for explaining actions. Hempel (1962) has argued that explanations by intentions and reasons are not to distinguish logically from the general scheme of scientific explanation. His argument is that an explanation of action implies statements of laws.

But how could we explain an action by reasons without knowing the relevant event (explanandum), that is, the event that is caused by an action?

In the general scheme of scientific explanation, such "explanations" always refer to the relevant law.

How can we apply the scientific explanation to actions in such a way that we could deduct the explanandum?

But the decisive question is:

In what way does the explanation of actions by reasons entail laws?

This is doubted by primary reasons. Rationalization means a relationship between reasons and actions, and the specification of the pro attitudes and beliefs explains the action: the reason explains the doing of a person: "In brief, laws are involved essentially in ordinary causal explanations, but not in rationalizations"(Davidson 1980 (1963): 15). In so far as explanations by reasons entail laws, they are nothing but generalizations that we imply for an ascription of dispositions. But these laws are, in difference to Hempel, only valid for individuals, that is, they are generalizations for the ascription of attitudes and traits of character that make such ascriptions informative for us. The generalizations that connect reasons and action are not laws having the power of predictions. It is possible that our ex-post considerations show that the reason we ascribe to an agent was one among many other reasons. Such generalizations are always hypothetical. But Davidson agrees with Hempel in the point that explanations imply empirical generalizations. In this point there is no difference between the two.

An explanation unconditionally predicts what it explains (in the sense that the sentence to be explained can be deduced from the law and the statement of antecedent conditions), and conditionally predicts endless further things. So by asking what an explanation of a particular event conditionally predicts we learn what sort of law is a reason explanation, let's say of Ford's compromise on the energy bill in order to curry favor with the voters. If the assumption of rationality is the important empirical law, then this explanation of Ford's action should tell us what (conditionally) to expect of all mankind. But if I am right, it mainly tells us what (conditionally) to expect of Gerald Ford. For what I have suggested is that the relevant generalizations are just the ones that express dispositions like wanting to curry favor with the voters, or believing that compromising on the energy bill would make the voters like him. To me the case seems clear; knowing the explanation of Ford's action tells us a lot about him but almost nothing about people generally. (Davidson 1980 (1976): 273-274)

7.4.2. The Limit of Integration

Hempel's integration of the explanation of action in the general scheme of scientific explanation leads us to difficulties, because in the covering law-model the description of antecedents is to expand to a law. In the case of explaining actions, the antecedence entails the ascription of attitudes. The description or ascription of attitudes respectively is a singular premise (condition) for the conclusion. A similar problem arises in the teleologic explanation because it is not possible to explain any action from its end, for example, we could not explain the killing of James by the event that his death has occurred. A part of the singular antecedence of teleological explanations, is the description of intentional behavior like beliefs, desires, intentions, knowledge. If we accept Hempel's solution, we ask:

What happens if the law is false or the statistical likelihood is low?

On the other hand, intentional actions are also to perform without any reasons like, for example, Peter goes to the railway station without any further reason, he simply does so. In the general scheme of scientific explanation a causal description is covered by a law. For an explanation of action this means that this explanation attributes attitudes to an agent.

How do we carry out such ascriptions?

Hempel's answer is: we refine a law with wider statements about the conditions of their application (the given antecedent). Surely Hempel's proposal is to accept in many cases. But it is not to apply to the explanation of action, if the explanation by reasons implies laws in the sense of empirical generalization for the attributive ascription of dispositions and we ascribe a given behavior or a certain property to an agent.

What do we presuppose for the ascription of dispositions? Is it only a given individual action that is an evidence for the ascription of dispositions (beliefs, desires)?

Hempel and Carnap have assumed that we accept the inductive logic as rational. The warrant of such reasoning is the totality of evidence. Yet, this principle is not to apply in general to the explanation of action, because such explanations are to instantiate to a relationship between primary reasons and actions in which laws only refer to *individual* agents. The empirical generalization about mankind does not inform us about the attitudes of "Ford" if we make his "compromise on the energy bill" intelligible. Yet, when we make action intelligible we apply a comparable principle to the totality of evidence of inductive reasoning, the principle of *execution of intentions* and making true beliefs. If we want to integrate explaining action in the general scheme of scientific explanation, the problem is:

... no single action can prove that a disposition like a desire or belief exists; desires and beliefs, however short lived, cannot be momentary, which is why we typically learn so much from knowing about the beliefs and desires of an agent.

This is the point, I suggest, where general knowledge of the nature of agents is important, general knowledge of how persistent various preferences and beliefs are apt to be, and what causes them to grow, alter and decay. Such knowledge is not used in giving reason explanations, but it is surely part of why reasons are so satisfying and informative. (Davidson 1980 (1976): 274).

This shows us the limit of the unification explaining of actions with the general scheme of scientific explanation. When we explain actions by beliefs and desires, the feature of desirability of the content of such attitudes from the agent's point of view comes into play, and this makes a difference to physical explanation. This feature has no echo in natural sciences. Therefore we presuppose another universe of discourse of instantiation of our redescription. The problem is in principle whether we also change our ontology.

Part III
Radical Contextualism

> First meaning, as revealed in a correct theory of truth, and discovered by radical interpretation, is all that a formal theory semantics can hope to recover. It is the foundation of a theory of meaning, but it does not touch all those further things a speaker may 'say' in uttering a sentence.
>
> *Davidson 1999c: 119*

Understanding any particular utterance of sentences in someone's language is the analysandum of the theory of meaning. There are, to portray it in simplified terms, two accounts of theorizing the understanding of one's language. For Grice, the basis for constructing a theory of understanding linguistic behavior is meaning. For others, especially Davidson, also Searle, saying is the main component and linguistic meaning is autonomous. The steps to a radical contextualism are a consequence of *RI*. Understanding of linguistic behavior by redescribing it makes such behavior intelligible by elaborating the significant relationship between an interpretation of the uttered sentences, the attitudes and background theories of individual speakers. Ascriptions of attitudes are concluded from the interpreter's theory of interpretation. The guarantee of all correct interpretation is a referential transparency of causing individual utterance in triangulation between speaker, interpreter and what happens in their surroundings. All evidence making behavior intelligible is given by holding-true, that is, the assent or dissent to sentences. This is the basic theory of *RI*.

Davidson has argued that intentions and propositional attitudes are not the evidence of radical interpretation or of a semantics of natural language because we cannot interpret utterances without interpreting speech and sentences. But the circle is not to smooth out, even if *RI* successfully evolves a theory of belief and meaning in one step. The theory is indetermined by the ascription of beliefs and the interpretation of uttered words we give. Davidson in fact modified Quine's view because, if our theory is tested successfully, the resulting indeterminacy is a small one. But he agrees with him on the indetermination of translation in principle. Therefore, propositions are to refute in semantics. Davidson's solution is the redescription of saying that requires the holding-true of a speaker's sentence as a semantic supplement. Ascriptions of propositional attitudes, intentions, and the function of linguistic conventions are dependent on the concept of literal meaning; especially the convention of sincerity (truthfulness) for performing illocutionary acts does not fix their meaning. All specifications and ascriptions of speakers-meaning and elementary propositional attitudes make sense only on the basis of theorizing literal meaning and the selection of behavioral evidence caused in the triangle. This is the hard core of Davidson's empirical semantics. But the redescription of utterances and its interpretation has to refer not only to beliefs, but also to linguistic contexts and situations as its frame of reference. Davidson presupposes that the interpreter has understood such contexts and that the situational features are obvious by triangulation. Any ascription of attitudes requires a more or less referential transparency of semantic contexts. The questions of contextual and situational reference give the opaqueness of reference that is born by RI a further turn.

Davidson's version of RI is not a generalized solution of the multiplicity force utterances because the utterance meaning (force) itself is, in this account, ultimately indeterminate; and it is not his claim to do this. From my point of view, a wider frame for the task of interpretation is to elaborate. In the following it is essential to make a distinction between the content of utterance $u(p)$, its redescription referring to the set of sentences the given utterance implies, situations, and the utterance as event. I make the distinction between the content of utterance $u(p)$, the utterance as event and the things and events that fulfill the utterance of the propositional content. Without true or fulfilled utterances there would be no language and communication. Yet, an interpreter always searches for a pattern of behavior to make a given piece of it comprehensible. An adequate theory of meaning must treat speakers' propositional attitudes, linguistic meaning, and situational references as separate but also coordinate factors in the performance and understanding of utterance meaning.

8. The Elugardo-Problem

A total theory of behavior makes the assumption that the interpretations of linguistic and non-linguistic utterances are combined. To recognize the meaning of an utterance $u(p)$, we redescribe it as an intentional doing from a speaker's belief system and with reference to a situation in which $u(p)$ was uttered. In this way we also understand the force of $u(p)$. But the propositional content of "that-clause" cannot be reduced to any propositional attitude or intention.

The feature of the force multiplicity of illocutionary acts is shown to us by the following example:

(1) Peter said: (that) snow is white in c_0.

* He makes a statement about natural things.

(2) Peter said: (that) snow is white in c_1.

* He wants some cocaine.

(3) I say that Peter said: (that) snow is white...

* The redescription of the content of Peter's utterance "snow is white" by my utterance as a "statement" or "want" is only given by considerations of linguistic context of uttering (c_0) or (c_1) and so on and by reference to the uttered proposition in given situations (speaker reference, intended content).

Therefore, the meaning of $u(x)$ of Peter's saying (doing) at the level of redescription is not completely given by:

(4) ($\exists x$) (Peter's utterance "snow is white" and my last utterance "snow is white" make us to samesayers) this is Davidson's account of samesayers.

The meaning of utterances and the language content are given by the redescription of saying that ... with reference to attitudes and contextual features of utterance meaning. The logical form is to bring into line with these items, and the application of this form gives us an instrument to interpret any utterance of natural speakers. But the worsening of this runs the risk of making a fault. To make this clear enough, I will discuss Elugardo's (1999a, 1999b) critique on the holistic truth-centered theory of *RI* and its paratactic account of reported speech.

RI is the intelligible redescription of linguistic behaviour reporting from a radical interpreter.

How do we redescribe such utterances in such a way that we give a report of the proposition-like content samesaying and also of the same token of utterance?

Attitudinal reports make two assumptions: we assert a relation between the speaker and a proposition-like content, and the report is true only if the radical interpreter redescribes the proposition-like content of the utterance by the complement clause.

But is the paratactic account of indirect discourse successful to bridge the gap between literal meaning and speaker meaning, that is, the intended force of the utterance, and the recognition of utterance meaning from an addressee in particular circumstances?

The leading question is:

What does it mean that one sentential utterance samesays another utterance by indirect discourse?

One answer by Davidson is that samesaying is a relation of synonymy of utterances. From the truth-condition of "Peter said that", we conclude synonymous utterances of our reporting. Yet it is not Davidson's proposal that utterance-tokens samesay one another if and only if they have the same meaning and reference. In the response to Foster he argues:

But what is this relation between utterances, of stating the same fact or proposition, that Foster has in mind? ...if both reference and meaning must be preserved, it is easy to see that very few pairs of utterances can state the same fact provided the utterances contain indexical expressions ...I cannot twice state the same fact by saying "I'm warm" twice. (Davidson 1984 (1976): 177)

Another differing answer is that the paratactic approach analyzes the indirect discourse of "Galileo said that the Earth moves" as two sentences whereby the "that" refers to a second utterance, and we report on the same content as a translation given by the truth-condition of uttered sentences. In the last case it is not a necessary condition that the reported sentences have the same literal meaning of the speaker's sentence-token. In general it is the task of RI to convey the content of $u(p)$, that is, what a speaker has said.

Elugardo argues:

1. If samesaying between the utterance of a speaker and a radical interpreter is a relation of synonymy, the paratactic proposal ascribes wrong or different truth-conditions with its indirect discourse. To synonymous utterances we ascribe the same truth-conditions, and such utterances have the same meaning. But it may be that an utterance is an accurate translation of another utterance without having the same meaning.

Elugardo gives the following example:
I report Peter's utterance "I am tired" by pointing to him and saying "you are tired". Yet, the meaning of the sentence of my report and the meaning of Peter's utterance are different. The report of samesaying as a translation (interpretation) is also possible if both utterances are different in their literal meaning and truth-condition. For Elugardo it is not the problem that the paratactic proposal is wrong, but it leads to the difficulty that samesaying is defined by the same meaning of pairs of utterances. Synonymy is not sufficient for samesaying.

2. If we make the assumption that the report by the indirect discourse is a pragmatical relation, it is possible that the truth-conditions of utterances in the analyzed language are also ascribed rightly if no natural speaker is interpreted in a correct way. Pragmatic features are intentions, particular circumstances of the talk, assumptions of shared beliefs and expectations or the past history of the speech.

The example by Elugardo is:
Cassius said in his well-known address: "Brutus is an honorable man". Nero who heard it and did not understand its rhetorical effect reported to his friend: "Cassius said that Brutus is an honorable man". But with none of Cassius's utterances the same was said that Nero said. Elugardo concludes that the paratactic analysis of Nero's utterance is wrong. Nero's literal report of Cassius's utterance is in fact true, but he did not redescribe the intended force of Cassius's speech. Elugardo concludes: the problem of a paratactic analysis is that the content of the redescribed utterance has to take pragmatic features into account. In difference to that, the T-theorems of a truth-theory in the style of Tarski are not determined by such factors. The intent of the utterance of Cassius is to recognize only by reference to the particular circumstances and the past history of his utterance, and, moreover, if and only if I know that Cassius wants to say the following with his utterance: Brutus is a villain.

Elugardo asks us:
What does any finitely axiomatizable, semantically compositional theory of truth achieve to interpret linguistic behavior?

He points out in his argument that we cannot conclude the intended force of an utterance from a theory of truth, for example in the case of Cassius the intended meaning that Brutus is a villain. The hard core of Elugardo's argument is the multiplicity of the intended force of an utterance.

3. In respect of Lepore's and Cappelen's (1999) analysis of mixed

quotation, Elugardo argues that they do not give the correct truth-condition, because the reporter and the speaker may mean different things
(intended meaning) using the same quoted expression. Mixed quotation
as a modified paratactic analysis interprets "Galileo said that the earth
moves" as

* There is an utterance u of Galileo such that u samesays that and some
part of u same-tokens these. (The earth moves)

In mixed quotation the marks play the role of quantifiers ranging over
utterance-tokens. Its mentioning role is to show the logical form of
reporting speech, such is, "same-tokens (u^*,x)" and "samesays(u,y)"
whereby the first argument-place of predicates is to grasp as a quantified
variable ranging over utterance-tokens; the second argument place is the
position for a demonstrative to the utterance, such is, the demonstrated
utterance of some expression. In the expression in the case of "samesays
(u,y)" it is the sentence following the complementizer, for example, "the
earth moves". Mixed quotation claims to capture the logical form in a
way linking paratactically the complement with a quantified sentence
containing demonstrative elements (without "that" and quotation marks):
therefore, the quotation marks are eliminable by the logical form.

Elugardo argues that Cappelen's and Lepore's account of mixed quotation does not work well in the cases where samesaying is a semantic
relation or a pragmatic relation, and mixed quotation does not give us the
right truth-condition for the entailed quotation. His argument is concluded from the multiplicity of (intended) force of utterances, that is,
the reporter or radical interpreter has to grasp the intended meaning that
may differ from its literal utterance. Elugardo concludes that the mixed
quotation may be true, but the two utterances do *not* samesay each other.
Therefore: difference in intended meaning entails a difference in what
the reported utterance and the reporting utterance mean. And just this is
the case if mixed quotation may be true.

Yet: is Elugardo right in his criticism?

I do not at all think he is. *RI* copes the circle between belief and meaning with respect to the first meaning. The redescription of linguistic behavior as regards samesaying and the same token of an utterance apply
the principle of the autonomy of meaning. First meaning is the subject of
RI and of the theory of truth. Only if we have such understanding, we
can handle the Elugardo-problem in the right way. Surely this is a serious
question. It is the task of radical contextualism to give a solution. Seman-

tics can help us to do this: "Language is the instrument it is because the same expression, with semantic features (meaning) unchanged, can serve countless purposes." (Davidson 1984 (1968): 108)

9. Analyzing Utterance Meaning

9.1. The Decomposition of Utterance Meaning

It is often argued that in natural languages there is a multitude of speech acts. Evidence of this is that there are similarly large numbers of verbs that have the function of designating speech acts. But linguists and philosophers of language agree that most verbs do not designate single speech acts, but features, roles or modifications of speech acts like, for example, "to answer", "to dispute", "to invite" and so on; other verbs designate types of discourses like, for example, "to tell", "to recount", "to advise", "to question", "to argue" and so on. Therefore, theorists of language also agree that the large number of speech acts is to reduce to such elementary speech acts that we characterize formally by a grammatical mood and not only by a particular verb. A concept of a speech act in L is to identify with the meaning of certain sentences in L. There is a general problem of the semantic analysis of explicit performative sentences. Sentences of judgement uttered as declaratives or interrogatives in the first and second person are widespread ambigious. For example, sentences like "I beg you to stay here" may be a plea or a statement that explains the utterance is a plea, "I want you to stay here" may be the utterance of a want or an expression of a motivation, or the utterance of "the coffee is cold" may be a statement or an evaluation. This is the reason why I do not analyze utterance meaning with a standardization of explicit performative utterances (sentences). The semantic decomposition of utterance meaning takes this trouble into account.

Every act, not as a type, but as an act-realization, is a particular result; also speech acts are such results. In the following I will give a sketch of how the intended meaning of $u(x)$ is to analyze, that is, a concept of a speech act as the meaning of certain sentences is a result-function of the utterance of such sentences $u(x)$ in certain circumstances, and every concept of a speech act is a part of a certain illocutionary type. Every concept of a speech act results from the application of an illocutionary type to a suitable propositional content. I call the decomposition of the meaning $(u(x)$ in $L)$ semantic form. Utterance meaning is to understand in this way on different levels of redescription. This form for analyzing $u(x)$ is an ordered 4-tuple:

* meaning $(u(x)_y$ in $L) = \{m : m = <s_{co,1...n+1}, p, a, p_{sito,1...n+1}>\}$

The utterance meaning $u(x)$ as a space-temporal token of $u(x)_y$ in L = any natural language is a subset of all ordered 4-tuples, that is, the logical form is a property of an ordered 4-tuple of s_c = uttered sentence in a 0-context or any other context, a = attitude, p = proposition like content (structure of such contents), p_{sit} = reference of the proposition like content in given situations, that is, the *particular circumstances u(x)* is uttered (speaker reference, intended content). If we assign attitudes to sentences and propositions, we make the assumption of general conditions of coherence. The logical form (structure) is to specify to the whole utterance, that is, this "form" is a semantic form (structure). This form connects the meaning of the whole utterance and the meaning of its parts. I call this the *intended interpretation*. The meaning of $u(x)$ or utterance meaning in L is to re-interpret by the ordered 4-tuple. Utterance meaning is therefore relative to a given language. Some philosophers might find the usage of the expression "proposition" odd. I agree with Quine's and Davidson's critique in principle. Yet, Quine has also introduced a harmless use of it:

...a usage of "proposition" that is useful and unobjectionable. It can be construed as denoting the sentences themselves, rather than their meanings, but it is used instead of "sentence" when we are concerned with the sentence as an object of belief rather than with its morphology and syntax. (1995: 77)

But we need a semantic answer to the question what a propositional content is (see 2. 3., in this chapter). In the following I will sketch the re-interpretation of utterance meaning. I assume here that the background theory is more or less well-known. The background theory may be expressed in different natural languages, but speaker and interpreter converge in the theory of interpretation in principle, for example, they do not pair different truth-conditions or other fulfillment conditions to utterances within different languages also. If we define the truth-(fulfillment) conditions of utterances of sentences $u(s)$ in L and we quantify over $u(s)^L$, then the logic-concept of the utterance in L is given. From my point of view, the classical logic is a powerful instrument to do its work for the theory of interpretation.

9.2. 0-Context and Linguistic Context*

The meaning of the utterance "snow is white" in L, in our example (1), is in s_{co} a statement about a natural thing. The 0-context is not to mix up with the particular (empirical) circumstances within which something is uttered. I will follow the concept of 0-context introduced by D. Wunderlich (1976: 133-134). Such context is not a general constant, but it is to introduce in relation to the utterance of a certain sentence $u(x)$ in L. The indexical expression shows in which particular extent the 0-context is necessary to understand the sentence: from here it is to conclude that the sentence *itself* determines the 0-context. Yet, it is to take into account that in a sentence its indexical determinations are not always explicitly expressed. There are "explicit" and "implicit entailed expressions" of indexical specifications that we have to filter out. An utterance like "Bring me the book!", for example, entails an indexical specification from the speaker's side by the verb "the speaker is the recipient", but it entails also an indexical specification of the addressee by the form of the verb. The utterance of "Bring me the book!" means advice in a 0-context. We take a sentence in a 0-context as literal. The force of the sentence is determined by itself. Therefore, in this context we cannot distinguish the force multiplicity of utterances, for example, to use the same sentence as an "order", an "instruction", a "question" or a "plea", and so on. To do this we have to construct further contexts c_1, c_2, c_3. One may call such contexts *linguistic contexts** of L, because references of the used expressions are fixed linguistically.

We find such contexts* of L by the specification of the explicit and implicit entailed indexical expressions, for example, "Bring me the book!" is uttered as some advice by a superior. Starting from the meaning in c_0 we find relative to the contexts*, the illocutionary acts that are performed by the uttered sentences. But also this context* is furthermore *not* to confuse with any p_{sit}, that is, the particular circumstance in which someone uttered a sentence. For example, the intent of the advice "Bring me the book!" may be to humble a subordinate. We have to make this distinction, because we could otherwise not distinguish between different forces of utterances and the intent speakers may have.

We assume for a redescription of an uttered or inscribed sentence in c_0 that the speaker knows the meaning of the uttered sentence, and so we understand the token of it in the sense of a semantic competence of

a speaker, which is expressed in the power of the used language. Therefore, for a radical interpreter the background theory is extensively well
known. In the first person attitudes there is in principle no error of any
speaker about the meaning of his uttered words. This is a knowledge
we have by our own standards. Yet, for the interpreter there is the
problem of semantic comparability of the heard utterances with his
own speech.

9.3. The Propositional Content and the Ascription of Attitudes

The problem of attitude semantics is in principle:

How do we analyze the semantics of attitude ascriptions to capture
speaker meaning (intended meaning) and literal meaning concluded
from the redescription of linguistic behavior?

It is not possible for *RI* to know attitudes of particular speakers without interpreting their linguistic behavior. Therefore, the independent
availability of evidence of the truth of a theory interpreting linguistic
behavior cannot be a research of speakers' attitudes empirically. If we
take this problem seriously, the solution to the problem of evidence of
the ascription of attitudes is to conclude from the structure of the propositional content and its fulfillment conditions.

It is of main importance that the analysis of types of illocutionary acts
goes hand in hand with the analysis of propositional content. It is a usual
thing among philosophers of language to make the distinction between,
for example, the sentence "p" and the nominalized sentence "that p". By
the singular term "that p" we take away from the sentence "p" the feature of the claim to be, for example, an assertion. If a speaker says "that
p", he does not utter a sentence with a particular intent, for example,
that p is true, "that p" may be, for example "true", "doubtable", in particular situations "desirable", and so on. With using predicates of the
metalanguage like "is true", "is fulfilled" we give back the ones we have
taken away, and the same is said as was said with "p" because "is true"
expresses the truth of "p". Therefore, it is to conclude that the meaning
of "p" is composed of the propositional content and the truth indication
whereby the propositional content is expressed in a nominalized way
by "that p". The propositional-like content of any illocutionary act has
a structure we grasp by its fulfillment condition expressed in L. Such

conditions are given by the used logic: the propositional content has the structure of "⊢$*p*$", "!$*p*$", "?$*p*$" and this is connected thereby that there is to every $*p*$ a $*non-p*$ ($*p*$ is the symbolization of a non-nominalized propositional content of "p"; see also Tugendhat, 1976: 64-70, the analysis goes back to Frege's analysis of negation). Yet, with taking this step we do not know *how* truth itself is to explain, and this concept of propositional content is without any structural differentiation of such content itself.

It is to emphasize that the analysis of illocutionary types and the ascription of attitudes goes hand in hand with the analysis of the relevant propositional content. This leads us to the truth (fulfillment) conditions and the semantic properties of propositional contents expressed by "that p" sentences, because such conditions are the structure of propositional contents, for example, of assertions, directives or other illocutionary acts. To distinguish these semantic properties, Wunderlich's analysis is helpful, and I will follow it in principle (1976: 70, 76). Four semantic properties of propositional contents are to distinguish that have a *predication*. Therefore we do *not* count nominal components or individuals to which they refer among the propositional content, even though they take place within the respective propositional contents on their positions. Furthermore it must be mentioned that propositional contents are not only to express by "that"-sentences but also by nominalizations of sentences, for example, "that Peter is coming tomorrow" has, with respect to "the coming of Peter tomorrow", the same right (yet the expressions are used in different linguistic constructions):

1. The *propositional content p* is, in the case of assertions, a connection between a singular term in a referential position and a general term in a predicative position by a predication (see 3., in this chapter). One may technically call it the proposition P or the statement that is made.

2. *Open propositional contents*: The propositional content p is an *open* one, for example in the case of directives. Such a content includes at least one *empty-place* that is to substitute by an individual in the particular situation within which, for example, the directive is addressed whereby the propositional content is given, that is, a directive to an addressee is uttered.

Informally I will introduce the following fulfillment condition, for example for representative and directive illocutionary acts; fulfillment conditions are conditions of interaction that characterize illocutionary types semantically:

Representative speech acts (assertions, statements, descriptions, explanations, reports, affirmations):

1. The propositional content p of, for example, the assertion >Fa< in a 0-context uttered by a speaker at the time t is satisfied *iff* it is true at the time t that the general term is verified by the entity which is given by the singular term. The predicates themselves are classifying expressions (as I will show in 3., in this chapter)

2. The verification of the general term by the entity that is given by the singular term satisfies the propositional content at the time t *iff* it is true at the time t that the predication is verified.

The generalized feature of representative speech acts is that the propositional content is a proposition, that is, should the situation arise it is true or not.

Directive speech acts (orders, instructions, advice, requests, demands, pleas):

1. Peter satisfies at time t the open propositional content p in 0-context that, for example, someone closes the door *iff* it is true at the time t that Peter closes the door.

2. The closing of the door by Peter at time t satisfies, for example, the open propositional content that Peter is advised to close the door *iff* it is true at time t that Peter closes the door.

If we have the condition of truth (fulfillment) from 1., we can conclude from 2. what the fulfillment condition is if we assume that the definiendum in 1. is identical with the definiens in 2., that is, "It is true at time t that Peter closes the door" (Wunderlich 1976: 76-77).

With this account it is coherent: if someone gives "Peter" a directive to do something, we do not describe his present or future actions. The speaker utters an open propositional content p. But this is not a proposition "p" that describes the action itself. We describe the circumstances which would be made happen if "Peter" had satisfied the directive in question. But the circumstances and motives of "Peter" are not relevant on this level of analysis. The analysis of directives to "Peter", for example, was forced, has to do, was committed to do something, is given in respect to any p_{sit}. The fulfillment itself is not effected by them.

3. *Concepts of predicates*, for example, of w-questions (who, where, when, which and so on) or complementing questions respectively. The concept of predicate is to complete with respect to a situation at a time t with an individual so that we have a propositional-like content p. There-

fore, the concept of predicate is also an open structure. The concept of predicate is to distinguish from the concept of propositional-like content p, therefore w-questions like "Who is coming now?" have some properties that are different from questions of decisions (and disjunctive questions). We do not select a propositional content p that is true or not, but we refer to individuals/entities that fall under the concept of predicate. "Who is coming now?" or "Whoever is coming now has found the way to us" refers to a concept of predicate, that is, the set of individuals that are coming at a certain time.

4. *Concepts of propositional-like contents p*, for example, of questions of decision (yes/no-questions) and disjunctive questions. The concept of propositional content is to specify to a situation s at time t by the propositional-like content p that has the respective property. The purpose of questions of decision is that the speaker can choose between p or non-p by the answer he has got, for example, by having got the answer to "Is Tom sleeping now?" the speaker decides to make no noise, therefore the question is closed by a property of a proposition P.

The propositional content p of a question is not true or false and therefore not to identify with such a content. But the propositional-like character p of questions is to analyze from this content itself, because the question is answered (fulfilled) by a particular proposition the speaker prefers (wants). If the propositional content p of a question is an *open* structure, then the fulfillment relation specifies what this relation satisfies relatively to the propositional content p of the question (on the analysis of question and the discussion of the different approaches, Wunderlich 1976: 181-250). Yet it is to mention that the difference between erotetic and directive illocutionary acts is that questions require a particular knowledge on the addressee's side. The open propositional-like content p of both speech acts is different in principle: for directives, the open content is to close by the addressee himself for questions, for example, such of decisions, the content is a concept of propositional content (a property of it). Therefore, a particular proposition p must be found that has the property in question, that is, the open structure is not to close by the addressee as an agent, but only by right proposition. For erotetic acts it can not be excluded also that the speaker himself removes his cognitive deficit.

Similar characterizations of fulfillment conditions are to give for other fundamental illocutionary types like commissive (promises, announcements, threats), satisfactive (excuses, thanks, answers, warrants), reactive (retraction of a promise, corrections of assertions, permissions), declarative (appointment, fixing an agenda, opening a meeting, verdict of guilty/ sentence, definitions), expressive (expressions of emotions), and vocative (calls, appeals, forms of addresses) illocutionary acts. With fulfillment conditions we have a general framework for their analysis.

What is to conclude from the structure of propositional content for the ascription of attitudes that are not to observe in our language in which we express our perceiving?

In a certain sense we can say that the attitude is not different from the structure of the propositional content itself that someone has uttered. Yet, if we redescribe linguistic behavior in different respects, we pair to the utterance of the sentence, for example, "Snow is white" the correspondent set of attitudes a on the basis of the fulfillment conditions of sentences that utterances of sentences "snow is white" in s_{∞} imply. In doing so, we give epistemic, doxastic, preferential, motivational, expectational, intentional, conative qualifications of the speaker or of the group under study. Every assertion and ascription of propositional attitudes implies particular conditionals how a speaker or a group would behave in certain circumstances. This is true only with respect to a given L. Within this frame we ascribe attitudes like a_0 "he holds-true that...", a_1 "he sees some white things", a_2 "he believes that there is snow", a_3 "he wants it to snow tomorrow" or in a particular frame, for example, in an absurd stage play within which a speaker utters "I order that it snows tomorrow" so-called comic attitudes. The machinery works without our studying its attitudes themselves.

The application of two-value logic structures the sets of attitudes and gives us explications of correlations between attitudes and behavior. The feature of attitude-connections implies that we apply generalized fulfillment conditions to utterances if we ascribe single attitudes. There are certain connections between attitudes and truth-conditions as well as other fulfillment conditions if we relate these conditions to the world we share or to the social universe in which we participate in particular positions (social status). An interpreter can only cope with the interdependence between propositional attitudes and meaning if he has an independent evidence not bound by individual cases to the ascription of attitudes and if he does not research what is happening empirically in the speaker's mind. We order all attitudes in a plausible picture of the speaker, and we decide upon the ascription of a single attitude only in this frame. This is also valid if we take particular background theories of the behavior under study into play, for example, in the case of religious and social behavior a theory of rituals, and also in cases of obvious contradictions between attitudes (utterances) from our point of view.

The essential feature of this account is that the analysis of any sentence s with these logical means shows: s literally implies, independently of the utterance meaning in particular circumstances (p_{sit}), at least one or more sentences $s_{1...n}$. Perhaps this is presumably valid for all natural languages. Without such implications, most sentences would not only be meaningless, but in the same way we could not understand the meaning of any utterance. In other words: the verification of the conditions of satisfaction of the sentence s' that s implies is the basis of the information for the ascription of attitudes, actions and therefore the meaning of the utterance. We could exemplify this also in the case of explicit performative utterances, for example,

(s) I advise you to hold your promise as a statement about an omission;

(s^1) it is true that the addressee gave a promise;

(s^2) there is an omission on the addressee's side (he has not held his promise);

(s^3) the addressee is a person to whom we ascribe that he can bind his will;

(s^4) it is true that the addressee is able to hold his promise relative to a situation sit_1 ;

(s^5) it is the case that the speaker is right to give the addressee some advice.

(In other *linguistic contexts** there is a variation of interpreting these sentences, and in different p_{sit} we would ascribe another meaning to the utterance.)

The conditions of satisfaction of the set of sentences s^{1-5} that s imply determine whether we ascribe to the speaker of s a certain action, for example, to give advice to do something in c_0, and what the speaker means, for example in difference to c_0 a warning in c_1 , and so on.

It is to emphasize here that the semantic characterization of types of illocutionary acts is a part of the general purpose of the speech act and what general conditions there are to fulfill for their success. These conditions are independent of any p_{sit}. We solve this problem of interpretation by the re-specification of the explicit and implicit entailed expressions of the indexical expressions (or other singular terms).

But with taking this step, we do not know the speaker's reference and have no evidence what he refers to, for example, a factual omission, a weakness of his will that is to overcome, to the commitment of the il-locutionary act, to an advance notice of punishment. The decision about the reference of a proposition-like content p that we have instantiated with the corresponded attitudes (speakter reference) is a matter of the reference (specification) of p in a given situation and their features = p_{sit} and the causal history. I call this indexicality whereby we specify the speaker reference that we redescribe. To identify/reidentify such refer-ence is the role of singular terms.

Now we can also answer the question:

How is truth (fulfillment) itself to explain?

It is not only the claim of speakers expressed in the propositional content "that p" that explains us what truth is. We understand truth (fulfillment) only by its expression in truth-(fulfillment) conditions in a metalanguage, and we give this expression an empirical turn by an explanatory redescription of behavior. Understanding of linguistic behavior is bound to the following: speaker or groups and interpreter have at their disposal the concept of truth- or fulfillment conditions, and we know more or less the background theory that comes into the play. This is only possible if the participants have a language in which they can express such conditions.

9.4. The Explanatory Redescription of Utterance Meaning

I make the general assumption, if someone utters $u(p)$, his intent is to recognize, and we can recognize it only to select the fitting context* of s_c and the speaker's reference p_{sit} of his utterance. This is also in harmony with the unified theory of meaning and action, because interpreting sentences and attributing attitudes goes along with the descriptions of actions "as having complex intentions" we ascribe (Davidson 1984:162). This is valid with respect to the explanatory redescription of actions, no matter whether they are linguistic or not.

To understand the meaning of $u(p)$, we make the following assump-tions for redescribing it and for the ascription of the intended meaning to $u(p)$:

1. Meaning $u(x)$ in Lc_o: a speaker S utters s (sentence) with the mean-ing $u(x)$ if x of S is uttered with a plausible propositional attitude a and intention in any p_{sit} we fit in the pattern of behavior.

2. If x is uttered literally in c_0 (first meaning), then a coherent correlation is given between x and:

(a) the uttered proposition or proposition-like content p;

(b) the assertion A in c_0 and the correspondent set of attitudes a;

(c) the directive (advise) D in c_0 and the correspondent set of attitudes a;

(d) the question Q in c_0 and the correspondent set of attitudes a;

(e) the promise P in c_0 and the correspondent set of attitudes a;

and x fits in the given circumstances.

The correlation is a regularity of linguistic behavior: whoever utters x intends with x in given circumstances to communicate y. Such regularities are a system of interlocking propositional attitudes, that is, the attitudes of a single participant presuppose that we also ascribe them to the other participants. Now we can give mixed quotation its place in the theory of interpretation, we redescribe the locutionary meaning of an utterance in c_0 like "Galileo said that the earth moves" as:

* There is an utterance, u, of Galileo and an utterance-part, u^* in c_0 samesays that and u^* in c_0 same-tokens this. (The earth moves)

Elugardo argues that Cappelen's and Lepore's account is semanticly or pragmatically not successful, because their version of mixed quotation does not have the power to represent the right truth-conditions for the indirect quotation that mixed quotation entails. The argument is that the same quoted expressions by which an interpreter (reporter) redescribes what the speaker has said may pragmatically have a difference in meaning, that is, differences in the intended meaning. Mixed quotation may be true, but the utterances do not samesay each other. If Cappelen's and Lepore's analysis goes in the right direction, as Elugardo has conceded, mixed quotation is to extend reporting different utterance meanings in context* and in p_{sit}. In different context* and p_{sit} we ascribe a different meaning using mixed quotation. And this is not a turn to pragmatics whatever, but it is in harmony with the principle of autonomy of meaning.

The question "Is Peter coming tomorrow?" may be uttered as a warning. In this case, a linguistic context c_1 or c_2 is to bring into play in order to recognize such an illocutionary act. This feature is different from a situation where, for example, the warning can be uttered with the intent: "For God's sake, there'll be trouble!" We may find this intent of the utterance only by the reference to any p_{sit} of the speaker, the causal history and the background of the utterance. This reference is comprehensible only by a mutual knowing about the causal history of the utterance and the adjustment of the theory of interpretation to the given circumstances. We alter our theory of interpretation and adapt the fulfillment conditions to any p_{sit}.

In this case, the speaker's utterance of words "Is Peter coming tomorrow?" is not a same-token of the same words an interpreter mentioned in his report if he recognizes the speaker's intent "For God's sake, there'll be trouble!" in any p_{sit}; and the mixed quotation can have different truth-conditions in this case. Yet, it is to emphasize that it is not the claim of mixed quotation to fix the truth-condition of such utterance meaning.

3. S intends and takes precautions that the addressee A recognizes $1-3$ in any p_{sit},

4. the fact that S intends the recognition of $1-3$ is, for the addressee A, a necessary condition for that:

   (a) meaning $u(x)$ in Lp_{sit}: S intends that A assumes/forms the belief that p,
   (b) meaning $u(x)$ in Lp_{sit}: S wants that A performs D,
   (c) meaning $u(x)$ in Lp_{sit}: S wants that A answers the Q,
   (d) meaning $u(x)$ in Lp_{sit}: S will hold his promise P,
   (e) meaning $u(x)$ in Lp_{sit}: S intends to give a warning W,
       and so on.

The natural way to analyze $s(u,p)$ and the intended meaning of u is: the theory of interpretation in $c_{o,1...n+1}$ and the reference of an uttered p in any p_{sit} determines the meaning $u(x)$. So we could also provide a solution to the problem: with respect to c_o, the two sentences like "Go!" and "I order you to go!" are not synonymous, but with respect to any other c the utterances of both sentences are to correlate with an act of ordering, and in any p_{sit} the utterance may be, for example, a threat.

10. Indexicality

Following Quine, recalling the canonic notation makes a distinction between singular terms in a referential position and general terms in a predicative position. An act of predication is a connection of both terms, but in a composed sentence the terms have different roles. The sentence is true if the general term is verified by the entity which is given by the singular term. The distinction of singular and general terms is a matter of their grammatical roles and not of grammatical forms. For logic, the difference of roles is relevant, but not the linguistic means that indicate them. Quine has argued that the difference in these two roles is shown in the case of faults of application of general and singular terms: if we have a correct application of a singular term to an entity, a fault of application of a general term leads to a false sentence, but contrary to this a fault of application of a singular term is not dependent on the application of a general term.

For Quine, the identifying function of singular terms is not significant. Reference is inscrutable. Therefore, identity is a matter of predication. The test of quantification is dependent on the distinction between the role of singular terms in a referential position and general terms in a predicative position. The proposal is that the position of singular terms is open for quantifiers and variables or expressions of natural language which correspond to the language of logic. Between both we distinguish the roles if we grasp the role of quantifiers or other linguistic expressions which correspond to the use of quantification. The solution is that any singular term, for example,

'Boston' designating Boston, can be reconstrued as a predicate 'is Boston', denoting only Boston. Anything said about Boston can be paraphrased using 'is Boston'. 'Poe was from Boston' becomes $\exists x(x$ is Boston. Poe was from x) or, equally, $\forall x(x$ is Boston $. \supset .$ Poe was from x). We can settle for this as an economical foundation and still derive our usual and more convenient idiom of singular terms by singular description: Boston = $\iota x(x$ is Boston). (Quine 1995: 59 sq.)

The logical form is universal. The word "term" is used along with the logical and not with the linguistic vocabulary. Terms have the property of being *universal* or *particular*. Their properties are dependent on the quantifiers like "all", "some", "for every x ...", that is, the properties of propositions which are to be transformed in positive or negative truth-values. Quantifiers could therefore express the difference between singular and general terms. In this point, there is no difference between Quine and Davidson in principle.

Yet, there is a reason why we do not, as Quine does, replace singular terms in the case of situational reference of p_{sit} in our ordered quadruple of semantic form to ascribe the meaning of $u(x)$ in L. I call this the problem of indexicality. This may go hand in hand with the inscrutability of reference. Tugendhat's (1982) proposal is helpful to show this. My considerations stand more or less on the shoulders of Tugendhat's approach. It is to mention here that it is the semantic or analytical account of reference that has changed the paradigm of mentalistic epistemology and semantics, that is, reference of signs (expressions) is not to assume as self-evident, and entities stand in a correlation to the pseudo-concept of representing something in our mind respectively; in contrast to that, referring to entities is to analyze within the medium of the use of lingual expressions: the understanding of their meaning. An expression that stands for an entity is not an absolute reference, neither proper names nor demonstratives have, as expressions themselves, the property to refer to something directly. It is the task here to analyze the semantic function (role) of singular terms, that is, how we identify something with these expressions. The traditional theory of representation is not successful in giving us an answer.

Singular terms and predicates do not assign their empirical content directly. Tugendhat methodically introduces the reference of singular terms with the following leading questions:

How do we understand 1. a *singular term*, 2. a *predicate*, 3. the *composition* of a singular term with a predicate, and 4. a predicative statement as a *whole*?

The second, third and fourth questions show us the problem of *non-entitative* reference to something, and the first question is a matter of a *verification* of singular terms, that is, their situational instantiation that we perceive. It is to show whereby a situation of perceiving is distinguished from a situation of verification. This does not contradict the inscrutability of reference, because the method of verification does not require a strong concept of reference (individuation) of expressions to entities, that is, an explanation of reference of expressions (words).

What are concepts?

Concepts are principles of classification that are correspondent in L general termini or predicates. By a progressive abstraction, for example, New Yorker, American, human, animal, organism and so on, we find predicates with a larger extension. These predicates are expressions of classification or of principles of classification respectively. This is a general feature because it is valid for *all* predicates. Therefore, the concepts (predicates) themselves fall under the description of these "classifications" but no longer the entities that fall under these concepts (predicates) or the application of predicates respectively. Therefore, the predicate "expression of classification" (the predicate "predicate") is found by picking out the use of predicates; and this is to decide semantically. Only by the use of predicates can we explain what concepts are, that is, by the use of lingual expressions, and these expressions do not stand for anything. (see Tugendhat 1976: 40-41. I will mention here that classification is not a successful exemplification. Exemplification is a method of verification but not one of fabrication of the intension of expression, see in particular W. K. Essler 2000: 57-59).

10.1. The Substitution of Singular Terms

The substitution of singular terms is a function (role) of such expressions. An expression is a singular term if we can substitute it with other expressions that are singular terms with the identity sign (=). A speaker who uses an indexical expression to identify an entity in a situation of perceiving can identify the same entity with other indexical expressions or other singular terms from outside this situation. This is a critique on Strawson's account. For him, the identifying reference is to be explained by an *identifying knowledge* of particulars (Strawson 1971: 77-78.) It is to emphasize in difference to Strawson that only the substitution of indexical expressions makes it possible to refer to the same entity without perceiving it. Reference of singular terms to other singular terms is a matter of their reference in a given situation. If we change the situation of perceiving we can refer to the same situation only by the substitution of singular terms. These terms must be completed with another (classificatory) expression.

10.2. The Specification of Singular Terms

Therefore, the leading question concerning the reference of expressions is:

Which particular, person, or collective does the speaker refer to with his use of a singular term?

To what single item among a given plurality must the reference of the singular term be assigned?

Strawson has called this "to single out" (identifying reference). This is the question of identifying reference in Strawson's proposal, and there is an analogy to the use of predicates in the context of the question what their function (role) is. It should be the function of singular terms to stand for entities. The function (role) of singular terms is to indicate from a plurality of entities of a domain which of all entities is referred to, that is, as something we apply a predicate to. We may call this *specification*.

Yet, it is to mention that it is an empty relation to say that singular terms *stand for* something: it is not a relation between a sign and its entity. If we analyze singular terms correctly, the specification of a singular term to an entity is a relationship of such terms to all entities. So it is shown that the specification of singular terms is not a relation, because we presuppose a relationship to all entities of the supposed universe. We would not need a specification of singular terms if it were not an open question *to what* or *to whom* the terms refer. Yet, if we use these terms in isolation, it is not clear what the functions of the terms are. We need another sign that can take this function. The use of a name, for example, makes sense only if we complete the name with a predicate. Therefore, terms make sense in a whole sentence only. The specification of singular terms is not restricted to *concrete general terms* like, for example, "blue" ("is blue") but is also to apply to *abstract singular terms* (abstract entities, universals), like, for example, "blueness".

10.3. The Incompleteness of Singular Terms

It is the essential feature of singular terms that they are to complete. Only in a space-temporal system in which positions are independent can they take a position. If this is the case, there is *no* rigid designation and direct reference like the meaning of names, as Kripke has argued. Therefore, to understand the function of these terms we need a situational-reference (indices) for their use. However, the use of "yesterday", "three hours ago" and so on, seen from the point of view of a speaker's o-coordinate, gives us no criterion for identification/reidentification of entities of perceptual beliefs. The subjective localization of the respective "here" and "now" is a o-coordinate from which we determine the non-demonstrative indexical expressions, that is, all other situations of perceiving are specified by their distance from and direction towards the given situation. Only by doing so we could, from the respective situation of perceiving, identify another situation, that is, we substitute the indeterminate expression, for example, "at that time", by "one hour ago". The point is that without an objective o-coordinate a subjective localization and therefore an identification is not possible: *there are space-temporal identifications in a system of objective localization only*. This explains us why we can refer to identical situations from a change of situations, for example, Peter says (from his o-coordinate) "here is a chair on the right side of the window", but now he is in New York and says (from his o-coordinate) "there is a chair on the right side of the window of my flat in Frankfurt am Main". It is a property of the semantic class of singular terms that they refer to each other.

But what is the connection of space-temporal identification and the function of predicates in assertions?

The connection is that predicates are expressions of classification. We do not explain the function of singular terms with reference to their use in situations, for example by exemplification. These expressions need to be completed with another expression (the predicate) that enables us to understand what is classified. This is the answer to the question "How do we specify singular terms?".

The difference between a situation of perception and a situation of verification is that the use of expressions of classifications is to complete with singular terms. This changes the situation of perceiving into one of verification.

10.4. The Extensionalistic Version

Nevertheless we can formulate an extensionalistic version of interpreting singular terms: *a predicate classifies what is to be specified by singular terms*. If it is the function of singular terms to indicate which entity is to be picked out, then we understand the word "all" in the same way as we understand the use of singular terms. The function of singular terms is to be explained by their *function* in the context of the *whole* sentence. The *specification* is the *situational reference* indicated by *indices* in a system of reference, that is, to say that p_{sit} is specified. This is the reason why I call the situational reference of *p indexicality*. It is the *function* (role) and the *meaning* of singular terms that we can *substitute* these expressions from different points of view. Yet, singular terms are not to be eliminated, because we use these expressions to recognize our position in an objective frame of localization, and *this is only possible if we complete the objective localization with indexicals.*

The given account is Quinean, because 1. the understanding of singular and general terms is on the sentential level, 2. singular terms can be substituted, and 3. general statements have been emphasized..Contrary to Quine, there are two reasons why singular terms are not eliminable: 1. identity is *not* a matter of predication and 2. singular terms are to be *completed* by general terms; they cannot stand alone. So we conclude: the interdependent reference is a substitution of singular terms under certain conditions (in a space-temporal system): this is a semantic feature of the class of singular terms. But for Quine, this indexicality of p_{sit} is not significant because meaning must be explained by behavioral (holophrastic) stimuli. If predicates are expressions of classification and their function is to complete singular terms, then the "asymmetry between particulars and general characters of particulars" (Strawson) is not an argument against Russell and Quine because reference is a successful classification under certain conditions. With the *extensionalistic version* of interpreting singular terms we have established an analytical understanding of the expressions being the *same as/is identical with* ... This will be shown in a further step.

10.5. Types of Singular Terms

It is essential that the reference of singular terms cannot be explained by exemplifications (ostentions) but by their function (role). Such terms are to analyze as semantic classes. It is to emphasize that the meaning of singular terms "their descriptive meaning", is not only to stand for something, but it is their essential feature also that they have a role/function in predicative statements.

There are four types of singular terms, apart from names, which have a meaning, that is, which are specified by objects of perceiving (on the analysis of name, see Tugendhat, C. Wolf 1983: 160-166). These types are informative for the specification of the reference of singular terms:

1. singular terms with a *demonstrative pronoun*, for example, this mountain, this car and so on;

2. singular terms with a *definite description* of space-temporal relations, for example, the mountain at the point of intersection of the y degree of longitude and x degree of latitude;

3. singular terms which stand in a *definite relationship to something* that was identified like, for example, the murder of Henry; and

4. singular terms which specify a *unique property*, for example, the highest mountain.

For Strawson, the *first* type is independent of the *second*, the *second* and the *third* types are not structurally different, but the *third* and the *fourth* types are to be sharply distinguished. Yet, in contrast to Strawson, the principal question of speaking on identification is:

How does the space-temporal identification function?

In other words,

How do we reach the individuation of the proposition p? How important is the specification of situational reference of p_{sit} by giving the indices for this process?

It is necessary to distinguish between the use of the *demonstrative* and the objective terms (space-temporal) on one hand and the *non-demonstrative* singular terms on the other hand. The specification of a singular term with a demonstrative expression (the *first* type) in one case and with a definite description of space-temporal relations (the *second* type) in the other case are *connected*, and therefore they must be sharply distinguished from the other *two* types. From here it follows that there is an interdependence of the *first* types of singular terms with space-temporal locations in their function of identifying entities of perception. Therefore, the meaning of singular terms is dependent on their reference to situations, that is, the reference to the proposition p_{sit}. Yet this does not annul the inscrutability of reference because the answer to the question "How do we state which entity a term refers to?" is a matter of an objectivity-localized reference. This reference, cannot be unsuccessful. The system of space-temporal relations is a system of demonstrative specification. Speaker reference is made explicit in this way, but we do not eliminate the inscrutability of reference, because there is no relation between signs and entities, but a successful classification under certain conditions. (For the identification of space-temporal entities we need also sortal predicates. I will not discuss their role here.)

Now we can also give an answer to the question "How do we understand a sentence-utterance with a predication as a *whole*?" Sentences have a meaning, but they do not stand for anything. The meaning is to grasp by the function (role) of singular terms, their verification in situations of perceiving to which the fulfillment conditions are qualified. If we dispose about the semantic class of such terms, we can distinguish between situations of perceiving that change in continuation and such of confirmation. Yet, we can see what the difference to Davidson's distal theory of meaning and reference is. It is the claim for the theory of truth that reference and satisfaction are theoretical concepts ("as are the notions of singular term, predicate, sentential connective, and the rest") ... "there is no reason to look for a prior, or independent, account of some referential relation" (Davidson 1990: 300). If we have an acceptable *T*-theory, no explanation of reference of singular terms is necessary. All we need to have is that its axioms are quantified to answer ontological questions. This is right with respect to a relation of signs and entities by satisfaction, as Tarski has already shown. Yet, if externalism works for our perceptual beliefs, particulars and events are to identify. This leads us back to the function (role) of singular terms, that is, their verification in a supposed universe we talk about. Reference as *reference-relative-to-a-sequence* can by no means explain that. But it is in harmony with a truth (fulfillment)-theory of interpretation to take the function (role) of singular terms into play. If we redescribe utterance meaning in any linguistic context* or p_{sit} , the objective space-temporal location and its specification is the guarantee that our re-interpretation of utterance meaning can work. However, it is another problem how successful we are. All this is not a modification in essence that reference is behaviorally inscrutable (the circle between belief and meaning is not to eliminate), and theories (the truth of a translation of a sentence by a theory about its utterance in particular circumstances)—all their expressions—are underdetermined. There is no last ontology of theories and no epistemic reductive basis of them.

What I call radical contextualism only works if the interpreter presupposes that the background theory is more or less well-known. We want to understand the utterance, that is, the intension of what is uttered. If we change our background theory, the fulfillment conditions are to re-interpret. This would be a drastic change of our theories of interpreta-tion and its ontology. I will mention here that I am not fixed to the verbal expression "radical contextualism". We are often embarrassed if we want to find the right word to declare terminologically what the proposal is. Yet, I think that what I mean is shown clear enough for sketching the problem of theories of interpretation of utterance meaning. Such utter-ances have a property to be true and/or to fulfill, or they haven't. We recognize this on the sententional level, and at the same time we link the mental, language and the social by compositionality (sub-sentential as-pect). If this is not the case, I can see no feature of semantic compatibility of making behavior intelligible.

Bibliography

Amoretti, C. 2008. *Il triangolo dell'interpretatione: Sull' epistemologia di Donald Davidson*, Milano.

Armstrong, D. 1973. *Belief, Truth and Knowledge*. Cambridge.

—. 2000. "Going through the Open Door again: Counterfactuals vs. Singularist Theories of Causation." Preyer, Siebelt 2000a.

Anscombe, G.E.M. 1959. "Thought and Action in Aristoteles." *New Essays on Plato and Aristotle*. Edited by R. Bambrough. London.

—. 1957. *Intention*. Oxford.

Antony, L.M. 1994. "The Inadequacy of Anomalous Monism as a Realistic Theory of Mind." Preyer et al. 1994.

Aristoteles. 1951. *Nikomachische Ethik. Werke*, Bd. 3. Stuttgart 1951.

Aune, B. 1977. *Reason and Action*. Dordrecht.

Austin, J. L. 1956/7. "A Plea for Excuses." *Proceedings of Aristotelian Society*, Vol. 57. 1959.

—. "Other Minds". *Logic and Language*, sec. Series. Edited by A. G. N. Flew. Oxford.

Avramides, A. 1999. "Davidson and the New Sceptical Problem." Zeglen 1999.

Bach, K. 2003. "Context ex Machina." http://online.sfsu.edu/~kbach/

Baker, L.R. 1993. "Metaphysics and Mental Causation". Heil, Mele 1993.

Bar-On, D. 1994. "Conceptual Relativism and Translation". Preyer et al. 1994a.

Bennett, D. 1965. "Actions, Reasons and Purpose." *Journal of Philosophy*.

Bennett, J. 1982. *Sprachverhalten* (1976). Frankfurt am Main.

Bezuidenhout, A. 2002. "Truth-Conditional Pragmatics." *Philosophical Perspectives* 16.

Bhargava. R. 1992. *Individualism in Social Science. Forms and Limits of a Methodology*. Oxford.

Bilgrami, A. 1992. *Belief and Meaning. The Unity and Locality of Mental Content*. Oxford.

—. 1993. "Norms and Meaning." Stoecker 1993.

Borg, E. 2004. *Minimal Semantics*. Oxford.

Brand, M. 1968. "Danto on Basic Actions." *Nous* 219.

Brandl, J., W.L. Gombocz eds. 1989. *The Mind of Donald Davidson. Grazer Philosophische Studien. Internationale Zeitschrift für analytische Philosophie*, Vol. 36. Graz.

Brueckner, A. 1998. "Content Externalism and A Priori Knowledge". *Proto-*

sociology, Vol. 11: Cognitive Semantics II – Externalism in Debate. Frankfurt am Main.

Burge, T. 1979. "Individualism and the Mental." *Midwest Studies in Philosophy*. Edited by P. A. French, T. E. Uehling, and H. K. Wettstein. Minneapolis.

—. 1993. "Mind-Body Causation and Explanatory Practice." Heil, Mele 1993.

Cappelen, H.1997. "Semantic Theory and Indirect Speech." *Protosociology*, Vol. 10: Cognitive Semantics – Conceptions of Meaning.

—. E. Lepore. 1999. "Semantic for Quotation." Zeglen 1999.

Carston, R. 2002. *Thoughts and Utterances: The Pragmatics of Explicit Communication*. Oxford.

Chisholm, R. M. 1966. "Freedom and Action." *Freedom and Determinism*. Edited by K. Lehrer. New York. 1977.

—. *Theory of Knowledge* 2nd rev. edn. Prentice Hall.

Chomsky, N. 1991. "Linguistics and Cognitive Science. Problems and Mysteries." *The Chomskyan Turn*. Edited by A. Kasher. Oxford.

—. 1994. "On Linguistics and Politics. Interview von G. Grewendorf." *Protosociology*, Vol. 6: Rationality I, Frankfurt am Main; *Linguistische Berichte* 153/1994. Open Access: https://ssl.humanities-online.de/en/open access.php

Clark, R. 1970. "Concerning the Logic of Predicate Modifiers." *Nous* 4.

Danto, A. C. 1965. "Basic Actions." *American Philosophical Quarterly* 2.

—. 1973. *Analytical Philosophy of Action*. Cambridge.

Donnellan, K. 1971. "Reference and Definite Description (1966)." *Semantics*. Edited by D. D. Steinberg, L. A. Jakobovits. Cambridge.

Davidson, D. 1980. *Actions and Events*. Oxford.

—. 1985 a. "Reply to Quine on Events." Lepore, MacLaughlin 1985.

—. 1985 b. "Replies to Essays X-XII." *Essays on D. Davidson. Action and Events*. Edited by B. Vermazen, and M. B. Hintika. New York.

—. 1984. *Inquiries into Truth and Interpretation*. Oxford.

—. 1990. "The Structure and Content of Truth." *The Journal of Philosophy*, Vol. LXXXVII, No. 6.

—. 1993 a. "Reply to Andreas Kemmerling." Stoecker 1993.

—. 1993 b. "Reply to Jerry Fodor and Ernest Lepore." Stoecker 1993.

—. 1993 c. "Reply to Richard Schantz." Stoecker 1993.

—. 1993 d. "Reply to Rosmarie Rheinwald." Stoecker 1993.

—. 1993 e. "Reply to Peter Bieri." Stoecker 1993.

—. 1994. "Davidson, Donald." *A Companion to the Philosophy of Mind*. Edited by Guttenplan. Cambridge USA.

—. 1995. "Law and Cause." *Dialectica* 49.
—. 1999 g. "Reply to Neale." *The Philosophy of Donald Davidson*. Edited by L. E. Hahn. Chicago.
—. 1999 a. "Is Truth a Goal of Inquiry? Discussion with Rorty." Zeglen 1999.
—. 1999 b. "Reply to Peter Pagin." Zeglen 1999.
—. 1999 c. "Reply to Reinaldo Elugardo." Zeglen 1999.
—. 1999 d. "Reply to Roger F. Gibson." Zeglen 1999.
—. 1999 e. "Reply to Gabriel Segal." Zeglen 1999.
—. 1999 f. "Reply to Stephen Neale." Zeglen 1999.
—. 2001. *Subjective, Intersubjective, Objective*. Oxford.
—. 2004. *Problems of Rationality*. Oxford.
—. 2005. *Truth, Language, and History*, Oxford.
Dummett, M. 1990. "Eine hübsche Unordnung von Epitaphen. Bemerkungen zu Davidson und Hacking." *Die Wahrheit der Interpretation. Beiträge zur Philosophie von Donald Davidson*. Hrsg. von E. Picardi und J. Schulte. Frankfurt am Main.
—. 1991. *The Logical Basis of Metaphysics*. London.
—. 1982. "Was ist eine Bedeutungstheorie (1975)." *Wahrheit*, Stuttgart.
Devitt, M. 1981. *Designation*. New York.

Elster, J. 1985. "The Nature and Scope of Rational Choice Explanation." Lepore, MacLaughlin 1985.
Elugardo, R. 1999 a. "Samesaying." Zeglen 1999.
—. 1999 b. "Mixed Quotation." *Philosophy and Linguistics*. Edited by Robert Stainton, Kumiko Murasugi. Boulder.
Essler, W. K. 1994. "Was ist Wahrheit." Preyer et al. 1994 a. Rep. Essler 2001.
—. J. Labude, S. Ucsnay 2000. *Theorie der Erfahrung. Eine Einführung in die Wissenschaftstheorie*. Freiburg i. Br.
—. 1999. "Truth and Knowledge. Some Considerations concerning the Task of Philosophy of Science." *Protosociology*, Vol. 12: After the Received View. Developments in the Theory of Science. Special Edition. Edited by G. Preyer, G. Peter, A. Ulfig.
—. 2001. "*Unser die Welt*". Sprachphilosophische Grundlegungen der Erkenntnistheorie. Hrsg. von G. Preyer. Frankfurt am Main.

Feinberg, J. 1968. "Action and Responsibility (1965)." *The Philosophy of Action*. Edited by A. L. White. London.
Feyerabend, P. 1962. "Explanation, Reduction, and Empirism." *Scientific Explanation, Space and Time*. Minnesota Studies in the Philosophy of Science 3, Minneapolis.
Fiengo, R., R. May. 2002. "Identity Statements." Preyer, Peter 2002a.

Fodor, J. 1970. "Troubles about Action." *Synthesis*, 21.
Fodor, J., E. Lepore. 1992. *Holism. A Shopper's Guide*. Oxford.
—. 1993. "Is Radical Interpretation possible." Stoecker 1993.
—. 1994. "Meaning, Holism and the Problem of Extensionality." Preyer et al. 1994 a.

Geach, P. T. 1972. "Ascriptivism (1960)." *Logic Matter*, Oxford.
Gibson, R. F. 1994. "Quine and Davidson. Two Naturalized Epistemologists." Preyer et al. 1994a.
—. 1999. "McDowell on Quine, Davidson and Epistemology." Zeglen 1999.
Goldman, A. I. 1970. *Theory of Human Action*. Prentice Hall.
—. 1971. "The Individuation of Action." *Journal of Philosophy*, 769 LXVIII.
Grandy, R. 1973. "Reference, Meaning and Belief." *The Journal of Philosophy*, 70.
Grewendorf, G. und D. Zaefferer. 1991. "Theorien der Satzmodi." *Semantik. Ein internationales Handbuch der zeitgenössischen Forschung*. Hrsg. von D. Wunderlich und A. von Stechow. Berlin.

Haack, S. 1987. *Philosophy of Logics*. Cambridge.
Habermas, J. 1975. "Handlungen, Operationen, körperliche Bewegungen." *Vorstudien und Ergänzungen zur Theorie des kommunikativen Handelns*, Frankfurt am Main 1984.
Hacker, P. M. S., Raz, J. eds. 1977. *Law, Morality and Society*. Essays in Honour of H. L. A. Hart. London.
Hampshire, S. 1965. *Freedom of the Individuals*. Princeton, N.Y.
Hart, H. L. A. 1949. "The Ascription of Responsibility and Rights." *Proceedings of Aristotelian Society*, XLIX.
—. 1958. "Legal and Moral Obligations." *Essays in Moral Philosophy*. Edited by A. I. Melden. Seattle.
—. 1961. *The Concept of Law*. Oxford.
Heil, J., Mele, A. eds. 1993. *Mental Causation*. Oxford.
Heil, J. 1996. "The Propositional Attitudes." *Protosociology*, Vol. 8/9: Rationality II/III. Frankfurt am Main.
Hempel, C. G. 1962. "Rational Action." *Proceedings and Addresses of the American Philosophical Association*. Ohio.
Henderson, D. K. 1994. Conceptual Schemes after Davidson. Preyer et al. 1994a.
—. 1995. "One Naturalized Epistemological Argument. Against Coherentist Accounts of Empirical Knowledge." *Erkenntnis*, Vol. 43, No. 2.
—. 2000. "Epistemic Rationality, Epistemic Motivation, and Interpretive Charity." Preyer, Peter 2000c. Rep. from *Protosociology*, Vol. 8/9 1996.

Hintikka, J. 1975. "A Counterexample to Tarski-Type Truth-Definition as Applied to Natural Languages", *Philosophia* 5.

Hornsby, J. 1980. *Actions*. London.

—. "Agency and Causal Explanation."

Horwich, P. 1999. "Davidson on Deflationism". Zeglen 1999.

Hume, D. 1941. *A Treatice of Human Nature* 1749/50. London.

Jacob, P. 1990. "Semantics and Psychology. The Semantics of Belief-Ascriptions". *New Inquiries into Meaning and Truth*. Edited by N. Cooper, P. Engel. Hemel Hempstead.

Katz, J.J. 1995. "Logic and Language. An Examination of recent Criticism of Intensionalism." *Language, Mind and Knowledge*. Edited by K. Gunderson. New York.

Kenny, A. 1963. *Action, Emotion, Will*. London.

Kim, J. 1969. "On the Psycho-Physical Identity Theory." *American Philosophical Quarterly*.

—. 1993a. "Can Supervenience and `Non-Strict Law' Save Anomalous Monism?" Heil, Mele 1993.

—. 1993b. "The Non-Reductivist's Trouble with Mental Causation." Heil, Mele 1993.

—. 1993c. *Supervenience and Mind. Selected Philosophical Essays*. Cambridge.

—. 1996. *Philosophy of Mind*. New York.

—. 1998. *Mind in the Physical World. An Essay on the Mind-Body. Problem and Mental Causation*. Cambridge, Mass.

Kirkham, R.L. 1992. *Theories of Truth. A Critical Introduction*. Massachusetts.

Larson, D. 1988. "Tarski, Davidson and the Theory of Truth." *Dialectica*, 42.

Lepore, E., B.P. McLaughlin eds. 1985. *Action and Events. Perspectives on the Philosophy of D. Davidson*. New York.

Lepore, E. ed. 1986. *Truth and Interpretation. Perspectives on the Philosophy of D. Davidson*. New York.

Lepore, E., B. Loewer.1987. „Mind Matters." *Journal of Philosophy* Inc.

—. 1989. „More on Making Mind Matter." *Philosophical Topics*, Vol. XVII, No. 1.

Lepore E., K. Ludwig. 2002. "What is Logical Form." Preyer, Peter 2002a.

—. 2003. "Truth and Meaning." Ludwig 2003.

—. 2005. *Donald Davidson. Meaning, Truth, Language, and Reality*. Oxford.

Lewis, D. 1998. 1975. *Konventionen. Eine sprachphilosophische Abhandlung* (1969). Berlin.
—. "Index, Context, and Content." 1980. *Papers in Philosophical Logic*. Cambridge.
Loar, B. 1976. "Two Theories of Meaning." *Truth and Meaning*. Essays in Semantics. Edited by G. Evans, J. McDowell. London.
Ludwig, K. 1997. "The Truth about Mood." *Protosociology*, Vol. 10. Rep. in: Preyer, Peter, Ulkan 2003.
—. 1999. "Theories of Meaning, Truth and Interpretation." Zeglen 1999.
—. ed. 2003. *Donald Davidson*. Cambridge.
—. 2003. "Introduction". Ludwig 2003.

Macdonald, G., Pettit, P. 1981. *Semantics and Social Science*, London.
Manning, R. 1998. "All Facts Great and Small." *Protosociology*, Vol. 11.
Martin, R. M. *Events, Reference and Logical Form*. Washington 1978.
McDowell, J. 1976. "Truth Conditions, Bivalence and Verificationism." *Truth and Meaning. Essays in Semantics*. Edited by G. Evans, J. McDowell. Oxford.
—. 2001. *Geist und Welt* 1996. Frankfurt am Main
McGinn, C. 1977. "Charity, Interpretation and Belief." *The Journal of Philosophy* 74.
McGinn, M. 1981-82. "The Third Dogma of Empiricism." *Proceedings of Aristotelian Society*.
Meggle, G., M. Ulkan. 1997. "Grices Doppelfehler. Ein Nachtrag zum Gricemodell." Preyer et al. 1997a.
Meggle, G. 2001. *Handlungstheoretische Semantik*. Manuscript.
Melchert, N. 1986. "What's wrong with Anomalous Monism?" *Journal of Philosophy* Inc.
Melden, A. I. 1960. "Willing." *Philosophical Review*, Vol. 69. Rep. *The Philosophy of Action*. Edited A. R. White. Oxford 1968.
—. 1961. *Free Action*. London.
Mele, A. R. 1992. *Springs of Action. Understanding Intentional Behavior*. Oxford.
—. 2001. *Self-Deception unmasked*. Princeton.
—. 2003. "Philosophy of Action." Ludwig 2003.

Nagel, T. 1991. *Die Grenzen der Objektivität. Philosophische Vorlesungen*. Stuttgart.
Neale, S. 1999. "From Semantics to Ontology, via Truth, Reference and Quantification." Zeglen 1999.
—. 2001. *Facing Facts*. Oxford.

—. 2004. "This, That, and The Other." *Descriptions and Beyond*. Edited by M. Reimer, A Bezuidenhout. Oxford.

Nida-Rümelin, J. 1995. *Kritik des Konsequentialismus*. München.

—. 2000. "Die Vielheit guter Gründe und die Theorie praktischer Rationalität". Preyer, Peter 2000c.

—. 2001. *Strukturelle Rationalität. Ein philosophischer Essay über praktische Vernunft*. Stuttgart.

—. 2002. *Ethische Essays*. Frankfurt am Main.

—. 2005. *Über menschliche Freiheit*, Stuttgart.

Parsons, T. 1980. "Modifiers and Quantifiers in Natural Language." *Canadian Journal of Philosophy*, Vol. 6.

—. 1985. "Underlying Events in the Logical Analysis of English." Lepore/ MacLaughlin 1985.

—. 1990. *Events in the Semantics of English. A Study in Subatomic Semantics*. Cambridge. Peters, R. S. 1958. *The Concept of Motivation*. London.

Peter, G. 1997. "Zu Richtigkeit und Interpretation der Metapher." Preyer et al. 1997a.

Picardi, E. 1994. "Davidson and Quine on Observation Sentences." Preyer et al. 1994a.

Platts, M. 1979. *Ways of Meaning*. London.

—. 1980. "Moral Reality and the End of Desire." *Reference, Truth and Reality. Essays on the Philosophy of Language*. Edited by M. Platts. London.

Preti, C. 1998. "The Irrelevance of Supervenience." *Protosociology* Vol. 11 1998. Pietroski, P. 2003. "Semantics and Metaphysics of Events." Ludwig 2003.

Preyer, G, F. Siebelt, A. Ulfig. 1994c. "On Donald Davidson's Philosophy." Preyer et al. 1994a. Preyer, G. 1994a. "Rationalität. Absichten – primäre Gründe – praktisches Denken (Rationality. Intentions – Primary Reasons – Practical Thinking "). Preyer et al. 1994.

—. F. Siebelt, A. Ulfig (eds.) 1994a. *Language, Mind and Epistemology. On Donald Davidson's Philosophy*. Dordrecht.

—. G. Peter, A. Ulfig. 1996b. *Protosoziologie im Kontext. "Lebenswelt" und "System" in Philosophie und Soziologie*. Würzburg.

Preyer, G. 1996a. "Rechtsgeltung, Argumentation, Entscheidung." *System der Rechte, demokratischer Rechtsstaat und Diskurstheorie des Rechts nach Jürgen Habermas*. Edited by W. Krawietz, G. Preyer. Special volume of *Rechtstheorie*, 3.

Preyer, G., M. Ulkan, G. Ulfig Hrsg. 1997a. *Intention – Bedeutung – Kommunikation. Kognitive und handlungstheoretische Grundlagen der Sprachtheorie*. Opladen. Open Access: https://ssl.humanities-online.de/en/open access.php

Preyer, G. 1997c. "Verstehen, Referenz, Wahrheit. Über Hilary Putnams Philosophie." *Protosociology*, Vol. 10. Rep. in Preyer 2003.

—. 1997b. "Kognitive Semantik." Preyer et al. 1997a.

—. 1998b. "Interpretation and Rationality. Steps from Radical Interpretation to the Externalism of Triangulation." *Protosociology*, Vol. 11.

—. M. Roth. 1998a. "On Donald Davidson's Philosophy. An Outline." *Protosociology*, Vol. 11.

Preyer, G. 1998c. "The Received View, Incommensurability and the Comparison of Theories – Beliefs as the Basis of Theorizing." In Preyer 2005.

—. 1998d. "Sprachbedeutung ohne Regelbefolgung." *Wittgensteins Spätphilosophie*. Analysen und Probleme. Hrsg. von W. Kellerwessel und T. Peuker. Würzburg. Rep. in Preyer 2005.

—. F. Siebelt (eds.) 2000a. *Reality and Supervenience. Essays on the Philosophy of David Lewis' Philosophy*. Lanham USA.

—. F. Siebelt. 2000b. "Reality and Supervenience. Some Reflections on David Lewis' Philosophy." Preyer, Siebelt 2000a.

Preyer, G., G. Peter (eds.) 2000c. *The Contextualization of Rationality. Problems, Concepts and Theories of Rationality*, Perspectives in Analytical Philosophy New Series. Edited by G. Meggle, J. Nida-Rümelin. Paderborn.

—. eds. 2002a. *Logical Form and Language*. Oxford GB.

Preyer, G. 2002b. *Donald Davidsons Philosophie. Von der radikalen Interpretation zum radikalen Kontextualismus*. Frankfurt am Main.

—. 2003. "On the Legacy of Russell's Theory of Definite Description." In Preyer 2005.

Preyer, G., G. Peter, M. Ulkan eds. 2003. *Concepts of Meaning. Framing an Integrated Theory of Linguistic Behavior*. Dordrecht.

Preyer, G., G. Peter (eds.) 2005a. *Contextualism in Philosophy. Knowledge, Meaning, and Truth*. Oxford.

Preyer, G. 2005b. *Interpretation, Sprache und das Soziale, Philosophische Artikel*. Frankfurt am Main.

—. 2005c. *Review: D. Davidson. Truth, Language, and History*. Oxford University Press. Oxford 2005.

Preyer, G., G. Peter (eds.). 2007. *Context-Sensitivity and Semantic Minimalism. New Essays on Semantics and Pragmatics*. Oxford.

—. G. Peter (eds.) 2006. *ProtoSociology* Vol. 23: Facts, Slingshots and Anti-Representationalism. On Stephen Neal's *Facing Facts*.

Preyer, G., 2011a. "Evaluative Attitudes." *Dialoges with Davidson*. Edited by J. Malpas. Cambridge MS.

—. 2011b. *Intention and Practical Thought*. Frankfurt am Main.

Prichard, H.P. 1945. "Acting, Willing, Desiring." *Moral Obligations*, Oxford.

—. "Acting, Willing, Desiring." *American Philosophical Quarterly* 2.
Putnam, H. 1975. "The Meaning of 'Meaning'." *Mind, Language and Reality. Philosophical Papers* Vol. 2. London and New York.
—. 1978. *Meaning and the Moral Science*. London.
—. 1981. *Reason, Truth and History*. Cambridge.
—. 1992. "Replies." *Philosophical Topics* 20.

Quine. W. v. O. 1960. *Word and Object*. Cambridge.
—. 1969. "Ontological Relativity." *Ontological Relativity and other Essays*, New York.
—. 1981. "Things and their Place in Theories." *Theories and Things*. Cambridge, Mass.
—. 1985. "Events and Reification." Lepore, MacLaughlin 1985.
—. 1992. *Pursuit of Truth* rev. edn. Cambridge, Mass.
—. 1995 a. *Selected Logic Papers*. Enlarged Edition. Cambridge USA.
—. 1995 b. *From Stimulus to Science*. Cambridge, Mass.

Raz, J. 1975. *Practical Reasons and Norms*. Oxford.
—. 1978. "Reasons, for Action, Decisions and Norms." *Practical Reasoning*. Edited by J. Raz. Oxford.
Recanati, F. 1993. *Direct Reference*. From Language to Thought. Oxford.
—. 2004. *Literal Meaning*. Cambridge.Rescher, N. 1967. "Aspects of Action." *The Logic of Decision and Action*. Edited by N. Rescher. Pittburg.
Richard, M. 1990. *Propositional Attitudes*. Cambridge.
Röska-Hardy, L. 1994. "Internalism, Externalism and Davidson's Conception of the Mental." Preyer et al. 1994a.
—. 1997. "Sprechen, Sprache, Handeln." Preyer et al. 1997a. Engl. version "Language Acts and Action." *Protosociology*, Vol. 10.
—. 1997. "Interpretation und Erste-Person-Autorität." *Davidsons Philosophie des Mentalen*. Edited by W. Köhler. Paderborn.
Rogler, E. 2000. "On David Lewis' Philosophy of Mind." *Protosociology*, Vol. 14: Folk Psychology, Mental Concepts and the Ascription of Attitudes. On Contemporary Philosophy of Mind, Frankfurt am Main. Rep. Rogler, Preyer 2001.
Rogler, E. und G. Preyer. 2001. *Materialismus, anomaler Monismus und mentale Kausalität. Zur gegenwärtigen Philosophie des Mentalen bei D. Davidson und D. Lewis*. Frankfurt am Main.
—. 2003 a. "Physikalismus und die Autonomie des Mentalen. Ungelöste Probleme in Donald Davidsons Philosophie des Mentalen." *Metaphysica. International Journal for Ontology & Metaphysics* Vol. 4 No. 2 2003.
—. 2003 b. "Anomalous Monism and Mental Causality. On the Debate of

Donald Davidson's Philosophy of the Mental." Frankfurt am Main. Open Access: https://ssl.humanities-online.de/en/openaccess.php
Romanos, G. 1983. "Quine and Analytic Philosophy." Cambridge.
Root, M., J. Wallace. 1982. "Meaning and Interpretation." *Notre Dame Journal of Symbolic Logic*, Vol. 23. No. 2.
Rorty, R. 1981. *Spiegel der Natur* (1979). Frankfurt am Main.
Russell, B. 1950. *Inquiry into Meaning and Truth* 1940. London.
Ryle, G. 1969. *Der Begriff des Geistes* 1949. Stuttgart.

Schantz, R. 1993. "Davidson on Truth." Stoecker 1993.
—. 1996. *Wahrheit, Referenz und Realismus. Eine Studie zur Sprachphilosophie und Metaphysik*. Berlin
Searle, J. R. 1969. *Speech Acts*. An Essay in the Philosophy of Language, Cambridge.
—. 1986. *Geist, Hirn und Wissenschaft* 1984. Frankfurt am Main.
Segal, G. 1999. "How a Truth Theory can do Duty as a Theory of Meaning." Zeglen 1999.
Shwayder, D. S. 1965. *The Stratification of Behaviour*. London, New York.
Strawson, P. F. 1971: "Singular Terms and Predication." *The Journal of Philosophy*, Vol. 1 VIII. Rep. P. F. Strawson 1971: *Logico-linguistic Papers*, London.
—. 1976. "On Understanding the Structure of one's Language." *Truth and Meaning. Essays in Semantics*. Edited by G. Evans, J. McDowell. London.
Siebelt, F. 1994. "Singular Causal Sentences." Preyer et al. 1994.
—. 1997. "Zweierlei Holismus. Überlegungen zur Interpretationstheorie von Donald Davidson." Preyer et al. 1997.
Soames, S. 2002. *Beyond Rigidity: The Unfinished Semantic Agenda of Naming and Necessity*. Oxford.
Spinner, H. F. 1994. *Der ganze Rationalismus von Gegensätzen. Studien zur Doppelvernunft*. Frankfurt am Main.
Stoecker, R. 1992. *Was sind Ereignisse. Eine Studie zur analytischen Ontologie*. Berlin.
—. ed. 1993. *Reflecting Davidson. Donald Davidson Responding to an International Forum of Philosophers*. Berlin.
Stoutland, F. 1968. "Basic Action and Causality." *Journal of Philosophy*, 65.
—. 1970. "The Logical Connection Argument."*American Philosophical Quarterly*, 7.

Thalberg, I. 1967. "Verbs, Deeds and what happens to us." *Theoria* 33.
—. 1972. *Enigmas of Agency*. New York.
Tugendhat, E., U. Wolf. 1983. *Logisch-semantische Propädeutik*, Stuttgart.

Tugendhat, E. 1976. *Vorlesungen zur Einführung in die sprachanalytische Philosophie*. Frankfurt am Main. Engl. publication 1982: *Traditional and Analytical Philosophy*. Cambridge.
—. 1979. *Selbstbewußtsein und Selbstbestimmung. Sprachanalytische Interpretationen*. Frankfurt am Main.

Ulkan, M. 1997. "Kommunikative und illokutionäre Akte." Preyer et al. 1997a. Engl. version in: Preyer, Peter, Ulkan 2003.

Vermazen, B., M. B. Hintika eds. 1985. *Essays on D. Davidson. Action and Events*. New York.

White, A. R. 1975. *Modal Thinking*. Oxford.
Weinstein, S. 1974. "Truth and Demonstratives." *Nous*, 8.
Wilburn, R. 1998. "Knowledge, Content, and the Wellspring of Objectivity." *Protosociology*, Vol. 11. Wright, G. H. v. 1963. "Practical Inferences." *Philosophical Review* 72.
—. 1974. *Erklären und Verstehen* 1971. Frankfurt am Main.
—. 1977. *Handlung, Norm und Intention. Untersuchungen zur deontologischen Logik*. Berlin.
—. 1994. *Normen, Werte und Handlungen*. Frankfurt am Main.
Wunderlich, D. 1976. *Studien zur Sprechakttheorie*. Frankfurt am Main.
Woodward, J. 1986. "Are Singular Causal Explanations implicit Covering-Law Explanations?" *Canadian Journal of Philosophy*, Vol. 16 2.

Yalowitz, S. 1998. "Causation in the Argument for Anomalous Monism." *Canadian Journal of Philosophy*, Vol. 28.

Zeglen, U.M. ed. 1999. *Donald Davidson. Truth, Meaning and Knowledge*. London.
Ziff, P. 1960. *Semantic Analysis*. Ithaca.

Detailed Table of Contents

Name Index

Subject Index

Gerhard Preyer
Intention and Practical Thought
Humanities Online 2011
(www.humanities-online.de)
128 pages · Paperback · ISBN 978-3-941743-09-0

The philosophical questions about action concern it's nature, it's description and it's explanation. The leading questions are "What a theory of action is possible?", "Are reasons causes?", "What are practical thoughts?" and "What is the formal logic of practical inference?"

Gerhard Preyer offers new answers of some old question about the description and the explanation of action and the logical structure of deliberation or practical reasoning which results from the theory of action since the 1950s years. It is argued that a theory of agent can provide an alternative to any theory postulating actions as irreducible entities metaphysically. The author's account presents intention as states irreducible to beliefs and desires. The analysis places also a requirement on a fruitful description of the mind-body problem.

Audience
Teachers and students (graduate and advanced undergraduate) in philosophy, particularly in the field of philosophy of action, mind and moral philosophy. Also of interest to sociologists and psychologists. Can be used as a textbook for graduate and undergraduate courses in philosophy of action.

The Author
Gerhard Preyer is Professor of Sociology at the Goethe-University Frankfurt am Main, Germany. Among his publications are Donald *Davidson's Philosophy. From Radical Interpretation to Radical Contextualism* and *Interpretation, Language and the Social. Philosophical Articles*. He edits *ProtoSociology. An International Journal of Interdisciplinary Research* (www.protosociology.de)

www.ingramcontent.com/pod-product-compliance
Lightning Source LLC
Chambersburg PA
CBHW021808270326
41932CB00007B/106